PLAYS AND PLAYWRIGHTS

2002

edited and with an introduction by

Martin Denton

Published by The New York Theatre Experience, Inc.
P.O. Box 744
Bowling Green Station
New York, NY 10274-0744

Visit The New York Theatre Experience on the World Wide Web at:
http://www.nytheatre.com
e-mail: info@botz.com

ISBN 0-9670234-3-2
Library of Congress Card Number: 2001099532

Book designed by Nita Congress
Cover designed by Steven Waxman

PERMISSIONS

TABLE OF CONTENTS

ACKNOWLEDGMENTS

We're now at the third volume of the *Plays and Playwrights* series; it seemed especially important this year to get this now-annual book out on schedule—to offer evidence, I suppose, that in spite of everything, the theatre here in New York City and across the nation is as vibrant and potent and adventurous as ever. *Plays and Playwrights 2002* is the result of the labor and love of many, many people. This is where I get to say thank you to all of them.

First, my gratitude to the ten playwrights who have consented to place their work in my hands this year is huge and heartfelt: Kate Chell, Marc Chun, Curtiss I' Cook, Matthew Freeman, Chiori Miyagawa, Peter S. Petralia, J. Scott Reynolds, Marc Spitz, Brian Thorstenson, and Ken Urban.

I am also indebted to the individuals who helped me find these terrific plays: Christopher Carter Sanderson of Gorilla Rep (*The Death of King Arthur*), Stephen Sunderlin of Vital Theatre Company (*Match*), Timothy Haskell of Publicity Outfitters (*Woman Killer* and *Shyness Is Nice*), Barrett Ogden of Handcart Ensemble (*The Wild Ass's Skin*), Adenrele Ojo of Tupu Kweli Theatre Company (*Reality*), Tim Fannon (*The Resurrectionist*), Ron Lasko of Spin Cycle (*Bunny's Last Night in Limbo*), and Jeff Corrick of Wings Theatre Company, plus Sam Sommer and Amy Mueller (*Summerland*). For those who have noticed that that makes just nine plays, I thank, again, Ken Urban for letting me see early drafts of *Halo* while it was being developed and kept me apprised of its progress as it headed toward production last summer.

The creation of this volume is a collaboration involving many talented and dedicated people. Nita Congress designed, proofed, and edited this book. Steven Waxman designed the covers. Playwright Bill C. Davis, who has been an unflagging supporter of The New York Theatre Experience, Inc., for many years now, graciously wrote the beautiful Foreword. Rochelle Denton did all the behind-the-scenes nitty-gritty stuff that makes this publication possible.

The following individuals, each in his or her own way, have been instrumental this past year in making the *Plays and Playwrights* anthology series strong and vital: Jose Antonio, Julia Barclay, Arian Blanco, Kirk Wood Bromley, Patrick Burchill, Chris Campbell, Steve Caporaletti, John Clancy, Julie Congress, Sarah Congress, Dave Dannenfelser, Donna Davis, Richard Day, Eddie DeSantis, Ken Dine, D.P. Duffy, David Fuller, Katherine Gooch, Matthew Greer, Evie Harris, Omar Hernandez, Nicole Higgins, Dale Ho, Elena K. Holy, C.J. Hopkins, Elizabeth Horsburgh, Jeff Hylton, Rachel Jackson, Laura Josepher, Ron Lasko, Royden Mills, Jennifer Morris, Sandra Nordgren, Marella Oppenheim, Tony Pennino, Carrie Preston, Sean Elias-Reyes, Adrian Rodriguez, Christopher Carter Sanderson, Joshua Scher, Robert Simonson, Monica Sirignano, Baylen Thomas, Trav S.D., Jonathan Uffelman, Ken Urban, Marcy Valladares, Kate Ward, Stuart Warmflash, Tim Werenko, Bev Willey, and Garth Wingfield.

Finally, the truth is that none of this would have happened if, thirty-odd years ago, my sister Nita had not introduced me to the joy of reading plays. We both still have the habit. Did either of us guess we'd be carrying the torch in 2002? This book is dedicated to her.

Martin Denton
New York City
December 2001

FOREWORD

I applaud Martin Denton for searching the front lines of the American theatre and finding voices that are original and new. The off-off-Broadway theatre is the arena where writers can dare fearlessly. Playwrights, along with actors and directors, do not have to apologize for their originality. They struggle with the question, "What do I want to say?" as opposed to "What do you want me to say?"

Martin Denton is like a scout—a satellite with his sensors up listening to what a playwright is saying. He interprets with his own individual sense of humanity and reports what the experience has been. He doesn't insult artists and audience with thumbs up or thumbs down. He wants you to know what the experience was and you can take it from there.

A writer tries to frame a story that he or she feels needs to be told. A playwright forges and gives birth to characters who in some way are like figures in that playwright's dreamscape. These characters and the evolution of the stories that their impulses generate are specific and unique to each writer. That uniqueness and that inescapable DNA of a writer's fingerprint are the gold that very few know how to recognize. Discovering a great work of art or finding a new and original voice is not unlike falling in love. You wonder how you got along before and you want everyone to meet your new beloved.

This compilation is that introduction to these new playwrights in our lives. Like miners with lights on their heads, they mine the caverns of the human heart and the geography of the present landscape. They do this with that first rush of need and hope that they can nudge the world to witness human dilemmas, identify, and perhaps change in some way. Writers are great natural resources, and they are delivered to us through mysterious forces in the universe, and then—

in the case of this compilation—the universe relies on Martin Denton in New York to continue the process. The next step is for us to read what our honorable pilgrim has found.

Bill C. Davis
December 2001

PREFACE

The attack on the World Trade Center redefined time in the way that epochal events can. There's a Before and After now; a sense that things changed, that nothing can be quite the same. This book was begun in earnest in October, and so it's part of the After; and so a project that was once primarily about showcasing the spectacular talents of a group of emerging and generally unknown playwrights suddenly has, perhaps, added significance.

One of the last plays I saw before the attack was Chiori Miyagawa's *Woman Killer*, which appears in this volume. This drama, which explores the question "What makes a man do evil?," opened on September 6. Five days later, there was more than enough evil to ponder.

An immediate impact of September 11 was that almost no one saw *Woman Killer*. The theatre where it played was located in what was called the "frozen zone," and performances were suspended for several days.

It's still too soon to know what the long-range impacts of September 11 will be. We do know this: Theatre didn't self-destruct; American playwrights and directors and designers and actors and producers responded to events with courage and compassion; the words of those who write for the stage bring comfort and understanding to those who hear them.

All ten of the plays included in *Plays and Playwrights 2002* were written before September 11, and all but one had their premieres before that date. Yet now here they stand, resonating in new and powerful ways as signposts on a journey that no one expected to take.

So… please: hear them.

Martin Denton
December 2001

INTRODUCTION

Martin Denton

Plays and Playwrights 2002 brings together ten new plays by ten talented writers whom you've probably never heard of; I'm betting that soon you'll be hearing more about—and from—all of them.

One of the things I hope this volume does is present a picture of what the New York theatre scene looked and felt like during the past twelve months or so. To that end, you'll find on the pages that follow ten very different, very adventurous plays. There's a romantic verse epic about King Arthur and an intimate verse drama based on a novel by Balzac; there's a suspenseful tale of graverobbers and anatomists set in seventeenth-century England and a tale from Japan about good and evil recast in contemporary Brooklyn. There are experimental and innovative works that stretch and re-imagine our expectations about theatre: a pageant interweaving three very different plays into a single—and singular—dramatic experience; a comic mystery that morphs unexpectedly into a Pirandellian exploration of the nature of reality; an episodic collection of vignettes and sketches that add up to an imaginative and surprising look at a boy's coming of age. There's a hilarious and profane comedy that looks danger squarely in the eye and spits at it; a wise and touching piece composed of five interlocking monologues that gradually reveal profound truths; and a moving and insightful drama that points hopefully and heroically toward a renewed faith in the principles on which our country was founded.

The playwrights are just as diverse as their works: teachers, actors, directors, and writers who have all embraced the stage as the platform from which to share their unique voices and visions with the rest of us. These voices are as yet mostly unheard—in fact, two of the plays in this book are the very first ones written by their authors; at

1

least half of these playwrights are still in their twenties. Read and enjoy their plays, and revel in their talent; if you're a producer or an artistic director or a drama professor, help spread the word about these extraordinary emerging playwrights by mounting one of their works at your local theatre or university. (You'll find contact information for each of them on page *iii*.) That's ultimately what this book is all about, to bring some much needed recognition to terrific work that might otherwise disappear unnoticed: the future of the American theatre—or a portion of it, at least—is right here in your hands.

I knew Matthew Freeman first as an actor, mostly from Gorilla Repertory Theatre's delightfully energetic outdoor summer productions of Shakespeare. In fact Gorilla Rep commissioned *The Death of King Arthur*, the verse drama by Freeman that opens our book; the company's artistic director Christopher Carter Sanderson is to be congratulated for entrusting this assignment to this young man who has done such a thoroughly terrific job with it.

The Death of King Arthur was written to be performed by a company of Shakespearean actors and to be performed outdoors: it's big, ambitious, maybe even a bit daunting. But what you'll discover, as you get caught up in this spectacularly well-crafted drama, is how accessible it is: Freeman makes this familiar, sprawling romance entirely contemporary and entirely his own. He takes nothing for granted; he makes us look twice at what we think we know about famous characters like Arthur, Lancelot, Guenevere, Mordred, Morgan La Fay, and Merlin—and also at what we think we know about the nature of nobility, morality, and right and wrong:

> AGRAVAINE: The grail is found, and what? More life. You see?
> You like me plain, I'll tell you, I can be.
> What's plain? Did you see God? Did I? Those men
> Who want, by day, a little bit of bread…
> Did they the Messiah touch on their cheek?
> Do workers truly profit each to each
> By wonders done in Distant Arab Lands?

The easiness of Freeman's verse reminds us how much life there still is in a form that doesn't get used much nowadays. And the genuine excitement that *The Death of King Arthur* generates, whether read or performed, begs the question of why this material hasn't been adapted in this way before. No matter; Freeman has done it for us now, and I wouldn't be surprised to find this fine epic romance of his becoming a staple of summer theatres across the country.

Marc Chun's *Match* began its life in the summer of 2001 in *Alternation*, a festival of one-act plays sponsored by Angelina Fiordellisi and Eduardo Machado's Cherry Lane Alternative. I didn't see it then, and I almost missed it again when it was subsequently produced by the Vital Theatre Company in its semi-annual new works festival, *Vital Signs*. Embarrassingly, I arrived late at the theatre, too late to see the first three of five pieces on the evening's program. Luckily, I was in time for Chun's remarkable play, one whose intelligence and very special resonance demanded that it be included in this volume, even though we were almost ready to go into production.

For *Match*, though it was written and premiered before September 11, is the play in this volume that most directly addresses the issues that that catastrophe brought to the fore. It's a play about random events—some would call them chance; others, fate—and what they do to people whose lives are irrevocably changed by them. It's also about compromising, connecting, and figuring out finally what's important; it is, in other words, authentically about life and death.

Match is also a brilliantly conceived work. It's structured as five inter-locking monologues delivered by five unidentified voices, and a good deal of its power derives from the fact that it takes us a while to understand who is talking to us and where they (we) are. We take a parallel journey with each of Chun's characters, from disorientation to something approaching understanding.

Here's our introduction to one of the five protagonists of *Match*:

> THREE: The sky was *that blue*. That's just what I call it: "that blue." I never came up with something more creative because, well, you only name things you fear you might forget. There were three other days when the sky was that *exact* shade. First, when I was five; my mom and I made a kite and then we went up to Wallacker Hill to fly it. That was the last time I... well, I stared up at that sky the entire day. Second, the day I found out I got into RISD, which is when I started to really believe I was actually an artist. And the third? The third was the day I met her.

Are you hooked? I know I was, sitting in the Vital Theatre, in time to encounter Marc Chun for the very first time, thanks to the self-same random chance that *Match* deals in.

Like *Match* and *The Death of King Arthur*, *Woman Killer* trades in the most fundamental issues facing humanity. What's on playwright Chiori Miyagawa's mind, though, is the nature of good and evil:

what makes a man, seemingly just like you or I, commit murder? Miyagawa took a bunraku play by Chikamatsu from 1721 as the source for *Woman Killer*, transplanting it to contemporary Brooklyn, where a young man, obsessively in love with a prostitute, sinks progressively deeper into a life of debauchery, crime, and amorality. The title gives the play's ending away; Miyagawa is concerned here not with storytelling but with using the theatrical experience to explore the elements of human character that make such a brutal story possible.

She does this by creating a universe that is at once familiar and unpredictable. Characters whom we think we know—suburban housewives, doting parents, rebellious teenagers—suddenly pull away from us and say or do things we don't expect. Even the setting of the play—a cozy neighborhood in Brooklyn, just a short subway ride away from the theatre where *Woman Killer* premiered—may not be precisely what it seems:

> CLAY: Are you going to move away from this neighborhood?
>
> JAMES: It's not that far.
>
> CLAY: Brooklyn Heights. That's nice. Nicer than this damn place.
>
> JAMES: What're you talking about? This is the crossroads of Brooklyn: southeast to Nagasaki, northeast to Kyoto, southwest to Manhattan, northwest to the Temple Kanzeon. It's a great place. Just look at the Grand Army Plaza.

Miyagawa keeps us off-balance throughout *Woman Killer*; she never wants us to assume we "know" what's happening, either on the surface or in the increasingly disturbed mind of her riveting anti-hero Clay. Director Sonoko Kawahara underscored this disorientation by freely employing the techniques of Eastern and Western theatre throughout the play, reminding us that people everywhere in the world are neither as different nor as uncomplicated as we would like them to be.

J. Scott Reynolds's *The Wild Ass's Skin* is the third and last adaptation included in this volume. Reynolds is an intellectual and a bit of an iconoclast; he heads up his own theatre company, Handcart Ensemble, which produces spare, intelligent, and uncompromising productions of work with significant moral content. Reynolds is also a director, and his staging of *The Wild Ass's Skin* was stunningly inventive, applying almost a story-theatre approach to material whose weight and complexity would hardly seem to invite treatment that light or loose. The resulting production gave actors and audiences the opportunity to become engaged together in discovering the secret of the ass's skin of the play's title, as together we breathlessly witnessed the protagonist's literal and ethical journeys to their exacting, bitter ends.

The Wild Ass's Skin is, then, at once cerebral and dramatically adventurous. It begins when a despairing young man named Valentine, about to commit suicide, happens upon a shop where he obtains a magical donkey's skin that supposedly can fulfill all of his heart's desires. There's a price, however: for every wish the skin grants its owner, a corresponding amount of the owner's life span is sacrificed.

Reynolds's play reveals the events that brought Valentine to his current state as well as what happens to him after he comes under the skin's spell. Written in verse, the play is intimate, lyrical, and compact. Here Reynolds explores one of his central themes, condensing pages of the Balzac original to a few stunningly succinct lines:

> SHOPKEEPER: Its pledge to axe the years from one's own life,
> for me, too overweighs its offering.
> And, caveat aside, I'd not consent
> to have a thing so fickle as my wants
> conduct a thing so cherished as my fate.
> But as you only faintly prize your own,
> I doubt that you'd forgo the season's bliss
> this skin, how much exacting, would afford.

Ken Urban's plays exploded in small theatres around New York City and as far away as Seattle and Los Angeles in 2001; he's definitely a young playwright to keep an eye on. *Halo* premiered at the New York International Fringe Festival, demonstrating the breadth of his ambition and his talent. Urban describes *Halo* as a pageant, which is apt: the play encompasses three smaller plays, intertwined to create a startling panorama of life in Urban's home state of New Jersey at the very end of the twentieth century. Juxtaposing stories of a middle-aged woman, a pair of twenty-somethings who kill for thrills, and a modern-day Everyman (actually a successful businesswoman), Urban scores points about the empty, rudderless ship on which too many of us find ourselves adrift. He also provides vivid proof of the viability of his dark and somewhat eclectic vision of what theatre is supposed to accomplish. (Read the Afterword to *Halo* to learn more about that.)

Each of the three segments of *Halo* differs radically in terms of style and form. The Everyman section is aggressively postmodern. The story of Brandon and Sue has something of an MTV/punk feel and sensibility. The story of the middle-aged woman, whom we see at four different ages (in her twenties, thirties, fifties, and sixties), is lyrical and insightful:

6: How can you claim to see more than me, "From here," "From here," where are you? I'm the one at the end, I'm the one at the door of the great beyond, I'm the one who should be able to see

5: This belief, it simply isn't true

2: So the later years become the bitter years, do they?

6: My son now departed, a daughter never present to me, this is what the years have wrought?

2: In this world, you do what you have to.

5's line always knocks me out; Urban has the soul of a poet. *Halo* portends much fascinating work to come.

Shyness Is Nice is as blithely farcical as *Halo* is serious. This is an edgy, envelope-pushing comedy with an extraordinarily well-developed sense of the absurd; it's a post-everything sex-drugs-n-rock-n-roll farce; a hilarious cartoon laughing at and in the face of just about anything you can think of. Cartoon is particularly apt, I think, because despite all the major damage that occurs to the characters in *Shyness Is Nice* you always have the sense that—like Bugs Bunny or Daffy Duck—they'll get up, dust themselves off, and dive right into the next installment of their adventures.

The story, to whet your appetite, concerns Stew and Rodney, best friends who, at thirty, are still virgins, stuck in some weird alternate universe of perpetual adolescence and music trivia. Their pal Fitzgerald hires a prostitute named Kylie to deflower them. But complications— lots of them—ensue when Fitzgerald tries to cheat Kylie's pimp out of the promised payment.

This is a very funny script:

STEW: So what did the dingoes do in lieu of… eating you?
BLIXA: Nothing.
KYLIE: They buried her.
STEW: God. Who found you?
KYLIE: Another pack of dingoes.
STEW: No!
KYLIE: They dug her up and brought her home.
STEW: Rejected by dingoes.
KYLIE: Rejected by dingoes.
RODNEY: That's the rough.
KYLIE: It was front-page news in Sydney.

The playwright responsible for this merry mayhem is named Marc Spitz, who, like Aristophanes, creates brilliant comic theatre by throwing the sacred and the profane on stage together and letting chaos theory do its number on them. The resulting nearly non-stop laughter may be the best kind of therapy there is for this terrible troubled world of ours.

Spitz, whose day job is senior contributing writer for *Spin Magazine*, has been writing plays for just a few years, and he's already earned (deservedly) a rather rabid following among hip downtown New York types. It's time for the rest of the world to discover him.

I did not know, when I approached Curtiss I' Cook about putting his play *Reality* in this book, that his day job was playing Banzai the Hyena in the Broadway production of Disney's *The Lion King*. It wasn't that big a surprise, however, for the one thing that's certain about Cook is that he is a consummate man of the theatre. Cook is one of the hyphenated people: an actor-singer-dancer-director-producer-playwright. And his play reflects the questing sensibility of the Renaissance Man that he assuredly is.

Reality begins with a playwright, whose name is Curtiss, arguing with an unseen voice about the nature and purpose of theatre. Actors arrive on stage and Curtiss, like Seurat in Sondheim and Lapine's *Sunday in the Park with George*, arranges and rearranges them until he has them the way he wants them and the play proper can begin. That play starts out to be a comic mystery thriller set in an African American church in Dayton, Ohio. But the only thing to be sure of in *Reality* is that you can't be sure of anything. What Cook has actually concocted here is a witty, provocative, deliciously challenging piece about the nature of life and art and creation. Actors burst through the fourth wall and in and out of character; scenes are restarted and replayed in hopes that this time things will go according to some kind of plan.

Reality is a carnival of surprises, and it has depth, too: there certainly are no easy answers to be had here, though Cook does wrap things up with a devilishly clever—and satisfying—conclusion. He also creates vivid characters for his actors to play and supplies them with rich and interesting lines to say, like this funny exchange involving a man, his wife, and the other woman:

> LATHAN: Reverend, what do you expect us to do here?... We've been here for over eight hours, and I fail to see how this is benefiting anyone. I have to agree... This is a case for the authorities.

BERTHA: You're going to be a case for the authorities if you don't sit down… You shouldn't be saying nothing, other than who this Jezebel is with that tight cheap dress on.

CARMEN: Tight dress! First of all, sweetie, you don't know me well enough to be calling me out of my name! Secondly, I'm not the one you should be upset with! And as for cheap, I know you can recognize that, look at your weave!

On the opposite end of the theatrical spectrum is Kate Chell's wonderful drama *The Resurrectionist*, which is the most traditional two-act "well-made" play included in this anthology. It's here because its protagonist, Molly Lark, is a splendid character for young actresses to sink their teeth into: a fiery, spirited, smart, free-thinking, independent, wholly self-sufficient woman who doesn't need a man to define her and doesn't look to society for boundaries. All of this makes Molly something of a novelty even today, but when I tell you that *The Resurrectionist* takes place in England in the 1600s, you begin to understand what a wonderfully unconventional heroine she is.

The Resurrectionist is also here because it's a ripping good story: this is a nail-biting, edge-of-your-seat suspense story, loaded with adventure, intrigue, and just the right amount of murder and mayhem. Even more impressive, *The Resurrectionist* has real moral weight as it spins its tale of a young woman who runs a graverobbing business to supply corpses for anatomists prevented by law from obtaining bodies for study in more legitimate ways. The story of *The Resurrectionist* turns on the shrouded, horribly mutilated body of a young woman that Molly sells to an idealistic young doctor. As the circumstances of this woman's murder gradually come to light, it becomes less and less clear whether the graverobbers or the doctors for whom they procure are the more culpable:

MOLLY: It couldn't go to waste, could it? A perfectly good corpse. What hideous kind of world is this? Where graves spit forth their bellies for us to sell like scraps to hungry doctors? We devour our dead and sacrifice the living.

ERIN: What do you expect?… He deserved what he got. And don't get righteous with me, either. Smithfield's just a big market for selling dead meat. You live too long with the dead and maybe it ain't so good for you.

Chell delivers her unusual tale with economy, intelligence, and a generous helping of panache. Actors should be clamoring to play Molly and the friends and enemies who share the stage with her.

Bunny's Last Night in Limbo, by Peter S. Petralia, has a setting more exotic and rarefied even than *The Resurrectionist*'s Restoration era London. Petralia's fantastical play takes place in a seductive dreamscape, where its protagonist (the Bunny of the title) tries to sort out the strange, mixed signals he is receiving from his parents, his sister, the world in general, and a mysterious boy in particular. *Bunny's Last Night in Limbo* is a very contemporary coming-of-age/ coming out story, and also a reflection on the ravages of the suburban lifestyle. Most importantly, it points to intriguing new ways to explore topics like these in the theatre, using movement, songs, lights, and a virtually continuous soundscape to provide surreal comment on too-real problems.

Petralia assaults us on all fronts in this endlessly surprising play. Here's Bunny's sister, musing about makeup in an early scene:

> SISTER: …My mother thinks beauty is important. That's why she is so pretty. She lets me wear makeup because she wants me to be pretty, too. I'm glad 'cause being pretty is fun… and important.

And here are Bunny's parents, later in the play:

> MOTHER: It's another day. Isn't it dear?
>
> FATHER: I have been trying to tell you.
>
> MOTHER: Are you feeling sick, sugar bear?
>
> FATHER: Yes, I am feeling sick. I am feeling sick of this place.
>
> MOTHER: Why don't we watch TV.
>
> FATHER: I fucked Alice again today.
>
> MOTHER: Oh.
>
> FATHER: It wasn't as good as it was yesterday.
>
> MOTHER: Should we watch the news again?

There's desperation here, behind the subversion; Petralia depicts this part of the contemporary psyche with remarkable sensitivity.

Petralia is a director as well as a playwright, and his staging of *Bunny's Last Night in Limbo* at HERE in New York City marked him as a true visionary. He is continuing to develop his unique approach of melding sounds and images with more conventional elements of stagecraft to reveal unstated truths about the culture that his theatre mines with such acuity.

Brian Thorstenson's *Summerland*, the final play in this collection, reflects our culture in a different way. It tells the story of Doreen and Bud, a mother and son who live in a remote town in South Dakota where she runs a diner and he just runs. Both are hungry for connection in a place where opportunities for this are almost unbearably sparse. Bud's loneliness is exacerbated by the fact that he is gay, though the only male companionship he's been able to muster thus far has been with a renegade rancher in a rest stop parking lot.

Enter Sam, another trucker, who is immediately taken with Doreen's pie and coffee and, quickly, with the lady herself; and Skye, an enigmatic drifter with whom Bud falls in love. Thorstenson gives his play the shape of traditional domestic drama as the parallel relationships rise and fall and intercept; he also puts in a welcome scene in which a drunken gay basher gets his comeuppance, making *Summerland* something of a milestone.

What most distinguishes this beautiful play, though, is the presence of Aura, Doreen's dead grandmother, whose spirit haunts—or maybe infuses is the better word—the protagonists and the piece itself. Aura's spirit is the spirit of America and of the pioneers who created it:

> AURA: Couldn't have been more shocked when I first came to Dakota. Nothin but sky, endless endless sky and empty land. Couldn't see past that for a long time… Then I started noticin how bright the moon and stars were. How the air sat on my lips like ripe fruit. How that desolation became this quiet, a quiet that worked its way into my bones. Became a craving. Became a balm. You hesitate before you give that up.

Thorstenson ends this lyrical play with the stunning image of Bud and Skye at the geographical center of the United States, about to embark to an unknown destination to make a life together. Aura looks down at the two of them as they kiss and says "Don't really know what to make of that. Seem content though. Seem, seemly." Here, just when we thought we'd lost it, is the true heart of America.

Brian Thorstenson, in *Summerland*, reminds us, with compassion and sincerity, who we are. So, in their own wonderfully divergent ways, do the rest of the playwrights whose work appears in this book. Their voices are resonant and original; their visions clear-eyed and unfaltering. Their moment is now: these are the plays and playwrights of 2002. I hope you enjoy getting to know them as much as I did.

THE DEATH OF KING ARTHUR

Matthew Freeman

MATTHEW FREEMAN received his BFA in acting from Emerson College in 1998, studying with Kristin Linklater and playwright David Valdes-Greenwood. His play *The Message* was produced by the late Gary Newton at The Player's Ring in Portsmouth, New Hampshire, in 1999. He recently contributed a piece ("RU4KGB?") to Elite Fighting Crew's evening of connected shorts *Are You Four Eighty-Sixed?* In addition to his work for the theatre, Matthew has written television reviews for *Maxim On-Line* and was a regular columnist for *Wrestleline.com*, an online professional wrestling magazine affiliated with CBS Sportsline. He has appeared as an actor in Gorilla Rep productions of *Macbeth, Twelfth Night, As You Like It, A Midsummer Night's Dream, Ubu Is King, Story of an Unknown Man,* and *Cymbeline*; in productions with Earle Hyman and Austin Pendleton at the Frog and Peach Theatre; as Romeo at the New Hampshire Shakespeare Festival; and as Jeff in *SubUrbia* with Boston's Other Theatre. As a director, Matthew was part of the team that assembled *Washington Square Dreams* (published in *Plays and Playwrights 2001*). Pennsylvania-born and a graduate of the Pennsylvania Governor's School of the Arts, he now lives in a basement in Hell's Kitchen.

The Death of King Arthur was first produced by Gorilla Repertory Theatre, Inc. (Christopher Carter Sanderson, Artistic Director), on September 28, 2001, in Central Park, New York City, with the following cast:

King Arthur	Sean Elias-Reyes
Guenevere	Sarah Dandridge
Lancelot	Michael Colby Jones
Mordred	Tom Staggs
Hermit	Tim Moore
Morgan La Fay	Rohana Kenin
Gawain	Aubrey Chamberlin
Kay	Bruce Barton
Bors	Greg Petroff
Bedievere	Matthew Trumbull
Lucan	Richard Scudney
Agravaine/First Baron	Zorike Lequidre
Gareth/Second Baron	Tom Flaherty
Gentlewoman	Lynda Kennedy
Page Boy	Kina Bermudez

Director: Christopher Carter Sanderson
Stage Manager: William Koski-Karrell
Fight Director: Carrie Brewer
Assistant Fight Director: Bevin Kaye
Assistant Director: Matthew Freeman
Costumes: Sean Elias-Reyes and Rohana Kenin
Publicity: Rohana Kenin

EDITOR'S NOTE: Guenevere's song in Act III is from Tennyson's *Idylls of the King.*

This play is dedicated to my mother, father, and David Valdes-Greenwood.

CAST OF CHARACTERS

KING ARTHUR: son of Uther Pendragon
QUEEN GUENEVERE
SIR LANCELOT DU LAKE
SIR GAWAIN: Arthur's nephew, son of King Lot of Orkney
SIR AGRAVAINE: Arthur's nephew, son of King Lot of Orkney
SIR GARETH: Arthur's nephew, son of King Lot of Orkney
SIR MORDRED: Arthur's nephew and son by King Lot's wife
SIR BORS DE GANIS: cousin to Lancelot
SIR KAY: son of Ector, Arthur's foster father
SIR BEDIEVERE: brother to Lucan
LUCAN THE BUTLER: brother to Bedievere
A PAGE BOY
GENTLEWOMAN
A HERMIT
MORGAN LA FAY: A sister of King Arthur
Two BARONS from London

PROLOGUE

The HERMIT.

HERMIT: Merlin the Wizard, dead by this late date,
       Raised Arthur, son of royal Pendragon.
       Once passed was then King Uther, stolen son
       Supplanted and the story tells itself.
       King Arthur rose to take his father's place
       Through foster fathers numerous and wise.
       A great conspiracy seemed to unfold
       Beneath him, a red carpet to the throne.
       This Arthur sat head of the Round Table,
       The Knights of Camelot, "Triumph" their name.
       These knights quested to Saras, found the Grail,
       This Sainted Sipcup of a Heavenly Host,
       That Merlin barely knew, though often served.
       Did Merlin know the Future Knights he made
       Would gather up a realm of Christian Right?
       Was that his plan, to win a sight of Christ?
       The mystery of Merlin lies wherein
       His motives and his loyalties had been
       Before his wanderlust confined him lie
       Beneath a great stone and to there remain.
       Is Merlin manifesting England's fate
       From even now beneath his stony tomb?

For Arthur's greatest knights are now returned
From a Dark Age's greatest tale yet told.
The climax was behind and Dénouement
Is what the mage's magic now unfolds.

ACT I
SCENE I

KING ARTHUR's Court. All of the court in attendance.

BORS: Great God be praised, and Arthur at his hand!
My life is now beyond the Palest Ghost
For I bear witness to the ascended!
Both Percival and Galahad, the purest
Were raised above their bodies by the Host.
Joseph of Arimethea himself
With arms outstretched did send them tired up
To Highlands, greatlands, Avalon beyond.
I aside was lone left, for once did sin
To make a child, in my distant home France.
I do repent though still saw them ascend.
The servants, savants, open mouthed and awed
By what the Round Table makes proof of:
Men are Good! Arthur their Leader, their King!
Not cruel, not fiefdom, not axeheaded brute
But sent by Merlin, nature, destiny
To build the peace from hordes and chaos grown.
We have risen, we have proved pure again.
This moment, as I speak, is paragon.
We, paladins, proved pure through gallantry!

ARTHUR: And further go We. Onward, up to heaven.
I am in full prayer as each breath passes
To have the Carpenter's Cup as my symbol.
The Sangrail humbles all of me, and every part
Is better, but now less, for we are one.
Sir Bors de Ganis, to thee we are in debt.
Let me hear of the others. Of your efforts.

LANCELOT: Our failures, sire.

ARTHUR: No failures my knight. None.
Lancelot you are great in warlike craft
And honored every way in all our pasts.
No shame that others come home with their gold.
You battled hard, and so was your charge sent.

LANCELOT: It was my sin that kept me from the Grail.

ARTHUR: All men's sin is somewhere, excepting three.
    And even Bors could little else save stare.

LANCELOT: My unrepented sin, my Lord, forgive.

ARTHUR: Forgiveness is not mine to give, my friend.
    That is the Lord's station.

LANCELOT: But I ask yours.
    Your word that you forgive.

ARTHUR: You have more, Knight.
    You have my Love, so all my words combined.

KAY: My brother speaks you fair, Lancelot. Rest.
    Your madness took you not, The Round Thank God.
    Now onward toward new quests, more suited you.

GARETH: Might I remind the court of the hairshirt
    That Lancelot shouldered upon return,
    Crazed with his losses and unkempt wonder?
    You must rest your aching. Find then some pride
    That God chose you to test above all else.

GAWAIN: Well spoken, brother. God gives Grace.

GARETH: Amen.
    To one so great as Lancelot I speak
    Only the truth and likewise would Gawain.

GAWAIN: I, too, was humbled, but please God forgo
    Grieving, pity, sorrows, and talk of loss.
    The Round Table together searching found
    The Sangrail, Cup of Peace, the Sainted Glass.

MORDRED: And like a glass, a mirror. To us all.

GARETH: Yes brother Mordred.

GAWAIN: Smartly spoken words.

MORDRED: Gawain, my brother, I so dote on you
    And all the men returned.

AGRAVAINE: He speaks for me.
    We four, Gawain and Mordred, Agravaine,
    Gareth, long parted, are in arms again.

ARTHUR: There will be time for personal welcomes
    But let us now speak collectively of
    The blight that's cured by our most gallant Quest
    As Merlin foresaw before vanishing
    To what was sure his death. His charge the Grail
    Was made to us, and by that word we searched.
    Merlin has not seen what we have achieved

So for him we should raise our voices now.
As for your triumph did Camelot cry
For all contributed to noble feats,
Advises, tragedies, hardships, and leaps
To bring the Cure of All and make us whole.
To Merlin, to all men, to old Sir Bors
To Galahad the Pure, and Percival
Who from above now smile on Arthur's Court.
We thank the Lord!

ALL: We thank the Lord above!

ARTHUR: And Sir Bors, your story pleases our ears.
　　　　Sayeth the Queen how amazed she stands here.

GUENEVERE: I am amazed my friend. Kneel beside me.
　　　　Let Guenevere kiss your cheek for her pride.

BORS: A Kiss from the Queen? The Lord blesses indeed.

ARTHUR: A deserved pleasure, for a man so chaste.

(She kisses him.)

BORS: Thank you, my lady.

AGRAVAINE: A kiss for Gawain too. And Lancelot.

ARTHUR: Do you volunteer the Queen's mouth for her?

AGRAVAINE: I was in spirit Uncle. No harm meant.

ARTHUR: Let's go forth to the feast in spirit, too.
　　　　The stories here told need some bread and meat.
　　　　Some wine and water, in tribute imbibed.
　　　　Come all, inside. More stories tell your King.

KAY: Let's sit around the Round Table again.
　　　And as old strangers that were childhood friends
　　　Let's gaze and hazy memories define.
　　　Then, new pages in our stories we'll write
　　　After remembrances are paid their true due.

ARTHUR: As older brother says, let's go inside.
　　　　I love this Camelot, this rising tide.

(All exit except BEDIEVERE and LUCAN.)

BEDIEVERE: I look forward to drinking wine, Lucan.

LUCAN: And I, my friend. To drink away my shame.

BEDIEVERE: Your shame for staying home to guard your wife?

LUCAN: I have no wife. I feared my life, brother.
　　　　Bedievere, tell me you knew not I lied?
　　　　For years we've stood beside each other shaking.
　　　　Did in this time, you meet my wife?

BEDIEVERE: No sir.

LUCAN: At least you're small enough these days to duck
        Away from service, but I simply know
        Without excuses I'll be sent to die.

BEDIEVERE: Why Merlin brought us to this place I wonder.

LUCAN: Well, food inside. Let's go with all and drink.
        I've better things to do than sit and think.

(They exit.)

SCENE II

A nearby chamber. GAWAIN, GARETH, and AGRAVAINE.

GAWAIN: Though kin and King proclaim in public laud
        This deed done by all soldiers to confirm
        The greatness of our cause and of our God,
        I feel its completion brings harder tidings…
        Although the battle's done and battle's won.

GARETH: Why labor you in doubt when we have proved
        The very face of God smiles on the earth?

AGRAVAINE: You're simple, brother, and you love the war.

GAWAIN: How so simple? Agravaine, hold your tongue.

AGRAVAINE: My tongue or my peace? Gawain, let's not argue.
        You'll note we're from the same blood and we act thus.
        Our hands move much the same, our eyes set near
        Like our father, King Lot of Orkney, but different
        Not in love, but in interpretations.

GAWAIN: Say not simple, my Agravaine, say plain.
        And that I'll ask from you. Speak thus and plain.

AGRAVAINE: The Grail is found, and what? More life. You see?
        You like me plain, I'll tell you, I can be.
        What's plain? Did you see God? Did I? Those men
        Who want, by day, a little bit of bread…
        Did they the Messiah touch on their cheek?
        Do workers truly profit each to each
        By wonders done in Distant Arab Lands?

GAWAIN: Do they profit? Yes.

AGRAVAINE: In some way, yes.
        They gain respect and love and faith and trust
        But what do these aims achieve by themselves?
        What is the end, brother? What is the goal?
        Which path does admiration lead us down?

> I know Arthur maintains it's cured an ill
> But that ill cured itself two months before
> The Holy Grail sent Percival upstairs.

GAWAIN: The goal has been achieved.

AGRAVAINE: For its sake? Or ours?

> Our Fortune spins and just as it comes up,
> We feel it, as you feel, turn downward, pulled
> By th' unwritten rule that no man lives forever
> Or forever in his glory. Glory fades.
> And, though we know it, still we call it good.
> The end of glory, as if done the Quest.

GAWAIN: To what end do we fight then?

AGRAVAINE: Can't it change?

> Invert and cancel and become the war
> On war and warriors?

GAWAIN: The simple trade?

> You overvalue thought and cut by rating
> The cause below the *profit* of the cause.

GARETH: Know comfort brother. He is indisposed
> To battle. He feels his fault as his own.

AGRAVAINE: Here is our Mordred, fourth of our family.

(Enter MORDRED.)

MORDRED: My two, my loved, the Opposites embraced!
> And you, the youngest Gareth, too I love.
> Gawain, at last I can tell you how I favor you
> And love to see you back at home again.

GAWAIN: You told me once before, Mordred. In court.

MORDRED: I said, in court, the truth. But that is nothing.
> My voice sang praises to the Table Round
> But you are mine, more than any before.
> My strong brother, magical and alive.
> How could you know how we thought most of you
> And how the single wonder of your journey
> Agravaine and myself did re-invent
> Night in and out, whenever we thought worst
> To keep ourselves in hope that this strange challenge
> Had not robbed us of you. We told new tales
> Of how you'd plan and plot advantages
> To keep your battles happening before noon
> So that the strength you bear would never wane
> And you would be back in your family's arms.

AGRAVAINE: It was quite near to mathematicals
    How we would stand the possibilities
    Upon their heads so never we'd believe
    You would be overmatched at any time.

GAWAIN: I am no plotter, and I never planned.
    My faith would take me where I needed hope
    And saved me, now you see, to bring me home.

AGRAVAINE: I love your answer, and your humorlessness.
    I told you he would find us both affected.
    He thinks our weeping comes from girlish hearts.
    Gawain, you know our tongues are made of muscle.
    The muscle that your brothers bruise and build
    The only muscle your body abhors.

GAWAIN: Come sweeter youth and let us talk
    Of true faith, undiscovered by the mind.

GARETH: I know my wife Lyoness awaits us both
    To kiss us and to love you as a host.
    We part you brothers, pardon us.

(Exit GAWAIN and GARETH.)

AGRAVAINE: He goes.

MORDRED: He hears the way you mock him with a smile,
    And someday, when his hand is through your throat
    I'll laugh at having warned you in advance.
    Pulled punches still find targets my Pugilist.
    Too bad your sword fails to back up your mouth.

AGRAVAINE: He bluntly blunts me even in deep thought
    He does it bluntly. I tried to calm him
    But he can smell you on me, that I know.

MORDRED: Now I'm a stink? Fortune for you made us kin
    And fortune that I trusted you not him.

AGRAVAINE: Your trust sticks to me like Luck to the Irish:
    A doubtful constant, quoted never seen.

MORDRED: And my stink is doubtful too.

AGRAVAINE: Too suspected.

MORDRED: You bring suspicion by your clamoring.

AGRAVAINE: As we agreed my clamoring should bring.

MORDRED: Not upon yourself, you thoughtless jabber.
    You never let a flower grow in peace.
    Our ascensions blooming bud is hindered
    When you pull't open, too ripe for the sun.

AGRAVAINE: The seeds of doubt are sown through Camelot.
Lancelot's failure makes our tongues sound true.
While only coincidence makes us truth-sayers
It's somehow satisfying to be on the side
Of righteous indignation, though we know
That righteousness is for our gain alone.

MORDRED: Evil is petty, Agravaine. Evil.
Have you heard a more maddening small word?
Does it contain the reason for your turns?
The anti-antihero Agravaine?
Does this give you the pride you lack in Christ?

AGRAVAINE: Do you believe in Christ?

MORDRED: No, Agravaine.

AGRAVAINE: I do. That is our difference, friend.
I know that Christ wants justice done in souls
Not by the knife or by the joust or horse.
I know that Christ loves all the minds he made
And soon, the men whom he loves best will rule.
Each time there is a good, it comes by war,
And our war is just illicit, spoken.
We'll bring, as you said, Parliament to England.

MORDRED: Evolution of the English honor.
We'll tempt the Good King to discover Lust.
In that action we'll serve your righteous lies
Turned truth by luck, and with your Christ
We'll turn his Holy Grail to memorial.
Go off, and prepare arguments and twists.
I'll meet thee in due time before the King.

(Exit AGRAVAINE.)

Before the King? Before my father-uncle
I'll report and turn the prevailing tides
As tide and moon together seem to meet
Conspire and plan their constant connection.
So I, the moonchild, pull the waves of fire
Upon my devil daddy Arthur of the Water.
If there is anything true about father
It is he is a myth. He's smoke and mirrors
Raised unregal farmer and placed to rule
On warrior throne by succubus son.
By British fools he's praised as Christian king,
Though sons abound, his married life newfound.
But this strange religion is lost on one
Who is a king's unrighteous incest seed

And born of prophecy to crush and lead.
When before Arthur his friends kneel in shame
And Guenevere is shown as skin and bones
We'll see who England loves as ruler loved
And who she shuns as all too far away.
Good night, old Knight, is all that they shall say.
(Exit.)

SCENE III

GUENEVERE and LANCELOT, in the Forest.

LANCELOT: I am not him that I would have you see.

GUENEVERE: You are not he that I would have you be.
How do you follow me on broken branches
And not make a sound until you mouth it?

LANCELOT: I have learned silence on my humbling course.

GUENEVERE: A humble sinner?

LANCELOT: I am not rare, now.
My sword and shield I lay down to expose
The common man that knelt before the King.

GUENEVERE: This is a place of quiet.

LANCELOT: Yes, I feel it.

GUENEVERE: And you are not of silence.

LANCELOT: I have learned
The virtue of a moment passed unspoken
And failure of a man who cries for grace.

GUENEVERE: This earth is silent. Are you like this dirt?

LANCELOT: The crying man is never pridelessly
Begging the heavens for his dignity.
All dignity is only pride made proud.
The prettier pride.

GUENEVERE: So you keep no dignity?
Does not this dirt show stern and unwav'ring
Contempt for all that would convert it else?
Does not a plant reach upwards to its growth?
Are you like flowers?

LANCELOT: I am like a man.
I cannot surmount the blooming flower
Of my sin, which is inherent in me.

GUENEVERE: We are not good. Not certain like the trees.
'Tis no comfort, but you are comfort to me.
I do not know why.

LANCELOT: For we are beloved.
           I am your same, although returned in shame.

GUENEVERE: Should not we take the sign of your failure
           As one from God that He sees how we act?

LANCELOT: Knew you not before what He saw was all?

GUENEVERE: He sees both what was and what will befall
           And a warning was made for us to quit
           Before not only hell but while we live
           The end comes tragically and we are found.

LANCELOT: Found how? We have for years met in this way.

GUENEVERE: Before the King and all, you nearly told
           What your sin was, as I sat and held breath.
           You heard the one who called for us to kiss.
           That was a mock to use us.

LANCELOT: Abuse us
           If they will, they cannot break my bonds.

GUENEVERE: When will you ever see that you are not
           Infallible, and your brash youthfulness
           Does not match the lines etched across your face.

LANCELOT: So I am what? Not Sir Bors, that old horse?

GUENEVERE: Do you claim childhood beside other men?

LANCELOT: At least I have the strength to raise my sword.
           Remember when I wooed in tournament
           For Bors, who barely could defend your name?

GUENEVERE: With you, my champion, off in sullen sulk
           And no man by my side could raise his hand
           Because the accusation was the poison of their kin.
           Even then were you my absent champion.
           Bors showed his love, how can you question him?

LANCELOT: I question him not, but make comparison.
           Would you that I were even keeled and calm?
           Would you that I were sturdy, tried and true?
           The dullest housewife in the quiet stead?
           A trusty breadknife, sitting in the cupboard?
           Would you your love was his? His safe old hands?

GUENEVERE: I would my love was Arthur's back again.

LANCELOT: Arthur? Bors? These old men, pious peacocks
           Who sit aloof and make grand gestures far
           From battlefields, from jousts and from Dragons.
           Bors saw the final moment of a great quest

But only watched. Other men sacrificed
So he could tell their tale as conqueror.

GUENEVERE: I'm jealous too, of those that can see God.
As we are now, we're far from such a goal.

LANCELOT: How so? Because we're in love with each other?

GUENEVERE: Have you taken Christ's love into your heart?

LANCELOT: My Guenevere.

GUENEVERE: Have you made me but flesh?

LANCELOT: You are flesh.

GUENEVERE: More.

LANCELOT: I love your flesh, it's warm.

GUENEVERE: I'm more.

LANCELOT: Yes. So much more.

GUENEVERE: But flesh is least.

LANCELOT: It's your body. How can it be said least?

GUENEVERE: My soul is more.

LANCELOT: Where's that? Show me your soul.

GUENEVERE: I'll show you everyday, and then it's less.

LANCELOT: Your spirit lessened by my eyes' discovery?

GUENEVERE: My spirit?

LANCELOT: By my eyes?

GUENEVERE: Is made too bold.
Too naked, I am naked in your eyes.

LANCELOT: Yes always naked. I see through your clothes.

GUENEVERE: You see through more and further still inside.
So Lancelot, I love Arthur. I love him.
I will find a way to love him ever more.
I will touch Arthur better than before.
Because by God, I'm his Queen, his Guenevere.
And by your right, it's safer for you gone.

LANCELOT: Safer? Do you love me safely? Distantly?
Shall we observe our lives in retrospect
And calmly say we lived them safe from harm?
Where is the glory in your safety, Love?

GUENEVERE: Glory resides in chivalry, in love
In worship and in sacrifice, in prayer.
Why marry you defiance and Glory?

LANCELOT: What victory is won by constancy?

GUENEVERE: Whose throat is cut by constancy? There's none.
You shame me, and you shame yourself beside.
Before the court, you ask for forgiveness
Of Arthur who smiles and bows his head, too true.
You see? The others know that we are two.

LANCELOT: This Sangrail quest has tamed you to my heart.
You blame me only for the failure past.
I wandered mad, bloodied by lesser men
I cared not for any quest but Guenevere.
I slept by churches, each one turned me out.
My horses stolen, my shield stoned *broken*.
No God smiled upon me. What God is He
That turns a simple love to want for pity?
How dare He challenge me, this God, for you?
I'll best them all, I best them still, no God
Is so vast He may crumble my stone will.

GUENEVERE: You condemn me to vow heresy by me!
I will run from thee to escape your fate
And never see thee in this Camelot.
I deserved a champion, deserved heaven.
Lancelot too deserved it but in test
Forsook the only Love that could raise him.

LANCELOT: No I did not. Only you raise me above
A woodcarver of balsam men, none else.

GUENEVERE: Can you compare me to God and not see
That this will hurt me more than compliment?

LANCELOT: I mean to show you where you are in me
And cannot call you else but gracious sent.

GUENEVERE: Alone again, with Arthur, home again.
Now in thy milky mind do remember
That in respect I bid you see me never.
(She exits.)

LANCELOT: Guenevere. From she, my body's center
Can never leave too long. I love and lover
Must be despite myself. I know this God.
He forgives me as I rage, for he knows
Who put these tempests inside my boiling breast.
Why did he make us with these parts inside
If only to mock us for their plainest use?
These hearts, these bodies, are all built broken
And wordless fervors fragment when too spoken.
(He exits.)

SCENE IV

The King's Chamber. ARTHUR and KAY.

KAY: My brother, where is your Queen gone tonight?

ARTHUR: She spends her nights renewing peasant faith
        By seeding gardens once barren of smiles
        By gazing on them from her forest path.

KAY: She walks alone at night. Without your hand.

ARTHUR: She has done this to meditate on flowers
        And kiss the ground in barefoot trysts untold.
        The best lovers keep secrets just to tempt
        Their partner from his possible boredom.

KAY: You'd never tire of Guenevere, Arthur.

ARTHUR: How could I when she is tempting me?
        When she is offering me mysteries
        Of how she spends her sweet night's loneliness.

KAY: Since you were farming, you have been in love
        With a girl that lived past the stony wall
        Or hidden in the wheat, or up a tree.
        You've chased your girls from when you were knee-high.

ARTHUR: My lovely Kay, you know me too well now.
        I am unsure of why I have the crown
        When I am younger than you and less wise.

KAY: I'm not wise. I'm older and less gifted.
        We compensate by looking confident
        We elder statesman, woodsman, carpenters…
        We, older brothers, we are talkative.

ARTHUR: So talk to me of Guenevere some more.
        When spoken of, she's water and music.
        A song shimmering still, yet never rests
        She glistens, vibrates, pours herself from me
        From my tongue and from my chest she streams.

KAY: You push your poetry, and I can't listen.
        You bring me smiles by foolish rambling.

ARTHUR: If but for you, no one would hear them.
        Not even she, so distant and so light
        She dances from me every night.

(Enter AGRAVAINE.)

AGRAVAINE: Sovereign.

ARTHUR: Approach my friend.

AGRAVAINE: Are you in private talk?
    I'll not interfere brotherly conference
    For I have recently partaken of such loves,
    My brother Gawain, returned to me at last.

KAY: So speak then, sir. You're bidden do by both
    The King and the King's friend, not true bloodmates.

AGRAVAINE: Your foster self is no less respected
    By all the realm as by Arthur himself.

ARTHUR: My brother bids you speak, so do it sir.
    Nothing is interrupted fatally.

AGRAVAINE: A careful phrasing sire, but I protest.
    Your politeness suggests I do infringe.

KAY: Speak what you will, or I'll remove your ears.

ARTHUR: No, Kay. He's scared to speak his words.
    That's why he protests and sputters excuses.
    Agravaine, you are welcome. Speak your mind.

AGRAVAINE: My mind deduces undercurrents quickly
    My eyes burdened with visions unrevealed
    To less observant, less suspicious men.
    When in a time so calm I feel unrest
    I question questioning, but question then, myself.
    Why do I even bring these matters forth
    If they carry consequences so grave?

KAY: What are the matters that you mean?
    Is there a threat to peace in this kingdom?

AGRAVAINE: Not now, there is no threat, and yet not yet.
    For as I do see, others do still note
    And underneath their smiles are shaken faiths
    Compounded by hidden meditation.

ARTHUR: The matter, nephew. What is its name?

AGRAVAINE: Lancelot, my Lord. The name is his we fear.

ARTHUR: We fear?

AGRAVAINE: I speak for unaccounted friends.

ARTHUR: Explain this quickly now. Explain your fears.

(Enter MORDRED.)

MORDRED: Agravaine! I had thought to reach you sooner.

ARTHUR: Mordred, we are in conference. Get you gone.

MORDRED: May I be bold and disobey the King?

KAY: For seconds you may be, before I'm at you.

MORDRED: What brings this tone of voice from my uncle?

ARTHUR: A name spoken from one less fortunate
        That he has not yet been excused, now go.

MORDRED: Agravaine, you made the accusation?
        I had hoped to keep the name unknown.
        We talked, my Lord, upon this very name
        A name I know you love, and so we mulled
        We worried at our very thoughts unworthy
        To challenge such a friend and man of men.
        I ran in desperate misgivings to you
        Hoping in vain to cut off Agravaine.

AGRAVAINE: I wish you had, brother, but I'm undone.

ARTHUR: Mordred, I want your pensive explanation.
        Our eager Agravaine should wait for my verdict.

MORDRED: As I said, I do not want to speak.
        The graces undone by the story told
        Would send our Camelot to disrepair.

ARTHUR: Kay, do you hear the King make small requests?
        Arthur says tell your story, make it so.

MORDRED: Your Lancelot, your friend and confidant,
        The man who serves you with the might of ages,
        Power nonpareil and speed that's set apart
        From other strong knights, hence struck down…
        This friend has taken to your Queen.

ARTHUR: If you want this hand removed from your neck
        You'll shake your head in disgust of yourself!

AGRAVAINE: He speaks upon your order, release him.

ARTHUR: Kay, kill my nephew Agravaine for this!

(Enter GARETH.)

GARETH: My uncle, I heard cries from within filled
        With violence and ran to aid your voice.

ARTHUR: Your brothers, child, have driven me to rage.
        So say you Kay? What stays your execution?

KAY: Arthur, I share your anger, but no murder here.

MORDRED: Did I not say I feared your hand at this?
        Did I not warn you, run here to keep quiet?
        You must release me, sir. I am not wrong.

ARTHUR: My marriage brought to questioning?
        My favorite's betrayal imagined by two fools?

MORDRED: He has been missing days, you have to see.
        You see his sin pronounced in court, yet hid.
        The Queen moaned for his absence publicly
        To embarrassing lengths, as most said after.

AGRAVAINE: Mordred.

MORDRED: No, now I am angered to truth.
        You are my greatest love, your reign the cure.
        You are the center, soul of Camelot.
        To see you mocked, to see your eyes go blind
        While confined my eyes, though I'd pluck out
        Anyone, no matter who, offending.

ARTHUR: I see this. I understand. But do you?
        Do you know what you accuse me of?

MORDRED: My accusations aim for others, sire.
        And while you struggle inward with these truths
        Know that I'd not risk death but for a cause.
        And what cause have I given my life to?
        To you, your cause, your honor, I'm for you.

ARTHUR: I know that Mordred, but how can that be?
        What proof have you except your traitorous word?

AGRAVAINE: I suspect it by a thousand glances,
        Coincidences, I have thought it through.

MORDRED: He speaks on her, protects her honor more dearly
        Than he seems to do you, his own sworn King.

KAY: Chivalry favors women by honor
        And Lancelot's chivalry exceeds all else.

AGRAVAINE: Why does she walk at night most when he's gone?
        Remember how he championed her cause
        When poison was accused? See how they fought
        And from the land he like a scorned child flew?
        When from her graces fell he was soon gone.
        If by your day he rises, by your night
        He falls, he sleeps and kills to keep you King…
        Why at her words would he abandon you?

MORDRED: This is too much. 'Tis too much that we've said.
        I see the pain in my uncle's sweet face
        And never wanted this, not called for sin
        To trace its circle round our holy place.

KAY: Your concerns are well taken and sound true.
        Still this lacks evidence.

ARTHUR: Yes. Evidence.

MORDRED: That's true. But we could act to find it then.

AGRAVAINE: Act? Is't not enough that doubt is fading fast?
Perhaps if we wait they will be revealed.
Why chase them down like witches, if we're wrong?

ARTHUR: I don't believe that my closest transgress.
His love for her, while storied, comes by way
Of his devotion to the English cause.

MORDRED: He's French, my King. He's always been of blood
Foreign to us, and not so brotherly.

ARTHUR: Kay is my brother, and yet not so born.

KAY: By Arthur I am treated brotherly.
And so as brother to England, I am.
Why not extend this Christian courtesy
To Lancelot, who's earned our trust tenfold?
He's slashed and shamed and been himself ashamed
For our ideals and to uphold the Court.

AGRAVAINE: All mortal men are sinful, our flesh fails.
It breaks a thousand ways against our wills
To bring the strongest bull to his dark knees.

MORDRED: Sir Kay, I doubt not that you love England
And would die for a man who'd die for you.
All of us love King Arthur as the Light
That lifts his kingdom and makes us divine.
Even Lancelot would never have fought so
If he did disdain and distrust the King.
I call not into question his good faith.
But if he takes the married Queen to bed...
All is in doubt. This is a treasonous act.
And less politically, it is unfriendly.
It is disrespectful to my uncle.

ARTHUR: What say you Gareth to what you have heard?

GARETH: Agravaine has a mind sharp and hot
As any crusader that Quested for you.
While he may rile a man to anger quick
'Tis rarely for a lack of reason.
The loyal Mordred in his ire seems rash
But he claims this grows by his love for you.
I wonder why they would invent this risk?

ARTHUR: My brother, can you say that it is not so?

KAY: My King, I cannot. I have seen and heard
These rumblings, but dismissed them just as quick

As they would swell and dissipate in secret.

ARTHUR: You kept this from me, Kay? Why did you so?

KAY: Unconfirmed rumor surrounds a regal life
And each suspicion need not go checked too far.
That way lies tragedy, breeds only fear.

ARTHUR: My marriage should not be stuff of rumor,
My love not talked of unkindly at court.
Her maiden love and honesty questioned
Must by her husband be defended now.
We shall discount false rumors with the truth.

KAY: I counsel caution. Discov'ring too much
Will give you no peace, and may ruin more
Than truth, if found, can bring you by itself.

ARTHUR: No more rumors. We must put them to rest.
She is mine and none other's, all shall see.

AGRAVAINE: The rumor is that at her cabin oft
They meet in secret, when he's gone from sight.
For days he's been away. Now is the time.

ARTHUR: You think in secret they meet presently?

AGRAVAINE: Upon some nights recently, they could be
Together, at her cabin, in the wood
Tonight, tomorrow, or another day
But that is where they'd be if they astray.

ARTHUR: Go Mordred, Agravaine, and bring your knights.
Go Gareth, bring your might to bolster them.
Observe her and you'll see that I am right.
She'll not betray her King or her true love
With any man, not even Lancelot.

GARETH: For Love so great it is unthinking pure.

MORDRED: We'll go straightaway Uncle, bring you peace.
But what if we find him there with your Queen?

ARTHUR: Then bring him here. Use the force you are lent.

MORDRED: If we must, Uncle, I anon repent.

(Exit AGRAVAINE, GARETH, and MORDRED.)

KAY: I fear this course of action is too brash.
And its effects too uncertain to match
The frail peace that we have taken so dear.

ARTHUR: My brother, without truth I'll live in fear
That Lancelot has taken Guenevere.
I wish to call my three nephews back now

But I confess, Kay, even I've some doubt.
Have I been blind, that I not questioned them?
Did I notice this but leave it aside
To my detriment and hid my suspicions,
From even my own heart, which would near burst
On nights that I laid lonely in my bed?
Let this be put to rest, let mistrust cease
For secrets are the end of all my peace.

ACT II
SCENE I

The Queen's Cabin. GENTLEWOMAN appears.

GENTLEWOMAN: My lady?

GUENEVERE: Yes. Here I am.

GENTLEWOMAN: Arise both.
        There's clamor at the gate. Knights on horseback.
        Awake Sir Lancelot! It's you they call.

LANCELOT: They call my name, or arms?

GENTLEWOMAN: They call your name.
        They call you villain and that you're found out.
        Ten or more men, who wear the garb you wear.

LANCELOT: The cross of Arthur? Knights of the Round Table?

GUENEVERE: Hide yourself lady, and wait for my call.

GENTLEWOMAN: My Queen, I will.

        (She exits.)

GUENEVERE: Oh what are we to say?

LANCELOT: Have you inside this cabin armor kept?
        What shame to face them unarmed and naked.
        Such proof of a tryst rightly discovered.

GUENEVERE: They haven't seen you here. They do but guess.
        If I deny your presence as their Queen,
        By order they must hold their tongues and go.

LANCELOT: They call my name.

GUENEVERE: To bring you forth they call.
        But none have seen you come to me before.

LANCELOT: And never were there armed men hereto come!
        The hunters smell their prey, cannot be swayed.
        'Tis proved your word on doubting ears falls oft
        So talk less of dealings, instead make haste
        To find me a sword that I may employ.

GUENEVERE: To prove them true by coming forth requested?

LANCELOT: I'll stop their throats.

GUENEVERE: You rogue. They are my knights.
    Retreat is nearer to retribution.
    If shamed we are, all shamed, even Arthur.

LANCELOT: No Arthur mine. He sent this raid to you.
    His militant spite rears its head again.
    And further falls his claim to nobility.

GUENEVERE: He's noble still. Curse our baseness, not his.

LANCELOT: Remembrance made of my Quest for the Grail
    Will story me sinner, failure, every age.
    My hope is only your defense, my Right's
    Tale only storied by my strong arm style.
    The vision of my victories falls left
    Of what my legend would have been before,
    Save my broken unloved soul betrothed—
    Though unbetrothed love to King Arthur's Queen.
    What should I do? Shun remaining history?
    Without this hand to raise, I'm less and less.
    And would you have me in the end, a lover?
    A simple man who's concubine to queens?
    Lancelot du Lake of France, a kept boy? No.
    Instead of wither, my knighthood must grow.

GUENEVERE: Speak quietly and stop your selfishness.
    Inside these wooden walls is Britain's heart
    And you would for pride be the dagger thrust
    From within outward spilling Arthur's blood
    And mine, your own, these knights, the loyal men
    The wicked men, divines, the very mice
    The gentle nuns, the memories, old men
    Lost ones, Christians, pagans, moors and French,
    Those cured of ill, Gawain, your friends, Sir Bors.
    All pierced when upon these men you drop
    To indignantly kill for naught but show.

LANCELOT: This Camelot, these people, all my friends
    Those mentioned, move me, as you do, my heart.
    But they are living with the luxury
    Of blinding graciousness and thoughts unbound.
    Why must I earthbound only sit in flesh
    And confront each day lonely viscera?
    The blood inside is hidden by the flesh
    And flesh, the plate mail, seems scriptured to shame.
    No longer shame will I endure for you.

GUENEVERE: I love your words, hate the effect they take.
          Do not convince us both this is the best
          To run outside and kill yourself for me.

LANCELOT: Prepare for proof that my love's past the limit
          And will not hear their cursing you too much.
          (He exits.)

GUENEVERE: By madness otherworldly we are touched.

SCENE II

A farm near Camelot. The PAGE BOY.

PAGE: Today my trusty blade lays lonesome siege to the stronghold
          of a Beast. Why lonesome? The blade, my wooden rapier,
          is alone today, but does a valiant hero need more than
          strength and purity? Ah no! A man once told me that if I
          kept my intentions pure and course just, I would be re-
          warded. The only thing I questioned is the reward! Is honor
          and goodness not its own reward? By Arthur, I have learned
          that courage makes a Knight, and that might comes after
          right. I could be with him, one day, not too many years.
          When I am taller, and battle beasts, and travel to the Land
          of Gore, to save the Maid Melinda, a pretty girl, from the
          wiry bloodroots and the Black Sorcerer. My wooden ra-
          pier made sharper with use, you see, so that I know its
          weight and wield it skillful. The sweet Melinda leaps into
          my arms and as she loves my goodness and my dedica-
          tion, is married to me before the King. But not before I've
          faced above a pit of fire, her captor and outwitten him
          with charms and riddles. He'd say: "Stand down, small
          knight! Your age impedes your might!" And I, with the
          Maiden's hand in mine, quip: "Mother says as much and
          told me so before, as early as this morning... long before
          I felled the Sorcerer and Roots! But you know as much as
          Mother, villain, there's none too young for bravery!" And
          by Excalibur, he'd pause for thinking of a retort, and in
          his leg! Then ARM! Then... other ARM! Then heart! I'd
          stick him with my blade. A married, holy, truthful hero.
          Can you see me then? I'm not noble, I know. But Arthur
          was raised by farmers, as was I. I'll see him, and he'll see
          me in him and likewise. And, I'll carry what I must, I'll
          teach them all a move or two with my cutter! Some will
          tell him No... like mother... but kings know who is good.
          When I am older, just a few short months, I'll go to
          Camelot and serve the King. I will be the Child of the
          Round Table.

SCENE III

The Forest of Gore. MORDRED and MORGAN LA FAY.

MORDRED: I have never seen a knight so brutal
             That called his actions valiant.

MORGAN: Raise your arm.
             Beneath it is another deep-set cut
             That this cool cream should wet and disinfect.
             It's made from all the leaves you find and some leaves
             Found in the Land of Gore, where many grow
             Above my husband's grave.

MORDRED: It feels like fire!
             Aunt, your cures have never cured my hate
             And never calmed a wound, but just prolonged
             My life for your own ends.

MORGAN: For both our ends.

MORDRED: How can I argue? You've taught me who I am
             And so I am.

MORGAN: I did as Merlin, served
             Broad winds, long Lakes, and gave my will to theirs.
             Their gravity, their growth, their roots and wraiths
           . All have direction, which will never alter.
             Nephew, we all are not unlike the roots
             Which grow from grandeur and sink sucking low.

MORDRED: Sir Lancelot has ruined what he loves
             With what he is. His sword is all he knows.

MORGAN: So will we all, the air is poison, child.
             The world's deep guts ingest themselves each day
             And heal with poison, kill with sugar cane.
             You, maybe, are a rare earthsop that sees
             The rivaling fate's own eccentricities
             That rain and burn at once, to the same end:
             To wash and clear the mess that is itself.

MORDRED: The scabbard saved me, its magic was plain.
             I felt my body move, my skin stretch hard
             To resist harm despite his awesome rages.
             I pitied him for flailing blindly, caught,
             As each of his friends fell by his own hand.

MORGAN: It was forgiven as soon as was done.
             Betrayal, Mordred, enters each tale told
             To mete it out and make the story whole.
             The death of Arthur, and of other boys,

        The earthsopped sobbers sinking by the sand
        They built their castles from, were and will be
        Dead from the past and present, presciently.

MORDRED: You speak no sense.

MORGAN: My speech is of senses.
        You've grown too old to hear me, child of dirt.

MORDRED: I hear you, but old Aunt, what would you teach?
        That I should act by how the branches break
        And whether it should rain on Sabbath days?

MORGAN: What Sabbath day? Whose?

MORDRED: What does it matter?
        It's not a toad that will bring on his death.

MORGAN: No, it will be a snake.

MORDRED: Are you not real?
        Have you not flesh? Are you not earthly born?
        You patronize me, as you heal my wounds.
        I know that I deserve no angry tones.

MORGAN: Take any tone you like, play a pan flute!
        Just watch this balm as it goes towards your throat.
        Do not breathe in, it's not to go inside you.
        Good, keep quiet for a moment, loving lad.
        Keep still and let me stroke your throat with this.
        You see? Where are these roots inside his castle walls?
        He'd never know a knitleaf from its mother.
        You're safe here with me, better than all others.

MORDRED: You're safe with me. I am trained perfectly.
        With hate, with justice, and immodestly
        I can spin spears, axes and chains so well
        That magic or no, Arthur I can kill.

MORGAN: Like Moses you were saved by water from
        A King who killed all that would do him harm.
        Too early to face them himself, he thought
        He'd strangle dangle stab and grab
        The babes he made that Merlin said to fear.
        Now Mordred, my sweet nephew, Arthur's son.
        His perversion and his dark paranoid acts
        Are you incarnate.

MORDRED: Abused in my birth
        But better for it, as I'm bathed in wrath.
        I'll cut him mercilessly as I'm taught
        And leave what he has made an afterthought.

SCENE IV

The King's Court. ARTHUR, GAWAIN, LUCAN, KAY, BEDIEVERE, and ATTENDANTS.

LUCAN: You live my friend! I heard you were cut down!

BEDIEVERE: No. I was not near what ensued just past.

LUCAN: Nor I. Thank heaven for our luck again.

BEDIEVERE: No, Lucan. We've no luck. We see the end.
        Lancelot's bravery has betrayed us
        And killed the brightest fellows that I knew.

LUCAN: As Gareth fell, Gawain's fury redoubles.
        And Agravaine, might have gone under too.

BEDIEVERE: I wish that I was home. Under my sheets.

LUCAN: At least you're not yet used as wormy meat.

KAY: Quiet all. Arthur addresses you. Stand tall.

GAWAIN: What has happened to us? Tell us straightaway.

BORS: I fear my friend, Sir Lancelot unsheathed
        And brandished his famed blade wrongmindedly,
        Since we know that he cannot bear mocking
        And his pride is a vice that burdens him.
        He bursts out anger suddenly when pressed.

ARTHUR: Patience. The event will be exposed here,
        With audience of Mordred, who was present.

(Enter MORDRED.)

        I sent you, Mordred, unto bloody acts
        And now you return undone, split in half.
        Tell the Court what occurred from out of sight.
        If there are horrors, please look to your spleen
        And force the words out. Do not choke the truth.
        Then, tell us why so many men are gone.

MORDRED: If I had listened to the Christian adage
        And learned not to pick apples from the tree
        My brothers would be living now, our Garden
        Could still by learned men be called Eden.
        Agravaine is gone, and others gone. Dispatched.

GAWAIN: My brother, you went to see Lancelot
        To find what sin was secretly on him.

MORDRED: That I did. So did we all. To find him out.
        As so we did. He was with our Guenevere.
        The cabin near the lake, that she rests in
        Is where we came upon the knave undressed.

KAY: Undressed?

MORDRED: Yes. He stole armor from another knight
⠀⠀⠀⠀⠀⠀⠀⠀And took at us with that dead Knight's weapons.
⠀⠀⠀⠀⠀⠀⠀⠀I am the only living witness of this act
⠀⠀⠀⠀⠀⠀⠀⠀Except Guenevere, who was hid within.

ARTHUR: What said Lancelot before the fight ensued?
⠀⠀⠀⠀⠀⠀⠀⠀Did he confess directly to a crime?

MORDRED: He waited until a man came within
⠀⠀⠀⠀⠀⠀⠀⠀And once he'd taken his life, ran outside
⠀⠀⠀⠀⠀⠀⠀⠀With eyes blood red and colorful mad scream
⠀⠀⠀⠀⠀⠀⠀⠀He raced at closest combatant, then maimed
⠀⠀⠀⠀⠀⠀⠀⠀The first, and then the second, each stuck down.
⠀⠀⠀⠀⠀⠀⠀⠀We called to him, forewarned him he was caught
⠀⠀⠀⠀⠀⠀⠀⠀But once unleashed, he would not hear our pleads.

ARTHUR: Were accusations levied from the trees
⠀⠀⠀⠀⠀⠀⠀⠀Or did a man reveal his charge from me?

MORDRED: My brother Agravaine stepped forward straight
⠀⠀⠀⠀⠀⠀⠀⠀And held your symbol high, to show his charge
⠀⠀⠀⠀⠀⠀⠀⠀Was from England itself. Lancelot frowned
⠀⠀⠀⠀⠀⠀⠀⠀Within the cabin of your wife, he scowled
⠀⠀⠀⠀⠀⠀⠀⠀And ducked away from sight most chillingly.

GAWAIN: Agravaine was slain as well? Gareth felled?

MORDRED: Each man lies headless in the woods, or bleeds
⠀⠀⠀⠀⠀⠀⠀⠀His insides on streams nearby. It was the worst
⠀⠀⠀⠀⠀⠀⠀⠀Of man that I have ever seen performed.
⠀⠀⠀⠀⠀⠀⠀⠀And that is much.

ARTHUR: You haven't seen enough.
⠀⠀⠀⠀⠀⠀⠀⠀Lancelot is known for bloody deeds,
⠀⠀⠀⠀⠀⠀⠀⠀But in the name of justice and of God.
⠀⠀⠀⠀⠀⠀⠀⠀This story confuses its motivations
⠀⠀⠀⠀⠀⠀⠀⠀For those of lesser men. He's still a friend.

GAWAIN: Sir Lancelot killed thirteen of your men.
⠀⠀⠀⠀⠀⠀⠀⠀My brothers, Uncle, your nephews lay dead.
⠀⠀⠀⠀⠀⠀⠀⠀Why does it matter why, or who, it's done!
⠀⠀⠀⠀⠀⠀⠀⠀We're lucky that he failed to kill Mordred,
⠀⠀⠀⠀⠀⠀⠀⠀Or of this tale we'd never know the truth.

ARTHUR: He's served us all, and saved us and our lands.
⠀⠀⠀⠀⠀⠀⠀⠀His muscle and allegiance courts my graces.

MORDRED: You trust me, Uncle?

ARTHUR: Trust? I do not know.
⠀⠀⠀⠀⠀⠀⠀⠀It's only used to make a man a slave

To promises he made oft while confused.
My nephew, you were valiant for your blood
But still I love the butcher you describe.

GAWAIN: I ask you for your word that Lancelot
Will answer for the acts he has performed.
If you let thirteen deaths pass through your eyes
Unblinking, while you love the butcher best
You precedent a lenience for sin.

MORDRED: Look to the Queen for answers, you trust her.
And, she knows better what drove him to slice
My brothers and his brothers of the Round.

GAWAIN: She is accused of something else than murder.

ARTHUR: Be careful how you address Guenevere.
She is more than the Queen, she is the air
That flows inside the kingdom's chest.
Inside my chest, more than even England.

MORDRED: Arthur, my hurts demand an explanation,
My losses seek revenge.

ARTHUR: More awful words.

GAWAIN: They're for your ears. So rise and act the King.

ARTHUR: Fetch the Queen. She'll need to address deaths.
Lucan, old friend, you are well-liked here
And comfortable to my Queen, so if you please
Take up the center of the floor and be our arbitrator.

LUCAN: Me? Take center stage? Right at this moment?

ARTHUR: In moments such as these, we find our calling.

LUCAN: Yes. Bedievere is more learned than I.

BEDIEVERE: I'm happy now to stand idly by.

LUCAN: Are you so sure that I should be the one
To talk now for you, and ask her these questions?

ARTHUR: Yes.

LUCAN: That's all? Just "Yes?"

ARTHUR: Yes, Lucan. That's all.

(Enter GUENEVERE.)

My love.

GAWAIN: You must stand and be questioned.
Lucan the Butler has been made fulcrum
For the proceedings. You shall address him as us.

GUENEVERE: Are all united of King Arthur's Court

        That I must answer to every man here?
        Who else gives answers to the Court today?

LUCAN: Mordred spoke up.

MORDRED: But she does not speak with me.

ARTHUR: This is not dialogue, it is examination.
        Not of you, Guenevere, but of events
        That passed erewhile, and you are said to have
        Some knowledge of the passings of thirteen.

GUENEVERE: Am I accused?

ARTHUR: You are examined.

GUENEVERE: Ask me.
        Lucan, I trust you would not be unjust.
        Please, ask me what you must.

LUCAN: And ask I must.
        I have no choice. Please note that in my voice.

ARTHUR: The deaths of my men are upon your voice,
        So ask the questions they would ask in life.

LUCAN: If courtly duties not assigned me thus
        To question that my Queen is pure—I'd not.
        But this grim doubt has fallen on us all
        So please you lady, pardon all of us
        By pardoning yourself. As written here:
        The many deaths that lay upon his head
        Need not lay upon the crown you bear.
        The evidence is self-defending blows
        Sent to the right-minded from Lancelot
        Who, killing kin, has fled and you remain
        To cut away the confused circumstance
        And place the blame upon the proper face.

GUENEVERE: I know what you speak of. I was present.
        I did not witness directly the engagement
        And only heard the battle cries outside.

LUCAN: The acts that Lancelot executed
        If I might mention them before your grace
        Were rather unbecoming of defense
        As none were sworn to hurt you.

GUENEVERE: I know this
        And I grieve each of them that he mistook.
        He is too mighty to be trifled with
        And with a blindness he in error struck.
        No doubt he is absent from shame himself.

LUCAN: Those knights, claim Mordred, looked for you alone
        And found you, to their consternation, kept
        In company by Lancelot.
        They were enraged by what they thought they found.

GUENEVERE: Which was?

BEDIEVERE: Brother, be careful of such talk.
        This is the Queen. My Lord, I do protest
        And fear, fear so much, that this talk is wrong
        For public ears.

ARTHUR: My Bedievere, silence.

LUCAN: They thought they found the Queen in company
        With her knight Lancelot in secret… tryst.
        I hope that I do not misspeak my Queen.

GUENEVERE: Am I the Queen?

LUCAN: You are. No one protests.

GUENEVERE: That I am Arthur's Queen no one protests?

LUCAN: Why proclaim you the mantle at this time?

GUENEVERE: If to Lucan I called, would he not come?

LUCAN: I'd come of course.

GUENEVERE: For I am she you serve.
        Am I but wife? Or am I Queen alone?

ARTHUR: Are these distinct stations? Do you divide?
        You are my Queen. Not alone, never left.

GUENEVERE: My word, like yours, is under God's word. True?

ARTHUR: Yes. Lucan, on.

LUCAN: Your word is under God.
        And Arthur's word.

GUENEVERE: So sayeth our Good Book.

LUCAN: Did you witness the slaying of the Knights?

GUENEVERE: I did witness defense of your Queen's word.
        And actions at her orders, nothing more.

LUCAN: Lancelot struck down Knights in your employ.

GUENEVERE: I did not see their faces, I heard them.
        Their venom accusations, bile and barks
        From outdoors, did not recognize the voice.
        I've never known a man from Camelot
        To speak in such a manner of the Queen.
        I thought myself in danger, all alone
        Save one defender, and a gentle maid.

LUCAN: The lady attending claims no knowledge.

GUENEVERE: We held each other as the fray ensued.
        She knows as I know.

LUCAN: You heard the battle, saw the arms drawn to?

GUENEVERE: One man approached the door, but just his arm
        Before Lancelot smote him and was dressed
        In the large man's armor, taking his blade.
        I saw this gallant act.

LUCAN: To steal from fallen foe?

GUENEVERE: He was unarmed, and set upon to fight.

LUCAN: You say he was there to defend?

GUENEVERE: He was.

LUCAN: Why absent was his own armor?

MORDRED: Answer to this! Claim not we died in vain!

ARTHUR: Be quiet all. Please, Guenevere. Answer.

GUENEVERE: I called him come unlabored by armor.

LUCAN: Why?

GUENEVERE: Do you accuse him?

LUCAN: No. Not accuse.

GUENEVERE: Am I allowed a whim? May I not call
        The page boy in a dress, or Bors with harpist come?
        My King, to me, has come at odd hour oft
        To calm my moving woman's temperament.
        So did the hero Lancelot, to quell
        My sudden whim, as a good subject would.
        These deaths, mistaken, Yes, were for the Queen,
        Brought by the calling. He is chivalrous.
        At each point as I turn the room I gaze
        Upon the eyes of men Lancelot saved.
        Use you those preserved parts to condemn him?
        Call you him a traitor?

LUCAN: This is his name.

GUENEVERE: That name unsay. He served to his own fault.

ARTHUR: Were you laying with Lancelot beside!
        Do you whore yourself and then scold the court?
        You cannot, you have lost all claim to scold
        To godly condescension and to me!
        No loving wife, no headstrong beauty none.
        Not Queen, not woman, barely what you were.

> I loved thee so. I love thee still, as you were.
> Here, before all, you lie and protect him.

GUENEVERE: He was there at my call, and killed at my whim.
> I protect no one. I tell the truth.

ARTHUR: Burn.
> Burn as a traitor, murderer, if you claim
> The truth beyond these words is nothing.
> You say you are the cause, you are the culprit.

GUENEVERE: I do.

ARTHUR: Where is your Knight to condemn you?
> Where did he run?

GUENEVERE: I bid him run.

ARTHUR: Please, love.
> Speak the truth:
> Out all! Out says Arthur. Out! Out! Out! Out!

(They all exit, save GUENEVERE.)

> Now, lonely, there is none on trial. I beg just words.
> Let mouths be free, and tongues relaxed uncurl.
> My rage is nothing. You don't fear it. I'm tame.
> I bound for them. I pound the seat for show.
> Who listens to a thoughtful king? These armed guards?
> You see? I must make show to get them out.
> They are listening, I fear, at the door even now.
> But that is what we've taken on. That is what we are.
> And I am burdened, tired, of talking in high language.
> Guenevere, you have been unfaithful to me?

GUENEVERE: Do you ask the question or accuse?

ARTHUR: Does it matter what I do to you at all?
> Has Arthur ever mattered, been the King?
> I sit here, now confused and open to failure.
> Where is my mind Merlin? Still dead? Perhaps.
> Where is my wife, my only Love, my closeness?
> Where is my sword? The great quest is done.
> I was here, sitting here, only here, eating.
> What did I do but lift a sword from a still place?
> What did I do but lead armies East when told?
> With all this, I am the Son of Uther Pendragon.
> The son of a massive legacy, and yet I surpass all?
> Why did this come to pass?

GUENEVERE: I don't know why, sir.

ARTHUR: Look at me. Look at my eyes. My chin. I waver.

 I shiver, cold, alone and only spoken to by devils.

GUENEVERE: This England is a good place, built by God.
    You are chosen ruler, hold your head high.

ARTHUR: Do you know me?

GUENEVERE: Yes.

ARTHUR: Do you love me, too?
    Do you love only my friend Lancelot?

GUENEVERE: I love you both.

ARTHUR: But him, you do love.

GUENEVERE: Yes.

ARTHUR: Are you not married to me still?

GUENEVERE: Yes. By law and grace.

ARTHUR: What passes law and grace?
    What overwhelms you so? The heat of his body?
    Tell me true.

GUENEVERE: The heat of mine, my love.

ARTHUR: No.
    Do not call me Love. Not now.

GUENEVERE: But Arthur
    I love you more, by grace and law, than he.
    Say why must you talk now of this with me?
    Can we not walk backwards through time
    And unsay all these things? Can we live
    As we did, with all the things we had?
    How were you set to change our lives so?

ARTHUR: Guenevere, do you know what a man will give
    For his love? What a King is when love arrives?
    A boy. A child. A page to her. A poet.
    The heart of a girl is all this boy entreats.
    So strange to you that I feel this? So wrong?
    Why turn you so?

GUENEVERE: I'm only angry that you speak!
    Why when I say to Lancelot be calm
    He calls it weakness, and too regal thought
    And when you speak to me, you dare remind
    Me that my heart is as a youthful wish?
    You both make me the worst that I can be.
    You turn me backwards, only reacting
    Always lost in begging and explaining
    Entreating for the other, much as both

Entreat to me now with each hand outstretched.
If I reciprocate both I do prove
That I say true and still that damns me too.
Enough of this. Do what you must, your grace.
I weary of your weeping words and tearing face.
(She exits.)

ARTHUR: Guards, take the Queen who leaves and to her room
    Should she be bound, my finest eyes on her.
    Damned Carlisle waits for her traitorous soul.
    Do not this room enter on pain of death
    For your King must sit by himself and rest.
    These weeping words and this same tearing face
    Are the last evidence my love had grace.

SCENE V

In the public square of Carlisle. BEDIEVERE and the HERMIT.

HERMIT: There's talk that the Round Table is in ruin.

BEDIEVERE: In ruin. Quite the phrase.

HERMIT: Appropriate.
    If Lancelot has brained some half the knights
    That he has sworn himself and his might to.
    There's talk.

BEDIEVERE: Whose talk?

HERMIT: Who's silent in this kingdom?

BEDIEVERE: The Table stands, as tall I as I do, man.

HERMIT: Some five foot six? And thin, I'd say. And pale.

BEDIEVERE: You're strange and unfamiliar and you smell.

HERMIT: I smell like earth.

BEDIEVERE: Look down. The earth can stink.

HERMIT: Much like the wind and sex and rotten food.
    It's all the earth, like you and me. But Bedievere,
    Our stink, either fresh grass or horse's ass,
    Will all be ripe when Lances make their pass.

BEDIEVERE: You know my name?

HERMIT: I'll tell your future, too.

BEDIEVERE: You are a devil, or insane?

HERMIT: Say you?

BEDIEVERE: I'd kill you in the street, a professed witch
    As your cackle warrants cutting down,

But as a fighter I'm not storied much
And you seem far too dim to earn your death.
I'll let you walk away, the fight is worthless.

HERMIT: My argument's complete. You should not fight
Unless the fight is reasoned by a king.
Or Destiny puts you before your maker.
Your maker waits beside an aging bed,
Unless you cross the sea to kill your friends.

BEDIEVERE: My friends? I'd kill no man that I call friend.

HERMIT: You'll see, my pasty knight, the lake unsheathed
And fire rise in France, near Joyous Gard!
A new-made King usurp himself, Arthur
Cross to you, like the Cross he holds so dear,
He'll tell you who you are.

BEDIEVERE: I've heard enough.

(Enter ARTHUR and train, with GUENEVERE beside. She's bound.)

The procession approaches, all grim faced.
I must attend our lady's tragedy.
Your assumptions and rumors are too close
But it's not Lancelot that causes death.
It's she that Arthur loved will be destroyed.

LUCAN: Here bound is once the Queen of Camelot
Of England and of all lands that she saw.
She was the Queen of all that look on her
And she has refused to refuse her guilt.
Now, as a murderess and here condemned
The Kingdom tearfully removes her rights
And turns her back to earth where she begs go.
Does the King speak for her, or on this matter?

ARTHUR: No public statement, Lucan. Continue.

GUENEVERE: Nothing to say, my love? Not in my name?

ARTHUR: No.

LUCAN: So to the fire of life we all return,
And even queens must end their days on earth.
So Guenevere, whom we have all loved fair
A last moment's repentance do you claim?

GUENEVERE: I do repent it all. I loved this place
And for you all would I undo my grace.

LUCAN: Bring her unto the sticks, and torches bring.
Of her good life will all our sad songs sing.

(Enter LANCELOT, brandishing his sword.)

LANCELOT: The Queen is saved, and all things will be right.
    If you stand crossed with me, you stand against
    The freedom, life and justice I defend.

BORS: All calm and comfort yet I plead to all!
    For the same love do we call up our hate.

MORDRED: Be silent, Bors, no man can make this peace.
    The stand he takes now proves his guilt tenfold.

LANCELOT: I, of all the knights, am the most true
    And defend Camelot more faithfully e'en as
    I am accused of slicing her apart.

KAY: You hypocrite! Your false tongue used for lust
    Should chide less boldly those that save the King
    From traitors such as you and Guenevere.
    My mourning brother, Arthur, wanted you
    To stand where his love stands before us now.
    And where were you, you noble gallant? Hid?
    Where was your voice to stand up for the just?

LANCELOT: We have been friends, Kay, do not tempt my wrath.

KAY: Bring forth the burden of your transgression,
    And see what color drips from righteous sin.

(They fight. KAY falls. BEDIEVERE and LUCAN enter the fray, but LANCELOT avoids them and takes GUENEVERE.)

BEDIEVERE: I trust my fear, and should not come to blows.

LUCAN: Why did he spare my life and not Sir Kay's?

ARTHUR: My brother falls!

GUENEVERE: No!

GAWAIN: I'll take up the Cause.
    Foul Lancelot, run not away from me.

LANCELOT: I run not From, but Toward the safer Joy
    Of Joyous Gard, my stronghold on French soil.
    As long as Camelot burns queens for love
    There is not perfect peace, not Table Round
    And no King Arthur, just a vacant crown!

GAWAIN: Offensive fraud, we will chase thee to France
    And deeper into earth, I'll chase thee down
    For Gareth, Kay, for Arthur, for myself.
    Your failings on the Grail did show your Sin.
    At last, your blight can be cured from our land
    As did the Cup of Jesus promise.

GUENEVERE: Hold!
        Oh Arthur what will you do for my sake?
        Will Carlisle burn more than the wicked Queen?

LANCELOT: I will not fight the pitied and meek.
        I will be gone, with Damsel in Distress
        And fear no man when I am free from Britain.
        This challenge contains all her recompense
        And I pray God Arthur shall be forgiven!

(Exit all save ARTHUR, KAY, and MORDRED.)

ARTHUR: All broken, every piece, every brother
        Who is adopted, but less than you Kay.
        Not endured, not outlasted.

KAY: Not so strong.
        As I confessed, I would be harder edged
        and not weep for fear of oblivion.
        This betrayed wound saps me of heaven's gifts
        and I mourn, Arthur, for being alive.
        I die before we are restored to grace.
        Pray on my bones for counsel after death.
        (He dies.)

MORDRED: Uncle, who weeps, let me commit our friend
        To Earth in your absence, my wounds still bleed.
        As you Excalibur brandish away
        I'll deputy as nephew on this Isle.
        Take heart that family buries family
        As Mordred adopts Kay as uncle now.
        Also, remaining, I'll rule as a show
        So your subjects know you leave them in care.

ARTHUR: Kind nephew, tend your wounds and tend lost Kay.
        Send in a ceremony all those lost.

MORDRED: The dead shall be unequaled in glory.

ARTHUR: Not glorified, but invoke their true selves
        And it shall be enough, as all were perfect.
        Oh I feel his last wordless shudder now
        As my arms coldly gather him to breast.
        I shall give chase, but be given no rest.

ACT III
SCENE I

France. Outside Joyous Gard. GAWAIN.

GAWAIN: The siege round Joyous Gard seems without end,
        And daily struggles whittle down reserves.

The faces, one by one, fall by my side
And good men fall in legion beside me.
Our brothers, and our cousins, cut us down
And we, in turn, give them the peace of death.
If men beneath him will kill those they loved
Why can their coward cutthroat not respond in kind?
LANCELOT! Your doubtful nature tires
With every passing day, and stifles pity!
Where once I was distraught to wage upon
Your castle this unnatural, sibling siege…
Now I am hotter than the blood I spill!
Where once the sight pulled weeping woman drops
From eyes which looked only to peer on you,
Now their dry desire overtakes their fountains!
I'll cut until I cut your flesh at last!
You will release our good King's stolen wife
And cease dishonor on the Round Table!
You've taken every thing I made my life
And turned it inside out, till who can tell
What paradise was once? Camelot spits
And salts its soil with blood dripped spears in spite!
Your crimes surround you now, your faults compiled!
Soon I will judge thee as Jesus judges me
For each new soul I send to heaven's gates!

SCENE II

Inside Joyous Gard. LANCELOT and GUENEVERE.

GUENEVERE: When we betrayed my husband and your King
A child of fury born began to grow.
No matter how our human voices sing
His destiny and spirit earn him woe.
Yet, all the true parts of this tale offend
And all his grandiose mistakes conspire
To burn my life's wax candle at both ends
And drip me like a seal till I retire.
I do not love him when I am with you
And hate you when I am with him alone.
Arthur and Lancelot each time renewed
Whenever one from me has newly flown.
The flowers and the earth do each contain:
Who would give up the heavens for the rain?

LANCELOT: Arthur would end you and I would you lived.

GUENEVERE: Tell me you never loved him as I do?

LANCELOT: I love him, love, but not as any else.
        A wife's love to a husband is unmatched,
        And still unmatched a paladin's to God.

GUENEVERE: I cannot say that I hate him for you
        Or for myself.

LANCELOT: Hate no one in my name.
        His qualities inspired a people, true,
        But those same ones did try to burn his love
        And kill his own heart.

GUENEVERE: 'Twas we killed his heart.
        To him I'll go, and look upon Justice.

LANCELOT: To send you out to him would never suit
        For he intends return you to Carlisle.
        His name for you remains The Traitorous.
        An anger nonsuch in a man rare fails
        To stay inside his belly till it's quelled.

GUENEVERE: We did incite his rage though not passion:
        His sadness overtook him on that day.
        I, like you, freed my shackled or bound whims
        And judged his judgments harsher than he mine.
        So crestfallen was he, and so wilted
        That he did pray for solitude and wept.

LANCELOT: I cannot see how you create a tale
        Of being set to die as mournful inaction.
        He's not of Denmark, he is just a fighter
        And as I am flawed so he seeks revenge.

(Enter BORS and the GENTLEWOMAN.)

        My old friend Bors who do you bring to us?

BORS: We have your Guenevere's handmaid from England
        Who loyal stowed herself upon the ship
        Of Britain as their soldiers did depart
        To be with her Queen despite fear of death.

LANCELOT: How came she past our gates in our defense?

BORS: She came as one of our own, and as female
        Unsuspected to bring battle inside.

GENTLEWOMAN: I would not trade my death if I had gone
        In lieu of the adventure you gave me.
        These men may love you, my Queen, but women
        Are more suited to soothe each other's strife.
        No matter what's been said of you as wife
        I will protect your heart above your life.

LANCELOT: My girl get warm and right you have well been
That I have no such women to take care
Of delicates which queens of England need.

GUENEVERE: Your life I have endangered lovely one.
For that I beg your forgiveness, now come
And put on better clothes. Become your beauty.
Likewise let me comfort thy sweet soul.

GENTLEWOMAN: It is my honor, madam, to do so.

(Exit GUENEVERE and GENTLEWOMAN.)

BORS: What duty she inspires in all she meets
My gracious Queen, even so far from home.
I, too, am here from loyalty to he
That Inspires me to protect his best whims
And keep his hot head under careful watch.
Your expressionless countenance reveals
That my sweet cousin, your thoughts are too kept.

LANCELOT: I show my outward peace.

BORS: True that you do.
Your breast bursts with a need to let it bleed.

LANCELOT: Do you remember Elaine of Shalott?
Elaine the White, who rested on the water
And died for loving me?

BORS: I do remember her.

LANCELOT: Her face, and lovely Gareth, Arthur's Kay,
They sing at me from heaven, where I'll never sing.
Why do they smile at me, and resist curse?
I would easy vindictiveness instead
Which I could shoulder better than their love.

BORS: Did not your Love comfort you on these names?

LANCELOT: To her I'll confess nothing but my strength
And to her I'll seem never to show fear.
Our broilings come from our stubbornness, Bors,
And inside our locked horns lies our passion.

BORS: Joyous Gard was once named Dolorous Gard
And you retrieved its namesake, made it yours.
You spun it into gold, as in a tale
Of straw, you'll spin your hairshirt into grace.
This Dolorous Gard and you are the same
And Joyous will you be when you are saved.

LANCELOT: Before salvation I must true repent
So I repent these murders that mark me.

I do this as I loved sweet Gareth so.
I loved old Kay, and will not have another
Lady begone from life for this brash Knight.

BORS: To find this love inside the raging siege
Is more than I can say would give me pride.

LANCELOT: Let them rage as they will from out of doors.
They'll never budge this family inside.

BORS: Our men begin gamely to push them back
And let those who bring food to our gate through.
But you must know that Gawain has killed tens
Of men he loved and will keep doing so
Until you answer his cries from the field.

LANCELOT: I cannot go to face him. Never, Bors.
I fear that I would kill those I respect
In battle that comes magic and natural
To both myself and to Gawain the True.
And what if Arthur came upon the field?
What should I do if he would come at me
With Excalibur in his hand hell-bent?
No, I shall wait until they see their wrongs
Or when my French men have shoved back their throngs.

SCENE III

MORDRED in England.

MORDRED: How many wars in France will England wage?
How many times will French soil burn beneath
The feet of British soldiers, just because
It's nearer to us than is Istanbul?
But, wait, you say, this time bears a grudge?
Not arbitrary action, but good sense
Should send a King to recapture his Queen
And punish he that breaks the kingdom's laws.
If soldiers meet each other, on a month
That's hotter, than we say was for a reason
That the sun beats down, and so makes foreign blame.
As each day passes, more passes his might,
His memory slips gently from each mind,
And I am more and more the active King.
But, deep debate is now ensued that slices
Deeper than he could have ever known.

(Enter two BARONS.)

FIRST BARON: We've come to thank you.

SECOND BARON: Yes. We appreciate all you've done.
>   For the people... of Britain.

MORDRED: Of course. What else should I do?
>   But protect the land and offer it freedom?

SECOND BARON: Freedom. Yes.

MORDRED: Yes. Gentlemen, what counties are you from?

SECOND BARON: We're from the West End, my liege.

MORDRED: Of London?

FIRST BARON: Yes. London.

MORDRED: I asked which county.

SECOND BARON: Which county is London?
>   You must pardon me, I am such a neophyte
>   Of these counties.

FIRST BARON: We both live in London.

MORDRED: Yes, well, I see. Go check a map.
>   We'll have some new ones issued soon enough,
>   So voting for your ilk is accurate.
>   Either way, I need your help my Lords.

FIRST BARON: Yes sir.

SECOND BARON: We will sire.

MORDRED: The tyrant, still in France, will soon return.
>   I am not certain if the man himself
>   The Arthur is alive, but old forces
>   Which having razed the castle of a thief,
>   Will return expecting venerable treatment.
>   Our armies' bare bones now shall meet their ships
>   And make bones where they once had meat and sinew
>   With Greek Fire, catapults and with archery.
>   We must pull babies from their mother's grips
>   To make them men, and teach them to give list
>   To our orders, our cause and to our history.
>   They'll swing down what's left of the former guard.
>   Even a boy of twelve will have the strength
>   To saw down those seaworn soldiers exhausted
>   By the spiritless protection of past pride.

FIRST BARON: I'm honored to be asked. But Mordred
>   Sire
>   What do I know about the army?
>   What do I know of battles?

SECOND BARON: Or me?

MORDRED: You will be my first, the general counsel
    And leaders of my ranks.

FIRST BARON: I've never raised a sword.

SECOND BARON: Nor I.

MORDRED: I said counsel. Let others kill.
    Just keep in mind how unworthy you are
    To make a battle scheme and execute
    Unless you listen closely to your King
    Who is for now, the Mordred that you see.
    You will survive and thrive, under this guise.

FIRST BARON: And thrive?

SECOND BARON: Yes sire. Yes. Thank you. King of England.
    Wisdom is reborn as intellect
    A much more revealing prospect
    If each of our sideways glances connect.

MORDRED: Leave me, Barons and to Parliament
    To see how well this new body
    Works.

(They exit.)

    England is like a woman. Best when paid for.

SCENE IV

France. SIR BORS, LANCELOT, and GUENEVERE in Joyous Gard.

BORS: Sir, all the men, the hundreds, thousands fall
    And blood on both sides streams intermingled.
    The clock ticks on. What is't you wait upon?

LANCELOT: I do regret that I cannot abide
    Surrendering Queen Guenevere outside.
    To send her out the front gate, during war
    Or even into Arthur, back to fire.

GUENEVERE: The siege must end. 'Tis hopeless hope to stand.
    My love, forsake protection and free me.

LANCELOT: Do not betray me, love, it's now too far
    To back away from this battle in fear.

GUENEVERE: Should I not die, by Faith, I'll not outside
    And if I do, then deserved that fate's end.

LANCELOT: You will not die inside my Castle.
    You are not queen here, not my wife.
    I defer nothing to you, Guenevere.
    You're safe and shall remain, that I will tell you.

(Enter the HERMIT.)

        Who comes here?

HERMIT: Draw nothing. He's not here.
        I am not here save Guenevere.
        It's only her ears give me hear
        And Lancelot forgets I'm near.

LANCELOT: Come weapon to my hand and then… rest too.

BORS: My Friend, art bold towards no one? Sit you down.

GUENEVERE: Bors, see you no man there to draw upon?

HERMIT: He hears no reference to me. He cannot.
        No matter, you can hear me. Let me say
        That I am magical. Make no delay
        To mark me, and in moments take no time
        To sing your Lancelot to rest and go with me.

LANCELOT: What say you, Bors? There's siege. Of course I draw.
        At any moment, there could be a foe.

HERMIT: No foe here Lady Guenevere, well met.
        Green-grass and soot, my wizard foot
        Is cowled from just below my head
        I'm bent so low, my face in shadow
        Keeps you staring, glaring, wondering.
        Still, to these men, you seem attentive, good.
        It's necessary, for they cannot see
        That which I hope to bring through trickery.
        Sleep Lancelot, and Bors, away.

GUENEVERE: They cannot see our conversation?

HERMIT: No.

GUENEVERE: Are you a devil?

HERMIT: No. I love you, Fate.
        You are too close to all that one could feel.
        Can you choose between these harsh-tongued men?

GUENEVERE: I am assumed to choose a champion.
        But it's impossible, and unceasing.
        Hermit, you tell me, devil or no, a plan.
        Devise escape from Stronghold to my land.
        For now, at last, I never can see fit
        To love any. Myself, Arthur, or Him
        Are lost in labyrinthine turns and tales.

BORS: More shouting from outside, more Gawain threats.
        I fear I must take arms myself to him.

I'll come to thee soon. Comfort him, Lady.
(Exit BORS.)

HERMIT: You are, as your name means "The White Phantom"
and may float from this Castle when he sleeps.
Comfort him, Lady. Sing the sweet sad song
Bring him to Idle gently, dream you gone.

GUENEVERE: *(Sings.)*
"Late, late, so late, and dark the night and chill!
Late, late, so late, but we can enter still.
Too late, too late! You cannot enter now.
No light had we; for that we do repent
And learning this, the bridegroom will relent.
Too late, too late! Ye cannot enter now.
No light! So late! And dark and chill the night!
O, let us in, that we may find the light!
Too late, too late! Ye cannot enter now.
Have we not heard the bridegroom is so sweet?
O, let us in, tho' late to kiss his feet!
No, no, too late. You cannot enter now."

(LANCELOT sleeps.)

Rest Lancelot du Lake. In Camelot, find me.

HERMIT: As safe in France, in Britain will you be.

(Exit the HERMIT and GUENEVERE.)

SCENE V

ARTHUR and GAWAIN on the Battlefield. Enter BEDIEVERE.

BEDIEVERE: My Lord!

ARTHUR: I'm here.

BEDIEVERE: The gates of Joyous Gard
Spring open like a trap reversed and loose
The Great Lancelot and his good friend Bors
Who pass the field, yell they will have conference.

ARTHUR: Friend, lead them here, and they will find my ear.
Gawain please keep you by my side this time.

GAWAIN: I would not be anywhere but beside you.
Bedievere make sure their path is clear
And lead the betrayers before the wronged.

BEDIEVERE: I could send others to the task you seek.

ARTHUR: I trust you friend, and know your competence.
Forgo your questions and fetch Lancelot.

(BEDIEVERE exits.)

ARTHUR: This is a quiet moment, hearty friend.
        I thank you for the time you have fought long
        So if this meeting should soon go awry
        You'll know forever that we are good friends
        And never have I met a finer man.

GAWAIN: You humble me, but there is no need Lord.
        No harm will come to you or I this day.
        Not while I watch this steaming field with you
        Will you need think on harm by any man.

(Enter LANCELOT, led by BEDIEVERE.)

BEDIEVERE: Here sirs, is our old friend we have besieged.

ARTHUR: Keep all the men away, though stay close by.

BEDIEVERE: I will my Lord.
        (He exits.)

ARTHUR: Where is Sir Bors de Ganis?
        I miss that old man. He must have more white
        In his hair since we were together last.

LANCELOT: I sent him back inside, assuredly safe.
        No man would touch him wantonly I'm sure.
        They love him more than they love any man
        And revere him as he that saw the Grail.
        I stand before you both, at last, alone.

ARTHUR: We both, Gawain and I, have waited long
        To have you in our sight, with Guenevere.

GAWAIN: This waiting cuts me deeper than you could
        With your dulled blade, out of rehearsal now.
        You cannot fight? Is that why you stay hid?

LANCELOT: No, Gawain. That I can. Hear my warning.
        I feel that this fight is not by the book
        And would avoid further damnable acts.

GAWAIN: You are already damned.

ARTHUR: Both rest your mouths.
        Why do you choose this time to come forward?

LANCELOT: My cause is at an end, and yet unspoken
        You have defeated me through thievery.

GAWAIN: Let me at him! Already my blood boils.
        His sin is hot and has been baked too long
        Inside that oven that he calls a Gard.

ARTHUR: Your King thieves nothing from you, Lancelot.

LANCELOT: Where is my love?

GAWAIN: Your love is murdering.

ARTHUR: She is inside, as far as I have heard.
        Have you lost her as I did her to you?
        Did she escape us both?

LANCELOT: Where is my love? How did you spy her out?

ARTHUR: Consider whose love that you come to seek.
        If she is released, let us end the siege.

LANCELOT: Am I worth all these bloody feuds boiling?

ARTHUR: I must confess, I see an old friend there.
        But it is not a friend I fight this for.

LANCELOT: All for a love, Arthur, we do conflict.
        Why not let her stay with me? What shame?
        Why steal her from beneath my nose instead?
        Would you be happiest when we're all dead?

ARTHUR: Do you ask me to surrender my wife to you?
        What say you to his plea, Gawain?

GAWAIN: My King,
        Do not be lowered to confer with a cur.
        This man's loving service is long past
        Before us rides a failure on all fronts.
        He steals the wives of all men, and douses
        Dribbling pious pleas upon the evil he has made.
        Let me go to him.

ARTHUR: My favorites in arms?
        No, Sir Gawain, I will draw blades myself.

LANCELOT: I cannot fight you Arthur, and will grant
        Submission to the swirling fateful wheel.
        You know we should never by sword be wed.

GAWAIN: And what of We? The favorites we're titled.
        Unglorious but warlike, we are one.
        We, fated on this moment to bring battle
        Here in France, and prove our mettle thus.
        'Tis early yet, and my strength peaks this morn
        Like a mountain in eastern mythic tales.
        I am a match for you at any time
        But are you match for me at my best brawn?

LANCELOT: This will not answer my question, Gawain,
        Of where my love is taken, and what for…
        This will only be tribute for your loss
        That I accept to touch my blade to yours.
        Favorite, your heights bring forth to match my lows.

(GAWAIN approaches and they begin to fight.)

GAWAIN: Until the sun is at its peak I'll rise
            In Power and your Shield will drop away.

LANCELOT: Never will I die on my own land
            Or by a freak of nature's petty hand.

(They fight on. The battle is even.)

GAWAIN: I'm hurt by you, but I will never cease
            Until at last your head is on the ground.

LANCELOT: Do your greatest and call me the worst:
            Language for you is use for naught save curse.

(They exit fighting. Enter BEDIEVERE.)

BEDIEVERE: The men stand numb to see so great a struggle!
            Even those on opposite sides of war
            Are standing dumbfounded, their arms aside.
            By the sad awesome sight they're all entranced.

ARTHUR: I have heard once that only noble loss
            Is noteworthy for books, for as the King
            Each loss he takes reflects the kingdom more
            Than any loss of simple peasant men.
            While there is logic in this, what then said
            Of the King as a Man who has his friends
            Stabbing blindly at victory for Him?
            What if the King's failing is their true cause?
            What difference, I ask Bedievere, is there
            Between me and these men who will fight for me?

BEDIEVERE: You cannot see it for yourself, perhaps
            But I do see it, and I feel it too.
            I won't be the last that would die for you.
            Even though I fear death more than most might
            For Arthur I would give Cerebus fight.

ARTHUR: When this battle is done, for we are helpless
            To end it by our own hands (Yes even I)
            Then call to me. I'll be inside the tents
            Awaiting some news of apocalypse.
            The rage in us has now the love eclipsed.

(Exit ARTHUR and BEDIEVERE.)

ACT IV
SCENE I

GUENEVERE and MORGAN LA FAY in the Tower of London.

MORGAN: The Queen is betrothed.

GUENEVERE: Not so. Not Queen.

MORGAN: Soon to be, if Grace, by bed, forsook
    Its regal poses, for those more earthspread
    Your grace will soon return into the arms
    Of trifles, twitches, touches, and tart's names
    And marry once again an English king.

GUENEVERE: The English King awaits his throne from France
    And will return to his still wedded woman.
    I came to Mordred expecting escape
    But find only the strange truth surfacing.

MORGAN: You find his consorts suspect, wince at me?
    My murder eyes and tiny frame of old
    Wood turned like tree branches too long...
    You see my ugliness and my stark voice
    And note that in Mordred's ear I can speak...
    This worries you?

GUENEVERE: You are the witch of Gore.

MORGAN: I'm so much more.

GUENEVERE: Begone from my small room.

MORGAN: I'll to your tomb, which is all else but here.
    Instead, take Gentlewoman who flew France
    And threw herself upon Mordred's pity.
    We had thought better to keep you locked up,
    But in your humor, perhaps she should come.

GUENEVERE: Again she comes? From England and then France
    And back again, she follows me so fast?
    She is like you, a magic thing, I think.

MORGAN: Loyal girls are a dogged thing indeed.
    I'll go so you can confer here in peace.
    Make peace with that peace you have former known
    For there is much you have yet to hear from me.

(Exit MORGAN. Enter GENTLEWOMAN.)

GENTLEWOMAN: My Queen, I see you are imperiled again.
    Why are you kept in the Tower like this?
    This place is worse than Joyous Gard in smell
    E'en after the dead field men began to leave odor.

GUENEVERE: Do not speak so vulgarly, Gentle love.
    Though we are in distress we are still women
    And must keep ourselves as ourselves above all.
    How many hardships this time have you seen
    So that you could come once again to me

In time of need, as if called from above?

GENTLEWOMAN: None, madam, as your son did bid me stay
And gave me clothes and kept me too well fed.

GUENEVERE: Son? I've no son.

GENTLEWOMAN: Is Mordred not your son?
Perhaps I do confuse, he is but half your son.
As he is your nephew.

GUENEVERE: Tell me how then
He could be called my own born son?

GENTLEWOMAN: But half
Your son, but all your husband's son
And also that of his sister, her son.
Your son, by marriage, and not of your blood
But also, as you've known him, nephew too.
Do I tell you things you've not heard before?

GUENEVERE: You do, my sweet. It's doubtful to my ears.
Who told you these things?

GENTLEWOMAN: Why he himself told.
He whispered to me secrets, I now see,
Though when he told me, there were told in tongue
Shameless and so it seemed revealed ere now
That he was Arthur's son of incest born.

GUENEVERE: My King should sin thus and not tell me so?

GENTLEWOMAN: His sister, King Lot's wife, is the mother
Of the four brothers, Mordred in the fold.
Arthur, in sleep, knew not this same seedling
Was to this same sister and not from Lot.
His other aunt, Morgan, did protect him
After his birth was called a damned thing.

GUENEVERE: How could a man mistake his sister's body
For one unknown to him? How can this be?

GENTLEWOMAN: By will o' wisps so carefully in place
That it would breed a most specific child
To bastardize itself and its producer.

GUENEVERE: Where do these stories come from that you tell?

GENTLEWOMAN: By illusions incanted for the cause
Of setting Fate's wheel spinning twice as fast
And serving it best by listening close
To that Fate calls to happen and makes so.

GUENEVERE: I do not believe this, and will ask you
To stop this talk and comfort she you love.

GENTLEWOMAN: Have I forgot myself, my Queen, this hour?
         Perhaps I am no longer fit to brush
         the hair beneath your neck, or fan your cheek?
         I wonder if it was Sir Mordred's charms
         That caused me to rethink my tone of voice?
         Or perhaps wonders never cease for we
         That are so wind thrown by other's decree.

GUENEVERE: Have I mistreated you in some cruel way?

GENTLEWOMAN: Your friendship is so mild that I grow tired
         Of inventing the ways to fawn on it.
         Let me simply say that you cannot know
         How it was trying to consort with those
         So petty and fleshlike inside this form
         For all the days that I was inside skin
         As I was corseted for all her life.

GUENEVERE: Who speaks inside you? What is this strange sound?
         Why do you tell me lies about my husband?

GENTLEWOMAN: They are not lies. In fact, this is the end
         To every lie that I have ever told.
         So know that you, like Arthur, have bedded
         That you should have not, and in other means
         Confided in a girl who was not dear.
         Think on this until in truth I do appear.

(Exit GENTLEWOMAN. Enter MORGAN LA FAY.)

MORGAN: Like you the games we play with these small shapes
         And how pretty that we can be when pressed?
         The only pain was how oft she was blessed.

GUENEVERE: What is this that I've seen? A form of you?
         What shall I take this to mean, how to confront this?

MORGAN: Know that your heart can recognize her truth
         Or mine, as you can see it is the same,
         That Mordred is your son, by Christian marriage
         But most unchristian was his saintly birth.
         Much like Merlin did turn Uther his wife
         So did Morgan turn Arthur to sibling.
         Such justice makes a woman want to sing.

GUENEVERE: You are a vile and most perverted thing.
         Begone and let me wail here in the tower.

MORGAN: I'll leave you once again, but this you know
         That your wedding to my nephew is set
         And he will come for you to make it done.
         Be ready like good child and stand tall

When your next ManGod enters your small room.
Girls like you are the queens of decorum
So act it or you risk losing the favor
Of he that can make your comfort his labor.
Sleep if you will, he'll not come on this night
Nor will your best handmaid, she's taken flight.

SCENE II

In ARTHUR's tent. KING ARTHUR and the PAGE BOY.

PAGE: My King?

ARTHUR: My boy.

PAGE: My King. They sent me in. They said you needed me. I met them and they said you needed a page.

ARTHUR: I have one. Who are you? Are you French?

PAGE: English. British. Arthur's subject.

ARTHUR: How old are you?

PAGE: I am twelve years old, now. When I came to France, much younger. Oh how evil he must be inside these walls, to keep me here so long I've had a birthday! But that is how Knights are. Even birthdays cannot make me pause.

ARTHUR: Are you a Knight yet?

PAGE: A knight?

ARTHUR: You said that Knights are how *you* are, I think. Did I hear you right?

PAGE: Yes. I am. Or No. I'm not. You heard me right, but I'm afraid I'm not.

ARTHUR: Do you want to be a warrior?

PAGE: Well, yes. For you, I'd be one.

ARTHUR: For God?

PAGE: For you. May I confess my father was not a Christian? That's not to say he was a Pagan, but he didn't like the church. It wasn't God that he disliked. It was the Church. He'd talk to God all day. I'd hear him. But just like him my mother stayed away. And she says things like In the Name of the Lord and for Jesus's Sake and Thank You Father in Heaven. But really, deep down, it wasn't the Father or Son or Lord or Jesus Bread that I wanted to invoke. It was you.

ARTHUR: Why?

PAGE: You are real.

ARTHUR: And then not worthy of such things, tiny sprite. Do you know the wars I've waged? The men I've killed?

PAGE: By heart. Each one. Each bad man, witch and dragon felled. Each black knight, churl and Kraken broken. And the wonder of it is, you are like me. Born from a farmer.

ARTHUR: Born?

PAGE: Raised by the land. Not dropped by God but you made yourself a hero. A king. I do love you so for this my King.

ARTHUR: Why did you come? Tell me plainly boy. I thank you for the loveliness you speak, but there is news you bring me. Is that true?

PAGE: The news I have been sent with is of Gawain and Sir Lancelot my Lord.

ARTHUR: Please tell me they both live child.

PAGE: Yes they do. They both lay finally exhausted down, and Lancelot was dragged inside the castle. I wondered why myself, for he is Good, and that castle is not. I was not told plainly he was kidnapped, but I do see it must be so.

ARTHUR: Do you?

PAGE: If armed men dragged him inside this stronghold. Yes. It must be. Still, he breathes. The mettle that they tested, sure for sport, left both Gawain and Lancelot exhausted. It was the most amazing display that I ever saw. When on their backs, too tired and spent to stand, they made great shows of trying to heft up their weapons and still be at each other. Still, they are only men... you see? And could not fight anymore.

ARTHUR: This is better news than some I could have gotten. Still, it does not bring me happiness.

PAGE: They must have been quite bored as many of us are. To sit so long outside the castle walls. Even after the waves of fighting stopped, we simply waited. I wondered what for.

(Enter the HERMIT.)

Who comes here? Face my sword to hurt the King.

HERMIT: Begone sweet boy, and mind a strange old man.

(Exit the PAGE.)

ARTHUR: The boy leaves without argument. Why so?
Who are you, stranger, that you're past the posts
And come to me appearing as a beggar.

(The HERMIT removes his cloak, and reveals himself as MERLIN.)

ARTHUR: Merlin the Wizard that was dead before!

MERLIN: Does my disguise and guile surprise you, son?
       Is't not my currency to be oblique
       And reappear more clearly afterwards?

ARTHUR: With you, my teacher, there is no respite
       And every river flows only downstream.
       I feel each moment racing and so said
       I barely blink before you're gone again.
       'Twas spoke your thoughtless passion was your end.

MERLIN: A common destiny for priests and slaves
       And even you and I, my handmade King.
       Are you so gone? Spoken of as if vanished?
       Do you tarry with pages to forget
       The noble cause for which your birth was made?

ARTHUR: No. I do not forget. I am reminded.

MERLIN: Too often, by your voice.

ARTHUR: This dirt still bleeds
       From all my foolishness. Each word I speak
       Kills twenty men, their sons, and all their sons.

MERLIN: That is the joy you get and that is grandness.
       That is the aspiration and the quest
       Of every man that perishes to be remembered.
       Where can you be when Mordred, your bred whelp
       Of litter predisposed and prophesied,
       Can piecemeal pick at England's parts unchecked
       And hold your Guenevere while you are chin to fist?

ARTHUR: Every land I have walked on you led me.
       Each Black Knight, Red Knight, taken by magic.
       This Excalibur, all my visions, Grails
       Amount to nothing but a distant hope.
       Even if I could find the favored Lord
       He could not love me as I break his rules?
       I puzzle on this, and on everything.
       Why did you prop me as a fragile king?

MERLIN: To save the day, as heroes must do forever.
       To save the world, and give it simple hope.
       Is that so strange, you fool? So unnatural?
       You call the world a puzzle, well then Think.
       Unravel what you can with what you're given.
       Call your God what you will, it's all the same.
       The selfless battle selfish once again,
       And in each other do the same contain.

> The parallels ambivalence forsake
> And some men damned must Goodness undertake.

ARTHUR: I cannot hear your answers anymore.
> I could not understand them if I did.

MERLIN: You cannot unmake yourself, nor unwrite
> The page all inky summoned by great quills
> That finish us both purely out of time.

ARTHUR: So I am just an old song I can hear
> That wasn't written yet? How can I act
> With faith and truth and certainty of cause
> If I must observe my confined array
> Of choices burst before me, partly splayed?

MERLIN: 'Tis a pity that you are a man of thought
> And heavy aches inside your breast untold.
> For Warriors are not designed to note
> The strangeness of each thing, but to Go Forth.
> Take solace that your despair is common
> And yeoman cross this fatal sea with you.
> Look to my spell and know yourself in it.
> Here's dust of courage, roots of luckiness
> Here is a blue drink which I keep for cures.
> These magics often true, now look so dull
> As roots and grass and plain mud now observed.
> Like you, they are but roots, though invested
> They tingle with a purpose for the taking.
> Arthur, address these men and be their hero.
> As a man, a son of farmers and of Kings.
> In this way, like the boy said, be all things
> And be none that you are not quite naturally.
> For in you is the champion you were.

ARTHUR: Your words bring fire in me and I am
> Ashamed to be so pensive before now.

MERLIN: Now here, I'll say, you must to London go.
> I was he that took Guenevere from France
> And by my magic her journey was hastened.
> She has been there for months without your knowledge.
> But news is hard from England: sly Mordred
> Subverts you and rules with Morgan La Fay.
> You make hasty sail with armed men
> And make your challenger tremble with fear.
> Still, note the prophecies of this bastard
> Who I past warned was from your sister born.
> He is foreseen your dread, so King take care

And heed Merlin's soothsaying this last time.
Beware you fight on Trinity Sunday
Where dreams may make you quake in bed on truth:
If war you on that day you will perish.
When on the English soil your forces meet
Bargain for any day but that Sunday
For I have seen it is a fateful time.

ARTHUR: I will draw up my men with common prayer
And draw up myself with faith in your word.
So brandish I unbroken Excalibur
And take up the right cause with the right sword.

SCENE III

GUENEVERE and MORDRED, the Tower of London.

MORDRED: Will you take me, step-mother, to your bed?
You are without a child, save me but half.
A child could be the remedy you seek:
A child has forgetfulness in its eyes;
Save those eyes will resemble both fathers.

GUENEVERE: No remedy is near you, you're disease.
I've seen your remedy, this parliament
Which already proves quarrelsome and base.

MORDRED: Is not war base and quarrelsome, my love?
This body politic acquits itself
By shedding no man's blood, if any yet.

GUENEVERE: Yes. My blood may it claim, as yet I die
Inside to see the peace divided up
And given to a thousand prattling jesters.
And even more, I die as you set deep
Your skewer into England's fleshy breast.

MORDRED: If you refer to yourself, not as yet
Have I enjoyed the white meat or the dark.

GUENEVERE: I'm not supper for you, glutton-pig.
Bastard bloodkin, humbled by your dwarvish set,
You beg for murder by my husband's hand.

MORDRED: Oh which husband is that? You left them both.
The froggish concubine and crippled myth
Wrapped sword to sword because you wrapped your legs
Around whomever's sword you thrust upon.

GUENEVERE: Is this your way to woo? To entreat grace?
To ask for marriage, that's your subtle touch?

MORDRED: Did father comfort you when your unrest
            Would sweat your sheets and underwhelm your feet?
            When Southern Northbound courses blew
            You from your conjoined queensbed out of doors
            Where you would bash your beauty 'gainst another?
            And then that other unmade, dirty man,
            Would service you to footsteps even faster?
            Could not this tempest be termed a disaster?

GUENEVERE: The pure disaster found there was my heart
            Could love too much, a problem lost on you.

MORDRED: Sweet mother by the church but not by blood
            Except by Christianess, and I am none
            Of that religion, but from earth and grit…
            You are as Mordred, teetering between
            Your saintly nature and your noxious Fate
            Which forced you upon animal four legs.

GUENEVERE: What saintly nature's in you, precious fool?
            You blame Fate for the worst things of your mind.
            Our difference clearly is I see my fault.
            What four-legged thing can blame its savage self?

MORDRED: Blame is uniquely man's lot, sad woman.
            Let men decide the fates, you're more to earth
            As is shown by your want to piety
            That's never stopped you from straight lechery.

GUENEVERE: God made all and made us all with choice.
            Even the broken, Mordred, hear his voice.

MORDRED: There are no Gods, nor Angels, nor great Floods.
            Just physical, and only pulsing Bloods.
            The wounds inside you, who has tended them?
            What doctor mends the nothing in a breast?

GUENEVERE: The only nothing's in the fallen man,
            Who thinks his accidental birth a Fate.

MORDRED: I see you feel such pain, and yet do hold
            To old thoughts, never seeing what is wrong.
            The medicine you seek lies in release
            Of what conflicts you, tears your heart apart.

GUENEVERE: The least release would be a second marriage
            To he that loves not even his own life.
            An aberration in so many ways,
            It would make hoarse the speaker of them all.

MORDRED: Why should there be marriages? Why so live
            To serve to nobody or keep glances lean?

The words like aberration disappear
When Heaven and that Christ man are dispelled.
The reason, so remaining, to unite
In law is safety, and insurance from
The stupid scanning of the blind believers
Who would hang those who think above the fray.
So marry me, and you will be kept clean
Kept safe, a kept woman, an English queen
And free from Mordred, from England, from God
From all the pain you've caused by elegance
By piousness and perfect pale white skin.

GUENEVERE: What must I say to you to cease your talk?
I'll never yield nor yield you likemade fruit.
Can pity find no home in you? Away.

MORDRED: So weep you now to hear the reason spoke?
I'll cut through all these lies and free your soul
To use your mind and make those heartbursts stop,
Then drip only to drip your last wet drop.

GUENEVERE: You are a dead man, and yet you are kin.
You are a dead man, and yet you can speak.

MORDRED: I am a dead man, and would kill you too.

GUENEVERE: Well said meek dead, both mummified and small.
This marriage that I have, this broken dial
Will pass by sun the wrong time still awhile.

MORDRED: Enter my aunt and perform the true rights
To silence her spitting and end this night.

(Enter MORGAN.)

MORGAN: Cry not as you curse, it makes your threats lose teeth.
And if you must kneel, at least pray silently.

GUENEVERE: You know my will, and cannot be wavered.
Speak what impresses your trees and hag priests.

MORGAN: Delight of daughter, cresting waves unite
And become larger, whiter at their tops,
Then still for second creaking like the wood
Of old doors opening, they break and flow
Unto the shores together, wet the earth
And make the grey rocks glow with slick water.
All the same, the waves unite, and become waves.
The stillness and the silence, then the shouts;
The bud inside the flower bursting forth.
The wedlock interlocking girls and men
Like boys to women, babies uterine.

The dust and darklings, locust swarms untold
The stilllife deadlife comes and goes and lives
Until we are rebirthed as undivine.
The minerals composing souls come rough
And toilings, bloodlets, crashing all your brains
Will not refine the better parts you seek.
You cannot alchemize your leaden gold.
Therefore, I Morgan La Fay, do entreat
The natural wedding of all things to this room
And make their shows by all that we believe:
These two were wed before and are still wed
Without consent, for who was born consenting?
Who living before was asked questions of
The sort that grant permission to make flesh?
We are will-less before hastening death
That asks nor tells its intentions, it Is.
So has this marriage, between those two haters
Been whispered of in temples and in books
That others read in histories yet seen.
All it needs is action and 'tis truly done
For more than simply two people are one.
So she takes you, Mordred, to wed and hold
From this day forward, and as days before
For richer or more rich, for sick or sick
Until your parting by the organs failing.
This is her solemn vow, and you vow too
To keep her in your ring of righteousness
Bound like the band of gold that others build.
The money they contribute to the petty
Contrivances of love and other nonsense.
And may the clouds above grant mercy here
Benediction and their rain to fall
To cleanse each day this dirty living lie.

MORDRED: Call you this a marriage, my old aunt witch?

MORGAN: As good as any other that I've stitched,
          If perhaps chaotic in its intent.
          I read not from the books my religion
          But speak its tenets as they scape my breath
          And so I say this marriage is made here.
          All it needs is public shows of grace.
          So when my Guenevere from this tower goes
          The announcements of marriage will be made.
          And all will see the Queen and her new King
          Who both defy the ancient regal rites.

MORDRED: You need not come unto my royal bed
        As I know that you have no maidenhead.
        But come from here when all your weeping's done
        And forget argument with compliment.

(MORGAN and MORDRED exit.)

GUENEVERE: This stale air, this mossy stone I smell
        This taste of ground is all the lips left me.
        My hands and knees once scraping now caress
        The cell of prospect accorded to this Queen.
        Down the spiral staircase will I never
        Descend to confirm what has happened here.
        These portals each betrayals unpermitted.
        Without the natural power to subvert
        And failing overcoming impotence
        The only weapon left to me is choice
        And I choose rest forever, final death.
        I choose the moss and rock, I choose this room
        To hide from food and hide the rituals
        Thrust into me as rape upon a maid.
        Perhaps I should to nunnery begone
        But why should I divine myself as chasten?
        Guenevere sleeps here, free from distant men
        Whose love I, in my final moments, doubt
        Could ever have turned justice inside out.

SCENE IV

France. ARTHUR, GAWAIN, LUCAN, BEDIEVERE, and all the BRITISH SOLDIERS.

BEDIEVERE: A parliament?

LUCAN: This is the word that came from London.

BEDIEVERE: Why would a king usurp himself?

LUCAN: They say that half of England loves him more than Arthur.

BEDIEVERE: For all Arthur has done?

LUCAN: What's he done?

BEDIEVERE: Made peace.

LUCAN: Look at all these men. This isn't peace.

ARTHUR: My men.

BEDIEVERE: God save you, once and future King.

ARTHUR: Shall I be King again? Am I not King?
        Did Mordred truly take away my crown?

BEDIEVERE: No sir.

LUCAN: He's taken nothing but the word.

ARTHUR: Line up, and take Gawain in arms beside.
    All men know that we today return Britain's Day
    To take what has been stolen in the night.
    We must have faith that we are chosen men
    Who storm Salisbury and claim fated ground.
    Like Archangels we must dispel the cruel
    Drop Lucifer from Heaven, Camelot.
    As the war in heaven, let no one stand
    That dares resist the thunder in our clouds.
    Let none by God who challenge reverence
    Persist past his foolish and prideful fall.
    So bless your weapons, your axes and spears.
    Raise them to Saint George and pray his blood milk
    Drip from the veins, nourishing their noble cut.
    Now kneel before your swords and pray to God.
    Blessed be the Lord, my rock and my fortress.
    He trains my hands to fight and fingers battle.
    My help, my stronghold, my deliverer
    My shield in whom I trust who subdues foes.
    O Lord are we those that you care for fair?
    Mere mortals that you should so think of us?
    We are like a puff of wind, a shadow.
    Bow your heavens, my Lord and come down
    Touch the mountains and they shall smoke full fire.
    Hurl lightning and scatter those that fight against
    Shoot out your angels' arrows and rout them.
    Stretch out your hand from up in Heaven Tall
    And rescue all our souls from the great waters
    That would drown us by foreign leaders
    Whose mouths speak deceitfully of Arthur
    And all his British perfect soldiers' work.
    We will sing you a new song this day Lord
    Of victory, like you gave to Saint George
    And salvation like Daniel in the Den.
    Rescue all from those foes' hurtful swords
    And may we plant our feet full fast upon
    Our old ground unbeaten by intruders.
    May a good life be granted once we prove
    Our passion for this play we act for you.
    May there be no need to breach the walls or cut
    The sinners into exile, but forgive us all.
    Then, let there be nothing but a new love
    Won by the Sword and ending with the dove.

GAWAIN: Our Arthur is the teacher, and his prayer
        Has set my heart afire once again!

ARTHUR: My soldiers, lift Gawain and hurry to the water
        Be worthy of the Son that was our Martyr!

ACT V
SCENE I

Trinity Sunday. The BARONS scan the Battlefield on British soil.

FIRST BARON: This is strange, this day we stand
        And look upon a battle we won't fight.

SECOND BARON: That's true. You see the forces of Arthur
        And they are
        Tired and they debate for time
        To fight on a day that's not Trinity.

FIRST BARON: Mordred says keep a look for all who draw
        And if they draw
        So do and go at them.
        Do not be taken unawares, says he.

SECOND BARON: It would take a whirlwind
        To make me draw
        An act of nature so primitive
        That would encourage me start this war.

FIRST BARON: Still, we simply fall behind and we will live
        Is what our King said.
        He said the forces come forward for us
        The youths with passion for their first bloodshed
        And in the swirling black, we'll to the tents.

SECOND BARON: Stand tall. Here come the Kings.

(Enter MORDRED and ARTHUR from separate sides. They meet formally, to discuss terms.)

MORDRED: Father-Uncle.

ARTHUR: Mordred. Come step near me.
        Our conference must be solitary.
        The fewer eyes upon us the less shame
        Our courage might not be turned into blame.

MORDRED: I'm King of England, that you'll never change
        Without you bring your forces, tattered there
        Against my fresh young nation in the field.

ARTHUR: No army can win England's heart, my son.
        A hero's welcome is all I need today.
        Can you give me that much, and to my men?

MORDRED: And what? That's all?

ARTHUR: My Camelot is gone, a memory.
    I killed a piece myself, we all did slice
    It's loveliness, it's hope, but not its light
    In history. All I want is that flight
    Of wings about my castle, to the sky
    And leave the earthly parliaments to men
    Who care more for the day to day affairs
    That my heaven seems now unfit to serve.

MORDRED: Do you repent?

ARTHUR: Some things, yes, I do.
    But not the visions, no those I do not repent.
    Not the love and that hope that destiny.
    I know you will not let us to London
    So at least let us rest off Trinity
    And so the battle is not unholy.

MORDRED: Care I for naming battles after your old God
    Or naming them for evil laughing children?
    This is a foolish request and I hate you
    For leaving the war's inciting to me.

ARTHUR: My son, know that if you start this war
    And your men should feel damned, it's on your hands.
    On Trinity Sunday we should not fight.

MORDRED: If I should win, and I shall, I still must
    Maintain the dignity of my decrees.
    For that reason I do hear your request
    And see it may not be unthinkable.

(FIRST BARON draws his sword.)

FIRST BARON: My! A snake is in the grass which I do fear!
    Kill it with this! This sword I cannot use!

SECOND BARON: Look what you do! You draw!

MORDRED: What has happened? These men draw up their swords!

FIRST BARON: My King, I did see a slither and
    I did shiver and reflex made me jump
    So I did draw my weapon to kill it.
    The snake
    Do you see it?

SECOND BARON: Let us run
    Unto the tents where we may be made safe!

(Exit FIRST BARON and SECOND BARON.)

MORDRED: Well Arthur, so it matters not who claims.
          The day is begun and there is no hope.
          Now face your son who seeks his due birthright.

ARTHUR: My righteousness is not questioned by you
         Or any man, though I do cry for this
         That all my men seem to go fast to fight
         And I must too draw up Excalibur.

MORDRED: I came to conference without a dagger
          So that your men would let me to your side.
          I have oft wished look at your white eyes
          Before your arrogance would help me slit their juice.
          I will return here with my arms and hot
          To slice your throat and drink my blood inside.

ARTHUR: I repent only that poor Mordred lived
         Past his base birth and to face father now.
         But Grace be kind, and God be listening
         Our blades, once retrieved will be glistening.

(Exit both, in opposite directions.)

SCENE II

The Battlefield. LUCAN, GAWAIN, and BEDIEVERE.

LUCAN: My temper tantamount to the war waged
        Confuses my cowardly inner self
        With one more ready to lay down his life.
        Like you, Gawain, I feel the righteous rage.

GAWAIN: You must go then and find more men to fight
         And find, too, Arthur where he may yet stand.

BEDIEVERE: I pray he stands in this insane exchange.

GAWAIN: With Excalibur in his hand he lives
         For with it is the King invincible.
         But still, I feel my own heart leaking out
         And I would have him by me 'fore I go.

BEDIEVERE: Go where? Sir Gawain, take heart for your health
            And be assured your legs stand still sturdy.

LUCAN: Come brother, let us off, to find the King.
        Gawain's ague is better left unchecked.

(Exit BEDIEVERE and LUCAN.)

GAWAIN: Though wounded, I am still a match indeed
         for any that would come and face me here!

(Enter MORDRED.)

MORDRED: Where is my father, brother?

GAWAIN: Father? I know not.
        But look on me, troublesome coward, and quake.

MORDRED: Your uncle is my father, Arthur ours
        Is all the things he would not clear repent.

GAWAIN: My arms are weak, but strong enough for thee.
        My legs bleed fast, but not too paralyzed.
        Confuse me not with little, fitful words
        But brandish metals like a soldier would.

MORDRED: Do not my sword entreat, not in this heat.

GAWAIN: If by my Lancelot I've lost my strength
        It's for your sickness we are all made weak.
        Come pass with me, and turn your life to past.

(They fight. GAWAIN falls.)

MORDRED: The scabbard of Excalibur sheaths me
        From harm from any man, and much less you
        The half man that I killed in this vast war.
        Goodbye Gawain, your gallantry is great
        But I am destined for another fate.

(Exit MORDRED. Enter BORS.)

BORS: Gawain, my friend, what has become of you?

GAWAIN: The final word I have is Give me Grace.
        (He dies.)

BORS: To lose a knight of truth to falseness aches.
        Oh Arthur, Lancelot, would you were here
        To embrace grace as grace ceases to be.

(Enter ARTHUR.)

ARTHUR: By God Old Bors, I knew not you came here
        To fight with us this day and risk your death.

BORS: Unlike my friend Lancelot, I felt just
        In fighting by your side and so followed
        Closely behind you to engage this war.
        But just as Mordred left, I found Gawain
        Your nephew on his back, passing away
        Slain as a Paladin, fighting for Good
        I feel God's hand is near to lift him high.

(Enter MORDRED.)

        Behind my Lord, approaches.

MORDRED: Silence Bors.
        If you must see another great deed done
        And stand by, as impure to act yourself

Then see this moment as great as Grail newfound.
The Death of Arthur, and the Table Round.

ARTHUR: You bring about your own fate with your taunts
And while I may be destined here to fall
You, Son, will not outwear my life's armor.
So let Mordred be slain Arthur's hand
As I bred you by sin, by sin will end.

(They fight. MORDRED stabs ARTHUR in the stomach. ARTHUR brings his blade through MORDRED's heart.)

MORDRED: What joy that I should not outlive my purpose
As you did Father.
Do not mistake my silence for quiet.
(He dies.)

BORS: Art wounded, regal champion, in victr'y?

ARTHUR: Sir Bors, find my Queen where'er she may be.
As I will never outlast this deep wound
Please know in parting that all Camelot
Was better for your living by their side.
Now do not cry, instead complete my quest
And see that my love lives when fails my chest.

SCENE III

Elsewhere on the field. BEDIEVERE alone.

BEDIEVERE: Lucan my brother where are you yet living?
My Lucan we should not have gone to France.
The land is barren and I am alone.
I fought this day, though shakily, I did
And did my best to serve my kingdom grand.
But now, at last, there's little left to cleft
And I would be informed of who has won.

(Enter LUCAN, carrying KING ARTHUR behind him.)

LUCAN: My brother come and help me with my burden.
The King has asked to see you in this time.
I found him upon Mordred's body broken
With this fatal wound deep inside his breast.

ARTHUR: Beloved Bedievere somehow I knew
Despite all things, that I could count on you.
Please, in these final moments that I live
I need you to perform the final task
That I must perform 'fore my dying gasp.

BEDIEVERE: Pray God my brother Lucan is here too
To give me courage to continue through.

ARTHUR: My knight, I fear his best moments are past.
Look now to his stomach and see the wound
That he ignores to carry me to you.

LUCAN: Yes, brother. Here it is. I am undone.
My guts would from me fall like ribbons now.
But this, I promise, brings me no more fear.
This is the finest day that I have seen
And I am happy to be at my rest.

BEDIEVERE: Who wounded my brother?

LUCAN: Do not him seek.
I left him with heart upon the grass
With all the others, that I butlered to
Their graves in the name of our King this day.
To find him would be fruitless
And revenges are all washed to the sea now.
This battle is renewing all of us.
Now do I see that I was meant for this:
To find the King and carry him to you.
My brother, I am proud for we have lived
To see our fate displayed as if through glass.
How rare a thing, and yet, I am so tired.
Do not feel lonely, brother, but be brave
And save the gentle Arthur, after death.
(He dies.)

BEDIEVERE: My heart is full of pride for his demise
But in the same moment, I cannot breathe.
My brother reawakened by his heart
Which was dormant until his final stroke.
O how I loved him and do weep for him.

ARTHUR: Do not end your weeping, but still come close
So you can hear my words where I lie down.
And know this is the quest you're fated for:
That you should take Excalibur with you.

BEDIEVERE: Excalibur, I should now take in hand?
And take it to London to make a show
Of what you did to raise the Table Round?

ARTHUR: There is a Lake just north of where I lie
That is near the cottage of my fair Queen
In the forest upon Camelot's borders.
Many times the men will have passed it by
And noted it, but never dipped their feet
For it is always cold and full of fog.

BEDIEVERE: I know this place by heart and have been there.

ARTHUR: Take up the sword and throw it in the Lake.
        When you are finished return to this place
        And tell me it is done.

BEDIEVERE: Discard the magic that proved you divine?
        Discard the blade that made you King of Might?

ARTHUR: Do as I say and you shall see my mind.
        Go! Tell me it is done, and when it is
        Tell me what your eyes were witness of.

BEDIEVERE: I cannot perform this, yet not resist
        The entire reason that God made me here.
        It seems a tragic folly to your jester
        That you would have me lose what is a treasure.

ARTHUR: Do as I ask, fair one, and do it fast
        For each minute I breathe is nearer last.

(Exit BEDIEVERE.)

SCENE IV

Further into the field. MERLIN meets LANCELOT.

LANCELOT: Old man, I thought you dead for years and years.

MERLIN: I will be soon, and was oft past deceased.
        Much like old Britain, risen just to fall.

LANCELOT: Who is now England's king?

MERLIN: None claim it yet.
        You sir, perhaps, can take the mantle up.
        In the future days these will be repeated
        So be Arthur or Mordred or yourself.
        Be Guenevere to some French warrior queen.
        It matters little.

LANCELOT: You riddle with me.

MERLIN: I never riddle, that's my curse and charm.
        I'm old and ageless and the riddle wastes
        The precious timelessness.

LANCELOT: Then you confuse.
        Is Arthur felled?

MERLIN: He is.

LANCELOT: I know no answer for this. Where is he?

MERLIN: In moments, Avalon.

LANCELOT: Gone and entombed?

MERLIN: Absorbed and taken up. Up then up again.

LANCELOT: Where is Guenevere? Where is my heart Bors?

MERLIN: Together in the London Tower holding
    Each other close as she weeps in his arms.
    Next he will take her from there, feed her well
    And in a nunnery will that Queen dwell.

LANCELOT: So Guenevere's to Amesbury at last?

MERLIN: The opposite of Carlisle's burning death
    Is Amesbury.

LANCELOT: Are not my arms the opposite?

MERLIN: The illnesses beset her must be cured.

LANCELOT: You can see this with your eyes?

MERLIN: It is breathed
    By all the books that will be written yet.

LANCELOT: What says your magic of the reasons why
    She goes to convent and not Lancelot?

MERLIN: If this is not clear to you, then I fear
    That you are unlearning inherently
    And so will men not learn from this sad state
    For centuries, and will repeat this war.

LANCELOT: I know only she is the reason that
    I defied all my better senses and
    Denied her to my best friend in his dires.
    Why else should I not have the right to her
    And not the God that kept us all apart?

MERLIN: When found she was in the tower she screamed
    That each soldier was that which he claimed
    Cried her that each was Morgan La Fay
    In form to fool her and to make her come
    And eat and surrender her love.
    She scratched until she felt the arms of Bors
    Who unmistakable, she cried upon
    And wondered to him that she was not sane.

LANCELOT: She will be well, and be again with me.

MERLIN: There is no will in her to love again,
    And she would not recognize former passions
    For fear of a transgression from forgiveness.
    Her heart rebuilt as penitence beats slow
    As if forever it would like to sleep.

LANCELOT: This will I trust when after she sees me
    And when I can to her entreat to France.

Reunited with her shall I be soon
So all these tragedies were not in vain.

MERLIN: If ever you were counseled, be so now.
That these proceedings were as in the court
And each human failing evidence of that
Which makes the living drama in your heart.
The race of man, and all its Evil ways
Are wrapped up in its Good, they are The Lovers.
So should you have her in your arms again
Soon to this point with new names we will come
And stand again, all repeated and broken.
Let lie that love you bury in this field
And mourn her as a heroine begone.

LANCELOT: You counsel me to forgive and forget.

MERLIN: I counsel you to quiet all these wailings.
Are you not content to be yet alive
When others die from being swept away
In the great fortune tree that grows
Beneath them, to lift them to the sun?

LANCELOT: Wizard, my Love is Gone, and my King too.
This final act has cut my fool's heart through.
This is not what Lancelot should see.
I am not content, and will never be.

SCENE V

ARTHUR and BEDIEVERE.

ARTHUR: Is it done at last?

BEDIEVERE: The deed is done my Lord.

ARTHUR: You'll lie no more?

BEDIEVERE: I hope never again.
The first time did I hide and return here
And tell you that I tossed it, but did not.
The second time I tried but could not bring
My hand to throw the beauty to its end.
At last, my failing I have overcome
And faced the ending of our Camelot
Like the man my brother would have me be.
This third time I cast the sword off to swim
As you decreed and balked not this mad need.
For my hand curled it back, then upward flew
Excalibur, which slew the heart of war.
The perfect and the golden blade turned upside

And then downside, circling End to End.
Then as if by Merlin's own devices
She raised away till hilt to point it stood
And lowered, gently, to a watery hand
Which, blue and fleshy burst from the still Lake.
Think not me a fool, as my eyes did attest
And this is not the madness of your passing
But wonderful and certainly the fate
Intended, I hope, by you all along.
So did the hand lower Excalibur
And drink it like a wine.

ARTHUR: The sword is Gone.

I own no sword.
Both strange and sage to finally turn and see
My long-worn, war-torn life entirely.
Have I been good?

BEDIEVERE: You are good.

ARTHUR: How so said?

My victories, my peace was made by blade.
Could history translate the peace from war?
Or was it true peace? For a little while?
Camelot, Ideal, made brief to be
Admired as too brief, too long away?
Forever never Camelot will stand
And remembered as what will be again.
Wind took me as a child of Kings
And blew me to the ground like a lost leaf.
And what then Knight? To sink as I did fly?
A boy again, an old man from the start?
I renew and I end, I Arthur all
Am nothing, once again, as I was once.
Then sisters three, in white, my sister, wife,
And yet another, veiled come by your boat,
And Avalon, as my mind rises, Sees!
There, Bedievere, sweet lonely, there they come.
They sweep me in their arms, the bold furies
With softness torn apart, and like the sword
Drawn into water, drowned within women.
Does it mean that I am men, or just a sword?
Or swords are men, or women furies soft?
Are visions rising riding to my eyes
On waves of darkness, liquid lullabies?
I see you sister, and another eye

Or fifty, or a hundred, or the child
Who came to me and told me he loved good.
Well, good will everlast and never found
But for a moment, lying on this ground.
The cause is never over, save last rites.
Good enough for Knights, is a last good night.

(He dies. The women come for him as BEDIEVERE watches.)

BEDIEVERE: Why did I see this, of all other men?
I flawed and shiv'ring, one unfit to send
Mythic Excalibur unto the end?
Does not the tale end with a new great power?
Camelot renewed? Not on this hour.
How will this tale be told in later years?
Well, we shall see, the ghosts and Bedieveres.

(The women carry ARTHUR away. As they do, they chant and sing the words: "Hic iacet Arthurus, rex quondam rexque futurus.")

(End.)

MATCH

Marc Chun

MARC CHUN was born and raised in the San Francisco Bay Area. He holds degrees in sociology and education from Stanford University. *Match* is Chun's first play; his only prior experience was writing term papers, writing tuition checks, and writing letters home to Mom to ask for money to cover his tuition checks. Other plays include *Beep* and *The Conference*. Chun's plays have been produced by the Cherry Lane Alternative, the Vital Theatre Company, and the Emerging Artists Theatre Company. Chun lives and works in Manhattan. He welcomes your feedback about the play; please e-mail him at Play_With_Matches@hotmail.com.

Match was first produced by the Cherry Lane Alternative (Angelina Fiordellisi and Eduardo Machado, Artistic Directors; Tracy S. Johnson, Producer) as part of its festival of one-act plays, *Alternation*, on July 17, 2001, at the Cherry Lane Alternative Theatre in New York City, with the following cast and credits:

One	Shawn J. Davis
Two	Tanya Clarke
Three	J.C. DeVore
Four	Blythe Baten
Five	Doug Simpson

Directed by: Steven Gridley
Lighting Design: Pamela Kupper
Stage Manager: Sara Sahin

The author gratefully acknowledges the contribution and support of the original cast, Playwrights Horizons Theatre School teachers Glyn O'Malley and Jeni Mahoney, writing group members, and Tracy S. Johnson and the Cherry Lane Theatre community.

Special thanks to Steven for his directorial vision, to Gretchen for the inspiration, and most importantly to his family for inexhaustible support and encouragement.

The play is dedicated to all those who tilt at windmills.

CHARACTERS

VOICE 1/ONE (male)
VOICE 2/TWO (female)
VOICE 3/THREE (male)
VOICE 4/FOUR (female)
VOICE 5/FIVE (male)

PLACE AND TIME

Here and now.

SETTING

The stage should be completely black, and set with just five stools or chairs. (Additional production notes at end of play.)

In the darkness, the following is heard.

VOICE 1/VOICE 2/VOICE 3/VOICE 4/VOICE 5: *(Whispering at different paces in round-robin fashion such that any one voice and any one phrase cannot be fully distinguished.)* I'm so sorry. It's all my fault. Please forgive me. Why did I do that? I didn't mean to. *(Repeat.)*

(This chorus continues. Each voice leaves the chorus to say each of the following lines, and then rejoins the chorus. Lights slowly come up as each line is said, the pace quickens throughout, and the lines begin to overlap. By the end, the lines are said in rapid fire, and the lights are at the highest intensity.)

VOICE 4: Would you like to lie down…

(Beat.)

VOICE 3: …yes, I know that…

(Beat.)

VOICE 1: …the whole truth…

(Beat.)

VOICE 2: …on location in Niagara Falls…

(Beat.)

VOICE 5: …enough acts of charity…

(Beat.)

VOICE 2: …welcome back…

VOICE 3: …welcome…

VOICE 4: …have a seat…

VOICE 5: …would you like a seat…

VOICE 3: …please have a seat…

VOICE 1: …nothing but…

VOICE 2: …would you like a seat…

VOICE 1: …please be seated…

VOICE 3: …my child…

VOICE 5: …how long since…

VOICE 1: …do you swear…

VOICE 4: …do you care…

VOICE 2: …do your hair…

VOICE 1: …so help you…

VOICE 4: …how can I help…

VOICE 5: …I'd like to help…

VOICE 3: …deal with aggression…

VOICE 4: …end of our session…

VOICE 2: …it's an obsession…

VOICE 1: …state your profession…

VOICE 5: …in my possession…

VOICE 4: …would you like to lie down…

VOICE 3: …yes, I know that…

VOICE 1: …the whole truth…

VOICE 4: …lie down…

VOICE 1: …whole truth…

VOICE 2: …on location in Niagara Falls…

VOICE 3: …yes, I know that…

VOICE 4: …lie down…

VOICE 1: …whole truth…

VOICE 2: …in Niagara Falls…

VOICE 5: …enough acts of charity…

VOICE 3: …yes, I know…

VOICE 4: …lie down…

VOICE 2: …Niagara Falls…

VOICE 5: …enough acts…

VOICE 1: …whole truth…

VOICE 3: … yes, I know…

(By now, the lines are being said at a fever-ish pitch, and the lights are at near full in-tensity.)

VOICE 4: …lie…

VOICE 5: …enough acts…

VOICE 1: …truth…

VOICE 2: …Falls…

VOICE 3: …yes, I know…

VOICE 4: …lie…

VOICE 5: …—nough acts…

VOICE 1: …truth…

VOICE 2: …Falls…

VOICE 3: …yes, I know…

VOICE 4: …lie…

VOICE 5: …—ough acts…

VOICE 1: …truth…

VOICE 2: …Falls…

VOICE 3: …yes, I know…

VOICE 4: …lie…

VOICE 5: …facts…

VOICE 1: …truth…

VOICE 2: …Falls…

VOICE 3: …yes and no…

VOICE 4: …lies…

VOICE 5: …facts…

VOICE 1: …true…

VOICE 2: …false…

VOICE 3: …yes and no…

VOICE 4: …lies…

VOICE 5: …facts…

VOICE 1: …true…

VOICE 2: …false…

VOICE 3: …yes and no…

VOICE 4: …lies…

VOICE 5: …facts…

VOICE 1: …true…

VOICE 2: ...false...

(Lights down. Long pause. Lights up on the five actors sitting on five stools or chairs. Each is bathed in a separate pool of light.)

THREE: The sky was *that blue*. That's just what I call it: "that blue." I never came up with something more creative because, well, you only name things you fear you might forget. There were three other days when the sky was that *exact* shade. First, when I was five; my mom and I made a kite, and then we went up to Wallacker Hill to fly it. That was the last time I... well, I stared up at that sky the entire day. Second, the day I found out I got into RISD, which is when I started to really believe I was actually an artist. And the third? The third was the day I met her.

TWO: Thanks a lot! Thanks for having me! *(Beat.)* When did I meet him? *(Beat.)* It seems like we've been together forever. The two of us complement each other perfectly: a mix of class and sass! *(She laughs.)*

THREE: That's her. She's beautiful, isn't she? I'm going to miss... I mean I hope she knows... *(Beat as he changes the subject.)* You know, it's a very particular shade. I tried for years to get it, and I almost had it once: I mixed five parts titanium white, two parts ultramarine, one part Prussian, and just a dab of pthalo.

FOUR: What am I feeling? A combination of sadness and anger and just a bit of regret.

THREE: But when the paint dried it... well, it wasn't right. *(Beat.)* Anyway, so that morning—May fifth—the sky was *that blue* again. *(Beat.)* There was a sweet mixture of star jasmine and dew on the breeze. Now we're talking not a single cloud in sight, we're talking birds singing, we're talking flowers blooming. I mean, c'mon: throw in a bright golden haze on the meadow and I could've broken into song. A day like that: of course it's not going to last. Nothing lasts forever. But I always figured you should enjoy things while you can. *(Beat.)* The smells, the sounds, the colors: I remember it all just like it was yesterday.

ONE: The afternoon of May fifth? I actually don't remember much of it at all. *(Beat.)* Now, did I mention that I was 250 days sober? *(Beat.)* I was driving to the hospital to see my mother. *(Beat.)* I did have the envelope. *(Beat.)* To the best of my knowledge, that's right. *(Beat.)* Right.

FIVE: Wrong! Completely wrong! I was totally fu—... oh, I'm sorry. Sorry about that.

ONE: Mind you, we're talking 250 *days*.

FOUR: A *week*. Maybe more.

TWO: A *month*. Maybe less.

FIVE: It's been probably really more like twenty *years* since my last... *(He changes the subject, and looks around.)* I don't remember these things being so cramped. Were they always like this?

ONE: Yes. *(Beat.)* No, she had already been admitted, so I didn't tell her. *(Beat.)* No, it *was* an accident. *(Beat.)* How was I supposed to know that? *(Beat.)* It's difficult to say.

THREE: It's difficult to put it into words. Just so... so...

TWO: Oh, and Kip? It's difficult to describe him. He's so... smart. And generous. And good-hearted. And... and...

THREE: ... pretty.

TWO: And witty.

FIVE: And hey! The *Enquirer* was bound to break the Kip story. And no one is going to pay $8.50 to see an action hero who is, well... you know.

TWO: Sorry, ladies, you're out of luck! *(Beat.)* He's all mine.

FIVE: Not that I care. Some of my best friends, you know.

FOUR: He was my best friend, you know.

TWO: Didn't I tell you this story before?

THREE: So, my story?

FIVE: She and Kip became good friends in what seems like a *lifetime ago*.

TWO: Kip and I fell in love in what seems like a *lifetime ago*. We met at a candlelight vigil peace rally. Turns out we have the same activist spirit.

FIVE: They met in a waiting room. Turns out they have the same plastic surgeon.

TWO: I had this defective box of matches—it was full of matches, but there wasn't one of those flint strip things on the side. He had used up his last match but still had the empty box.

FIVE: Nose job, lipo, cheek implants, chest implants. *(Beat, as he tries to remember.)* And, um, she was having *something* done... What was it?

ONE: I don't remember.

TWO: Useless apart, but together: sparks fly! Our love is true blue.

FIVE: Anyway, so she did it to help him out when people started to ask questions.

ONE: I don't understand your question. *(Beat.)* See, it wasn't like that. Appearances can be deceiving.

FIVE: But over time, they both grew to really resent lying about it. In fact, a couple of years ago, they seriously talked about Kip going public once and for all. I knew that she'd be fine, but Kip might not work again. So for the good of their careers, I convinced them that they should just keep it up. To be a celebrity, you have to pay an exorbitantly high price. So whenever the rumors would start up again, I would send the two of them out on the circuit to do damage control. They come off as this loving couple that needs to set the record *straight. (Chuckles.)* If only they acted *one-fifth* as well on set.

ONE: Can I take the fifth?

FOUR: The fifth. I've been like this since the fifth.

THREE: Call it fate. Call it destiny.

TWO: It was inevitable. Once Kip and I saw the script, we knew we had to do it. It was the kind of story that keeps you guessing until the very end. And now this *(Gesturing, as if setting up a movie clip.)* is from "Match Made in Heaven"... *(Beat, and then in response to an unseen audience's round of applause.)* Oh, thank you! Thank you very much! We're all so proud of it.

FIVE: We're all so *embarrassed* by it. The film was one of those ridiculous, cookie-cutter star-crossed lover stories; like who do *you* think she ends up with: All alone? With the goofy sidekick? *(Sarcastic.)* Or *maybe* with the leading man?

THREE: We always knew we were going to end up together.

FIVE: We couldn't figure out how to promote it. But for her sake, I knew that I had to come up with something. And then she told me what happened with the *Marie Claire* thing, and I had a brainstorm.

This is the angle. *This* is how we could spin it. And the media would devour it. They would absolutely eat it up.

FOUR: I haven't been able to eat. I can't sleep. I cry every hour on the hour. *(Beat.)* That's not normal, is it?

THREE: So, when I saw the sky that morning, I knew it was a sign. I knew something *unbelievable* was going to happen that day. It was a sign.

ONE: Since the separation... well, I guess officially the divorce now. Well, I'd visit my mother each week. So I could tell her the numbers.

FOUR: What I want to know... I mean what I *need* to know... maybe what you can help me figure out is... how could he leave me? Here. Alone.

TWO: Now, what kind of question is that? "Sexiest Man on Earth" or not, he's just Kip to me. *(Beat.)* Well, it's always uncomfortable doing love scenes, but it's *really* embarrassing when you have to do them with your husband! *(Beat.)* Now, cut that out! My mother is going to watch this!

ONE: My mother can't watch, so I make sure to catch the draw. They always announce the numbers just before 7:00. *(Beat.)* Yes, that's correct.

FOUR: And what am I supposed to do now?

TWO: Again, where do you get these silly questions?

FIVE: We could turn this into a fantastic PR event. With that many flops in a row, she desperately needed some good press. I mean, holy sh—sh—sure, sure, it's a good cause, so she can help people out, it's noble, you know, blah blah blah.

TWO: Ha, ha, ha! Very funny. *(Beat.)* Actually, I had just finished the song for the soundtrack, and then did this fabulous piece for *Marie Claire* about my research for the role. I met a woman who was donating bone marrow to save her sister's life, and I learned so much from her. See, the recipient has to have radiation treatment to kill off her own white blood cells because they would otherwise attack the donated marrow. The body is stripped of all its defenses. The recipient is as close to death as possible. And if the body doesn't recognize the marrow, it will reject it. Reject it outright. *(Beat.)* In the operating room I held her hand, and she had this aura of peace about her. There were tubes down her throat and tubes into her arms, and I watched as they drew three cups of marrow out of her hip. Through it all she had this look of... of *fearlessness* that I'll never forget.

ONE: I don't actually remember.

FOUR: I don't want to remember.

THREE: But instead of just waiting for something unbelievable to happen to me, I decided this time I was going to do something.

TWO: In the recovery room she was groggy and in so much pain. I asked her if there were something I could do for her. An autograph, anything! *(Beat.)* And she turned and whispered, *(She uses a very scratchy voice.)* "How about if you just sign up for the bone marrow registry?" *(Beat.)* Well, how could I say "No"?

ONE: No. No, I didn't mean it that way. *(Beat.)* No. There was that other guy. *(Beat.)* See, no one told me that. *(Beat.)* No, I didn't know I had to do it.

TWO: I just knew I had to do it.

THREE: I just knew I had to do it. But I didn't have much time. Things had taken a turn for the worse. They had been searching for years, but the doctors wouldn't give up. They told me to just hang in there because everything was going to be OK. That's what they kept saying.

FIVE: But this wasn't just another publicity stunt for her. She was really taking this seriously. She started reading up on this, she met with doctors. I had to try to squeeze in one meeting after another. Which meant another scheduling *nightmare* for me.

FOUR: Sometimes I feel like it was all a *dream. (Beat.)* We could practically read each other's minds. Sometimes I hear him. Is that weird? *(Beat.)* It's almost a whisper, but I swear I can hear his voice. *(Beat.)* What does he say? Different things. Sometimes he reads me his poetry. Sometimes he just tells me that things are going to be OK.

THREE: *(Almost a whisper.)* Everything's going to be OK.

FOUR: It's comforting.

FIVE: It's a nightmare!

TWO: It's important.

ONE: It's silly. She picked the same numbers every week: one, two, three, five, eight, thirteen, bonus twenty-one. They're called the Fibonacci numbers. My dad was a mathematician, and that's what he studied. He found this pattern in the numbers. The same pattern, that went on and on. He said that if he kept going, the pattern would eventually have to stop. He figured there was no way it could go on forever.

FIVE: Of course, it couldn't go on forever.

ONE: He loved those numbers. My mom loved him. For my Mom, playing those numbers gave her a chance to remember him.

TWO: Playing the role gave me a chance to remember her. While she was going through the procedure, I worked on a sense memory: the pain, the fear, the commitment. I wanted to bring the truth of her life to the movie set. I could feel how brave·she was. So selfless.

FIVE: So selfish. So *her* little five-minute blood donation was becoming *my* logistical headache. *(Beat.)* A lot of people say she can be a real pain in the butt, but the thing about her is she has a good heart. And she cares. I think her best quality is that she just does what she believes is right, regardless of what anyone else says. And when she gets really excited about something, she… *(He smiles as he trails off.)* You know, why couldn't I have… She has no idea how much I lov—… *(Pauses before saying "love".)* …look out for her best interests. Someone has to. In this business? *(Beat.)* But when it comes to stuff like this, I don't get it. We never seem to connect on these things, she and I.

THREE: We would always connect on these things, she and I. I could tell when she was calling just by the way the phone rang. I could tell what she was thinking just by the way she'd tip her head or squint her eyes. And we'd finish each other's…

FOUR: …sentences. Stories. Poems. I hear him all the time.

FIVE: I look out for her all the time.

THREE: Our lives were always in sync. Up together, down together. Good news happened in tandem. The very day I sold my first painting she got into Stanford.

She got the job offer from UCLA one morning, and then that afternoon I found out I got my first gallery showing. *(Beat.)* But it worked the other way too. When we were down, we were both *down*... but we knew that better times were coming. It was the law of averages or probability or something, but it had to happen.

ONE: It was never going to happen. Statistically speaking? My dad would have had an aneurysm.

FIVE: *(Counting them off on his fingers.)* So, she'd take the blood test, we'd finally get some good press, and she'd fall madly in love with the man who really cares for her.

ONE: There's no chance she could have *won*.

THREE: She would have good news *too*.

FIVE: Well, two out of *three*.

ONE: One, two, three, five, eight, thirteen, and bonus twenty-one.

TWO: I took the blood test, and all I could think was: maybe this could somehow save a life.

FIVE: Maybe this could somehow save her career.

THREE: When I was really getting sick, she had a string of major crises in her life. Everything was falling apart. She hated her job, she was fighting with her parents, and her sister was driving her crazy.

FOUR: Everything was coming together. I loved my job, I was finally getting along with my parents, and my sister was doing great.

ONE: You know, she was more likely to be hit by a meteor than to win the lottery.

FIVE: She was more likely to win the lottery than get a good review.

TWO: It was weeks later, and the donor center called and told me I was a *first-level* match. So, I went back to the hospital for an actual blood draw. That's when I told my manager I wanted to become a spokesperson to try to get other people to register. We'd turn it into a big ol' campaign.

FIVE: She was going to turn it into a big ol' campaign. But, since she has the attention span of a five-year-old, as soon as she got interested in saving the spotted owl or freeing Tibet, I'd be left to pick up the pieces.

THREE: Up together, down together.

FIVE: Of course I was the first person she tried to get to sign up. I'm a good guy. I do what I can. I give money, I recycle, I usually remember to order *dolphin-safe* tuna. Now, that's a lot more than other people do, am I right? *(Beat.)* But she kept asking me to do it. And I heard that if there were a match, we're talking about major surgery. Major pain. I'm not into pain.

TWO: The blood draw would check to see if the proteins matched, which would determine if I were a *second-level* match. The nurse kept asking me if I was sure I wanted to do this. Was I absolutely, completely, totally positive? At first, I thought she was trying to talk me out of it, but then I realized that it would be far worse to get the recipient's hopes up and then back out. I should have been scared, but then you start thinking you are the *one* who could save another life. So of course I did it.

FIVE: So of course I didn't do it.

FOUR: I didn't mean to do it. Not at first. Is this all my fault? *(Beat.)* He knew me like no one ever did. Or ever will.

ONE: I didn't know him from Adam. I never saw him. What was I supposed to do? He just came out of nowhere.

THREE: Out of nowhere, I called her and told her there was something important we needed to talk about.

FOUR: He called me and said there was something we had to talk about. He said it was something he couldn't tell me over the phone. But there was something in his voice. Something. I thought maybe they found someone. That was reasonable, right? They found someone. Or maybe his condition started getting better.

ONE: Her condition started getting worse. She started talking to my dad. He's been dead almost ten years, and she talks to him as if he's right there in the room. She would tell him she still believed in me. My mom would say, "You get what you deserve, and you deserve what you get." And she'd always tell him she knew *some day* I'd make her proud. And I will. See, I have some pretty big plans. Big plans. Fate has thrown me some curve balls, one thing after another that's been out of my control. But I've got sort of a blueprint for things now, and it's all going to happen.

FIVE: I tried to talk her out of it, but she was convinced it was going to happen.

TWO: It almost didn't happen. With the risk of surgery and the health concerns, my manager warned me there was no way the studio's insurance people would have signed off on this. So I didn't tell them. I had to keep it completely confidential. See, I didn't tell anyone.

THREE: See, I didn't tell her how really bad things were getting. The neutropenia, the anti-emetic, the side effects from the new meds. I didn't want to worry her. It would've upset her.

ONE: And she started giving me two crisp new dollar bills each week to play the lottery: one for her, one for me. She said she was determined to hang on long enough to finally win. She was so sick, but she was just going to hang on. She'd never admit it, but I'm sure she hoped it would be a way to provide for her grand disappointment of a son. But I got my big plans. I'm getting my life together, and I don't need the lottery to— *(Beat.)* I'm sorry, yes, I'll stick to answering the question. *(Beat, and clearly not answering the question.)* But it's just that my dad would have flipped. He called the lottery the "tax on ignorance." He held gamblers, day traders, and lottery players in utter… *(Searching for the word.)* contempt. *(Beat.)* Yes, sir, that was an unfortunate word choice.

FIVE: I called the doctors to check, and they said it was extremely unlikely she'd be *the* match. What a relief. I was prepared to talk her out of it, but now I figured what's the point? When the test comes back negative, she can do her patented disappointed shtick, which the public loves. Now, everyone gets what they want: she gets to do her little spokesperson thing, I only have a few more days of this scheduling torture, and the press gets the perfect story. Not too bad, if I do say so myself: a win-win all around. No one gets hurt.

THREE: But my situation was pretty bad.

FIVE: And the story was right out of the movie: there she is, willing to save this guy's life with her own bone marrow. It was life imitating art imitating life. A big, fat self-serving lie masquerading as honest-to-goodness truth.

THREE: I probably should have told her my condition wasn't getting any better, but...

FOUR: I probably should have just been honest with him all along, but...

TWO: I probably should have just told the studio and said this was more important than being a celebrity, but...

ONE: I probably should have just told her I couldn't stand to see her throw away her money, but...

FIVE: I probably should have told her there was no chance of a blood match, but...

THREE: ...what's...

FOUR: ...the...

TWO: ...harm...

ONE: ...in...

FIVE: ...telling...

ONE/TWO/THREE/FOUR/FIVE: ...a little white lie?

FOUR: So I went down to the hospital to meet him. There was this huge crowd out front, so I called and said I'd meet him in the back.

TWO: So we went down to the hospital. My manager went with me.

FIVE: We went down to the hospital. I went with her. It was *fantastic*. There was a media circus out front. "Entertainment Tonight," "Extra," E! It was crazy.

TWO: It was a *nightmare*. There was a media circus out front. "Entertainment Tonight," "Extra," E! It was crazy.

ONE: Yes, sir. That is correct.

THREE: She said she'd meet me in back.

TWO: So I made them drop us off in the back.

FIVE: But they ended up dropping us off in the back. So, change of plans: she could do the procedure first, and I'd get her to talk to the press afterwards. This was a big deal, and I was worried about her, of course, so I had a hair and makeup person on standby for a quick touch-up.

ONE: No, I had no control over that. *(Beat.)* I don't recall that.

FOUR: All right. He still wouldn't say anything on the phone, but now I'm getting this feeling. That he's going to have good news. Maybe they really did find someone. That there was finally something to celebrate.

ONE: No, I was not drinking.

THREE: When you really think about it, I mean, what are the odds? A million to one? A billion to one? What are the odds that someone actually finds his soulmate?

ONE: Yes, sir, I did take a breathalyzer test.

FIVE: So they took the second blood test.

TWO: And then they took the blood test. I knew it wasn't likely. I mean, what are the odds of a marrow match? A million to one? A billion to one? The doctor said I had to match eight out of eight proteins.

ONE: One, two, three, five, eight, thirteen, and bonus twenty-one.

FOUR: There was practically no chance for a marrow match. You know what one in a million is? That's point-oh-oh-oh-oh-oh-one.

ONE: Yes, I believe it was point-oh-one; at least that's what the officer said.

FIVE: What are the odds?

THREE: No, really, what *are* the odds?

FOUR: But we always knew that if there were a match, that would only be the first step. He'd have to start getting prepared. Tests and more tests. Painful procedures and radiation that would leave his body without the ability to defend itself; so close to life, but so close to death. The preparation alone would be so scary, so risky, so complicated.

TWO: The preparation was so simple. Being an actor really prepares you for such situations. All you need to do—and folks, don't try this at home—is ask yourself "What would I do if I were in that circumstance." *(She closes her eyes and meditates.)* See, there! Prepared! It's Stanislavski, the "Magic If."

THREE: If I really thought about it, I knew the timing wasn't great. I didn't have the ring. And with the meds, there was no way I could get down on one knee, but I was going to do it. I just had to do it. I just can't explain!

ONE: But I can explain. I was at that bar, but I didn't drink. She didn't say she saw me drink. *(Beat.)* I might've had some cold medicine earlier, which could have explained that, right? That's reasonable, right?

FOUR: That's reasonable, right? He had been through so much. I feel horrible about it now, but it seemed to make sense at the time. And at first it *was* all true. When his white blood cell count dropped they put him in isolation, and he got so depressed. At the same time, I couldn't get my book published, my student evaluations were horrible, and my third year review looked grim. When I saw him, he

knew how down I was, and he just wanted to take care of me. He felt he could do something. And it boosted his spirits. *(Beat.)* For the first time in a long while, he had something to give.

TWO: Now, the odds of finding a match are increased if the marrow comes from a family member. But this poor man didn't have brothers or sisters or parents. He was all alone.

THREE: Just thinking about her, I was never alone.

FIVE: At first, she was livid when she saw all the media there. Although she was happy to talk to anybody on any other day about the registry, she wanted to do the procedure privately because she felt it was personal. But I convinced her that we could have a press conference to try to get people to register, that greater good could come from this, and that by tying it into the movie, it's almost like this was a big public service announcement. A five-hundred-dollar-million, PG-13, make-or-break the studio, public service announcement. So she finally relented.

ONE: But then that's her word against mine.

FOUR: It was touch and go for a while. He had a bad reaction to the chemo and he was nauseous and vomiting. It was just so much. And I'm not proud of this, but I started to make up some, um, well, some *stories*. I don't know why, they just came out of the blue: I told him I had a big fight with my parents, I told him I was having problems with my department chair, I told him my cat died! And each time we would talk for days. He'd give me advice. He'd hold my hand. He'd try to make me laugh. And through it all, he didn't focus on how his body was being ravaged by the radiation. That's not wrong, is it? *(Beat.)* You have to be willing to make great personal sacrifices to protect the ones you love. It's what he needed. To be able to think about something else, to be able to make things better for me. Right? He could be there for me.

THREE: She's always been there for me in this true, pure, honest way. The two of us, we have this… this… *(He can't find the word.)*

FIVE: While she was off doing press, the doctor came back with the results. I figured we'd have the little press conference about how disappointed she was, she could encourage people to register, and then we could finally move on. She had the blues album to work on, scripts to read, the big fashion shoot with Kip. But of all the luck: the doctor told me there was a perfect match: *eight out of eight* proteins.

ONE: What are the odds? My dad would have had an aneurysm.

THREE: We were a perfect match.

FOUR: We were a match made in heaven.

TWO: I was waiting for the results, and somehow I really thought there was going to be a match.

FIVE: A perfect match. Now I'm thinking it's a whole new ballgame. This was a miracle. If she's getting this much press by just being a spokesperson, imagine what she'd get if she actually donated bone marrow to save this poor guy! Now we've got cover of every magazine! First story on the evening news. Boffo box office for the movie. This would be unbelievable! *(Beat.)* But then I started thinking.

THREE: It was time to stop thinking. If I told her there wasn't much time left,

then she'd feel obligated. She'd accept not because she wanted to, but because she felt she had to. If you think too much about something, you always end up talking yourself out of it. When it comes to things like this, you just have to act with your heart. You have to just act.

FIVE: She doesn't just act. She's a singer. Her bread and butter is her recording career. *My* bread and butter is her recording career.

THREE: I knew what I was going to do.

FIVE: I didn't know what I was going to do. I remembered the lady from *Marie Claire* could barely talk. The tubes they put down her throat scratched her vocal cords. Permanent damage. My mind started racing.

ONE: No, I wasn't racing down the street. *(Beat.)* There was a glare, so I was driving at or below the speed limit.

FIVE: One wrong move and they could scratch her vocal chords. And then what do we do if she can't sing? I should have seen this coming and could have nipped it in the bud. But by now there was no way I could talk her out of it, so I would have to track down the best anesthesiologist and get the best specialist to do the procedure. I could take care of it. I wouldn't tell her about the risks to her voice, and would just convince her the procedure was completely safe.

FOUR: And I lied to him. *(Pause.)* What horrible kind of person lies to the people they love?

ONE: What kind of person lies to the people they love?

FIVE: What kind of person *doesn't* lie to the people they love?

TWO: While I was waiting, I met with the press. I wanted to tell people that this could very well be the most important thing I've ever done. *(Beat.)* No, even *more* important than that miniseries.

FOUR: On the drive over I started thinking. If there had been a match, the doctor would have called me too. It had to be something else. And then it hit me. He had figured out I had been lying all that time. I mean it was only so long I could fool him. He knows my every thought, he can tell. But by then, one lie had led to another. And then another. I'd try to explain, and I'd beg his forgiveness.

THREE: She'd never forgive me for not having a ring, for not doing this right. But I couldn't wait. I bet she had already figured out I was going to propose.

FOUR: I got to the hospital. I parked the car, and saw him across the street. I started walking towards him.

THREE: She started walking across the parking lot towards me.

FIVE: So, everything was under control. I would handle it. As always. I went to find her to tell her the good news. She was going to save a life.

THREE: I couldn't wait. She was on the other side of the street, and when I saw her face, I had to ask her right then.

FOUR: He was on the sidewalk in front of the hospital. And when I saw his face, I knew. He'd never be able to trust me again. How do you apologize for that?

ONE: I'm sorry, I'm sorry. I'll just answer the question. *(Beat.)* Yes, I was listening to the radio at approximately 6:55 when they drew the numbers.

FIVE: You can't script stuff like this. Against all the odds, there was a bone marrow match.

TWO: I was talking to Mary Hart when my manager approached with this look on his face I'd never seen before. This was it. I'd find out if there was a match. I braced myself. *(Beat as she takes a dramatic breath.)* In the next minute, lives would change forever. *(Pause.)* And then he said...

FIVE: And then I said...

ONE: And then they said...

THREE: And then I said...

FOUR: And then he said...

ONE: One...

THREE: *(Shouting excitedly.)* "Will you marry me?"

ONE: ...two...

FOUR: *(Solemnly, as she remembers.)* "Will you marry me?"

ONE: ...three...

FIVE: *(He closes his eyes, and there is a long pause as he tries to finally say the words.)* "I just talked to the doctor and there... wasn't... a bone marrow match."

ONE: ...five...

TWO: *(Remembering FIVE's words.)* "There *wasn't* a bone marrow match."

ONE: ... eight, thirteen, bonus twenty-one!

FOUR: Oh my god!

FIVE: Why did I say that? I can't believe I did that.

THREE: *(Excitedly.)* I can't believe I actually did it. I asked her to marry me!

FOUR: I couldn't believe he did it. He asked me to marry him. I was caught completely off guard. I didn't know what to do.

THREE: But then she just stared at me. With this blank look. Like she didn't know what to do. Like she didn't know who I was.

TWO: *(Recalling.)* If the body doesn't recognize the marrow, it will reject it.

FOUR: I just stared at him. I didn't… I just couldn't… believe it.

ONE: I couldn't believe it. The jackpot! After all these years, listening to those stupid numbers every single week for ten years. And then they actually drew her numbers. They drew her numbers! Hanging on all this time, and they drew her Fibonacci numbers!

FIVE: I can't believe it. Why? Why?

FOUR: He had this look on his face. Like he had used up every last ounce of emotional energy to ask me that question. He was willing to give me everything. He had nothing left.

TWO: *(Recalling.)* The body is stripped of all its defenses. The recipient is as close to death as possible.

THREE: I could tell. That look, that silence. I can't really blame her. I mean nothing lasts forever. I had so little time, so I'm not even sure if it would have caused more or less pain if we… well, I don't know why but I wandered out, I stumbled towards her.

FOUR: He started to walk towards me.

ONE: The jackpot! Fifty-five million dollars! *(Beat.)* But of course…

TWO: Of course, I was disappointed, but I always knew it was a long shot. But sometimes you just have to do the things that

matter. The things that are important to you. But Kip would have… *(Beat.)* What's that? *(Beat.)* The rumors about Kip?

ONE: …I didn't buy the ticket! I never bought any tickets! Every single week I just put the dollars in this envelope. I was going to save the money for her. It was for her own good. For once, I thought I wasn't a complete screw-up. So that night I was going to give her that tattered old envelope with a thousand crisp one-dollar bills. Talk about your *grand* disappointment. I felt deep down in my bones that I was finally doing something right.

TWO: About Kip? *(She thinks about doing something right.)*

FOUR: He had this look in his eyes as he walked towards me.

FIVE: What's wrong with me? Why wouldn't I let her help save this guy's life? *(Beat.)* But it was for her own good, right?

ONE: What's wrong with me? What was I going to do? I started to panic.

TWO: All right. Enough is enough. Can't you see there's something bigger going on here? Something more important? We're talking life and death here. We're talking about regular people demonstrating amazing compassion and generosity and heroic acts in everyday life. Everything doesn't have to be about Hollywood and gossip and box office receipts. *(Beat.)* You want to know the truth about me and Kip? You want to really know what's going on? The studios, my manager, and the record company are always telling me it's best if I don't… it's just that it's nothing to be ashamed of, and by pretending otherwise is just wrong. If I've learned anything from this, it's bravery. So, once and for all I just want to come clean and let people know…

FIVE: *(Looking in direction of the "priest" in such a way that he's looking directly at TWO.)* It was for her own good. She just doesn't know how to look out for her own good.

TWO: *(Looking in direction of the "talk show host" in such a way that she's looking directly at FIVE.)* ...I'm absolutely, completely, totally positive...

FIVE: *(Looking in direction of the "priest" in such a way that he's looking directly at TWO.)* To be a celebrity, you have to pay an exorbitantly high price.

TWO: ...it's time for someone to tell the world...

FIVE: So why did I do it?

FOUR: And out of nowhere...

THREE: And out of nowhere...

ONE: And out of nowhere...

FOUR: This car comes speeding by and hit him.

THREE: This car came speeding by and hit me.

ONE: This guy came out and I hit him.

TWO: ...there are things you do...

FIVE: I did it because I... I... I love her!

TWO: ...to protect the ones you love... *(Beat.)* There are things you have to do...

FOUR: You have to be willing to make great personal sacrifices to protect the ones you love.

FIVE: But like who do *you* think she ends up with? Not the goofy sidekick. *Maybe* the leading man?

THREE: What are the odds of finding your soulmate?

(Pause.)

TWO: *(Catching herself, and composing herself.)* ...such as come out... and tell you that this movie is the best work Kip and I have done together. *(Smiles weakly.)*

FIVE: Or all alone?

FOUR: I'm all alone.

FIVE: What have I done?

ONE: What have I done?

FOUR: What have I done?

ONE: I swerved, but it was too late.

FOUR: *(Angry.)* I need to tell him. I need him to know. I need him to understand. *(Beat.)* Because. *(Beat.)* I need him to forgive me. Maybe I just need to forgive my— *(Beat.)* What? Are you implying I was being selfish? *(Beat.)* No, just say it! What was I avoiding? *(Beat, as therapist asks if telling the lies was a way to make it so THREE would take care of her.)* No, it was a way that *I* could take care of *him*! *(Beat.)* That's not what this is all about! But that's not... I didn't mean... I do not! *(Beat.)* Who are you to judge me?

FIVE: *(Looking up toward heaven.)* So tell me, who are you to judge me?

ONE: Yeah, well who are you to judge... *(Beat.)* Oh, yeah.

THREE: The doctors operated right away. I was in surgery for almost fifteen hours. *Fifteen* hours.

TWO: *(Trying to get back to celebrity guest banter mode.)* Yeah, maybe I am still a little light-headed. *(Beat.)* I'm a little off! I don't even know what I'm saying. *(Beat.)* You're right, thank goodness for editing! *(Laughs.)*

ONE: It was an accident. I didn't mean

it. I just felt, down to my bones, that I was doing the right thing. It was part of my big plan. *(Now speaking about the accident, the lottery, and his life.)* This wasn't supposed to happen. This really wasn't supposed to happen. *(Pause.)* What? My mother? *(Beat.)* She'd probably say that I should… that I've had enough chances. Probably that… I need to stop making excuses. *(Pause.)* That all it would take to make her proud would be… You know, she didn't really need the money. I think my mom has actually just been hanging on all these years hoping…

THREE: Now that's a really long time.

FIVE: Of course it couldn't go on forever.

ONE: *(Saying for the first time in his life.)* …Sir, I'll take full responsibility.

FIVE: So you see, it wasn't my fault. And I'm sure they can find another donor. She can help. I'll help. We'll get everyone to register. *(Beat.)* That's what I should do now, right? *(Beat.)* It's just that I've been pretty stressed out since then. My stomach's been in knots. My back. I've been having trouble sleeping. My heart has been pounding. And these migraines. It's just so much pain and— *(Beat.)* I was doing what I thought was the right thing. It was the right thing. Does God… you know it was the right thing. It *was*. It's just…

ONE: You get what you deserve. And deserve what you get.

FIVE: …do you think I'm being… punished?

FOUR: What? *(Beat.)* What? *(Beat.)* Oh my god. *(Begins to cry.)* I want to feel cheated, but not after what I've done. Look what I've done. What have I done? *(Beat.)*

There aren't the words to explain. *(Beat.)* It's too late. What am I supposed to do now?

TWO: I'm sorry, but I need to run to get back to the studio. Thanks, though. So go see the— *(She stops herself before saying "movie.")* …, um, everyone get registered! Kip, honey? I love you.

(The light over TWO slowly dims and goes out.)

THREE: They took my organs. My lungs, my eyes, my kidneys… *(Beat.)*… my heart. Maybe they can learn something. They had a nice funeral. She was inconsolable. I would have done anything just to hold her hand. She was there with her sister and parents. I think somehow this might have brought them back together. I'm glad they're there for her. So she's not alone.

FIVE: Maybe I shouldn't have… how are we supposed to know whether or not, well, I mean, if there's a lesson I'm supposed to get that… what am I supposed to do?

ONE: Is there anything else I should say? *(Pause.)* So I can step down now?

FIVE: I understand.

FOUR: Our time's up? Already?? All right. *(Pauses as she composes herself.)* How about three sessions a week? *(Pause.)* Thanks.

ONE: Thank you, your honor. *(Pause.)* What was that? *(Beat.)* I think she will be. *(Beat.)* I will. Thank you.

(The light over ONE slowly dims and goes out.)

THREE: So, that's pretty much my story. I wasn't sure if I'm supposed to ask you or if there were some forms or something, but… *(Summoning up the courage to ask.)*

Do you think there might be *any* exceptions about getting to, well, you know, go back down to— *(Beat.)* Even though— *(Beat.)* I mean, just for… a day, even a day, that's all… *(Beat.)* But… even when it's… I mean, c'mon… your *soulmate*— *(Beat.)* When I saw the sky, how was I supposed to know that… I mean, if I had known, I would have… *(Long pause.)* What? Yes? *(Pause.)* OK, I'm sorry. I understand. Just thought I'd ask.

FIVE: Yes, father? *(Pause.)* I don't know. *(Beat.)* Actually, I do. I'm… sorry. I'm really sorry. *(Beat.)* For everything. *(Pause.)* Thank you, father. *(Crosses himself.)* In the name of the Father, the Son, and the Holy Ghost. *(He looks up toward the light.)*

(The light over FIVE slowly dims and goes out.)

THREE: Well, in that case, can you tell me one thing? One thing. I really need to know. Could you tell me, well, why did this have to happen? No, wait, if it weren't for that car, would there ever have been a match? Or why wasn't there anybody with the same… I mean, even if there weren't, how much longer would I have had… no, how much longer would *we* have had…

(He trails off.) … *(Pause.)* You know, actually it's all right. I don't think I want to know.

FOUR: I want him to know, wherever he is, I want him to know that I loved… *love* him. And that I would have said… *(Sotto.)* yes. *(Beat.)* Do you think he knows? Oh my god, I just hope he knows. *(She starts to walk away.)*

(The light over FOUR's stool slowly dims and goes out, and she slowly walks into another pool of light.)

THREE: Well, I just hope she doesn't forget. The two of us, we will always have this, well, I still don't know what to call it… it's just, well, *that connection. (Beat.)* You know, even now, sometimes I still hear her.

FOUR: *(Pauses, and says over her shoulder, in the general direction of THREE.)* Goodbye.

(FOUR disappears into the darkness. Pause.)

THREE: I know. Here's the one thing. Instead, how about just telling me what *you* call that color. *(Beat.)* Oh. That's nice.

(Lights out. End of play.)

A NOTE ON STAGING

The play takes place simultaneously in a courtroom, on a late-night talk show, outside the pearly gates, in a therapist's office, and in a confessional. Under no circumstances should the staging be literal. At the beginning of the play, the audience should *not* be able to tell where each of the characters is or to whom each is speaking. This play consists of five overlapping, interlocking monologues. The journey the audience will take is through hearing the stories unfold, trying to figure out to whom the characters are talking, and experiencing the stories intersect and then ultimately diverge. This is a play in which five characters are desperately seeking connections to others, but the only connection they actually have exists ephemerally in the void between their shared spoken lines. Experimentation in production has found that the most successful staging embraces this ambiguity for as long as possible.

WOMAN KILLER

Chiori Miyagawa

CHIORI MIYAGAWA met actor/director/teacher Paul Walker at the Actors Theatre of Louisville, and with him she created a theatrical event that changed her life, *A Passenger Train of Sixty-one Coaches*, for the 1991 Humana Festival of New American Plays. She later collaborated with Walker on her first play, *America Dreaming*, which was produced after Walker's death by Music-Theatre Group and the Vineyard Theatre in New York City in 1995. In 1998, Miyagawa was granted a private audience with His Holiness The Dalai Lama. Her deepest inspiration comes from the forty-five minutes she spent with him in northern India, and she continues to write to keep her promise to him; making small attempts to change people's minds about violence and hate. Her other plays include *Awakening* (Performance Space 122 in co-presentation by Dance Theater Workshop and Crossing Jamaica Avenue), *Nothing Forever* and *Yesterday's Window* (both at New York Theatre Workshop; *Yesterday* published in *TAKE TEN*), *Jamaica Avenue* (New York International Fringe Festival, published in *Tokens? The NYC Asian American Experiences on Stage*), *FireDance* (Voice&Vision Theater), *Broken Morning* (Dallas Theater Center), and *Stargazers* (commissioned by The Public Theater, translated into Japanese and presented in the 2001 Asian Women and Theater Conference in Tokyo). Miyagawa lives half the time in New York City, managing her theater company Crossing Jamaica Avenue and the Playwriting Fellowship program for New York Theatre Workshop where she is an Artistic Associate; and the other half in Annandale-on-Hudson, New York, managing the undergraduate playwriting program at Bard College as Associate Professor under JoAnne Akalaitis.

Woman Killer was first produced by Crossing Jamaica Avenue and HERE on September 6, 2001, at HERE, New York City, with the following cast and credits:

Clay .... Crispin Freeman
Anne .... Hope Salas
Rebecca .... Kristin DiSpaltro
Mother .... Corinne Edgerly
Timothy .... Michael Braun
Amy .... Kei Arita
Father .... Ronald Cohen
James .... Shawn Randall
White Fox, Michael, Joe .... Paul H. Juhn

Directed by: Sonoko Kawahara
Music: Daniel Sonenberg
Lyrics: Mark Campbell
Sets: David Korins
Costumes: Theresa Squire
Sound: Crispin Freeman
Stage Manager: Luisa Bieri
Assistant Director: Maryam Mehrjui
Associate Producers: Hillary Spector, LeeAnne Hutchison
Press Representative: Timothy J. Haskell (Publicity Outfitters)

This production was supported in part by Lower Manhattan Cultural Council, Bossak/Heilbron Charitable Foundations, and the board members of Crossing Jamaica Avenue, Rande Brown, and Sue Shapiro.

Music for "Some Years from Now" may be ordered by contacting Dan Sonenberg at 25-59 38th Street, Astoria, NY 11103, or via email at Shnootre@aol.com.

Woman Killer was inspired by *The Woman Killer and The Hell of Oil*, a Japanese Bunraku puppet play from 1721 by Monzaemon Chikamatsu.

CHARACTERS

CLAY: a man in his mid-20s

REBECCA: Clay's girlfriend

TIMOTHY: Clay's younger brother, 20

AMY: Clay's younger sister, 17

FATHER (HENRY.): Clay's stepfather

MOTHER (ELIZABETH.): Clay's mother

ANNE: a woman in her early 30s

JAMES: Anne's husband

WHITE FOX

MICHAEL

JOE

CO-WORKER

TIME

Today.

PLACE

Brooklyn.

SCENE 1

Lights up on ANNE. Singing.

ANNE: When we're in our golden years
    Some years from now
    Our lives will not be so complex
    We can up and get away
    Or stay in and read all day
    Maybe even rediscover sex.
    Looking at our golden years
    Some years from now
    The day-to-day will be a breeze.
    Though the children will be grown,
    They'll have children of their own
    We can spoil as rotten as we please.

Until then
There are mouths to be fed,
And shoes to be tied,
And beds to be made.
Until then
There are skirts to be hemmed,
And tests to be passed,
And boys to fend off.
Until then
There are a million wrongs to make
    right,
And a million kisses good night.
It will be our golden years
Some years from now
Although it's hard to say just when.

But imagine how sublime
When we look back at this time
Some years from now
And laugh at how
Serious we used to be—back then.

(Lights down. ANNE disappears.)

(Music, violent. Lights up. CLAY's dance in shadows, violent. Music cuts off. CLAY becomes still. A light on his face.)

CLAY: But how can I go home? How can I get off this train and walk toward the beginning, when it never began in the first place, and where is this first place, and what is *it* that never began?

(Black.)

(Lights up on CLAY and his girlfriend REBECCA. Dream scene. Threatening.)

REBECCA: What do you want?

CLAY: Nothing.

(CLAY advances on REBECCA menacingly. REBECCA senses danger.)

REBECCA: Stay there.

CLAY: Why are you scared?

(They circle each other.)

REBECCA: Clay, it's me.

CLAY: I know who you are.

REBECCA: Go home.

CLAY: I can't.

(They stare at each other. Tense. Black.)

SCENE 2

Halloween. Lights up on ANNE's apartment. ANNE is putting away children's costumes. The doorbell rings.

CLAY: Trick or treat!

ANNE: Clay! Come in.

(CLAY enters. He is wearing a large pair of feather wings of mixed odd colors.)

CLAY: I was on my way to a party and thought I'd drop by and see you. Where is James?

ANNE: He's still at work. What kind of a bird are you?

CLAY: I'm not a bird.

ANNE: The wings.

CLAY: I'm an angel.

ANNE: *(Teasing.)* I don't know if it's the right costume for you.

CLAY: What should I be instead?

ANNE: Devil?

CLAY: There is no irony in that.

ANNE: I suppose. Did you make the wings yourself?

CLAY: Bought them white. I added the colors.

ANNE: I don't seem to have the time or desire to do those things for myself anymore. I have to do them for my children now. It's like I'm reliving parts of my life over through them. Only now I'm watching, walking parallel to the actual path of life's discoveries.

CLAY: Is that strange?

ANNE: Sometimes. Sometimes even sad. But most of the time delightful.

CLAY: Hey, do you want to go to this party with me?

ANNE: What am I going to do with my kids?

CLAY: Bring them.

ANNE: Don't be silly.

CLAY: *(Half-serious.)* It's the night of the devil. The only night that you can be something other than yourself. Without consequence or punishment. Shed your fears, Anne. Sacrifice your children. Abandon your beliefs. Bite the candied apple. Come with me.

ANNE: *(Laughs.)* We already had our spooky Halloween outing. Would you like some chocolate?

CLAY: We used to party. James too.

ANNE: Yes. We used to. When we were carefree and privileged.

CLAY: We are still.

ANNE: Not carefree. I have a lot to care for. James. The kids.

CLAY: It's boring.

ANNE: Some of us grow up.

CLAY: You deserve a medal for growing up.

(CLAY plucks a fake feather from one of his wings and goes up close to ANNE. He threads the feather through a buttonhole on her shirt. He then holds her wrist and examines her bracelet.)

CLAY: Very nice. A gift from James?

ANNE: For our tenth anniversary.

CLAY: Diamonds and gold. It sparkles on you.

(During this JAMES enters. He stops and looks at them silently until ANNE looks up and sees him.)

ANNE: *(With joy.)* James.

(ANNE goes to kiss JAMES as CLAY turns around to see him.)

CLAY: Hey, buddy.

JAMES: Clay. Didn't recognize you with your wings.

CLAY: A costume party.

JAMES: What are you doing here?

CLAY: Came by to see if you wanted to go with me.

JAMES: Me? Or Anne?

CLAY: You. Both.

JAMES: We can't get a sitter with such a short notice, you know that. Especially on Halloween.

CLAY: Right.

ANNE: Don't you have a date, Clay?

CLAY: That's such a bother.

ANNE: I'm sure there are many women who would be happy to be your angel mate for the night. Carefree and privileged.

CLAY: Not really. Anyway, I should get going. Out to the haunted city!

(He kisses ANNE, shakes JAMES's hand and exits. Pause.)

ANNE: Are you hungry?

JAMES: Yeah.

ANNE: Hamburger ok?

JAMES: I'm tired of hamburgers. Can't we have a little more imagination?

ANNE: We?

JAMES: Ok. You. If you didn't spend all afternoon yakking with Clay, I wouldn't have to live with hamburgers again.

ANNE: The girls and I were out trick or treating this afternoon. Clay was only here for ten minutes before you came home. Besides, you like hamburgers. And we don't have it that often.

JAMES: Did you know he was coming over?

ANNE: James. What are you asking?

JAMES: Nothing.

ANNE: Clay lives five minutes away. He comes over all the time without notice.

JAMES: Not so much anymore.

ANNE: Did you have a bad day?

JAMES: I've been hearing things about Clay.

ANNE: What things?

JAMES: He got into a fight at a bar about a month ago. Injured someone with a broken beer bottle. His parents took out their checkbook to fix the situation.

ANNE: This isn't the first time they had to pay Clay's way out of trouble.

JAMES: The fight was over a girl. Someone who works as an escort or something.

ANNE: Where did you hear all this?

JAMES: I ran into Clay's uncle. He has a hard time trying to keep Clay out of trouble at the job too.

ANNE: Clay has always been restless.

(Pause.)

JAMES: Did you want to go to the party with him?

ANNE: No.

(Pause.)

ANNE: How about some pasta?

JAMES: Sounds good.

(ANNE turns to go to the kitchen.)

JAMES: Anne?

ANNE: Yes?

JAMES: Did you miss me today?

ANNE: More than usual?

JAMES: I don't know.

ANNE: You go to work everyday.

JAMES: Right. Everyday.

ANNE: I miss you everyday.

JAMES: Today more than yesterday?

ANNE: What's wrong?

JAMES: Time passes between us.

ANNE: Time passes with us, James.

JAMES: I'm hungry.

SCENE 3

REBECCA and CLAY in bed. CLAY takes off a locket from REBECCA's neck. He fumbles when he attempts to open it and drops the locket. Pause. They both look at the locket on the floor. REBECCA picks it up and opens it.

REBECCA: The glass is broken.

CLAY: I'll buy you another one.

REBECCA: It was my grandmother's.

CLAY: I just wanted to see what she looked like.

REBECCA: I think it's bad luck. It feels like death.

CLAY: No, Rebecca. Breaking a mirror is bad luck.

REBECCA: It's glass with an image of a person inside. It just makes destiny more specific.

CLAY: It's not destiny. Just a superstition. Besides, your grandmother is already dead. Nothing else is going to happen to her.

(Pause.)

CLAY: I'll make it up to you. For the loss of your grandmother.

REBECCA: I want a silver locket from Tiffany's.

CLAY: Anything you want.

REBECCA: Two. An oval one and a heart-shaped one. I saw them in a catalogue.

CLAY: Anything you want.

REBECCA: Anything?

CLAY: I love you.

REBECCA: You broke my locket on purpose. Because I liked it. Because I wore it everyday. It touched my flesh more than you ever did.

CLAY: Strange thing to say, Rebecca.

REBECCA: I know you.

CLAY: If you had to choose between the memories of your grandmother and a future with me, which would you choose?

REBECCA: I can't choose between something I already have and something that's yet to exist.

CLAY: I exist. She doesn't.

REBECCA: Why are you jealous of my memories?

CLAY: I don't want you to look away.

REBECCA: We all live with memories.

CLAY: I want you to look at me. Always.

SCENE 4

Thanksgiving dinner. CLAY's parents' house.

MOTHER: Timothy made the cranberry sauce.

TIMOTHY: From scratch.

ANNE: It's delicious. I'm impressed.

TIMOTHY: I went to the farmer's market for fresh cranberries.

ANNE: And what did you contribute to this Thanksgiving dinner, Amy?

AMY: I watched.

MOTHER: I made her help me with everything. When she gets married, she will have to do all this herself. She should start learning it now.

AMY: I'll pick everything up at Balducci's. Including the cranberry sauce.

TIMOTHY: Don't you like my cranberry sauce?

AMY: I do. But it's too wholesome and good for when I have to become a housewife. I need a little bitterness.

ANNE: Being a housewife can be sweet, Amy.

JAMES: How's college treating you, Timothy?

TIMOTHY: Good. I'm playing soccer this year.

FATHER: His grades are excellent. He is thinking about going to law school.

TIMOTHY: Dad, I don't know about that yet.

MOTHER: Clay just had an interview for a new job.

CLAY: It's nothing, really.

JAMES: You didn't tell me about this.

CLAY: Because it's not a big deal, James. I'm just looking for something that pays better.

FATHER: I will pay you more if you show me that you're serious about our family business.

CLAY: We've been through this before.

FATHER: You have to earn money, just like trust.

MOTHER: Henry. You can't pamper him forever. He has to be on his own eventually.

FATHER: I'd like him to be by my side.

CLAY: *(To ANNE, indicating that this conversation is over.)* I have to miss your pumpkin pie this year. I have to go now.

ANNE: Where are you going?

CLAY: I'm having dessert with my girlfriend's family.

(Awkward pause. CLAY's parents are tense.)

ANNE: I'd like to meet your girlfriend sometime. What's her name?

CLAY: Rebecca.

ANNE: I'm sorry she couldn't be here today.

CLAY: Me too. I'm also sorry that you didn't bring your kids. Where are they?

ANNE: They are with my parents in Oregon. They wanted to go on an adventure on their own. So I put them on the plane and sent them off.

JAMES: It was very brave of her.

ANNE: It was brave of our girls. They are only six and eight. I didn't get on the plane and leave home until I was twenty.

JAMES: It was very brave of you.

CLAY: I agree. You are a good mother, Anne.

ANNE: Thank you, Clay.

SCENE 5

Late at night, the same day.

AMY: You didn't really go to Rebecca's for dessert, did you?

CLAY: If you go into Manhattan, you can always find a bar that's open, even on the day of judgment.

TIMOTHY: Why do you need to do that? You know it upsets Mom every time you leave a family gathering in the middle.

CLAY: I couldn't sit there for one more minute. I don't have the enormous capacity for bullshitting that you have, Timothy.

TIMOTHY: It's called being decent.

CLAY: All those decent people around the table being decent to each other makes me want to puke. Every Thanksgiving we do the same thing, eat the same food, and have the same people over for the same conversation.

TIMOTHY: Don't you like Anne and James?

AMY: I can't imagine how Anne stands being at home all the time. Cooking and cleaning. I thought women stopped doing those things for men.

TIMOTHY: You know she has two daughters. And she and James are very much in love.

AMY: I think she likes Clay.

TIMOTHY: That's insane. We've known her since her family moved into the neighborhood when she was in high school. A long time.

CLAY: It's really too bad she went and had a slew of kids. She's still young and attractive.

AMY: A model housewife. A picture of domestic simplicity. It's very boring.

TIMOTHY: You are jealous of her.

AMY: Now who is insane?

CLAY: Anne is pretty to look at, but I don't think there is any passion left in her.

TIMOTHY: Tell me what you think passion is.

CLAY: Something you wouldn't know, Timothy.

TIMOTHY: I don't think you know me well enough to say that.

CLAY: When have you known passion? Tell me one incident when you felt passion.

(Pause.)

AMY: It's not necessary.

TIMOTHY: You have no idea.

CLAY: Tell us.

TIMOTHY: I scoop a handful of sharp jagged crystal pieces from my dream, and scatter them on my bed on the nights I can't sleep because I'm choking on the ashes of my fantasies. You are wrong if you think it's easy to get it right, to be a good student, to look good, to respect women, to save money, to plan for the future. You are wrong if you think these are the things I really want in life.

CLAY: What do you want then?

TIMOTHY: I try not to want. I spend all my passion trying not to want the wrong things.

(Pause.)

CLAY: You're mixing up boredom and passion.

TIMOTHY: You've been mixing up harm and passion all your life.

CLAY: Yeah. I want so much, want so much, I can hardly stand it. It's blue, sharp clear icy blue, and so scorching hot it burns my eyes. Blue fire. I am so thirsty I can taste my own death.

(Pause.)

TIMOTHY: Clay. Passion will kill you in the end.

(Long pause.)

AMY: Anne is very pretty. And a good person. I like her. Really.

SCENE 6

A few days later. MOTHER is holding a credit card statement. She shows it to CLAY. TIMOTHY comes in during their argument.

MOTHER: Would you explain this to me?

CLAY: It's a cash advance for one thousand.

MOTHER: I did not give you permission for this.

CLAY: I'm tired of discussing money.

MOTHER: We're not discussing money. We're discussing your stealing.

CLAY: I'm tired of that too.

MOTHER: What did you do with the money?

CLAY: Sounds like we're discussing money to me.

MOTHER: Are you in trouble?

CLAY: No, Mom. Don't worry.

MOTHER: Don't mock me. You owe me an explanation.

TIMOTHY: Answer her, Clay.

CLAY: I don't have an answer. You're the one with all the answers, Timothy.

TIMOTHY: Was it for drugs?

CLAY: You think you're smart, don't you?

TIMOTHY: It wouldn't be the first time.

MOTHER: If you get caught again with drug possession, you will go to jail this time.

CLAY: I'll try not to get caught.

MOTHER: Clay, tell me the truth!

CLAY: It's not that serious. I rented a limo and went out with Rebecca. I'm sorry, but you know all my credit cards are maxed out, and it was her birthday. I had no other choice.

TIMOTHY: That is absurd. You could have just stayed home.

CLAY: No. I couldn't have.

TIMOTHY: No mater how much you want it, how much you think you need it, at any given moment of your life, something will be out of your reach. You have to live with that like the rest of us.

CLAY: Not me.

MOTHER: Why does Rebecca have to go out in a limousine? Doesn't she know you can't afford it?

CLAY: But you can afford it.

MOTHER: That is not the point.

CLAY: Mom, I'll pay you back. I promise. Ok?

(He kisses MOTHER's cheek.)

CLAY: I'm sorry. But no one got hurt. And Rebecca and I had a really good time. Don't stay angry with me. I won't do it again.

MOTHER: Be careful with someone who asks for more than you can give. In materials or emotions.

CLAY: There is no need to worry. *(Exits.)*

TIMOTHY: Are you going to let him just walk away from his responsibilities again?

MOTHER: I'm tired, Timothy. I don't have in me to discipline him anymore.

TIMOTHY: You're not helping him by always covering for him. Let him grow up, for god's sake.

MOTHER: He is grown up already. Sometimes I wish he would just go away. He has worn me out.

(Pause.)

MOTHER: I'm glad you are home.

TIMOTHY: You know I'm going skiing over Christmas. Are you going to be ok without me?

SCENE 7

Music, violent. CLAY's dance in the shadows, violent. Music cuts off abruptly. CLAY becomes still. Lights up on AMY's room. Three weeks later.

CLAY: You have to help me.

AMY: Why are you so stupid to borrow money from somebody like Joe?

CLAY: Because I have no money. I haven't been paying my credit card bills. The collection agency is after me. I'll have to declare bankruptcy pretty soon.

AMY: If Joe doesn't get his money back, he will kill you.

CLAY: He won't. But he'll hurt me. Embarrass me.

AMY: Explain it to Mom and Dad. They'll cover it for you, I'm sure.

CLAY: You want me to tell them I owe a drug dealer sixteen thousand dollars?

AMY: You said it wasn't for drugs.

CLAY: Not all of it.

AMY: It's Rebecca, isn't it? What did you buy her? What did she ask for?

CLAY: Everything she deserves.

AMY: Clay, Rebecca is dangerous for you. She has no limits to her desire. She will devour your longing, your illusions, your sex, and your money. The empty space in her is bigger than yours. You'll disappear in her.

CLAY: That's what I want.

AMY: She's not worth giving up the chance for normal life that Timothy talks about. She's only a whore.

CLAY: Shut the hell up!

AMY: You know she is. If you don't, tell me she isn't a whore!

(CLAY goes for AMY. He grabs her neck. AMY gasps. He slowly releases her, but keeps his hand on her. He changes his energy from violent to sexual.)

CLAY: Do you remember when we were kids, we went back everyday to the school ground after everyone had gone home, and played until the sun was dead and the air was dusky?

AMY: Some days, the sky would go orange before turning grey. Hours after that, I still had orange in my throat.

CLAY: One time there was a big hole in the ground. I think they were in the process of putting in new swings. The workers had left for the evening.

AMY: I remember.

CLAY: I hopped into the hole, made you stand still on the edge of it, and threw a stone at you.

AMY: It hit me.

CLAY: I didn't think I could really hit you. I was looking up at you from the bottom of the hole. You were a silhouette against the faint faint orange.

AMY: You hit me. I cried.

CLAY: You promised to tell Mom and Dad that you fell. When we got home, Mom flipped out seeing blood on your forehead. As soon as she asked what happened, you said,

AMY: Clay hit me with a stone.

CLAY: I hated you.

AMY: I was just a little girl then.

CLAY: You have to help me. You're my sister.

AMY: Only half. Only the half that longs for darkness, for the shadows of the unattainable.

CLAY: You know I love you.

AMY: What makes you think they'll give me the money?

CLAY: Because you're the baby of the family. And Dad is your real father.

AMY: He's your father too. We are a family.

CLAY: I've asked for money too many times already. Do this for me. Sixteen thousand dollars. Get it for me.

(CLAY kisses AMY on the lips tenderly.)

SCENE 8

A few days later. The house is decorated with Christmas ornaments.

AMY: Talk to Dad for me.

MOTHER: Are you sure that's what you want to do?

AMY: What else do you think I should do, Mom?

MOTHER: I want us to be sure that we want to bring your father into this.

AMY: I don't think we can hide it from him, Mom.

MOTHER: Why do you want him to know? He has enough worries.

AMY: This should be one of them.

MOTHER: Who is the father?

AMY: It doesn't matter.

MOTHER: It matters. You did this together. It matters.

AMY: There is no father because there isn't going to be a baby. I just need the money.

MOTHER: We'll go see the doctor together.

AMY: No. I want to do this alone. Please just give me the money.

MOTHER: I want you to be safe.

AMY: Please just give me the money or you'll ruin me.

MOTHER: What do you need?

AMY: Sixteen thousand dollars.

MOTHER: You're not making any sense.

AMY: It's not just for an abortion. I need certain things.

MOTHER: What things?

AMY: I need a bridge, protection, sharpness, and silence, sixteen thousand dollars.

MOTHER: Amy?

AMY: I'm carrying a devil child. If I don't do this right, I will be damaged forever. I'll never be able to cook a Thanksgiving turkey. Do you really want to risk that, Mom? What is life for without a turkey? Huh?

MOTHER: Amy, please.

AMY: I'm pregnant with everything that was ever wrong with this family. It was inevitable. The only way out of doom is money. You agree, don't you?

MOTHER: Calm down, Amy.

AMY: You and Dad fix the world with your checkbooks, don't you? You send money to cancer research, to children of the third world, to the animal rights people, and to the relief efforts for the disaster in Indonesia. For years you wrote checks to keep Clay out of juvenile halls and to keep Timothy in private schools. You can write a check for me for once to save me from becoming the devil's concubine, can't you?

MOTHER: Don't be ridiculous. Let's concentrate on how we can get help for you.

AMY: Yes! Let's concentrate! I need a cow and a needle and a noodle and toilet paper by the truckloads. I need sixteen thousand francs, freaks. *(Screams.)* Ahhhh. I'm in pain. Mom! Mom! Where are you?

MOTHER: I'm right here. Henry!

AMY: I'm dying.

MOTHER: Henry!

(FATHER rushes in.)

FATHER: What's the matter?

MOTHER: Amy is sick. Call an ambulance.

AMY: No! You take me to the hospital, I'll kill myself. You know what I need. Save me, Dad.

FATHER: Shhh. It's all right. Whatever it is, I'll take care of it. Don't worry.

AMY: Punctured, burned, scraped, frozen. We are in the ice age and dinosaurs are extinct. The miracle of greatness is vanished, but I'll stain this planet with my blood before it's all over.

I'll kill myself. I'll kill myself. I'LL KILL MYSELF! MERRY CHRISTMAS!

SCENE 9

The winter streets. CLAY and JAMES run into each other.

JAMES: How have you been, buddy? You don't come around much anymore.

CLAY: I'm sorry about that, James. I've been busy. How's your family?

JAMES: Good. I think we are going to buy a house in Brooklyn Heights. We looked at one over the weekend.

CLAY: Are you going to move away from the neighborhood?

JAMES: It's not that far.

CLAY: Brooklyn Heights. That's nice. Nicer than this damn place.

JAMES: What're you talking about? This is the crossroads of Brooklyn: southeast to Nagasaki, northeast to Kyoto, southwest to Manhattan, northwest to the Temple Kanzeon. It's a great place. Just look at the Grand Army Plaza.

CLAY: *(Forcing an air of sincerity.)* A house in the Heights is better. I envy you. You've got it made. A good job, nice wife, kids. That's what life is all about.

JAMES: Bullshit. You don't envy me. I think you like your own life quite a bit.

CLAY: *(Exaggerated.)* You're wrong. I'm miserable.

JAMES: *(Teasing.)* You've got your tough friends to hang out and go drinking with. You have a sexy little girlfriend I hear. You really want to give that all up to be a responsible family man?

CLAY: Sure. Anytime.

JAMES: You're funny.

CLAY: Aren't you happy with your life?

JAMES: I am. I just know too much.

CLAY: I don't know enough.

JAMES: I guess that's the difference.

CLAY: When I was a kid, the future was a blank sheet of paper. Wait. No. I didn't even know the paper existed. I wasn't aware of the vast whiteness in front me.

JAMES: I guess we become adults when we begin to see that paper.

CLAY: Filling in the space is tedious. We can still end up with nothing in the end.

JAMES: Not nothing.

CLAY: What?

JAMES: Not nothing. Family. Loves lost and found. Images. Memories. Not nothing, Clay.

CLAY: Whatever. I'd rather be free.

JAMES: See? You like your life.

(Pause.)

CLAY: *(Sincerely.)* Go home James. While you still can.

JAMES: I will. Come over sometime soon. We'll watch the game. Drink some beers. Like before.

CLAY: Before what?

JAMES: I don't know. Just before.

CLAY: *(With an enthusiastic air.)* Sure. Sounds good. Sounds like fun. Sounds real good.

JAMES: Soon?

CLAY: *(Innocent.)* Yeah, I'm looking forward to it, buddy. Merry Christmas.

SCENE 10

New Year's Eve. CLAY waits for REBECCA in front of a nightclub. She enters with a man.

CLAY: What's up, Rebecca.

REBECCA: Clay. What are you doing here?

CLAY: I heard a rumor that you'd be at this club with this asshole, instead of at your sister's like you told me.

MICHAEL: Excuse me?

CLAY: I wasn't talking to you.

REBECCA: It didn't work out with my sister tonight.

CLAY: I thought it was a family tradition that you two spend New Year's Eve together.

REBECCA: It is. It just didn't work out this year.

CLAY: Why didn't you call me?

REBECCA: I didn't know how to find you.

CLAY: You knew how to find him.

MICHAEL: Rebecca and I have plans for the evening.

CLAY: You're crazy if you think you're going in to that club with her.

REBECCA: Baby, I'm sorry for the misunderstanding.

CLAY: Misunderstanding?

REBECCA: I'm here. You found me. I'm yours and yours alone.

(REBECCA moves close to CLAY.)

MICHAEL: Jesus.

CLAY: Get lost.

MICHAEL: Rebecca, why don't you tell him that two hours ago you said you were mine? Mine alone?

REBECCA: It was a dream, Michael.

MICHAEL: Slut.

(CLAY jumps Michael. They fight. REBECCA watches.)

MICHAEL: I'm not coming back. Do you understand me, Rebecca? This is the last time! *(Exits.)*

CLAY: There goes your rich boyfriend.

REBECCA: I missed you.

(Pause.)

REBECCA: Hold me. I'm cold.

(CLAY does so.)

CLAY: That's a nice dress. Did he buy it for you?

REBECCA: No. I put it on my Amex. Didn't you promise me a dress for New Year?

CLAY: When I thought you were coming out with me tonight.

REBECCA: Here I am.

CLAY: What do you want from me?

REBECCA: A silk kimono in red chrysanthemum patterns that I can wear with a sash on high waist like the courtesans of Tennoji House.

CLAY: Tennoji House?

REBECCA: Come on, I know you've been there. On 42nd Street off the Tokaido path.

CLAY: Silk kimonos are expensive.

REBECCA: I thought you said anything I wanted. I only want it for you anyway.

CLAY: What are we doing, Rebecca?

REBECCA: Can't we just hang out without promises or analysis? It's boring. You know you're special to me. We're like Siamese twins of the soul. No one can cut us apart.

(CLAY kisses REBECCA passionately.)

REBECCA: It will be midnight soon. Do you want to go see the Brooklyn Bridge?

CLAY: If you want.

REBECCA: We can take a cab on the Manhattan Bridge and see the Brooklyn Bridge from there. Man-made stars sparkling, bridging fierce needs across dull water, against the skyline of greatness. Then we can drive up Fifth Avenue. Did you see the Empire State Building tonight? It's blue.

CLAY: Deep blue.

REBECCA: Touch my lips, Clay.

CLAY: Why?

REBECCA: You open doors in me when you kiss me.

CLAY: Where do the doors lead to?

REBECCA: Places I've never been before. New places. Where my ghosts live.

CLAY: Ghosts?

REBECCA: Deep, disengaging my heart from years of wanting.

CLAY: I'm honored.

REBECCA: Fuck you.

CLAY: Don't leave me.

REBECCA: Why are you scared?

CLAY: I'm stepping around quicksand. At any time I can slip and fall into it.

REBECCA: What would happen if you fall in?

CLAY: I don't know. Rebecca, if you betray me, I will kill you.

REBECCA: Whatever is waiting for you in the quicksand has nothing to do with me.

CLAY: Doesn't matter. I'll kill you anyway.

REBECCA: I don't care. None of this is real anyway. I can give it up anytime.

CLAY: I doubt you'll be saying that when I have a knife against your throat.

REBECCA: You hate me, don't you?

CLAY: I love you. I will kill you.

SCENE 11

The next day. TIMOTHY enters the house with bags.

FATHER: Timothy! I didn't know you were coming home for New Year's.

TIMOTHY: Mom called me about Amy.

FATHER: She shouldn't have bothered you. Amy is going to be fine.

TIMOTHY: Where is she?

FATHER: She is in her room. Don't worry.

TIMOTHY: I also got a call from Uncle David. He thinks Clay is trying to embezzle money from the company.

FATHER: Why didn't David tell me this?

TIMOTHY: He didn't want to upset you. He wanted me to talk to Clay. But I thought you should know. Dad, you need to make some decisions about Clay.

FATHER: Deep in my heart, I knew I could not trust him.

TIMOTHY: Fire him. Throw him out of the house. You have been too lenient and forgiving with him, with both of us. When we were small, the only one who got punished for mischief was Amy. I know she is your blood child. But you're Clay's and my father too. We have had no other.

FATHER: Your father was my best friend. Clay looks so much like him now. Sometimes I have to stop myself from calling him Walter. Sometimes I'm back in time, before the accident that killed him, before the sorrow that buried me, and I see Walter. I want to say, where have you been, Walter? Twenty years have passed. But in that moment, no time has passed in us. We are both young and strong. Time is frozen. I want to reach over and grab his shoulder, and just that moment, I realize it's Clay.

TIMOTHY: All my life I have covered for him, cleaned up after him, and apologized for him. I'm sick of it. You've spoiled him rotten with the best stereo, the best bicycle, and the best clothes. Made him rotten.

FATHER: I've given you the same.

TIMOTHY: But I'm grateful.

FATHER: I know.

TIMOTHY: He hurts you. I don't.

FATHER: I know. You are good.

TIMOTHY: Mom wants you to be firmer with Clay. She thinks you're hesitant because you're his stepfather. Dad, Clay has tortured her soul. How many times has she told us that she doesn't care if he were gone from our lives forever?

FATHER: Your mother loves Clay.

TIMOTHY: She says she has no love left for him.

FATHER: Do you believe her?

TIMOTHY: I do.

(Pause.)

TIMOTHY: I want to believe her. His drinking, fighting, lying, dreaming of damage, taking souls, trampling, polluting, turning, cracked, broken, no way back, and his shame, his shame should make her stop loving him. But despite all that, I know she still loves him best. Still loves *him* best.

SCENE 12

The same place as Scene 1. They circle each other. CLAY is threatening. Dream scene.

AMY: What do you want?

CLAY: Nothing.

AMY: Stay there.

CLAY: Why are you scared?

AMY: Go home.

CLAY: I can't.

AMY: You can. You can still go home.

CLAY: After a certain point, there is no way back home. Home is a lie anyway. Life is a big lie. This stupidity, this resignation, two cars parked on the driveway, barbecues and beaches and funerals, meaningless, deprived, boring.

AMY: Clay, it's me.

CLAY: No one is true. You are not me, and I don't know you.

AMY: I know *you*. It's a new year, Clay.

CLAY: Happy New Year! Another happy lying year!

(*They stare at each other. Black.*)

SCENE 13

JAMES is in his office. He picks up the phone and dials. It rings. ANNE picks up on the other end.

JAMES: Anne.

ANNE: Yes, honey.

JAMES: I'll be late. Have dinner without me.

ANNE: Again?

JAMES: I have to catch up with work. I'm behind because of the holidays.

ANNE: Other people have holidays too.

JAMES: I have a lot to do.

ANNE: Always.

JAMES: I'll see you later.

ANNE: James?

JAMES: What?

ANNE: Would you like dinner when you get home?

JAMES: No. I'll just grab a hamburger on the way home.

ANNE: It's no trouble. I was creative today. I made roasted potato and fennel soup and poached salmon.

JAMES: Sounds good. But you don't have to wait for me.

ANNE: I'll wait for you.

JAMES: All right. See you later.

ANNE: James?

JAMES: What?

ANNE: Did you miss me today?

JAMES: More than usual?

ANNE: I don't know.

JAMES: I go to work everyday.

ANNE: Right. Everyday.

JAMES: I have to go.

ANNE: See you soon.

(*Click. Dial tone.*)

SCENE 14

Music, violent. CLAY's dance in the shadows, violent. CLAY becomes still. A light on his face.

CLAY: We sneak into my father's company building one o'clock in the morning and fuck on the floor of his office. Rebecca is menstruating; she drips dark blood mixed with milky semen on his plushy beige carpet. This is how it feels to live. My hands are covered with her blood. We baptize each other in the liquid of the mystery from which all human cravings arise.

(Lights up on REBECCA, half-dressed, lying on the floor.)

CLAY: Let's go.

REBECCA: Can't we just sleep here a little?

CLAY: We can't stay here. When the sun comes up, our lovemaking will become a crime.

REBECCA: That's what you wanted.

CLAY: You're wrong.

REBECCA: You have something raging and homeless in you.

CLAY: I recognize the same in you.

REBECCA: Not me.

CLAY: The first time we met at a party, I said I liked your rhinestone earrings. You looked at me, took them off, and threw them in the trash. You didn't say a word to me.

(Pause.)

REBECCA: I don't want to look like a fake, even if I am.

(Pause.)

CLAY: Go home, Rebecca. Your parents must be worried.

REBECCA: I doubt it. They don't ask themselves questions like "It's five a.m. in the morning. Do you know where your kids are?" *(Gets up and gets dressed. Her beeper goes off. She checks it.)*

CLAY: Who is beeping you at five in the morning?

REBECCA: Wrong number.

CLAY: Don't lie to me.

REBECCA: I'm going home.

CLAY: Tell me who it was.

REBECCA: Clay, who the hell are you? What claim do you have on me?

CLAY: I love you.

REBECCA: But you don't have a place of your own and you don't have any money. All you got is a soul raging and homeless. When I get home, my knees bruised, my back carpet burned, and step into a bath with dried blood caked on my inner thighs, where will your heart be, Clay? Will you be making plans for living happily ever after with me somewhere where there are white picket fences?

CLAY: You can't possibly dream about something so tame.

REBECCA: I want to. But not with you. Away from you.

CLAY: That will never happen.

REBECCA: We are flying without a safety net. We can crash at any time. Then what?

CLAY: You love the thrill.

REBECCA: Not always. I haven't given up on the other thing. Someday, I'm going to be a different person. I'm going to achieve a normal life.

CLAY: Why don't you leave me then?

REBECCA: I'm trying.

(Pause.)

REBECCA: What do *you* dream about?

CLAY: I dream about not here, not now, not me, not this. Nothing. I can't.

REBECCA: You think you're chasing me. It's you who is not mine.

CLAY: I like the smell of your blood.

(Pause.)

REBECCA: I love you, Clay.

SCENE 15

TIMOTHY enters AMY's room. She is in bed.

TIMOTHY: Amy, it's me.

AMY: Timothy.

TIMOTHY: What are you doing?

AMY: I'm in pain.

TIMOTHY: Did Clay put you up to this?

AMY: Are you asking me if Clay got me pregnant?

TIMOTHY: I'm asking you why you need sixteen thousand dollars.

AMY: You don't know anything.

TIMOTHY: Who does?

AMY: Me. Only me.

TIMOTHY: I don't believe you.

AMY: Life is so easy for you, Timothy.

TIMOTHY: How do you figure that?

AMY: Because you weren't born with *it*.

TIMOTHY: It?

AMY: It. That thing that eats your insides slowly, so slowly that you don't even notice until the hole is so big your entire being can crumple into it. And there you are, slipping, bleeding, cooking a turkey in the big hole until death do us part.

TIMOTHY: Us?

AMY: Me and *it*.

TIMOTHY: Why do you love Clay so much?

AMY: He has *it*. We are the same.

TIMOTHY: No, you are not. Don't go to him. Stay with me.

AMY: I don't think it's a choice. You don't understand.

TIMOTHY: How can you hurt our parents? Is he worth causing their agony? Especially Dad. He is so sad. You are his blood.

AMY: It's not all for Clay. My pain is true. They should notice it. They should notice me.

TIMOTHY: I'll stop you.

AMY: They have the money. And it's only money. It's not going to fix anything in anybody. It's only money.

TIMOTHY: It's not the money they are worried about. They don't understand your hostility. They don't understand what your demand really is.

AMY: They never have.

SCENE 16

CLAY's house. The doorbell rings. WHITE FOX, a mountain priest enters.

WHITE FOX: Is this the house of Henry of New York? I am the priest of fox god. I am calling at the request of the mountain brotherhood.

FATHER: I appreciate you coming, White Fox. I need your prayers for my daughter. Please wait here for a moment.

(FATHER exits. CLAY enters.)

CLAY: White Fox! Are you here to pray for my sister? It's a waste of time. Amy is mortally ill. No mountain priest can drive out what possesses her.

WHITE FOX: We'll see.

CLAY: What's that?

WHITE FOX: We'll see how she responds to my prayers.

CLAY: That's not satisfactory. We are paying a lot of money for your scam. I'd like to see some real exorcism, you know, her head turning and shit.

WHITE FOX: What's your name?

CLAY: Oh, no. You can't hypnotize me. I went to college. I know about these things.

WHITE FOX: What do you know?

CLAY: Do you ever speak more than one sentence at a time?

WHITE FOX: *(Laughs.)* Not when I'm with someone much wiser than me. You, for example. You are so smart and fast, you don't even breathe in between your desperate ranting to cover your guilt.

(CLAY tenses up. Pause.)

CLAY: You don't know anything.

WHITE FOX: Exactly my point.

CLAY: I'm not going to let you ruin me.

WHITE FOX: I'm just a simple priest who sits and meditates most of the time. I come down the mountain occasionally when I'm called upon to relieve suffering. You need not be threatened.

CLAY: Great! Why don't you relieve my suffering since you are here? And how about the people next door?

WHITE FOX: I cannot foretell the future, but I can see you are carrying a heavy burden of karma. It may defeat you if you don't dissolve it through purification.

(FATHER comes back.)

FATHER: She is ready for you.

CLAY: Dad. I have urgent business to discuss with you.

FATHER: I can't deal with you right now.

CLAY: Uncle David is in trouble. He tried to embezzle money from the company. I assured him that we would work this out as a family. He's in such a deep debt, if we don't help him, he will have to declare bankruptcy. For a man of his social position, nothing is worse than that. We don't want to share his shame either.

FATHER: What do you propose we do?

CLAY: If you give me a signed check, I'll take it over to Uncle David now. He probably needs a few thousand dollars right away just to get back on his feet.

FATHER: Have you always cared so much about David? I haven't noticed.

(Pause.)

FATHER: I don't give blank checks to anyone. If you want to save David, you should. You are not exactly destitute. You live at home without paying rent. You eat for free. The salary I pay you must be sitting in your bank account. You help him, Clay. Be a good man. *(To WHITE FOX.)* I'm sorry to have kept you waiting.

(WHITE FOX and FATHER exit.)

CLAY: White Fox, whatever you do, Amy is going to die! We all are!

SCENE 17

AMY's room.

WHITE FOX: Here I am. A listener, a healer, a prophet, a sympathizer of your eclipsing soul.

AMY: I don't know you.

WHITE FOX: I know you.

AMY: What do you know?

WHITE FOX: I know that rage lives in your throat. It's made of ancient things that we manage to make cloudy. Until the day memories come crisp.

AMY: It's like soaking in a lukewarm swamp. You can fool yourself for a long time, but all of a sudden memories come crisp.

WHITE FOX: Take my hand.

AMY: Now you notice it's nothing but slime, thick with vegetation, green and brown, that you have been sitting in for years.

WHITE FOX: When you were seven, you played with magic, and believed it true until winter. Then the white light revealed nothing but twigs. You've been suffering ever since.

AMY: Where do I fit in, this cycle of births, monsters, and angels? In this dense bright, my hands do not deserve to touch the clear sea. But then where else shall I wash off my red? How can I go home?

WHITE FOX: I am the messenger of the great Buddha Amitaba. Do not deviate from the truth. Believe in my incarnation as medicine. With Lord Shakyamuni, come home to safety.

(As the priest prays, AMY begins screaming. FATHER comes in when AMY starts screaming, followed by CLAY.)

WHITE FOX: Come to me, all who la-bor and are
heavy-laden, and I will give you rest.
Take my yoke upon you, and learn from me;
for I am gentle and lowly in heart,
and you will find rest for your souls.
For my yoke is easy, and my burden is light.

AMY: I'm in pain! I'm in pain! I need sharpness and silence. I need the truth!

(Silence.)

WHITE FOX: What is the truth?

(Pause.)

WHITE FOX: You know this. Nothing external possesses your soul. You have to kill your bastard child.

FATHER: White Fox!

WHITE FOX: The child is not actual. It is a phantom.

CLAY: Shut the hell up, you phony priest! Stop this charade!

(CLAY grabs White Fox and tries to throw him out of the room. FATHER tries to stop CLAY. WHITE FOX gets out of CLAY's grip.)

WHITE FOX: My work is not finished.

CLAY: You don't belong here. You're not family.

WHITE FOX: Amy, if you want me to help you, call me. I will show you the way to live with monsters and angels that you are so afraid of.

AMY: I'm not right.

WHITE FOX: Do not worry. You will recover from this.

CLAY: What is there to recover from? If she isn't pregnant, there is no problem, is there?!

FATHER: Clay, how can you disrespect White Fox?

CLAY: Because I don't believe!

WHITE FOX: Soul raging and homeless.

CLAY: Because I don't believe?

WHITE FOX: No, not because of that. I don't know the reason. I'm sorry I cannot help you. *(Turning to AMY.)* Winter will be over soon. Underneath the frost of your heart lies sound and color. Try to remember. *(Exits.)*

FATHER: The money she is asking for is for your girlfriend. Amy has been lying to me, hasn't she?

CLAY: I love Rebecca. I want to marry her.

FATHER: Amy is not pregnant then.

CLAY: Duh.

FATHER: Have you no shame? Putting your sister through the agony of deceit and lying viciously about your uncle all for a selfish desire. Who is Rebecca anyway? Who is her family? What is she?

CLAY: She is a student. She goes to the community college.

FATHER: Why do people say she is a prostitute?

CLAY: Who have you been talking to about Rebecca?

FATHER: People talk. It's no longer possible to save our family dignity with you going around with questionable friends and women.

CLAY: I want to know who said that about Rebecca.

FATHER: Are they wrong?

CLAY: I'll kill the motherfucker who said that. I can kill you for repeating it to me. If it was true, I'd have killed *her* already.

FATHER: Stop saying nonsense. Do you have any idea how worried your mother is about your relationship with Rebecca?

CLAY: She can go to hell.

FATHER: Clay!

CLAY: You're wasting your breath trying to make me feel guilty about Mother. I have no use for her right now.

FATHER: What do you want from me then?

CLAY: Money! I want to give Rebecca a certain life style. The money you have was my father's. You took his company. You took his wife. That makes you in debt to me, the rightful owner of the company. I'm blood.

FATHER: The company would have gone down if I didn't take over. Do you really think you deserve what I have built over twenty years?

CLAY: You would have ended your life as a clerk at my father's company if he didn't die. Tell me, when was the first time you fucked my mother? Was it really after the accident?

FATHER: There is nothing good about you, is there? You're damaged.

CLAY: Yeah, it's a sad story. Anyway, you took things from me. I think you need to give it back.

FATHER: You don't care about the business. Do you think I will allow you to destroy it all for the sake of your little tart?

CLAY: You stupid old fool!

(CLAY kicks his father down and stomps all over his body. AMY clings to CLAY.)

AMY: Stop! Stop! Are you crazy?

FATHER: Let him, Amy. Let him trample on me to his heart's content.

AMY: He is our father!

(CLAY stops, and turns to look at AMY.)

CLAY: What does it matter?

AMY: You are a depraved, degenerate human being. And there is no reason for it. You have no right to be so fucked up.

CLAY: Are you any less fucked up than me? Is anyone?

AMY: Yes, Clay! We belong to the human race. Where do you belong, huh? You look at Dad now and tell me that.

CLAY: What are you suggesting?

AMY: That I was wrong about you. You are not my soul, not my brother, not anything but a waste.

CLAY: You betray me in your heart, I will hate you.

AMY: I'm not betraying you. I'm cutting you out of my heart. Obliterated. Demolished. Burnt. Gone.

(CLAY slaps AMY. She backs away, but he goes after her. FATHER grabs him. They struggle.)

CLAY: You asked for it! This is how I content my heart!

(He stomps furiously on his father. MOTHER enters in the midst of the fury.)

MOTHER: Henry!

(She grabs CLAY's hair and topples him to the floor. She falls on him.)

MOTHER: Are you insane?

CLAY: He pushed me to it!

MOTHER: You're the meanest, vilest human being I know. I cannot believe that you came out of my own womb. I don't recognize you. Your soul is blind. You cannot see that with every outrage you cut me, cut my peace, cut my wish, cut my life.

CLAY: Isn't that what you did to my real Dad?

MOTHER: What are you talking about?

CLAY: Why did he get into an accident, huh? It wasn't raining, he wasn't drinking. He was a good driver. There was no reason for it except that he wanted to. How did you make him want death, Mom?

AMY: Clay, what are you doing? You don't even mean anything you are saying.

MOTHER: What do you think you know?

CLAY: I think maybe he checked out. And you drove him to it. I wondered about it all my life.

AMY: Liar! You never thought about it before this minute.

CLAY: Shut up! I think we are all guilty. Born guilty. It's in our blood.

MOTHER: Where does this fantasy come from? The accident happened more than twenty years ago. You were five years old. You barely remember him.

AMY: Mom, he doesn't care about any of that. He's just being evil.

MOTHER: Our family is crippled because of you.

CLAY: I don't think I made that happen all by my lonely self.

MOTHER: Look at us, Clay. Just look at all of us.

CLAY: We are the picture of a perfect American family. Just what you always wanted, I'm sure, since you were a little girl.

MOTHER: Get out. You're not staying one minute longer in this house. You are disowned. Get out!

CLAY: I have some rights to this place, this life style. I'm entitled to this life that you dreamt up. It's my birth right.

MOTHER: You renounced it by attacking your father.

AMY: He'll die out there.

MOTHER: *(To AMY.)* What do you know about it? Henry, why don't you say something? He has injured and humiliated you. Say something to him.

CLAY: I have nowhere else to go.

MOTHER: Go to that harlot of yours. Stay with her.

(CLAY slaps his mother. FATHER flies at him and slaps CLAY hard. A beat. They stare at each other. FATHER slaps him again. Silence. Stillness.)

FATHER: I don't know what force brought us strangers to be father and son. But I have cared for you. Cared for you deeply. Where did I fail?

MOTHER: You exasperate me, Henry. Don't waste your sorrow on him. He is incapable of understanding our language. Get out, Clay. If you don't, I'll call the police.

FATHER: Striking your mother is the last of your destructive acts in this house. You have no lower depth to go than you are right now. Get out.

(Pause. CLAY exits. The door slams.)

MOTHER: Loving him only harms you.

AMY: Maybe our loving him harmed him somehow.

FATHER: He looks so much like Walter. Sometimes I have to stop myself from calling him by his father's name. Where have you been, Walter? I see him, he is young and strong. I want to reach over and grab his shoulder, then I realize it's Clay.

SCENE 18

The next day. ANNE enters AMY's room. Evening. AMY is in bed.

ANNE: How are you?

AMY: Fine.

ANNE: Feeling better?

AMY: I guess.

ANNE: I brought some soup for tomorrow.

AMY: *(Sarcastic.)* Chicken noodle?

(Pause.)

ANNE: Your parents were worried sick about you.

AMY: They're my parents.

(Pause.)

ANNE: I thought we were friends.

AMY: *(Sarcastic.)* You are the most perfect friend I have.

(Pause.)

AMY: I'm sorry.

ANNE: What do you think you know about me?

AMY: I think you watch the Home Shopping Network.

ANNE: I do that sometimes when I can't sleep. Usually at four in the morning. I scrub the kitchen floor at that hour too.

(Pause.)

AMY: How do you put yourself to sleep again?

ANNE: I imagine the Milky Way on my ceiling. Stars fall on me, my left shoulder disappears into the white light. I remind myself that in the fabric of history, my blood is water. So I should sleep.

AMY: How many nights like that do you live?

ANNE: Infinite. Only one.

(Pause.)

AMY: Even when we were small, Clay was different. He took money out of Mom's purse to buy me silly things. Superman comic books. Sweet rice cakes in March for Hinamatsuri, painted cloth Koinobori in May for the Boys' Day, pink cotton candy on Memorial Day, white tree barks that were meant to be burned to guide the ancestors' spirits during Obon in August. I used to love the smell of those barks and kept them under my pillow. Every time Mom asked us where we got the money, I would hide behind Clay, but he would look straight into her eyes and say "I found the money on the street."

ANNE: Your mother probably knew and forgave you two.

AMY: Clay knew that all he had to do was ask her for the money. But he didn't.

(Pause.)

AMY: He wasn't afraid of anything. So I was fearless when I was with him.

ANNE: You love Clay very much.

AMY: He was my hero.

ANNE: He'll come home. It's always possible to start over.

AMY: I don't know if I want him back.

ANNE: You don't have to decide now.

(Pause.)

ANNE: Are you sleepy?

AMY: Yes.

ANNE: Sweet dreams.

AMY: You too, Anne. Sweet dreams.

SCENE 19

ANNE and JAMES's apartment.

JAMES: I'd feel better if you went to see a doctor. How long have you had this headache?

ANNE: It's really nothing to worry about. Because of the snow the girls have cabin fever. They are loud and demanding, which doesn't help my little headache. As soon as the weather is better, I'll get Jane to take them to the park with her kids, so I can have a little silence.

JAMES: I don't know about Jane's kids. They seem a bit aggressive. How old are they?

ANNE: The younger one is eight, same as our Jamie.

JAMES: Which means Sachiko is too young to play with both of them. Their older girl must be ten. Sachiko is only six.

ANNE: I know how old my children are, James. I thought this was about my headache.

JAMES: I'm sorry.

ANNE: I need something of my own. You have your work, the girls have school. I don't have anywhere to go.

JAMES: You wanted to stay home and be a full-time mother, remember? It was your own choice.

ANNE: Maybe I made a mistake.

JAMES: Anne? What's wrong?

ANNE: I don't know. I want to do something with my life.

JAMES: Ok. Let's figure this out. Maybe you'd like to go to graduate school.

ANNE: What will I study?

JAMES: You studied literature in college. You can continue that.

ANNE: I don't have to go back to school.

JAMES: A job then?

ANNE: Wear pantyhose and ride the rush hour train everyday into Manhattan and back?

JAMES: Volunteer work? You could teach reading and writing at the library maybe. They must have programs for children in need.

(Long pause.)

ANNE: I want to be here when Jamie and Sachiko get home from school. I want to take a big part in their growing up. I want to be here when you get home from work, too late to tuck the children in bed, the dinner I made already cold.

Every morning when I get up, I'm delighted to find you next to me. Delighted to meet my girls again in a new day. But once in a while I truly wish I had made different choices.

JAMES: How long do those moments last?

ANNE: Not long. Only a very small fraction of eternity. Then I come home.

(JAMES embraces ANNE.)

SCENE 20

The night streets. The same evening. Someone grabs CLAY's arm.

JOE: I've been looking for you, Clay.

CLAY: Joe.

JOE: Where have you been hiding?

CLAY: I was looking for you too.

JOE: Got my money?

CLAY: I'm getting it.

JOE: Better be tonight. Seventeen grand.

CLAY: Seventeen?

JOE: Interest. It's not free money. It's business. And tomorrow morning, you're gonna owe me eighteen. Day after tomorrow, I'm gonna have a talk with you. Day after that, I gotta have a talk with your old man.

CLAY: I know where I can get the money. I'll pay you back tonight.

JOE: Good. And if you need more money tomorrow after paying me back, I'll lend it to you again. But if you don't pay me back, we can't be friends anymore.

CLAY: I understand the contract.

JOE: Before the first siren of an ambulance tears the thin sleep of the city, get the money to me. I'll wait up. *(Exits.)*

CLAY: Ten million people in the city. Think. Think.

SCENE 21

JAMES is in his office. Late. He clears his desk and accidentally knocks over a framed picture of ANNE. The glass shatters. He looks down at the broken frame, and suddenly feels urgent fear.

JAMES: A breathless second of circular motion descending, then a universe is created with a big bang. I stand over the newborn stars. Everything I lost in my life is in this galaxy of a broken likeness of my love. ANNE! *(He grabs the phone and dials. It rings and rings and rings.)*

SCENE 22

ANNE's apartment. The doorbell rings. FATHER enters.

ANNE: Henry. Is everything all right?

FATHER: Have you seen Clay? I thought James might be in touch with my son.

ANNE: I haven't heard anything.

FATHER: If you see him, would you tell him to come home?

ANNE: Of course.

FATHER: I fear at any moment he can be beaten, arrested, or die in a ditch somewhere. His behavior has no safety latch. He's free with his idiocy and malice. I fear for his life.

ANNE: He has strayed from the normal orbit of life, but he will get back on course. You'll see.

FATHER: If he shows up, please give him this money. Three thousand dollars. It's the most I can withdraw from our account without making my wife suspicious. This should tide him over until he decides to come home.

(The intercom buzzer. ANNE goes to answer it.)

ANNE: Henry, it's Elizabeth. She is on her way up, ok?

(The doorbell rings. ANNE opens the door to let MOTHER in.)

MOTHER: What are you doing here?

FATHER: Hello, Elizabeth.

MOTHER: Is Clay here, Anne?

ANNE: No. He hasn't come.

MOTHER: So you're here to leave the money in case he shows up.

FATHER: He is out there flying without a lifeline.

MOTHER: He cut it himself, Henry. Your generosity poisons his mind.

FATHER: Flying without a lifeline. I'm afraid for his untimely death.

MOTHER: Of a despised life. Come home now. We still have Timothy and Amy. Remember?

FATHER: How can you consider him dead?

MOTHER: Anne, I'm sorry to bother you with our problems. Henry, let's go.

ANNE: Elizabeth, what can I do for you? Why did you come to see me?

(Pause.)

MOTHER: Perhaps Clay has taught me how to lie. I was going to hide this from Henry.

(She gives him an envelop.)

MOTHER: I cashed some Treasury bills that were in our safety box today. Four thousand dollars. I thought you may not notice it gone. I've become a thief, Henry.

FATHER: No, my dear.

MOTHER: Twenty years. Despite our heartaches over Clay, most of our lives have been music and delight. I fear I have compromised your trust.

FATHER: No, my dear.

MOTHER: For something so abhorrent to come out of my womb, I must bear in myself deep ruin. Many years ago I realized Clay's damage, and I have been afraid of looking into my own soul ever since.

A woman warrior will fight her inner fears. She will conquer the demons of her own heart. The victory is about being whole, so that she can change the world. I have not changed the world. I have not changed Clay. I have spent my life being afraid.

FATHER: No, my dear. You have spent your life weaving ordinary moments of joy and sorrow into our memories so our family can dream about it two, three hundred years from now. You have been brave. Very brave.

MOTHER: Shall we go home?

FATHER: Anne, please give Clay this seven thousand dollars. He may not accept it if he knew it came from us. He may be angry.

ANNE: I'm sure he will appreciate it.

FATHER: It's only money. It won't change him. Even so…

(FATHER and MOTHER exit. ANNE stands silent.)

SCENE 23

JAMES is in his office.

CO-WORKER: James, aren't you going home? It's late.

JAMES: Soon. I'm trying to finish some things so I can take a long weekend.

CO-WORKER: Are you going somewhere?

JAMES: Taking my family skiing.

CO-WORKER: That's nice. Well, I'm going home.

JAMES: Good night.

(Pause. He continues working. After a while, he begins to clear his desk and gets ready to leave. He knocks over a framed picture of ANNE by accident. The glass shatters. He looks down at the broken frame, and suddenly feels urgent fear.)

JAMES: In this one second of fracture, everything is possible. I can gain the world or lose everything in it. How can I rewind this second so I am not me at this moment but me a moment before. Something has pierced my heart, a doubt, a consequence, a fear, of my life lived in distraction. ANNE! *(He grabs the phone and dials. It rings and rings and rings.)*

SCENE 24

ANNE's apartment. The doorbell rings.

CLAY: Hello.

ANNE: Come in, Clay. I was hoping that you'd stop by tonight.

CLAY: Where is James?

ANNE: He's still at work. I have something for you.

CLAY: What?

ANNE: Money. You needed money. Seven thousand dollars.

CLAY: *(Showing no joy.)* Whose money is it?

ANNE: Don't ask. Just take it.

CLAY: Come on, Anne. Who says just take the money, no strings attached, no guilt required. Are you a saint?

ANNE: It's your parents'. They are suffering. Take their money and do some good. Don't waste your life. Don't waste their love. Do you understand? Do you understand anything?

CLAY: I understand perfectly. From now on, I will be a good son. I'll make you and my parents proud. But right now, this precious money, this gift of their love, is not enough.

ANNE: Clay!

CLAY: I have certain obligations. I'm sure you have credit cards and bank cards and checkbooks and such, don't you? Lend me seventeen thousand dollars.

ANNE: Are you insane?

CLAY: I beg you.

ANNE: I can't get you that kind of money. Even if I could, I would not do it without talking to James first.

CLAY: If you don't help me, I'll be ruined. I'll have to kill myself. Do you understand, Anne? I will be dead. I will be twisted, rotten, foul, dead, dead, dead!

ANNE: Why are you so selfish? Why do you torment me? Why do you torment everyone who cares about you?

CLAY: If you care about me, save my life. You have the power.

ANNE: Clay, pull yourself together. What did you do with so much money? Do you need to pay it all back at once?

CLAY: I needed the money because I didn't want anyone else touching Rebecca. Touching her, touching her, touching her with dirty hands, old hands, rich hands. I needed money to stop that.

So first I borrowed two thousand dollars and bought her a leather coat. Then I borrowed three thousand dollars to put down on a car. It's like that.

I know what's going on. She lies to me all the time. Lies about her beeper and her bra and her heels and her lipsticks. I need money, because she is mine. She is mine. No one else should touch her. When I can't have her, I drink my own blood, a scorching flame of blue rage.

ANNE: You have strayed so far from life. You anguish because you are attached to something that is not real. It's not too late, Clay. You can give up this suffering. You can go home.

CLAY: You think you know everything and that the everything you know is the right thing. James with his six-figure job and you, a stay-at-home-wife who goes to the PTA meetings, and two daughters who wear matching dresses. Who cares? The dark night is expanding and collapsing into a universe hostile and stupid. And I couldn't even get Rebecca to dress up on Halloween as death to parade with me to the flat edge of the planet. We should fall off the edge together. Fall a long long way into the unconscious delicious one-thousand-degree never-ending fire of blue hell. My wings are crooked.

(Pause.)

ANNE: Who should fall off the edge? You and Rebecca? Or you and me?

CLAY: You won't help me, will you?

ANNE: I'm trying.

CLAY: I need you.

ANNE: I'm here.

(Long pause.)

CLAY: Can I have a cup of tea?

(Pause.)

CLAY: You are right. I'm sorry. I won't ask you anymore.

(They look into each other's eyes. CLAY smiles. He sits down.)

CLAY: I'm thirsty.

(ANNE turns her back to him to go to the kitchen to make tea. She takes off her rings to wash her hands. After drying her hands with a towel, she puts the rings back on. CLAY watches.)

ANNE: I'll talk to James and see what we can do. He cares about you a great deal.

(CLAY stands up. As he approaches ANNE from behind, he picks up a large kitchen knife. He hides the knife behind his back. She turns around and sees his menacing expression.)

ANNE: What do you want?

CLAY: Nothing.

(CLAY advances on ANNE.)

ANNE: Stay there.

CLAY: Why are you scared?

(They circle each other.)

ANNE: Clay, it's me.

CLAY: I know who you are.

(She steps backwards, trying to get away from CLAY. He follows her. This goes on in silence for quite a while. Finally CLAY jumps on her and restrains her. She screams.)

CLAY: Shut up, bitch.

ANNE: Are you insane?

CLAY: Aren't we all? You think your little life is sane and safe? The hell is right around the corner, and you conjured me, your demon from the depth of darkness. You're the insane one.

ANNE: I did not. This is all your making.

CLAY: You're my partner in crime.

ANNE: Never.

CLAY: Don't argue with me. You know where you are going, don't you?

ANNE: How would you face James?

CLAY: Don't worry about me.

ANNE: I have children. You know them. You know my children. They are sleeping in their bedroom.

CLAY: Well then, you better be quiet not to wake them up.

ANNE: They need me. I don't want to die.

CLAY: I'm sure you don't. It's natural.

ANNE: Please.

CLAY: But I need the money. I know you have expensive jewelry. For every anniversary, birthday, Christmas, James has given you something that sparkles on you. Isn't that right? Because he loves you so much.

ANNE: Take it. Take anything you want except my life.

CLAY: It's too late now. After a certain point, there is no way back home.

(ANNE breaks free from him and tries to get away. He grabs after her. They struggle.

She picks up a cushion and swings it at him. The knife cuts in to the cushion and red feathers fly all over the room. She trips and falls. They are both covered in feathers.)

ANNE: Help! Help!

(CLAY grabs her.)

ANNE: No, no no. Don't! Don't! Save me. Save me. James!

(He cuts her throat.)

CLAY: Die quickly, Anne.

(He pulls her to him and slashes her body from right to left, down to her waist. Then lets go of her limp body. Long pause.)

CLAY: God, look on this your servant, lying in great weakness, and comfort her with the promise of life everlasting, given in the resurrection of your Son Jesus Christ our Lord.

(He stands over her body as the shadows deepen in the room. He shudders suddenly. His knees buckle as he tries to move. He goes through her things and gets what he wanted.)

CLAY: I'm free. I've left home behind, left sanity behind, left behind the chance I had to end peacefully this story that is my life. There is nothing to go back to, nothing to live for, nothing to prove. I am free.

For the blood I shed, one day I will be caught in a cycle, beginningless and endless, to live forever, to suffer eternally in the flickering blazing hell. But that's a faraway future. My luck in this world is just beginning.

(As he makes his getaway, he slips and slides in ANNE's blood. The phone starts ringing. It rings and rings and rings.)

(End of play.)

THE WILD ASS'S SKIN

An original verse adaptation of the novel by Honoré de Balzac

J. Scott Reynolds

J. SCOTT REYNOLDS grew up in eastern Washington state and attended Brigham Young University in Utah. He is the artistic director and a co-founder of Handcart Ensemble, a New York City theatre company. *David & Bathsheba* is his most recent play, produced by Handcart at the American Theatre of Actors. He has also translated Racine's *Andromaque* and co-translated Goldoni's *The Mistress of the Inn*. Reynolds also works as a director and actor. He resides in New York City.

The Wild Ass's Skin was first presented by Handcart Ensemble on August 11, 2000 at the American Theatre of Actors, New York City, with the following cast and credits:

Cardot and others .... Kevin Ashworth
Emile and others .... James Mack
Valentine .... Barrett Ogden
Foedora and others .... Christy Summerhays
Pauline and others .... Erin Treadway

Director: J. Scott Reynolds
Assistant Director and Stage Manager: Steven Gridley
Costume Designer and Choreographer: Mireille Enos
Lighting Designer: Tamara Shelp

CAST OF CHARACTERS

EMILE (actor also plays SHOPKEEPER, PORRIQUET, and BUTCHER)

CARDOT (actor also plays BOY, VALET, and MAN OF SCIENCE)

PAULINE (actor also plays YOUNG WOMAN)

FOEDORA (actor also plays AQUILINA and SOOTHSAYER)

A NOTE ON STAGING

Any number of spare approaches to staging might be serviceable for this play. The original 1999 production used a bare stage with a medium-sized movable trunk in the first half that functioned as a bridge, a bed, a coach, and as the visible place of storage for props and costume pieces used in the internal narrative. A Louis XVI replica was used as the chair in the latter portion of the play. No other sizeable set pieces were used. As much as half of the play's action was unaccompanied by speech, much of which is not indicated by stage directions. Stage movement was frequent and varied in pace, breadth, and intensity.

VALENTINE: The sky, unmellowed from its azure bliss,
        assumes this night a gown of mocking rose,
        untroubled by the groans that pulse below,
        which we of clay do poorly to restrain.
        Wink not at me, oh stars, I know your ruse.
        The dame you sequin has no mind to please
        beyond the fitful yearning she provokes,
        whose jabs are felt more keenly than its glees.
        Tempt elsewhere orbs, you bodies bright, you moon,
        who, sound within your courses, know no strife;
        These ossifying eyes are slow to shine
        when wrought upon by otherworldly glare.
        The things which writhe upon this nether-sphere—
        and chiefly those which cause a soul's decay—
        exact so unreprievingly my gaze
        that, were I not to leap now from this bridge
        (which forces a horizon to my view),
        your teasing glitter might have gone unseen.
        Bejeweled may be the dreams your grandeur births,
        but cobbled is the trail of their pursuit
        and I'll no more be bruised upon its rocks
        which, randomly protruding, foul my way.

Enough. Let waste be joined at last with waste.
And let the squalid waters down below
declare the matter with their icy smack.

(*Pause.*)

Perhaps not now; so many folk about.
As newly pallid corpses call for sheets
and baseness bids we kindly down the blinds,
this act, entailing both, were best withheld
till thickened night affords a better veil.
How best till then to dull the hours' pinch?
My pockets limp, distraction's means are slim…

(*A WOMAN appears, enters a shop.*)

My final glimpse of womanhood, perhaps.
Forever strange to her who gave me breath
(the gift of which expended all her own)
and foreign just as much to love's caress
(excepting what licentiousness can feign),
my zeal to leave this mud called Earth abates
not much, but some, on thinking I perhaps
may, with more fight, that flickering boon obtain:
a bosom that receives me without cost,
except that I delight to be received.

(*WOMAN enters from shop, carrying an urn. Exits.*)

Where came she by an urn so blast with age?
No antique, that—an artifact at least!
Unless my sense deserts me, it's a Ming.
She brought no purse, her gait's unlike a thief's…
Who barters relics so, like morning loaves?
And lights his shop despite the hour's hush?
—no vendor I've yet met along these banks.
Face-on examination this demands.

(*Enters shop.*)

Hallo?… No keeper guards this heaped array?
Or might these straw-filled apes with frozen snarls
and boas locked in pounce be so designed?
Well ought they—here's no shop, but more a trove!
And all the world condensed within it, too.
Here's Persia at my feet in royal weave;
there's Rome: a sculpted Mars with marble glare;
there China climbs the air with dragon's wings
across the red expanse of some lord's gown;
Japan demurs, a modest, preening stork

upon a white kimono nearby perched;
Byzantium's a jackal etched in brass
who cackles o'er his stolen leg of prey;
we've Greece, here prancing Bacchus on a jug,
and there a stern Minoean figurine;
all watched by an embalmed Egyptian lord,
who, heedless of his soiled and tattered wrap
and undisgruntled by his want of height,
upholds himself as though a very king.

SHOPKEEPER: *(Who has entered unseen.)* A corpse, we see, can
hold more life than some.

VALENTINE: And I am more cadaverous than most,
yet pale the more to be so crept upon.
Identify yourself before I strike.

SHOPKEEPER: The keeper of this shop, my cheery man.

VALENTINE: I'll own that your comparison was apt;
no vice nor passing thrill that I recall
has lately brought my face the merest pink.
Our Pharaoh, with his mummied-over traits
possesses more demeanor, I've no doubt;
my suicide's a mere formality.

SHOPKEEPER: Indeed, I feared the reaper'd come to call,
so hardly seems there flesh upon your cheeks.

VALENTINE: I more would fear arrest if in your stead;
a hoard like this requires rotten means.
I see now why you keep such night-clad hours.

SHOPKEEPER: The shadows are my favorite company
and yours no less; I doubt we'd else have met.
But, while I've never trembled or abhorred
to undertake the darkest enterprise,
my goods have all been conquered lawfully.
A thief pursues such things not for themselves,
but hoping they'll beget him greater gain.
I seek no end beyond mere ownership
and tire of an object once attained.
You're free, in fact, to take what likes you best.

VALENTINE: Munificence can bear the light of day.
What need then for this dusk-filled secrecy?

SHOPKEEPER: The rash despondent, craving swift release
from cares he deems too crushing to uphold
is who I seek and not who loves the sun.
Nor does my bounty rise from any glow

of feeling for my wretched fellow man.
Possession, I'll remind you, is my craft,
but since its pleasing tremor fast subsides,
the fat of all the Earth itself becomes,
with time, encumbrance, rather than delight.
I've lately therefore sought less tactile things—
a person's destiny not being least.
The objects I've amassed are of such worth
that, fell within the grasp of grasping men,
they without fail soon manacle their fates.

VALENTINE: I gladly would deprive you of a vase,
and pawning it, extend my days of vice;
but want of means by which to so indulge
is not what makes me seek my own demise;
I am the very prince of wretchedness
and, rather than awake each day to woe,
prefer inertia in a bed of pine.

SHOPKEEPER: Your father too reproached your birth, perhaps?

VALENTINE: Not so. A widower, he loved me more.

SHOPKEEPER: Then some disease puts fire in your bones.

VALENTINE: More near the mark. I feel as if aflame.

SHOPKEEPER: A woman.

VALENTINE: All their race. Not one alone.
The disregard of men is no less fierce.
My attributes may lack Davidic sheen,
my ingenuity may lack sheer might;
my aims are nonetheless Olympian,
and unfulfilled, I cannot wish to live.
If I must fail to penetrate those realms
where beauty and accomplishment reside,
then, I repeat, no morning luster holds
sufficient warmth to tempt me from the grave,
whose beckon I shall shortly give reply.
Good night. May passion's whips be still with you.

SHOPKEEPER: (*Beckoning to* BOY, *who brings a box.*) A moment,
please. I may have something yet,
which, though you seek what's set apart for kings,
has, of itself, more potency than they.
I see you've knowledge touching Eastern things.
Might Sanskrit fall within your tutored reach?

VALENTINE: An odd presumption, though it does, in fact.

SHOPKEEPER: (*Removing an animal skin from box.*) This skin,
      obtained from some uncertain beast,
      possesses an inscription underneath.
      Peruse, if your appointment brooks delay.

VALENTINE: (*Taking skin and reading.*) "He who possesses me
      possesses all.
      The forces that have born me so decree.
      Desire, and all you yearn for will be yours.
      But moderate your wishes as your life.
      Upon each wish, gargantuan or slight,
      I shall contract an equal measure's breadth,
      as will the span of all your living days.
      Desire you to have me nonetheless?"

SHOPKEEPER: You read your Sanskrit like the morning post.

VALENTINE: You doubtless mean to snare me in a prank.

SHOPKEEPER: A clumsy one indeed, if but a prank—
      the premise tortures credibility.
      And yet it seems to've netted your regard,
      behind whose flame all harbored thoughts of death
      have vanished like the noon-assailèd frost.

VALENTINE: You've never craved its powers for your own?

SHOPKEEPER: Its pledge to axe the years from one's own life,
      for me, too overweighs its offering.
      And, caveat aside, I'd not consent
      to have a thing so fickle as my wants
      conduct a thing so cherished as my fate.
      But as you only faintly prize your own,
      I doubt that you'd forgo the season's bliss
      this skin, howmuch exacting, would afford.

VALENTINE: Indeed, I'll wear it wrapped about my loins
      and moonward cry my whims without restraint!
      The studious and labor-soaking path
      I've kept upon in hopes of due return
      so twists and intersects lowhanging limbs,
      so turns to mire or mountain at each breath,
      so nestles snakes and all their vicious kin,
      my pace attains at best a numbing creep.
      I'll no more pass through rites that bolster scorn,
      laid down by those who seek to hold their thrones.
      My compass now resides upon my word,
      my heart's design determining its bounds.
      I'll have me now a banquet so immense,

the tables all shall keel beneath its mass;
and furnish it, you skin, with mirthful guests
whose spirits shall propel us into dawn,
emboldened by a wine whose trickling sting
shall blaze as fiercely when the stars have dimmed.
Come, come now, skin, enact your promised charm!
Shall writs be grimly etched but not upheld?

(*To Shopkeeper.*)

You're laughing, feeble toad. Am I deceived?

SHOPKEEPER: You want the planks we stand on to upheave
and wine-wet nymphs to surface from the gape?
Don't fear, good man, you'll have your bacchanal;
but know the powers that you've now unleashed
shall gnaw at you till bone at best remains.
The weight and ardor of your every wish
shall cause this hide to shrink reciprocally,
betokening your life's diminishment.

VALENTINE: You speak to one who nearly cut his throat
no more ago than half an hour's lapse.
To know all pleasures in a single quaff
and perish once the ecstasy has passed
is far from what I deem a worthy curse.
Farewell. You've not entrapped me, cease to leer.

(VALENTINE exits shop, is accosted from behind by EMILE and CARDOT.)

EMILE: (*Holding knife to VALENTINE's throat.*) Hail pig! Prepare
to meet a bitter end.

CARDOT: (*Blindfolding VALENTINE.*)Your choices are as follows:
a) be drowned
and b) be drawn and quartered while alive,
then left upon a hill for birds to peck.

VALENTINE: Emile and Cardot: Go. I've game to chase.
You're free to join but cause me no delay.

(CARDOT and EMILE lead blindfolded VALENTINE by the arm.)

EMILE: Your game, no doubt, is of the smallish kind.
We two have been at game since six o'clock
and happen to have called some numbers well.
In short, we've fallen into such a sum,
that recklessness demands its due be paid;
and as the night's still shy its dozenth bong,
yet lands upon the same on which you hatched,
we've booked this night a scarlet-draped salon

with dame and drink a Caesar might commend.
Be at your goatish peak, then, honored guest:
upon your form depends a night's debauch!

VALENTINE: I need no priming, gents. Let's on our way.

(The three enter a salon, where VALENTINE is approached by AQUILINA, who removes his blindfold. Carousal ensues in the form of dance and distribution of spirits, amidst which AQUILINA and VALENTINE remain in one another's proximity.)

VALENTINE: *(To AQUILINA.)* That we've not met, my certainty's as stone.
I know you, yet, as surely as my thumb
and with my inner eye beheld your form
the moment ere you lifted off that blind;
your visage often comes to me in sleep,
though never yet has image woke to flesh.
My wonder shall consume me: you are who?

AQUILINA: I'm none but Aquilina. Need you ask?

VALENTINE: The courtesan of Otway's bloody play,
precisely as I've fashioned you in dream.
That skin has far more reach than I supposed
if damsels made upon the written page
and added to by fancy's etching-blade
can show themselves upon my whim's conceit.
So: are you truly flesh or merely shade?

AQUILINA: I dare declare myself the very mould
of woman on whose granite stoop you've flung
both bone and soul since anxious youth began.
Too doted on by nature's partial wand
to fear your sex's gaze shall ever dim,
and having far too velveted a tongue
to see my needs for any length foregone,
I find a man's devotion to be first
among the things I ought, but fail to prize.

VALENTINE: Tranquility has never thus been mine.
It's true, whatever shape you've ever took,
I've never been too wise to shun pursuit,
Foedora having been the latest pearl
for whom I've sounded to the blackest low.

EMILE: *(Overhearing.)* A tale that bears recounting, if you're game.
Your party, though. Be wholly unobliged.

VALENTINE: "Be unobliged," you say, my dear Emile?
You little comprehend despondency;

nay, contrary to what is more believed,
who takes his life seeks less to flee his woes,
as much as to declare them shrillingly.

CARDOT: You wish to die? I've rope.

VALENTINE: I've better means,
the which I shall describe when further soused.
For now, let's have my newly supple tongue
dispense to you the tale of my decline.
To give it added furbish, I propose
we with the aid of all enact the thing.

YOUNG WOMAN: I fear I've not the aptitude you need.

VALENTINE: Don't fret your roles; I'll cue you mightily.

CARDOT: We're hardly thespians. You ask a lot.
I'll join if you assume an equal task.

VALENTINE: Such as?

CARDOT: Delivering all the tale in rhyme.

VALENTINE: Agreed. But let's begin. The moment stales.

(The enactment begins, the four principal guests assuming the various roles as needed.)

My father was a penny-hoarding sort
whose words were few, but genial enough.
Though nephew to a count, by broad report,
I never saw a link on either cuff
when handing him his evening glass of port
that gleamed of aught but brass (our life was rough).
And yet, before he died, I heard him call
"I've left ten thousand francs! Don't spend it all!"

My age fell, at the time, between those years
where nothing seems too bold to undertake;
I'd written odes which, met with patient ears,
bespoke a master wordsmith on the make.
And so, though nude ambition gathers jeers,
there rose in me a thirst I swore to slake:
to be, like Keats, a sudden man of letters
and raise a glass with those esteemed my betters.

EMILE: But poets have a stony patch to hoe:
a clerking job by day to keep you fed
and nights bereft of sleep in which your woe
comes not from the ideas that cram your head,
but knowing you've ten stanzas still to go,
with nothing penned before you fell in bed.

One leaps at means to ease the metier's curses,
not least of which a patron's ample purse is.

VALENTINE: Ten thousand francs… not much, and yet suppose
I kept my spending under harsh control
and went three years with but one pair of shoes;
or each day ate one bratwurst on a roll;
or if within the chillest winter's throes,
I wore my coat instead of burning coal;
I'd buy the time to write my *Gesamkunstwerk*
and (two birds) leave my job as a saloon's clerk.

Three years, then, of seclusion with the Muse;
Papà's remittant francs allowed the means.
Three years to let her influence suffuse
my soul and conjure blood-and-smoke-filled scenes
of Bonaparte at war—the source I'd use
to forge an epic meant for tougher spleens.
Napoleon I liked—at five foot four,
he made the Cossacks weep and claw the floor.

EMILE: And so our man set out upon his way,
belongings in a bundle neatly tied;
his father had a mortgage still to pay
almost in full the day his spirit hied,
which meant the ivied brownstone couldn't stay,
or rather, Val could no more there reside.
His only wish: to skirt the sort of places
where twenty queue at dawn to wash their faces.

And fortune, though we curse it, can be kind.
Five hours after traipsing in the snow,
his numbing fingers put him in a mind
to step inside a shop and there bestow
them stinging all before a stove, to find
there was, in fact, a space for rent below.
He learned this by Pauline, the keeper's daughter,
who, earnest-eyed, recalled St. Joan pre-slaughter.

PAULINE: You're cold. You'd like some hot milk in a bowl?

VALENTINE: No time. I have to find a place to live.

PAULINE: Your eyes are sad. They've no more shine than coal.

VALENTINE: They've been too long unlidded. Do forgive.

PAULINE: Then stay with us. You seem a gentle soul.

VALENTINE: An observation less-than-putative.

PAULINE: We've got a bed and basin in the cellar.

VALENTINE: My sous are few. I ask for nothing stellar.

EMILE: A cellar may at first seem unideal
        for even bachelors to set up house.
        Pauline, though, brought the place a hearthèd feel.
        Her sometime morning crumbcakes would arouse
        him with unfurled aromas that would steal
        to him with the mute footfalls of a mouse.
        He couldn't quite conceive her as a lover.
        "She's pure," he'd say. "Such things must be above her."

        Now settled, Val began to write his oeuvre.
        Come dawn, he'd with a flourish raise his quill
        and force a tepid stanza for to prove,
        regardless of the Muse's gracious will,
        he had at least the wherewithal to move
        reluctant ink and empty pages fill.
        Come night, he'd muse (without a trace of jollity),
        "The volume's there, but Muse, bestow some quality!"

VALENTINE: I'll mention, lest we fail to by neglect,
        my hound's pursuit of literary fame,
        though worthy (surely) in its own respect,
        was linked, for me, to a more urgent aim.
        Now, some are born with beauty to project,
        and others with the means to win acclaim.
        I, being born to Category Two,
        hoped, with its traits, the former sort to woo.

        That said, let's have our story recommence,
        whose pivot was my meeting you, Emile;
        in moments, you without a doubt could sense
        the coolness I did little to conceal:

EMILE: "Your verse is grand, but cannot recompense
        an utter lack of parlor guest appeal.
        A poet's life needs gentlefolk to fund it,
        who gladly worship wit, but flee a pundit."

CARDOT: The months ensuing thus became a school
        in which our grave protagonist was brought
        to boost his frigid bearing up to cool
        and keep his words vivacious, but unfraught
        with musings at which dilettantes might drool,
        yet by which others might feel overwrought.
        For pleasantry's the mightiest propriety,
        he learned, when penetrating high society.

        In time, Emile, whose coattails had some reach,

believed his friend sufficiently reformed
to nudge his prow towards a whiter beach:
a dame, into whose circle he had wormed
a cautious path, then kept at like a leech,
but learned was drawn to minds more stressed and
   stormed.
Her name, Foedora, wafted from the tongue,
but bricklike fell on hearts who thereto clung.

FOEDORA: I'm told that you're a poet; do I err?

VALENTINE: I am, but promise not to read aloud.

FOEDORA: I worship Poe. To whom do you defer?

VALENTINE: To such as like a cow more than a cloud.

FOEDORA: Your ruse won't work. You're not so earthbound, sir—
   your eyes have manic fire. Don't be proud.

VALENTINE: I'd not have thought a countess so insightful.

FOEDORA: Some words about your work would be delightful.

VALENTINE: I've taken on the little Corsican
   as matter for a poem of epic weight.

FOEDORA: What sort of man would choose Napoleon
   to charge his verse with needed mythic freight... ?
   Ah-ha. I know. The willful sort of man
   who vows he'll not recoil from any height;
   who can't abide that any not succumb
   beneath his itching, ever-probing thumb.

VALENTINE: I have a theory regarding Will
   (the sort whose double-u is upper case);
   a vaporous, outer entity, with skill
   it can be seized and made to build or brace
   whatever one is minded to fulfill.
   Its mastery more ranks than breed or race.
   Who owns it stands aloof from even nature
   and freely scoffs at man-appointed stature.

CARDOT: He, on returning home, felt some regret;
   His words, he feared, had come across as smug.
   As night drew on, he, sleepless, was beset
   by thoughts that he could neither chase nor shrug:

VALENTINE: What arrogance! We'd barely even met!
   I'd just as well thrown compote on her rug.
   I'll go and make amends upon the morrow.
   It's that, or immolate myself from sorrow.

CARDOT: When morrow came, he woke up with dismay.

He only had the dowdy set of clothes
he'd worn last night. He knew it wouldn't pay
to seem like the bourgeois a countess loathes
who change apparel every thousandth day.
His mandate clear, he moaned a string of oaths.
To buy a waistcoat (and his heart's requiting)
would cost a hundred francs and months of writing.

Recall that Val possessed a skimpy purse
and that the project he had undertook
demanded that, come pox or hail or worse,
all pleasures, for the most part, be forsook
and funds applied to keep him scribbling verse
—three years would barely do to fill a book.
But then, to wed a member of nobility…
Her eyes had shone. That boded possibility.

VALENTINE: Was not my father's uncle a marquis?
A count, perhaps. I don't remember which.
I'll have to go dig up my pedigree…
No. Sentiment, when fervent, knows no niche.
But don't presume a thing, or else she'll flee;
a woman won't be badgered, knave or rich.
Assume, at first, a dignified remove.
A heart full-bared wins pity, never love.

CARDOT: A moment's hell while at Foedora's gate,
and then the maid returned to let him in.
His fears began to instantly abate;
she greeted him as though her very kin
and kept him in her parlor until late
into the morning; Val exclaimed within:
Not bad at all for an initial foray;
maintain reserve, though—not so *con amore*.

Their meetings soon attained some frequency,
she welcoming him weekly (often twice),
he following a careful strategy:
to pique her sentiments at any price—
including that of geniality.
He liked her laugh, but anger would suffice:

VALENTINE: I mustn't let her feel indifference.
For vibrant sorts, to bore's the worst offense.

CARDOT: His time with her was never without cost:
a carriage here to send her on her way,
and there a full day's work forever lost;
a new cravat whenever one would fray,

a bootblack's fee to keep his footwear glossed,
and launder's fees when shirts began to gray.
One morning, nose in ledger, he was stunned
to find a year had trickled from his fund.

Some self-examination was in store.

VALENTINE: I've clearly cause to question my resolve.
When Father died, I reverently swore
that for three years, my life would all revolve
around my gift of Muse and nothing more.
My aged governess once told me "All've
we got's one life. One day it's gone."
As numbers go, there's none more bleak than One.

I think I'm more distracted than I thought.
My poem's only twenty pages thick;
my working days increasingly are fraught
with visions of the countess, all which stick
with garish weight upon a mind that ought
to be consumed with matters more epic.
I haven't the resources to adore a
phenomenon arresting as Foedora.

How is it she so ably captivates?
I've surely looked on beauty more endued.
Perhaps it's how she so ingratiates
when gazing at you, seeming to exclude
all others from concern as she relates
a sudden thought through lips so richly hued.
You for a moment fancy you're a king
and fear to feel her disaffection's sting.

The favor she extends me cannot but
be born of something fervent underneath.
Our discourse never slumps into a rut;
I either make her smile or make her seethe.
Those titled imbeciles who daily glut
her parlor merely make her flash her teeth.
I'll no more weigh the cost nor question why.
This woman shall be won, or let me die.

CARDOT: The weeks ensuing floated like a mist.
Foedora seemed increasingly to warm
to him; she'd much less glacially insist
he keep a blurred remove within the swarm
of suitors ever chirping for a tryst.
"She must," he thought, "be ready to disarm,"
and flew to their first evening rendez-vous.

The butler said, "Madame's beset with flu."

Unable to dislodge her from his brain,
he couldn't bring himself to trudge back home.
He turned his collar up and in the rain
set to the opera house, beneath whose dome
he'd hoped that night to make his yearnings plain.
He'd purge them watching seized Otello foam,
or so he thought; beside him on the right,
a too-familiar visage came to sight.

Without her, he'd not come, she'd understood
(her suitor being so bereft of means).
The moment where the Moor cries out for blood
was doubtless the most paramount of scenes,
but didn't help at all our hero's mood
—or calm the dame's. Their seats were mezzanines,
and, although pleasant (having been re-plushed),
would speed one to the morgue if therefrom pushed.

The curtain fell. She said, "Escort me back."
He did, and all the while cursed his name.
The coachman's fare he'd found himself to lack
had filled him with an acid surge of shame
that wouldn't cease for days to burn and rack.

VALENTINE: What deed could ever equally defame!

CARDOT: She asked him in, despite the tired hour;
        he, startled, briefly dropped his rueful glower.

FOEDORA: I'm sought out, at the moment, severally,
        and more than not by men of high prestige.
        Despite their make and monied agency,
        my heart is unassenting to all siege.
        There's none whose mind holds your agility
        and none whose soul has shown itself so liege.
        Regard it as a proof of estimation
        to be foresquarely shown disinclination.

CARDOT: A moment, then he realized he'd been spurned.
        Or if not spurned, a gauntlet had been thrown.
        A woman sometimes says such things, he'd learned,
        to let her flagging interest be known
        and signal her affection must be earned
        with greater verve or artfulness than shown.
        It's up to you to know which of the two.
        Use caution; one false move and all is through.

VALENTINE: I'm pleased to hear my mind and soul so praised,

but question how you view my heart's intent.
Your beauty, true, has on occasion raised
a wistful thought—but quickly I repent.
"This jewel on which I shamelessly have gazed,"
I say, "was not for vulgar longings meant!"
How dare I hold divinity so earthily?
A man may love you, true, but never worthily.

FOEDORA: You caustic ass. I ought to throw you out.

VALENTINE: I fear that I shall beat you to the door.

FOEDORA: You can't be earnest. All you do is flout.

VALENTINE: Confessing love while prostrate on the floor
would cause me to be banished, I've no doubt.
Indifference would paint me as a boor.
I'll choose for now, Madame, to hold my peace.
Suspense is often kinder than release.

FOEDORA: You're odd, but oddly fair. Good-night, my friend.

VALENTINE: Be glad I wasn't thrown out on the street.
A lover scorned can cause a ghastly end.

FOEDORA: I'd rather death than deprivation meet.
Against mere blows, I could more ably fend
than, say, a spouse who'd all my fortune eat.
Do leave. I've no more waking strength to borrow.
I'll be more genial when you call tomorrow.

CARDOT: On leaving her, he might have taken heart
for having rightly chosen artfulness,
yet couldn't help but dwell upon the tart
reality she'd hastened to address:
that poverty adorned him like a wart,
a fact he had endeavored to finesse,
but vainly; any feature so conspicuous,
when hidden, makes its bearer seem ridiculous.

(VALENTINE simulates slumping into bed. He is approached by PAULINE, who carries a pitcher and bowl.)

PAULINE: I heard you groan and feared you might be ill.

VALENTINE: If but. I'd gladly catch a croup and die.

PAULINE: The treatment you require knows no pill,
to judge it from the timbre of your sigh.
You wrote today how many stanzas?

VALENTINE: Nil.
My epic's not been worked on since July.

PAULINE: Ah-ha. A jealous Muse withholds her favor.

VALENTINE: The countess too allures. I cannot stave her.

PAULINE: Then fell her with your charm, you comely lad.

VALENTINE: I have. Ten others too. She wants us all.

PAULINE: And keeps you all, that she may keep unhad.

VALENTINE: What's more, my want of wealth has thrust a wall
I cannot scale between us; I'll go mad.
Whatever made me take up a vocation
that leaves one in so damnable a station?

PAULINE: Persistence in your craft may free you yet.
Acclaim in letters can be lucrative.

VALENTINE: To hear you say so cinches my regret;
the time retreats like wine within a sieve,
and in its place remains a widening debt
of means to make my dearest wishes live.

PAULINE: (*Pouring cream into bowl.*) You mustn't fret. You're life's
not half-expended.
Now down this cream and drift till night has ended.

(*Gives bowl to VALENTINE, who drinks it empty before returning it. PAULINE exits.*)

EMILE: He met the morning calm and resolute.
Foedora, he allowed, would not be his,
a fact he'd no more labor to refute.
"But equally as evident," he thought, "is
my readiness to rise into repute
by writing verse with eloquence and fizz.
Pen swiftly, though. Your funds are near-depleted.
And let that wretch from memory be deleted."

A month flew by, then two. The verses poured
with prim succession from his tireless pen.
His confidence had largely been restored;
the poem would be finished, although when
and if before he lost his room and board,
he couldn't say. He kept within his den
and swore to stay till work or bourse was over;
then came a letter from his would-be lover.

FOEDORA: (*Speaking the words which VALENTINE reads.*) "I've
missed your presence horribly, my dear.
Your wit, your lively discourse both have left
a cold and staid void. I darkly fear
my words, when last we spoke, were too bereft

   of kindness and fell harshly on your ear;
   to quit me with my heart, though, would be theft.
   I ask of you to consecrate a day
   on which to meet. I've things I wish to say."

VALENTINE: I find here little ambiguity.
   She's plainly said I have her heart in hand.
   My absence makes her see me differently,
   it seems, and smites her as a reprimand.
   What's more, she asks a day to spend with me,
   a better turn than ever hoped or planned.
   What better proof than this of one's virility?
   I'm stunned. I thought it outside my ability.

   Our tryst shall bring all feelings to the fore.
   I therefore can't leave anything to chance.
   I mustn't vex and neither must I bore,
   but lead her in a gentle, gliding dance.
   I mustn't seem too hurried. Furthermore,
   I can't approach her in these horrid pants—
   as well to ask a kiss while chewing rappee,
   as hope to then mold eros from agape.

EMILE: His funds would barely pay a year of rent.
   He nonetheless believed too much at stake.
   Upon a coat and trousers all was spent,
   and with the trade, his pledge completely brake.
   He told himself: I have to look a gent.
   This shall, in time, turn for my epic's sake.
   I'll, wedding her, do more than make a matron;
   till fame accrues, she'll be a ready patron.

   He made the fateful date; when it arrived,
   he suddenly was stricken with despair.
   In purchasing his suit, he'd not contrived
   to set aside an ample coachman's fare.

VALENTINE: (*Screaming.*) It's lost! That peak for which I grueling-
   most have strived!

PAULINE: (*Entering unhurriedly.*) My little friend, you're overcome
   with care.

VALENTINE: This life be damned with its incessant billows!

PAULINE: There's something, if you'll look, beneath your pillows.

EMILE: He did as was instructed; there he found
   a newly pungent bill for twenty francs.
   He skyward hurled a bleating, joyful sound
   and kissed her beaming cheeks in fevered thanks.

He made to leave her in a giddy bound,
then stopped and fell before her on his shanks.

VALENTINE: (*Taking her hand.*) I'll not forget the guileless amity
you've troubled for a knave as vain as me. (*Leaves.*)

EMILE: On greeting him, Foedora was all bliss;
it seemed as though they'd been apart for years.
He felt as though he'd climbed from an abyss,
enveloped all at once with the arrears
of joy he'd in seclusion had to miss,
the which profusion nearly caused him tears.
She, turning, said, "There's something I must ask."
Thought he: "The better in your breath to bask."

FOEDORA: Your uncle is the Viscount of Ozon,
or so I've heard. Confirm it, if you care.

VALENTINE: He's not a man I've ever met or known;
it's therefore not a fact I often share.

FOEDORA: You see, I've got an estate on the Rhone;
the title's in dispute—a grim affair.
I wanted to inform you of my need.
Do write to him and ask he intercede.

EMILE: His stomach lurched. Was this the pressing cause
that made him burn his savings for a suit?
He posed the question: Was it? Well, it was.
He, filled with a dejection absolute,
abruptly spilled his heart on all four paws.
Of grace, Foedora found him destitute
and fled—which comes of waxing histrionic,
the surest means of keeping love Platonic.

That very night, he quit Pauline's abode,
and stealthily so's not to say good-bye.
I found him on a bench when first it snowed,
so took him in and offered my supply,
which wasn't grand—my fortunes too had slowed;
I'd lately took to living by the die.

VALENTINE: I thus was introduced to dissipation.

EMILE: Compared to love, a great amelioration.

VALENTINE: Bravo! Enacted brilliantly by all!

AQUILINA: I never thought decay could so intrigue.

VALENTINE: (*After drawing at length from a bottle.*) Be watchful
then, for with encroaching dawn,
my days shall drop like scales from mongered eel!

(*Holds out skin for all to see.*)

This hide purports to give me all I ask,
most notably a cool, reposeful tomb,
agape and ever nearer galloping
the more I test its magnanimity!

CARDOT: Then ask it for the lice I daily host
where most I'd rather other company!

EMILE: And for a toothless concierge's cur!

AQUILINA: A horde of biting rats within the sheets
of such as will not adequately pay!

VALENTINE: (*Draws again at length from bottle. Drops to his knees,
lays down skin, traces outline of skin upon the floor.*) I'll have
Foedora pleading at my feet!
Ah no, I would forget her. I'll instead
content me with a fair annuity
of, say, two million francs. Let it be done!

(*Draws once more at length from bottle, passes out on floor. All becomes
momentarily dark and silent. A gradual, dim light signals the onset of
dawn, revealing the sleeping bodies of all who participated in last night's
bacchanal. A chime sounds repeatedly, awakening only EMILE, who arises
and exits. All but VALENTINE awaken. The chime ceases. EMILE returns
with sealed envelope, awakens VALENTINE, hands envelope to him.*)

VALENTINE: (*Reading enclosed letter.*) "Monsieur de Valentine, we,
the legally vested advocates of the Viscount of Ozon have
determined you to be the only living blood relation of his
recently deceased lordship. You are accordingly the in-
heritor of a thousand acre estate in the Rhone valley, the
Viscount's title, and all proceeds of the late viscount's Indian diamond speculation, payable in lifetime annuities
of two million… "

(*VALENTINE rises off the floor to look upon the skin. It has
receded within the outline he has traced.*)

EMILE: I've never seen a jest turn out prophetic.

AQUILINA: Nor I a lush who woke to sudden wealth.

VALENTINE: I read the skin's inscription self-possessed
and made myself its bondsman unconstrained.
Why then this terror clutching at my maw?
My days are far too wretched to be dear.
And whence this breath of winter at my nape?
If death's my fee, then let it come when due!
I'll not abide this mocking, spectral lurk!

EMILE: But why this sodden ranting, lad? You're rich!
   And titled, too. Be drunk, but merrily.

CARDOT: Mesdames and gents, Viscount de Valentine
   appears to have an odd prodigiousness:
   his wants take form the instant they're conceived!
   He being of a generous dispose,
   we all shall make our sundry wishes known
   and let him each accord with ampleness!

UNNAMED GUEST: I'll have, my dear, some pearlèd finery!

AQUILINA: I'll have a swift and cedar chariot
   conducted by a blood bay pair of steeds!

EMILE: Mere payment of my debts would please me much.

CARDOT: And lower all our rents—your name be praised.

VALENTINE: Cardot, you know the price of what you ask?

EMILE: You're far too glum—they only mean to tease.

CARDOT: And furnish us with duck down pillows, please!

UNNAMED GUEST: And have our nightwear made of tailored
   silk!

AQUILINA: And cover us in fox before the snows!

VALENTINE: Be gone, you fiends of hell! I'll hear no more!

(All retract as if smitten, then disperse.)

VALENTINE: Seclusion may allow me further lease.
   My windows sealed, my doors denying all,
   I'll keep desire distant, languishing,
   and cheat the reaper of all further gain.
   This hide, on a monastic, has no claim.

(CARDOT, assuming the role of VALET, places a cape on VALENTINE's shoulders, a top hat on his head, and a cane within his fist. He then brings out a large armchair in which VALENTINE sits. VALET exits, then returns.)

VALET: An old acquaintance wishes audience.

VALENTINE: As do they all. By no means let him in.

VALET: Demurring to my charge, I said as much,
   then learned he tutored you some thirteen years
   —identifies himself as "Porriquet,"
   insisting you'd except him from your ban.
   But there, I've mouthed his case, I'll send him off.

VALENTINE: Ah, Porriquet… he stated his intent?

VALET: Renewed association, he purports,
   and gives his word he'll nothing else pursue.

VALENTINE: He's little else to offer, I suppose.
  Allow him in. I'll brook a moment's chat.

VALET: You will indeed? I'll bring him straightaway.

(VALET exits, returns with PORRIQUET before again exiting.)

VALENTINE: It's years since last I looked upon you, sir;
  regardless, you're the first aspiring guest
  admitted here since first I was installed.

PORRIQUET: I'd heard about the solitary lord
  who'd bought him the hotel upon this street
  and keeps the windows blind both day and dusk,
  but only lately knew him to be he
  I used to drill in dates and formulae.
  You've kept with your pursuit of poesy?

VALENTINE: No more. My mind has fell to other things.

PORRIQUET: It's true you shun all sociality?

VALENTINE: Since having slipped into nobility,
  I've met with an insidious disease
  that worsens with each kindly splash of sun.
  On this account, I'm rarely elsewhere seen.

PORRIQUET: I'm humbled, then, to be at all received
  and straitly shall address my purpose here:
  My post at a provincial school for boys
  is soon to be eliminated, see,
  and knowing you to be of eminence,
  considered that your intervening hand
  might, if discretion bid you so to act…

(PORRIQUET continues to mouth words and to gesture, but suddenly no sound is heard from him. VALENTINE stands and paces while PORRIQUET continues to inaudibly speak at the chair in front of him.)

VALENTINE: Be wary, Valentine. His tedium
  shall make you wish him out of doors, which wish,
  as wishes must when yours, shall speed the creep
  of unretiring, ever-nearing death.
  The hateful talisman shall see to it,
  this tiger watchful of my every flinch.
  Excite it not. Take patience, hear him out.

(Returns to seat. PORRIQUET becomes audible again.)

PORRIQUET: … You see, therefore, my weighty circumstance,
  the which I'd not fatigue you with, except
  I have a nephew at academy,
  and…

VALENTINE: Sir, I wish you fortune in this cause, and…

> (*Realizing what he has said, his mouth falls agape. He withdraws skin from pocket and finds that it has shrunk considerably.*)

PORRIQUET: You seem in pain; perhaps your illness flares?

VALENTINE: My illness is yourself, you mongrel ape!
> They'll make you Provost now, you need not fear!
> A thousand francs of stipend might you asked,
> or board within an inn—nay, a salon!
> I'd all and more have gave, but no, you beast,
> you had to force a homicidal wish!

(PORRIQUET flees.)

> Distemper more and more becomes my state.
> Perhaps I'll venture out; indeed, I must,
> whatever fatal wistfulness aroused;
> no glad recourse from death is lunacy.
>
> *(To VALET.)*
>
> I'm going to the opera, Jonathas.

VALET: You're certain that your bearing shall persist?

VALENTINE: I doubt it much, but here I soon shall rave.

(VALENTINE leaves, chair is removed by VALET. VALENTINE approaches opera seats. Seats are simultaneously approached by strange WOMAN.)

VALENTINE: Oh Moor, fail not to clamor spittingly,
> my sentimental vicar thus to be
> and lend my inner gnashings some repose.

(He and WOMAN sit beside one another without taking note of each other. A moment lapses.)

VALENTINE: I know when I am haunted without fail
> and know that I am haunted presently,
> but not by that dread hovering to whose
> ill whisperings I've grown unduly used,
> and not by some other thing that oddly soothes…
> I dare not guess it's… could it? Yes! PAULINE!

PAULINE: My Valentine! My tenderness! My brooding Baudelaire!
> I've turned out rich! What mad event, my love!
> Papà, upon his death, bequeathed to me
> the cottage in Chalons for which he'd pined.
> Who'd in their dreams most fevered ever find
> a copper vein so baldly underneath?

I think my loving Lord believes me kind
and placed an over-bounty in my hands
for knowing I'd dispense it liberally.
No use for it have I, my wintry lad—
it's all for orphans' shoes and hospices.
Otello, too, whenever it's on stage.
You're sad, you always are, but cheer, my dove!
I've love enough for legions of your make!

VALENTINE: And I enough for none, I cannot doubt,
      but all I that I shall muster evermore
      is yours to pick or trample as you list.

(The two begin a dance, he leading her while speaking unheard.)

VALENTINE: How came I not to think my fondness love
      when back I lived beneath her every step?
      What gave my addling soul the gross miscue
      of worshipping the cause of its dismay?
      Where came I by such ill economy
      that longing had no worth without a pinch?
      She'll not elude me twice. Count me resolved.

(Now addressing her.)

Tomorrow shall our hearts again be met?

PAULINE: So late? Good then, for patience must be learned.

(They begin to part in separate directions. Once they are significantly apart, she freezes. He withdraws and examines a ring.)

VALENTINE: Too early… ? No. No, too belatedly!

(They turn toward one another and begin slowly walking in one another's direction. He becomes weak, coughing, stumbling, wheezing. The ring falls from his fingers. She freezes. He withdraws the skin and sees it has shrunk tremendously.)

VALENTINE: Well apropos. I've never yearned so much.

(Three personages appear behind him: a BUTCHER, a MAN OF SCIENCE, and a SOOTHSAYER. No words are exchanged in the following interactions. The BUTCHER attempts to hack up skin with cleaver, is unsuccessful; tries to dispose of it in meat grinder, is equally unsuccessful. BUTCHER exits. VALENTINE takes skin to MAN OF SCIENCE, who withdraws corked test tube, shakes it, hands it to VALENTINE. The latter places skin on floor, hurls contents of tube upon it, recoils as if preparing for a blast. Seeing that nothing has happened, VALENTINE shakes his head at MAN OF SCIENCE, who exits. VALENTINE is approached by SOOTHSAYER, who places her hands upon his temples and raises her head with eyes closed. She then, without speaking, in-

structs him to climb a mountain, then exits. VALENTINE climbs moun-
tain with great difficulty, hurls skin off the peak, climbs back down.
Appearing near death, he snaps fingers, signaling for VALET to come,
who does so with a pitcher and glass. VALET tips pitcher to pour. Instead
of liquid, out comes small flap of remaining skin.)

VALET: I know not what. I'll go and bring you more.

VALENTINE: (*Sitting on ground, breathing heavily.*) No, no. Allow
        me, rather, solitude.

VALET: A doctor you shall have. Go nowhere, sir.

(VALET exits. VALENTINE is approached by PAULINE.)

PAULINE: My cherub, you're not well. Where comes this blench?

VALENTINE: To speak or love or look upon you more
        is vanity unto the utter reach;
        my curse is such that ecstasy's mere name
        agrees with me like wrenching arsenic,
        and far more so with you to carry it.

PAULINE: You need a doctor's aid. Be on your back.

VALENTINE: No more! Your words are poignards in each lung!
        Another breath and see me carrion!

(PAULINE picks up flap of skin, examines it, slowly understands.)

PAULINE: There's none but I to save him. I alone.

(PAULINE flees.)

VALENTINE: The struggle ends. Come reaper, hew with ease!
        But wait. Could I not have a last embrace?
        Indeed I can! I've breath within me yet!
        Pauline!

(Looks around him, runs about haltingly, longly gasping. Comes upon
her: she is about to strangle herself with a scarf. He throws himself at her,
crying "No, Love!" She halts, he dies inches from her feet.)

(End.)

HALO

A Pageant
in which a woman looks backwards and forwards at her life,
in which a young man and woman commit a crime,
in which Everyman takes a journey from which she won't return.

Ken Urban

KEN URBAN holds a BA in English from Bucknell University and
an MA in Literatures in English from Rutgers University. His plays
include *Burners*, which was presented in the 1999 New York International Fringe Festival; *Bodies Are Floors* (Screaming Venus Kallisti
Festival, New York City, 2001); *I ♥KANT* (Premiere One Act Festival, Moving Arts, Los Angeles, 2001; also scheduled for production
in May 2002 at the Union Garage, Seattle); *The Absence of Weather*
and *Or Polaroids*, both of which received staged readings in 2001;
and the ten-minute play *My Good Leg*, published in *The Brooklyn
Review* (June 2001). He is also a director as well as a frequent reviewer for nytheatre.com. He has had scholarly articles on theatre
published in *Theatre Journal* and *Performing Arts Journal*. Urban
teaches in the English Department at Rutgers University in New
Brunswick, New Jersey.

Halo was first presented by Screaming Venus Theatre Company (Monica Sirignano, Artistic Director) on August 10, 2001, as part of the New York International Fringe Festival (John Clancy, Artistic Director; Elena K. Holy, Producing Director), with the following cast and credits:

6/Sam	Marilyn Beck
5/Everyman	Deborah Carlson
Daughter/Good Deeds	Ruth Darcy
Sue/Confession	Kelly George
Delivery Man #1/Steve/Talk Show Host	Matthew Lawler
Son/Fellowship/Delivery Man #2	Taylor Ruckel
3/Death	Monica Sirignano
Shadow/Homeless Man/Father Ed	Richard Van Slyke
2/Doctor of Philosophy	Leigh Williams
Brandon/Knowledge	Justin Yorio

Directed by: Jenny Schwartz and Sarah Stern
Lighting: Daniel Jagendorf
Production Manager: Erica Corenblith
Choreographer: Lauren Grant

Halo is for my mom and sister. And as always for Matthew. With love and gratitude.

Thanks to Mac Wellman, David Bucci, Susan Dunlap, Aime Hartman, Dana Lang, Joan Larkin, Julia Barclay, Elin Diamond, Ruth Darcy, and Monica Sirginano for their help and advice during the writing of this play.

CHARACTERS AND STRUCTURE

I-XI: In which a woman looks backwards and forwards at her life

2, a woman in her late 20s
3, a woman in her 30s
5, a woman in her 50s
6, a woman in her 60s
A DAUGHTER, Wendy, never present
A SON, Ken, now departed
A SHADOW OF A MAN, Walter, her husband, their father

A-K: In which a young woman and man commit a crime

BRANDON, a man in his early 20s
SUE, a woman in her early 20s
A DELIVERY MAN, late 40s
ANOTHER DELIVERY MAN, late 20s
STEVE, Brandon's father, late 40s
HOMELESS MAN, possibly 40s, looks older
SAM, Sue's grandmother, late 60s
FATHER ED, Catholic priest, late 40s
TALK SHOW HOST, ageless

i- vi: In which Everyman takes a journey from which she won't return

EVERYMAN, a business woman
DEATH, a normal person
FELLOWSHIP, a frat boy with a career in banking
CONFESSION, a homeless person
KNOWLEDGE, a homeless person
GOOD DEEDS, a gravedigger
A DOCTOR OF PHILOSOPHY, a secret writer of plays

PLACE

All three sections occur in that section of the United States wedged between New York City, Pennsylvania, Delaware, and the end of the world, known as New Jersey.

I-XI: The rooms inside a well-to-do home in Medford, a suburb outside of Philadelphia.

A-K: Various locations in and around Woodbridge, a suburb across the river from Staten Island.

i- vi: Various locations in Northern New Jersey, not far from New York City.

TIME

The last days of the twentieth century.

CASTING

The author suggests that the play's twenty-two characters be performed by an ensemble of ten actors (six women, four men), cast in the following manner:

Women: 2/Doctor; 3/Death; 5/Everyman; 6/Sam; Daughter/Good Deeds; Sue/Confession

Men: Son/Another Delivery Man/Fellowship; Delivery Man/Steve/Talk Show Host; Father (Shadow)/Homeless Man/Father Ed; Brandon/Knowledge

Other arrangements are encouraged.

TEXT NOTE

An * indicates that the following lines or speech begin to overlap at that point. Punctuation is used to indicate delivery.

BRIEF NOTE

This play completes the cycle of plays about New Jersey begun with *I ♥ KANT* and *Nibbler*. (Please contact the author for information about them.) The three sections of *Halo* should be very distinct in style, though the actors will overlap among the three. Think of it as a kind of jigsaw puzzle. The pieces should not, however, ever fully fit; they should just give the sense that they could fit. This is, in many ways, a pageant and should be staged in such a way. The story of the woman is the most obtuse, and this is intentional. Directors shouldn't feel the need to necessarily make everything crystal clear. The truth is that the most opaque things in life are often the most affecting. The story of *Everyman* (ca.1495), a medieval morality play, concerns Everyman preparing his way for a trial with God the Judge, while he looks to his "friends" for comfort. They are of no help. It is only through Confession and Good Deeds that he finds his way to God and Death. Unlike previous medieval dramas which tended to be lighthearted and bawdy, *Everyman* is a sober tale which emphasizes the importance of the priesthood and the sacraments in achieving salvation. The play, it is worth noting, ends before its audience gets to see any dramatic representations of the afterlife or heaven. I have taken great liberties with the play, but I have taken direct passages from the Middle English text and "translated" them into verse.

PLEASE REMEMBER: The setting of the play is crucial. Directors should find a means of creating the specific milieu of these figures.

FINAL PLEA: No symbols where none intended. And no blackouts where none noted.

Anti-natural morality—that is, almost every morality which has so far been taught, revered, and preached—turns, conversely, against the instincts of life: it is a condemnation of these instincts… Life has come to an end where the "kingdom of God" begins.

To derive something unknown from something familiar relieves, comforts, and satisfies, besides giving a feeling of power… First principle: any explanation is better than none.
　　　　　—*Friedrich Nietzsche*, Twilight of the Idols

I + A + i

Nowhere.

Numerous figures in the darkness. The sounds of a densely populated state.

The DAUGHTER, naked, shivering. A voice is heard, but her lips don't move. An older woman's VOICE cries in the dark.

VOICE: I don't want our children to hate you, I don't want our children to hate, Walter, I don't want them to hate you.

(A pizza DELIVERY MAN, shaking. His voice is heard, but his lips don't move.)

MAN: Please, man, c'mon. I ain't got any real money, please.

(A figure, the face of DEATH, a normal person, barely visible.)

DEATH: Lord, I will in the world go over all,
Cruelly search out both great and small,
He that loves riches I will strike with my dart,
His sight to blind,

All that live beastly,
Out of God's laws,
And from heaven they depart,
In hell for to dwell,
World without end.

(A shot. Blackout.)

(Emptiness. From the darkness, a VOICE.)

VOICE: Halo. A Pageant. In which a woman looks backwards and forwards at her life. In which a young man and woman commit a crime.

II

The bedroom.

3: The walks, the walks in the fall

5: The contradiction

6: The weight I was left with

5: When he comes in, the call must end

2: The days when it was all four

3: When the doubts creep in

2: What I was doing was what had to be done

6: Now having reached the end, I can see more

2: I cannot hear this now

3: The weight of that contradiction

5: Neither was what they said the other was

3: Now strengthening my faith, I proceed

2: I mustn't hear what is to come

6: The walks, the walks with my husband in the fall

5: The days past, days still to come

6: What I had done was what must have been

ALL: done.

B

An abandoned house.

SUE: No

BRANDON: Yeah

SUE: No

BRANDON: Yeah

SUE: Howlonghowlonghowlong

BRANDON: 25, 30

SUE: Address?

BRANDON: Here, where else?, God I got one

SUE: No? Now?

BRANDON: Yeah, I got one

SUE: Shit, no shit

BRANDON: Yeah

SUE: Plan?

BRANDON: Y'know, me, front, you, behind the door

SUE: No shit bout address, they don't know it's

BRANDON: No, no shit, he'll be here 25, 30

SUE: Guy knocks

BRANDON: I open, take a step back, hold out money, then

SUE: Then?

BRANDON: Y'know, then

(Beat.)

SUE: Lemme see it, Brandon.

(BRANDON exposes his erection.)

SUE: Never wanted one of those

BRANDON: Feels good

SUE: What I got, that feels a touch more, more sensations

BRANDON: Guess so, don't know, this always feels good, but better when you cum

SUE: The best

BRANDON: 20, 25, now

SUE: Can't believe it, can't believe it

BRANDON: He's the first

SUE: Can fuckin taste it

BRANDON: 20, 25, he'll be here

SUE: The first.

III

The living room.

2: I believe

3: It's not that the other groups are wrong, it's the same goal, different paths

2: The Jews, the Muslims, all of them

5: Jesus loves me this I know cause the Bible tells me so

2: I believe in God, and when I die, I will go to heaven, In God I believe

5: Do you?

6: Of course, we do, this is the constant

3: I have these flickers of doubt

6: I know, I remember them

5: They take my insides out

2: I do not want to hear this

3: I believe that Jesus died for my sins

5: I will not have any more babies

3: There is always faith

6: We didn't want anymore, all that blood, it's better that it's gone

5: I can't feel him inside now

6: We eventually do, the sensations come

5: When I touch down there, I wonder what's taken its place, or if there's just a void, a vessel that made warmth, now only cold

3: I like sex

2: I can't believe I say that

6: We do, we like his penis inside us

5: Warm and pumping, the way he can keep pumping, that's when he is his most warm

2: That's when all men are their most warm

3: That time

6: Do not say that, I cannot believe you'd say this, aloud

3: When he wanted to put it in our—

5: The way that hurt, but felt good

(They all giggle.)

3: And he held you

2: I have never been with another

6: No, we never will be

3: I have a been a good person, I have lived a good life, I have done the best I could for my husband and my children, this is what I have meant to do

5: But what about those moments

6: Close your eyes

5: I see all the things we've lost

3: The things no longer here

5: They are not gone

3: You will be with them again

2: I will be with them again

5: This pain around us now

2: It does not matter the cost

6: There is more than this

3: I will be rewarded

5: I will see my mother

3: Feel God's hand touching you

6: I will be rewarded

5: The split will be healed

2: I will be rewarded

ALL: Amen.

(The SHADOW appears in the living room and remains.)

5: The walks in the fall

3: He would talk to me

6: We'd hold hands, like lovers do

2: I would talk to him

6: I could see he was sad

5: He asked me to sacrifice my first-born

6: The other, in turn, asked me to sacrifice my husband, his father

5: I was waiting for God to give the sign that would stop them both

3: But on our walks

2: Yes, our walks

5: We didn't speak

3: The leaves were turning

6: The leaves were gone

2: The leaves now returning

3: We would walk and everything seemed right in the world

5: A part of me hates him

2: I'm not going to listen *(Leaves.)*

5: The sign, I knew, would come, there'd be no sacrifice, so I thought—I thought wrong.

C

An abandoned house. A pizza DELIVERY MAN stands shaking, food on the floor. BRANDON aims a gun at him, SUE has a gun to his back.

MAN: Please, man, c'mon. I ain't got any real money, please.

BRANDON: Don't want any money.

MAN: I got a kid.

SUE: He's fuckin old.

BRANDON: How old are ya?

MAN: 46.

BRANDON: Sue's right, you're old. This your job?

SUE: Don't fuckin use my name, Brandon—

BRANDON: What's it fuckin matter?

MAN: Please don't. *(Starts to cry.)*

BRANDON: Yes.

(BRANDON shoots the MAN's feet, left then right. The MAN is screaming. Blood.)

MAN: HELP FUCKFUCK HELP…

BRANDON: You drove here, you saw, ain't anyone around.

(The MAN keeps screaming.)

SUE: Can I?

BRANDON: You want it?

SUE: I want it

BRANDON: How much you want it?

SUE: I want it

BRANDON: How much you want it?

SUE: I fuckin want it so bad

BRANDON and SUE: I can taste it in the back of my fuckin

BRANDON: Mouth.

(SUE puts the gun to the MAN's chest.)

(Blackout. A shot.)

IV

The laundry room.

2: Why does he leave?

6: I thought you weren't listening anymore

3: Don't be like that

5: You know why

2: He's only a kid, I don't

3: We always knew

6: Knowing something, and *knowing* something, two different things—the second one, it's a very complicated thing

2: You do what you have to

3: Yes

2: I'm not going to listen

5: What's wrong with you, why are you so naive?

6: Let her be, she still has dreams

5: It's funny, I used to think I was that naive but then I decided I was seeing it all, from here, from the present—I saw naive when it wasn't that at all, wrong again, I was that naive

6: Yes I guess we were, we should let us be

3: Did I really know he was

6: Don't get upset, there's nothing you could've done

3: But of course, there was, I could

5: But you wouldn't, you wouldn't

6: I might have

5: No we wouldn't, we wouldn't have done anything—we didn't—it hurts to see this, but from here, where I am, I can—we didn't really feel that different from his father—we were embarrassed—we were—

6: No

5: Disgusted, we felt, we feel, it wasn't right, that it wasn't

3: I don't want to hear anymore *(Leaves.)*

5: I should think not

6: How can you claim to see more than me, "From here," "From here," where are you?, I'm the one at the end, I'm the one at the door of the great beyond, I'm the one who should be able to see

5: This belief, it simply isn't true

2: So the later years become the bitter years, do they?

6: My son now departed, a daughter never present to me, this is what the years have wrought?

2: In this world, you do what you have to.

D

An abandoned house. BRANDON, wearing yellow rubber gloves, holds the MAN's body. The MAN is still breathing, but it is shallow. Extremely dark now. SUE watches. Her pants are pulled down and she fingers herself.

BRANDON: *(Whispering.)* What do you see? *(Strokes the MAN's face.)* What do you see? Tell me. Whisper it. Here. In my ear. Here. Whisper. *(Puts his ear to the MAN's mouth.)* Can barely hear you. Speak up.

(The MAN dies.)

BRANDON: Barely made out what he said. But I heard enough.

(BRANDON kisses him. SUE shakes with orgasm.)

V

The kitchen. The MOTHER is on the telephone with her SON. The SON is there, but he is not there.

5: My son now departed

SON: Mom, it's me.

3: School's been busy

5: Working late hours

6: Your father, he's been campaigning

2: Report cards, grading

SON: How are things down there?

5: Fine

3: How are things at school?

SON: I've been busy, between

5: Working late hours

6: Your father, he's been

3: That's good

5: Feel a cold coming on, must have caught it from the children, they're always sniffling and sneezing

3: The man who came to check the septic tank told me:

5: Told me, I think I just ruined a marriage

3: At the last place, he found a bunch of condoms clogging the tank. He told her, and she looked at him and she said:

5: But we don't use condoms

3: He didn't know what to say. He told me:

5: I think I just ruined a marriage

SON: I've written a new play

5: Oh, Ken, really?

3: Between teaching and your father, I've been

SON: I want you to come and see it

3: I'm not sure

5: Of course, tell me what's it about

SON: It's called "The Charm of Desire and Regret." It's about

(The SON continues to speak, but he cannot be heard.)

3: Another one

6: My image on stage

5: I cannot bear this

3: My son, he will be remembered

2: He has surpassed me

5: Is this what he thinks of me?, then he must hate me

6: I do not take pills, I do not speak like that, it is not me, me?, no

5: This cannot be, he has left me, leaving this weight with me

(The SHADOW appears in the kitchen.)

5: I have to go, I have to go—

SON: Is he there?

5: Yes

SON: But I don't

5: I have to go

SON: Mom, don't hang up on me

5: I have to go

SON: Have you ever stood up to him, have you ever said no, have you ever, have you? You stupid bitch, I hate you

5: You're just like him

6: Ah, that magical gesture to make him quiet

5: I have to go.

E

An abandoned house. BRANDON, wearing yellow rubber gloves, holds a MAN's body. It is a DIFFERENT DELIVERY MAN, a young man. He has been shot numerous times. The MAN is still breathing, but it is shallow. Extremely dark again. SUE watches. Her pants are pulled down and she fingers herself.

BRANDON: *(Whispering.)* What do you see? *(Strokes the MAN's face.)* What do you see? Tell me. Whisper it. Here. In my ear. Here. Whisper. *(Puts his ear to the MAN's mouth.)*

MAN: I'm… s… s… sorry

BRANDON: Can barely hear you. Speak up.

(The MAN dies. BRANDON kisses him. SUE shakes with orgasm.)

VI

The bedroom. The DAUGHTER enters. She is there.

5: A daughter never present to me

DAUGHTER: Mom?

5: Yes

3: She has grown up

2: Such breasts

3: I wonder if she has sex

DAUGHTER: Mom?

5: Yes

DAUGHTER: I'm ready when you are

5: You are going to come?

3: She is going to come

6: She never lost her faith

2: She is going to come

5: She does not believe

6: Of course, she does

5: She goes with you, but she's never there

3: Of course, she does

6: She's there, so she's there, where else could she be, but there beside me, the same pew, the same line for the host

3: Wendy is going to come

5: She lives with her boyfriend, she lives with him, you know she lives with him, you know he sees her breasts

3: She's there, so she's there, where else could she be, but there beside me

5: She has sex, you took her to the doctor, you tell no one

2: She does believe

(The bedroom is empty except for 5 and DAUGHTER.)

DAUGHTER: Mom?

5: Yes

DAUGHTER: I'm ready when you are.

(A SHADOW appears.)

DAUGHTER: We are all going to go. There and then to breakfast

5: Yes

DAUGHTER: We are all going

5: Yes.

VII

Nowhere.

Numerous figures in the darkness. The sounds of a densely populated state.

3 emerges, naked, shivering. She cries as she speaks.

3: I don't want our children to hate you, I don't want our children to hate you, Walter, I don't want them to hate you.

(Blackout. A slap.)

(Emptiness. From the darkness, a VOICE.)

VOICE: Halo. A Pageant. In which a woman looks backwards and forwards at her life. In which a young man and woman commit a crime. In which Everyman takes a journey from which she won't return.

ii

The play Everyman. *A First Union financial center somewhere in Morris County. EVERYMAN enters. She wears a pink Chanel suit and holds a cell phone. DEATH, a normal person, waits for her.*

DEATH: You must take a long journey,
Before God you shall answer,
Your many bad deeds,
Good but a few,
How have you spent your life?,
For this you must answer.

EVERYMAN: Excuse me.
Unready I am to make such a reckoning,
Death, you come when I had you least in
    mind,
My goods I will give in the thousand,
Defer this matter for another day.

DEATH: Everyman, it may not be.

EVERYMAN: If I take this journey,
should I ever return?

(The financial center is quiet.)

DEATH: No, nevermore.

EVERYMAN: Oh, I see.

F

Kitchen. BRANDON sits, eating cereal. His father STEVE sits near, reading a newspaper.

STEVE: Where's your sister?

BRANDON: Playin with her giner.

STEVE: Sick fuckin world we live in, Brandon, y'know?

BRANDON: *(Mouth full.)* Yeah.

STEVE: Remember the guy went missin, pizza guy? Another's gone.

BRANDON: Yeah.

STEVE: Maybe just ran off. Sick of their wives and kids. Can relate.

BRANDON: Yeah.

STEVE: It don't seem likely though. More like some sick fuck did a number on the two of them.

BRANDON: Yeah.

STEVE: Better be careful out there, lotta fuckin sickos.

BRANDON: Yeah.

STEVE: That all you can say?

BRANDON: Gonna be late for work.

STEVE: Where's your sister?

BRANDON: Fingerin her twat.

(STEVE smacks BRANDON in the face.)

BRANDON: Gonna be late for work.

STEVE: Yeah.

iii

The play Everyman. *The bar of an expensive restaurant in Upper Saddle River. FELLOWSHIP drinks a whiskey. He adjusts his hair and crotch frequently. EVERYMAN finishes another Chardonnay.*

FELLOWSHIP: In faith, Fellowship won't forsake you.

EVERYMAN: Commanded I am to go on a journey,
A long way,
To give a strict account,
Before the Highest Judge.

FELLOWSHIP: Oh.
Tck, Tck, Tck…
Such a journey would cause nothing but pain,
No,
No,
No, No, No.
I'll deliberate here instead, I exclaim.

EVERYMAN: You said you would not forsake me.

FELLOWSHIP: I said so, in truth,
If you go to drink or make good cheer or haunt women with lusty company,
I would not forsake you,
But to that judging place,
…
No.
Fucking.
Way.

EVERYMAN: My heart is sore,
I shall see you nevermore.

(A patron drops a glass and it shatters.)

G

An abandoned house. The two dead bodies lie in a heap. BRANDON and SUE's song-and-dance number. BRANDON and SUE enter, both wearing yellow rubber gloves. The duo sing and dance to a big-band number, such as Louis Jordan and Louis Armstrong's "I'll Be Glad When You're Dead (You Rascal You)" or a similar tune. A HOMELESS

MAN is their attentive audience member.

DANCE and SING,
SING and DANCE,
DANCE,
DANCE,
DANCE!

Before the song is finished, BRANDON and SUE laugh hysterically and fall down. The HOMELESS MAN applauds. They bow. The song continues while BRANDON and SUE drag the bodies over to the homeless man. After a last look, the duo leave the house. The HOMELESS MAN rummages through the pockets of the corpses. The rest of the cast enter during the last section of the song. At first, crazy scat dancing, restrained ballroom, breakdancing, and such. As the song reaches its end, everyone does the gun dance for a big-band conclusion.

The corpses remain.

Blackout.

iv

The play Everyman. *An alley in Newark. EVERYMAN clutches her purse. Two homeless people, CONFESSION and KNOWLEDGE, are smoking crack. They show signs of having full-blown AIDS, and they are missing teeth.*

CONFESSION: I know your sorrow well, Everyman,
Because for Knowledge you came,
I will comfort you as well as I can,
For this journey a precious jewel Confession gives. *(Hands EVERYMAN a knotted scourge.)*

EVERYMAN: Now my penance will begin.

KNOWLEDGE: Look at your penance,
…

What pain it will bring to you.

EVERYMAN: My body sore,
Punished shall it be. *(Drops the purse and scourges herself. First slow, then with increasing violence.)*
My heart is light and shall be ever more,
Now will I smite thee faster than I did before.

(EVERYMAN is bloody. KNOWLEDGE and CONFESSION join in using their own scourges to whip EVERYMAN until she falls. CONFESSION goes through her purse, removing all the money. KNOWLEDGE takes off EVERYMAN's suit, then takes off his rags.)

KNOWLEDGE: The garment of sorrow.

(KNOWLEDGE's rags replace the Chanel on EVERYMAN.)

EVERYMAN: Now I have true contrition,
But friends let us not part.

CONFESSION: A priest's higher than an angel,
To him,
Open your mouth,
Accept in full,
Your heavenly host,
Now suck,
And swallow this
Down
Hole.

(CONFESSION inserts her fingers into EVERYMAN's mouth, as if forcing a bit into a horse's, pulling teeth from the gums. EVERYMAN's mouth bleeds. Then, she is left alone.)

VIII

The living room.

2: The later years are the bitter ones

5: Yes

6: No

5: I have a parable for you: A concentration camp, this Jewish man is on his way to a gas chamber. He hears this terrible screaming and crying as he's forced inside. Just before he enters, he turns to the naked guy behind him and says, "The food here *did* really suck."

2: What kind of thing is that to say?

6: Our departed son sends that to you on your birthday

2: He is a bastard who never believed

(2 is slapped. She cries.)

3: We need to hold out

5: Is that weight of contradiction ever sorted out?

6: Our departed son said we were like that German philosopher who thought that, in history, contradictions are eventually reconciled into one

3: In God, there will be that, a unity with our holy savior

5: It certainly never happens here

6: How would you know? I'm the one at the end

5: I know

2: Does it? I need to know, I haven't wanted to hear but I've heard too much. How does it end? Our departed son tearing me between him and his father. My daughter never present to me fading away the more she stays. This cannot be the way it ends. Please tell me. At the end, is there something that heals that which is to come to me and that which has already come to you?

6: I can't say

2: You can't, you can't! or you won't? Please.

6: I sit at what seems like the end. You think that if only there was a great height from which to survey all that has come before, then you could know, then you could see what you couldn't see before. There is no great height. There is no place devoid of blind spots and darkness. There is no great height.

5: I know this. I haven't made you yet

2: No

3: I haven't made you yet

2: No

5: Things could change, all this weight, I just don't know.

6: No

2: I'm the one at the end

5: Forever and ever, world without end

3: He is the beginning and the end

6: I am the beginning and the end

5: World without end

ALL: Amen.

H

A front porch. SUE and her grandmother SAM sit. SUE smokes.

SUE: On the screen there's this guy. Skinny limbs, empty eyes, and red-wing boots, nuthin else. He's naked, you get me. A swastika tat on his right thigh, no hair to be seen. And he's right there, then another guy's right there. No more screen, and no one moves for awhile, just stand there, looking. Then it's weird, I don't move and he don't, but then the guys are in different places. *(Deep drag.)* His ass's right in the face and the face's right up to the hole. The face just goes for it. He's like giving it to the face and even though it ain't this other guy's thing, it's the skinny one's gift. Mouth opens and the tongue slaps it and slaps it, the hole puckers and lets it in. The thing is, it tastes fuckin great, sweetest thing, pure and warm, the mouth wants more. Hands spread it apart, tongue goes deeper, but it's not enough. Mouth starts biting, gentle bites at first, then harder. Hands hold the ass in place letting it take in bigger and bigger mouthfuls. Taste changes, there's blood, more and more of it. Teeth are breaking through gristle, muscle, skin. Mouth wants more, more bites, savage ones, deep ones. Gore's boilin, slobberin, slidin down the throat. It's my face, my mouth, you get me. It's me. Not a guy, it's me. *(Puts out cigarette.)* I pull out, a face plastered with innards, feces, entrails, and I'm fuckin grinnin. This joy I feel, can't compare, Gram, it can't compare. *(New cigarette.)* Then I wake up. Still happy. Fuckin happy for days. The first thing's made me feel good in awhile. Don't mean nothing though. *(Pause.)* D'you think?

(SAM signs that she would like a glass of water. She is deaf.)

SUE: *(Face close to hers, nodding.)* Sure, Gram. I'll get ya some. *(Getting up.)* You see I learned somethin these last few months and I wanna share it with you before I go. Just cause you do fucked up things, think fucked up things, it don't make you fucked up. In fact, it's what keeps you from being fucked up. All part of the big picture. Still, it's time for me to move on. OK? You understand?

(SAM smiles and nods. SUE kisses her tenderly.)

IX

The kitchen. The MOTHER is on the telephone with her SON. He is there, but he is not there.

SON: I'm giving up, I can't do this anymore

5: I know this is a setback but you can't

SON: No, you don't see

3: Report cards, grading to be done

6: He has had so much, why can't he see

SON: I can't even enjoy it anymore. I watch these shitty plays that've been given these things, productions, awards. I'm bitter. I know my work is better than that. But you didn't give me a trust fund or send me to Yale—

5: We did the best we could

2: He's not even grateful

3: He has so much, why can't he see

SON: I'm sorry, I know you did.

5: I've done the best I could

SON: I've never wanted to turn into this, some two-bit writer, nobody wants to do my plays. A career in community theatre? I'd rather be dead. I turn 30 next year, if it doesn't happen, that's it, I'm not going to do it anymore

5: This is a setback, not an end

2: He will be home soon, must get his dinner ready

3: A long day campaigning

5: Who are you writing for?

SON: What?

5: Who are you writing for?

(He utters a short laugh.)

5: What was that for?

SON: He always says that.

2: He?

3: Yes, he.

5: You always lived for the future, you never noticed what you had now

6: He is the man that he loves

5: When you reach the end, you'll look back and see that this is the moment you've been waiting for, and what if at the end, you realize that, there's nothing after the end

2: He?

3: Yes, he.

5: That the end is just that, the end.

2: I am ended before I even begun

SON: He always says that.

2: I believe.

3: I believe.

6: I believe.

5: I don't know if I believe anymore

SON: I'm still writing. Now.

5: Maybe the now is all there is

SON: I can't keep waiting

2: Waiting? Waiting? What's he mean?

3: We are no longer talking about writing

5: I know you can't

SON: I have to go

5: I know

3: Is he there?

6: Yes, he is there, now

5: I know.

SON: Goodbye, mom

5: Goodbye

3: Don't let him go

SON: I'll call—soon.

5: Yes

2: He's not going to call, can't you see that?

5: Goodbye.

SON: Goodbye. *(Goes.)*

2: You fool, you fool, you let him go, you let him go

6: Our son now departed

3: Our son, you let him go

2: He's ruined our life with filth

3: And you let him

2: He hates us, he hates us

5: I know.

(A SHADOW appears in the kitchen.)

ALL: Your dinner will be on the table in five minutes. How was your day at work? Mine was busy. The children, the children are enraged, can't wait for

2: the *winter

3: the *spring

6: the *summer

5: the fall

ALL: Papers to grade. Reports to fill out. All in time, all in time. You're home so late. Too dark to take a walk, too dark for a walk today.

v

The play Everyman. *EVERYMAN, covered in rags, wanders along the side of the New Jersey Turnpike, near exit 13A. Cars speed past her.*

EVERYMAN: All have forsaken me,
Everyone,
I must be gone,
Debts paid in full,
My time near spent away,
Into His hands,
My soul I commend.

(GOOD DEEDS emerges. She is a gravedigger, the kind whose job consists mainly of collecting highway roadkill.)

EVERYMAN: Good Deeds, my true
    friend I see,
No, not all have forsaken me.

GOOD DEEDS: Be quiet,
I'll command you,
For to never come again.

(GOOD DEEDS pushes EVERYMAN down and begins to shovel dirt onto EVERYMAN.)

EVERYMAN: *In manus tuas, (A cough-ing fit. She spits out dirt and blood.)*
    commendo
        spiritum
            meum

GOOD DEEDS: Shut up and die, fucker.

EVERYMAN: Now have I suffered all I
    shall endure,
Good Deeds shall make all sure,
Now she makes my ending,
Hark, what's this?
Angels, and how they sing.

(EVERYMAN's face is now covered in dirt. GOOD DEEDS finishes and spits on the grave.)

I

A kitchen. BRANDON sits, eating a bowl of cereal. STEVE sits beside him, reading a newspaper.

STEVE: They caught him.

BRANDON: Hmmm…

STEVE: The guy, the one who was killin off all the delivery guys. Some Spic, they caught him.

BRANDON: Oh.

STEVE: Some crazy homeless guy or immigrant. They caught him, with the bodies. Must've lured the guys out there, fake delivery or somethin, and then he killed 'em. Those abandoned houses out by that development that went under, y'know where I mean? Wanted their cash I guess. I guess the pizza too.

BRANDON: Yeah.

STEVE: Must've been hungry. That's good though, they caught the fucker.

BRANDON: Yeah.

STEVE: Should fry the bastard.

BRANDON: Yeah.

STEVE: But they won't.

BRANDON: Yeah. Nope.

STEVE: You late for work?

BRANDON: Our job as proper and decent citizens must be to maintain order and civility by maintaining its borders so that every man has a right to his dream in this country that has taken its place next to God.

STEVE: *(Not hearing him.)* I said you're gonna be late.

BRANDON: Yeah.

STEVE: Wait. Fore you go. Whatta you use in your hair?

BRANDON: What?

STEVE: Gel? Mousse? Spray? Combination? Spray and Gel? Mousse and Spray? Gel and Gel? What?

BRANDON: I don't understand.

STEVE: Don't tell her, OK? But I was thinkin of surprisin her. Takin her somewhere nice. Maybe get a room maybe too. And I wanna look my best, y'know?

BRANDON: I don't understand.

STEVE: I just wanna try somethin new, impress her. Your lady friend obviously likes what you do, don't she?

(Beat.)

BRANDON: I don't get it.

STEVE: I'm just askin.

BRANDON: I just… I just… I mean I don't wash it for a couple of days. And it just stays. Like this.

STEVE: Oh.

BRANDON: I'm gonna get to work. Don't wanna get bitched out.

STEVE: Sure thing. *(Pause.)* Later.

BRANDON: Yeah.

X

The living room. The DAUGHTER sits alone.

DAUGHTER: My brother and I were about nine and eleven. He's older than me, less than two years. Close enough in years to be extremely far apart in life. We decorated the basement. We used to play school, we wanted to be teachers like our mother. We'd grade imaginary papers, make imaginary bulletin boards and paste things on the walls. Dad saw what we'd done one day. We weren't even there, we were upstairs watching TV, doing home-work, it was Sunday. He screamed and slapped Mom. Started ripping things down, knocking our stacks of old text-books over. He wanted to know why she hadn't watched us. We were sent to bed. My brother came to sleep with me. We huddled together while we heard them cleaning, steaming the stuff off the walls. My mother was crying. The whole house could hear it, sound propelled up vents. Then they came upstairs. We pretended to be asleep. All my mom kept saying was: I don't want our children to hate you, I don't want our children to hate you, Walter, I don't want them to hate you. Ken whispered in my ear: I'm going to leave and never come back. My brother did. I hate him for it. Now my mother and I have to suffer. I'm getting married to a boy I met in high school. My mother met my father in high school too, the same high school actually. Weird, isn't it? We take walks in the park. Sometimes he asks me about my brother. I talk to him about it and stuff, but I don't say much. Eventu-ally, I want to have kids, but I have a ca-reer now. *(Pause.)* My brother isn't even going to come to the wedding.

J

A field. BRANDON and SUE are working on a second six-pack.

SUE: You ever feel guilty?

BRANDON: No.

SUE: Me neither. Don't never think of it.

BRANDON: Seems like a long time ago.

SUE: You believe in God?

BRANDON: No. But there's somethin out there, some kind of higher power. Yeah.

SUE: Yeah, probably. Somethin. Me too.

BRANDON: Actually feel good, y'know, proud.

SUE: Same.

BRANDON: There was somethin holy bout doin it, religious.

SUE: Y'think?

BRANDON: Yeah. Like looking into God's face.

SUE: Made me feel good. But now I've done it, don't wanna do it again.

BRANDON: No, course not. Not a fool, they got the guy, ain't gonna go to jail. You ever tell anyone?

SUE: No. Yeah.

BRANDON: Who?

SUE: A priest. Guess after the first one, felt guilty. I went to one to confess. After we stopped. After the second one, I guess. No big deal.

BRANDON: What he say?

SUE: Should turn myself in, ask God's forgiveness, usual shit.

BRANDON: How you do that?

SUE: Just ask. I did. That was that. I for-got about it. Don't feel nuthin. Just did it. Then, sin's gone.

BRANDON: Me neither. Don't feel nuthin.

SUE: Got a new job.

BRANDON: Cool.

SUE: What they say?

BRANDON: What?

SUE: What they say before they kicked?

BRANDON: Nuthin really, just made sounds. A gurglin sound. Prayin or somethin.

SUE: I'm moving.

BRANDON: Where?

SUE: Cause of the new job, I'm gettin outta Jersey.

BRANDON: Cool.

SUE: We're like saints. It's purified me or somethin.

BRANDON: Holy.

SUE: I close my eyes, I see God. And he loves me.

BRANDON: Cause the Bible tells me so. Yeah.

SUE: If people knew, they'd think we sick. But we're not. Cause we believe. *(Pause.)* You gonna miss me?

BRANDON: Yeah.

SUE: Me too.

BRANDON: Do you think it's weird that we never... y'know... I mean that we never—

SUE: We did something better, man. Brought us far closer than just doing that. I mean our parents do that shit.

BRANDON: Yeah. *(Pause.)* You think we could though, just once, before you split Jersey?

SUE: No.

BRANDON: You're right. *(Pause.)* Could I maybe watch you finger your—

SUE: No. Ain't turned on.

BRANDON: I am. I got one.

SUE: OK. Wanna watch you.

BRANDON: OK. Cool. *(He tries to masturbate for SUE, but he cannot do it.)* Sorry... I just can't... I can't *(He turns away.)*

SUE: Hey. Look at me.

(BRANDON turns. SUE sticks her hand in her pants. She removes her hand and then puts a finger in BRANDON's mouth. BRANDON tastes her. BRANDON forces her hand on his growing erection. SUE resists. BRANDON turns away. Eventually, BRANDON gets hard again. This time, SUE decides to touch his penis. BRANDON's hand touches SUE's as it strokes him. His other hand touches her tenderly.)

SUE: Miss me.

BRANDON: Miss me too.

XI + K + vi

These sections overlap.

The play Everyman. *The side of the New Jersey Turnpike. A DOCTOR OF PHILOSOPHY stands on the grave of EVERYMAN, holding a book entitled* Halo.

DOCTOR: These moral men may have in mind,
At the last all do every man forsake,
Save for Good Deeds,
But beware for if they be small,
Before God they hath no *help at all.

(The bedroom.)

3: The walks, the walks in the fall

SON AS 5: The contradiction

6: The weight I was left with

SON AS 5: When he comes in, the call must end

DAUGHTER AS 2: The days when it was all four

3: When the doubts creep in

DAUGHTER AS 2: What I was doing was what had to be done

6: Now having reached the end, I can *see more

(A church rectory.)

FATHER ED: You ever molested?

BRANDON: No.

FATHER ED: Your parents alcoholic?

BRANDON: No.

FATHER ED: You ever molested?

SUE: No.

FATHER ED: Your parents alcoholic?

SUE: My dad, he sometimes drank *a bit.

(The living room.)

DAUGHTER AS 2: I cannot hear this now

3: The weight of that contradiction

SON AS 5: Neither was what they said the other was

3: Now strengthening my faith, I proceed

DAUGHTER AS 2: I mustn't hear what is to come

6: The walks, the walks with my husband in the fall

SON AS 5: The days past, days still to come

6: What I had done was what must have *been done.

(A church rectory.)

FATHER ED: You ever molested?

BRANDON: This uncle—

FATHER ED: Your parents alcoholic?

BRANDON: Yes, Father Ed, they drank—

FATHER ED: You ever molested?

SUE: This man, Father Ed, at the daycare center—

FATHER ED: Your parents alcoholic?

BRANDON: Yes, they were awful—

FATHER ED: Brandon, you played violent video games, you weren't raised in a faith, you were molested by your uncle, you are a repressed homosexual, you hate your father, you do not know God, I know your truth. Sue, your mother was overbearing, you weren't raised in a faith, you were molested by a man, you're an oversexed cunt, you hate your father, you do not know God, I know your *truth.

(The laundry room.)

ALL: Forgive me father for I have sinned, It has been

DAUGHTER AS 2: 2 months

3: 6 months

SON AS 5: 9 years

6: 1 day

ALL: Since my last *confession.

(The set of a TV talk show. BRANDON, FATHER ED, and SUE sit on comfy chairs. The TALK SHOW HOST holds a microphone into which BRANDON and SUE speak.)

TALK SHOW HOST: *(To BRANDON and SUE.)* Tell them what you told me during the commercial break.

BRANDON: The reason I did what I did are the following:

SUE: Not being raised in a proper loving family environment,

BRANDON: subjection to abuse at the hands of my cold father who did not provide me with the suitable amounts of affection and support needed by a male of my age,

SUE: listening to music that extols the virtues of the devil and the meaninglessness of life,

BRANDON: the playing of video games which has desensitized me to the true horror of gun violence and death,

SUE and BRANDON: etc., ad infinitum, Amen.

TALK SHOW HOST: *(To FATHER ED.)* You heard that, yes?

FATHER ED: All is *redeemed.

(The play Everyman. *The side of the New Jersey Turnpike. The DOCTOR remains on the grave of EVERYMAN.)*

DOCTOR: Thus endeth the moral play
    of *Everyman*,
But being not only a doctor,
But a writer too,
I have written, previous to you, some text
Which, in conjunction with you, we have
    now made,
A lesson learned,
A message since conveyed,
This now finished,
Seems fit then to end this play—

(Before the DOCTOR completes the thought, EVERYMAN's hand lurches from the grave and grabs the DOCTOR. The DOCTOR screams and screams. All of the characters begin to sing "Ave Maria." SUE and 6 are transformed into saints, tortured and magnificent, while the DOCTOR and FATHER ED are murdered and eaten. Wide open spaces. Mini-malls. Toll booths. Tax cuts. The future. No future. Final tableau.)

(Blackout.)

(End of play.)

AN AFTERWORD

"Why do you [Ken Urban] write plays?"

I once thought that the most pressing question facing artists revolved around a work's impact on an audience: Should art comfort or challenge? I saw my own work through this lens, always placing myself firmly on the side of wanting theatre to challenge its audiences. The art I enjoyed, the music I listened to, the novels that turned me on sprang from an aesthetic sensibility that defied or subverted the expected. I now feel, however, that we have reached an endpoint with "offending the audience," to borrow Peter Handke's apt title. When audiences crowd into galleries, theatres, and shows, gleefully anticipating titillation, subverted expectation is the only expectation. To avoid succumbing to cheap sensationalism, young theatre artists need to go beyond this notion of art-as-challenge-to-the-status-quo, but without giving into the comforting temptations that theatre-as-live-TV provides.

That the theatre is in a state of crisis is hardly a surprise, but its crisis is more dire than that of other creative media, such as painting or poetry. Theirs is a crisis of an expiration date perceived to have passed. Theatre's problem is not that it is outmoded. It suffers from the opposite problem, overexposure: It's everywhere. From the hallowed halls of the presidency down to our trips to the local shopping mall, the world is an endless testament to a theatrical imperialism. To some degree, this may always have been the case, as Shakespeare's Jaques informed us centuries ago. But never before has the over-theatricalization of culture been so ubiquitous. This creates a real need in playwrights to look inward at what makes theatre different from other art forms. Playwrights need to explore the theatre-ness of theatre and to create plays that draw from its quizzical nature. The eternal "What for?" needs to be conjoined with the "Why theatre?" Each play needs to answer this inquiry in ways that speak to theatre's innate weirdness. There is a room; there are chairs in that room; for a number of hours every night, that room becomes a theatre. Playwrights are indebted to the bodies filling those chairs. That debt need not be paid with comfort or confrontation. Rather, audiences should be treated to a constant reminder of theatre's unusual workings. Strangers come together in this place for that most prurient of activities: to watch other strangers do strange dirty things in strange dirty windowless rooms. Every time I sit down to write a play, I take as my starting point what a weird thing theatre is. I write with a sense of wonder and I hope it's contagious. But with that wonder comes the realization that an infection's effects on the body and mind are not necessarily pretty. If the theatre bug's bite hurts, then I hope that "it hurts so good," to quote Freud (via John Cougar Mellencamp).

"Why do you [Ken Urban] write plays?"

Imagine a play with two characters, one white person and one a person of color. (In the U.S., person of color tends to translate into black.) They are having a mundane conversation which, because of art's dictates, quickly turns heated. Inevitably, the white person says something racist. On cue, the audience, which is primarily white, makes an audible gasp. I doubt it takes much imagination to hear this play in your mind's eye, to imagine the stifled sounds that echo throughout a downtown theatre. Anyone who has set foot in a theatre in the last few decades has seen a variation of this theme. Mind you, there is nothing wrong with such a theme, though in truth, to realize that a majority of white culture remains racist is a surprise to no one except, perhaps, white culture. What is far more insidious in these plays is precisely the way that white culture (including myself) is let off the hook: "Did you hear what a stupid thing that (white) character said? Thank God, I'm not like that." The feigned surprise is really a sigh of relief. We have been exonerated. This is what the *theatre of consensus* does; its moral heart is that of a terrorist's, for there is no room for disagreement. The audience, the actors, the writer, the director, the theatre of consensus presumes we are all in on the joke. This theatre places our heels firmly on the moral high ground: We are not like that, we do not speak like that. Thus, we leave the theatre feeling better about ourselves, our world views confirmed. And if by some chance, you don't feel this same way, consensus places you outside the norm, and you have been effectively silenced. This kind of theatre sucks the vitality of conversation and debate from the world. If you are a person of color, and feel the audience's disingenuous sounds weighing in on you, you keep quiet for fear of looking hysterical. If you don't feel that any racial issue is reducible to a cheap and well-meaning joke, you keep quiet because it is not cool to side with a character perceived to be racist by the rest, and should you not simply dismiss such a character, your credentials become suspect.

Feeling good is a privilege we haven't yet earned. But to choke on guilt and despair is nothing but self-congratulation in a black turtleneck. To feel sickened, to feel comforted, to feel lost, to feel these things at the same time, this is what a *theatre of dissensus* desires: To have the person sitting next to you laughing as you weep. To place yourself morally above a reprobate character one moment, only to find yourself implicated in that same impiety the next. To not know who the writer wants you to "identify" with or with what politics she or he is aligned. That is dissensus. It is not so much an end point as a guiding force which one can occasionally achieve for a brief moment. But in those moments of complete uncertainty when the ground slips beneath our feet, we experience a *vital theatre*, a theatre that lives within us and that we need to live. "Let us wage war on totality; let us be witnesses to the unpresentable; let us activate the differences and save the honor of the name" (Jean-François Lyotard). The name I seek to honor is that of theatre and I write to wage war and bear witness at the same moment: a contradiction without a reconciliation in sight. Why turn two into one, when you can have three as more?

"Why do you [Ken Urban] write plays?"

Theatre should eat me, but it should also *not* eat me insofar as it should also feed me. With that in mind, theatre should be naughty, very naughty, but on occasion, it should dish out a little goodness, perhaps as a side dish or an after-dinner mint you pop in the mouth as you leave the place. Theatre should feed me and be good, but it also must eat me and be naughty, very naughty. To that end, the theatre should pay me. But usually the theatre steals from me. It steals all my clothes and dresses me in lavender. I'm not fond of lavender, and at some point, I will want all my stuff back, but for now, this will do. All this leads me to believe that theatre is really nothing. No thing. Not a goddamn thing. But nothing is more real than nothing, my friend. And so won't somebody eat me? At least, feed me. I'm cheap. Hence, I am a playwright. Poor bastard me.

SHYNESS IS NICE

Marc Spitz

MARC SPITZ holds a BA in creative writing from Bennington College, class of 1992. He is a senior contributing writer at *Spin Magazine*, and is the co-author of *We Got the Neutron Bomb: An Oral History of Los Angeles Punk Rock* (Three Rivers Press, 2001). His other plays include *Retail Sluts*, *The Rise and Fall of the Farewell Drugs*, *"...Worry, Baby,"* and *"I Wanna Be Adored."* He lives in New York City.

Shyness is Nice was first produced by Westbeth Theatre Center (Arnold Engelman, Producing Director) in association with PANIC, Publicity Outfitters and Kirsten Ames, on May 3, 2001, at Westbeth Theatre Center, New York City with the following cast and credits:

Stew .... Zeke Farrow
Rodney .... Andersen Gabrych
Blixa .... Sibyl Kempson
Fitzgerald .... Jonathan Lisecki
Kylie .... Camille Shandor

Directed by Jonathan Lisecki
Stage Manager: Rebecca Schraffenberger
Set Design: Andromache Chalfant
Costume Design: Jackie Baer
Lighting Design: Jonathan Lisecki
Sound Design: Megan Moore

EDITOR'S NOTE: The text of *Shyness Is Nice* includes references to various songs and recordings. Persons intending to use these songs and recordings in actual performance should contact the copyright holders for permission and/or royalty information.

CHARACTERS

RODNEY: A 30-year-old virgin with a great record collection.
STEW: A similar virgin.
FITZGERALD: A brand-new junkie.
KYLIE: An Australian prostitute.
BLIXA: An Australian pimp.

TIME

Present.

SETTING

New York City.

The title comes from the first verse of the Smiths' song "Ask."

Lights up on spare apartment. Couch, coffee table, two chairs, rug. Lots of books and records. RODNEY and STEW sit on the couch, both wearing cardigans and Smiths t-shirts.

RODNEY: I've got the light.

STEW: What light?

RODNEY: The hot light behind my eyes. Can you see it?

STEW: *(Looking, long, hard.)* No.

RODNEY: Look.

STEW: I am looking.

RODNEY: I have it. All artists have it.

STEW: I can't see it.

RODNEY: Really?

STEW: No.

(Long pause.)

RODNEY: Shit.

(Long pause.)

STEW: Come into the corner. Maybe the bulb's absorbing it.

RODNEY: Oh, okay.

(They move into the corner. STEW stares into RODNEY's eyes.)

STEW: Hmm. No. I still can't see it.

RODNEY: I saw it last night.

STEW: Really?

RODNEY: I was staring into the mirror and I totally saw it.

STEW: Maybe you were an artist last night. What were you doing?

RODNEY: Nothing.

STEW: Nothing?

RODNEY: No, I was in a chat room for a while. I made some dinner.

STEW: Oh, what'd you make?

RODNEY: Vegetables.

STEW: Oh. *(Beat.)* What kind?

RODNEY: Mushrooms.

STEW: Oh.

RODNEY: Broccoli. Sometimes I melt cheese on top of it.

STEW: Oh yeah?

RODNEY: Yeah. *(Long beat.)* Sometimes. When I'm feeling crazy.

STEW: What kind of cheese?

RODNEY: That's kind of personal.

STEW: Right.

(Lights down.)

(Lights up. FITZGERALD stands center stage, looking alarmed. He wears a shiny black suit, spiked hair. His small apartment is littered with books and records, mostly jazz and Beat literature. He is frantically searching for something while suppressing a severe asthma attack. The phone rings. It rings and rings again. He stops, tries to calm his breathing. Walks over to the record player and puts on some jazz. Lights a cigarette. Pauses. Finally, he picks it up.)

FITZGERALD: *(Super cool voice.)* This is Fitzgerald. *(Quick beat/long pant/complete crack in cool façade.)* Hello? *(Beat.)* Mommy? *(He extinguishes the smoke, takes the record off the turntable.)* Help me, Mommy. *(More panting.)* I can't find it. My inhaler! Listen to me! *(Wheezes.)* I'm having an attack. *(He continues to search while panting into the phone, finds some porno mags under pillows.)* Mommy! Can you help me, please? Well, bring me a new one. I know you're on Long Island, but I'm dying. I am *too* dying. I can't breathe. Please? I'm very scared. *(Beat/call waiting.)* Oh, wait. Hang on. *(He places the needle on the jazz again. Relights the cigarette. Regains cool. Smooth/cool.)* This is Fitzgerald. *(Beat.)* Mom? Shit, hang on. *(Clicks the receiver madly/smooth cool voice.)* Fitzgerald. Who? Blixa. Yeah, I remember you. Shit, baby, it was just last night. Yeah I'm still interested in the deal. Say what? Oh, yeah. No problem. Leave it to me. As long as you're cool, I'm cool. Don't worry bout it. Yeah, ha ha. You know it. Alright. Alright. Ciao, baby. *(Clicks/wheezes.)* Mommy? *(Extinguishes cigarette. Continues to rummage. Finds pill bottle. Unscrews it. Swallows pills.)* No, Mommy, I'm not going over there. No, Mommy, Aunt Susan scares me. No, Mommy, I'm not doing that either. No! Have you ever tried to wait on line for anything at CVS? No, Mommy. Mommy, will you let me talk? Will you please let me talk? Will you… will you let me… Thank you. *(Swallows more pills.)* I'm fine. I'm fine. No… it wasn't an asthma attack. No. It was a panic attack. Okay. Okay. No. Alright. I will. I promise. Okay. Mommy? Will you send me some food? Thanks. I love you too. Night night. *(Clicks receiver/lights cigarette/changes again.)* This is Fitzgerald! Hey, what's shakin' baby? Me? Just doing my thing. Yeah. Hey, dig this, right?. I got a major surprise for you. Yeah, yeah, the both of you. Shit, man if I spilled over the phone, it wouldn't be a major surprise, now, would it. Alright. Yeah, I'll meet you there. Be cool. Me? Always cool, baby, you know that. *(Beat/anger.)* I am too. I *am not* talking funny. Fuck off. Maybe I won't come over, Rodney. *(Beat.)* Alright… but watch it. *(Hangs up phone.)* Yeah, you better watch your ass. *(Paces apartment. Puts on shades.)* Or I'll… kick it.

(Lights down.)

(Lights up on RODNEY and STEW's apartment. FITZGERALD staggers in.)

FITZGERALD: Alright, alright. I've got one for you. Get ready.

RODNEY: Hi Fitzgerald.

STEW: Hi Fitzgerald.

FITZGERALD: Are you fuckin' ready?

RODNEY: I don't know?

FITZGERALD: I said are you cats fuckin' ready?!

(They stare.)

STEW: I'm ready.

(Long pause. Suspense.)

FITZGERALD: Hang on. I'm not ready. I gotta use the john.

RODNEY: Oh. You know where it is.

(FITZGERALD exits.)

RODNEY: Have you noticed?

STEW: Totally. You've noticed right?

RODNEY: What's wrong with him?

STEW: Maybe he's going through a phase.

RODNEY: Do you think he thinks we think he's cool?

STEW: Yeah. Ha ha.

RODNEY: But we don't right?

STEW: I don't know. He's kind of cooler. Don't you think?

RODNEY: I don't know. The smoking thing kind of worries me.

STEW: And the heroin thing.

RODNEY: Yeah.

STEW: The heroin thing kind of worries me.

RODNEY: Yeah. The heroin thing kind of worries me too.

STEW: You know he gave me all his Smiths records the other day.

RODNEY: Really?

STEW: Yeah, and all his cardigan sweaters.

RODNEY: Score.

STEW: And like three Judy Blume books.

RODNEY: *Forever?*

STEW: Yeah. I already have it.

RODNEY: Yeah.

STEW: But now I have two in case I lose one.

RODNEY: Yeah.

(FITZGERALD reenters.)

FITZGERALD: That was the cleanest motherfucking toilet I ever seen, ha ha.

RODNEY: Um… thanks.

FITZGERALD: Alright, alright, alright… I hired a prostitute to have sex with the both of you. *(Calling offstage.)* Kylie!

KYLIE: *(Enters.)* Hi.

(Long beat.)

STEW: Hi.

RODNEY: Hi.

(Long beat.)

KYLIE: You mind if I have a drink first?

STEW: No. I don't mind.

(Long beat.)

FITZGERALD: Offer her a fucking drink, man.

STEW: Oh. Okay… man. Would you like a drink? Something to drink?

KYLIE: I'd love one.

(STEW exits.)

KYLIE: Thanks.

(STEW returns with a bottle and a glass. Pours some booze.)

STEW: Here.

KYLIE: Thanks.

RODNEY: Do you want to hear some music?

KYLIE: Okay.

RODNEY: What would you want to hear? I mean, what do you want to hear?

KYLIE: Oh, I like all kinds of music.

RODNEY: Really?

KYLIE: Sure.

RODNEY: Me too. Well, lots of kinds of music.

KYLIE: Great.

RODNEY: Have you heard the new Mogwai album?

KYLIE: No. What kind of music is that?

RODNEY: They're from Scotland. I'm not sure where.

KYLIE: Great.

RODNEY: I can find out.

KYLIE: Great.

RODNEY: You wanna hear that?

KYLIE: Great.

RODNEY: Okay, I'll play that.

(RODNEY returns with a vinyl copy of the new Mogwai album. Hands it to KYLIE.)

RODNEY: This is Mogwai.

KYLIE: Wow.

RODNEY: Yeah. You can check it out. You can even borrow it too. But careful. Don't get them wet… right? Ha ha.

KYLIE: What?

RODNEY: Don't get them wet? Cause… um…

FITZGERALD: Shut the fuck up, Rodney, man.

RODNEY: Okay.

STEW: If you want a refill, Kylie… I mean, when you're done, I've got the bottle right here. Just ask. Or, you know, you don't have to ask. You can just pour it yourself, or ask me to pour it for you. And I will.

(Long beat.)

KYLIE: Thanks. Stew.

STEW: *(Giggling.)* You know my name.

KYLIE: Fitzgerald told me your names. You're Stew and that's Rodney, right?

RODNEY: Right. I'm Rodney. *(Long beat.)* That's Stew.

KYLIE: I'm Kylie.

RODNEY: Hi Kylie.

KYLIE: Hi Rodney.

(Long beat.)

STEW: Hi Kylie.

KYLIE: Hi Stew.

(Long beat. FITZGERALD sits on the couch, opens his coat, pulls out a rig and a glassine bag.)

FITZGERALD: I'm gonna get incredibly high. You cats don't mind.

STEW: Just... don't squirt blood onto the ceiling like you did last night, okay?

RODNEY: We had to borrow a ladder to clean it off.

STEW: It was a pain.

RODNEY: A total pain. Ha ha. *(Long beat.)* Ha.

KYLIE: Can I use your restroom, please?

RODNEY: Yes.

KYLIE: Great.

(Long beat.)

FITZGERALD: It's down the hall. Left hand side.

KYLIE: Thanks.

(KYLIE exits.)

STEW: *(To FITZGERALD.)* Seriously, don't squirt the blood up there again, okay?

RODNEY: She's a prostitute?!!!!

FITZGERALD: Yeah.

RODNEY: That's the surprise!?

FITZGERALD: Aren't you surprised?

STEW: Well... yeah.

RODNEY: Um, who's paying for this. This costs money, right?

FITZGERALD: I am. It's paid for. No worries.

RODNEY: Cause I can't pay for it.

FITZGERALD: You don't have to.

RODNEY: I just bought all those Dusty Springfield reissues.

STEW: And the Joy Division box set.

RODNEY: And the Joy Division box set.

FITZGERALD: Fucking is better than the Joy Division box set.

STEW: I don't know. It's pretty great.

FITZGERALD: Fucking is better.

RODNEY: We know why you're acting this way. Saying these things.

FITZGERALD: So.

RODNEY: Just don't think we don't know... cause we know. We figured it out.

FITZGERALD: Like I said... so.

RODNEY: You're going though some kind of turning thirty crisis.

FITZGERALD: What do you know about it?

RODNEY: A little. I'm going through crisises.

FITZGERALD: You don't know shit. Cause if you did, you wouldn't be pussy-footing around this ideal fucking situation like you are. You'd be thanking me for bringing you this beautiful whore to bang. So shut the fuck up and be a man like me... instead of a scared little bitch boy!

RODNEY: Please stop shouting. And please, just call her a prostitute. If my mother knew I was sleeping with whores... she'd... she'd... I don't even want to think about it.

FITZGERALD: Don't tell her.

RODNEY: I just feel like she'd find out somehow.

FITZGERALD: Fuck your fat ass mother. That woman made you a fucking mess. I'm telling you you're perfectly fine. All you gotta do is start fucking. The best thing you can do for yourself right now is to fuck that whore.

RODNEY: I don't think so.

FITZGERALD: If you don't fuck that whore, I'm gonna hit you Rodney. Right now, I'm gonna punch you in the face. I paid three hundred dollars for that bitch to de-virginize your shit.

RODNEY: You didn't… tell… her…

FITZGERALD: Yes, I told her.

RODNEY: Oh, Jesus. Oh, no. Really?

FITZGERALD: Yes.

RODNEY: Why?

FITZGERALD: Why not?

RODNEY: Cause… it's… it's not… *(Long beat.)* cool… it's not. I mean, I know it's not.

FITZGERALD: She was extremely excited, for your information. Touched even. I think she got misty. Now, you got me all upset. I gotta shoot up now cause of you. Go get me a Q-Tip.

(RODNEY exits without further prodding. Returns quickly with a Q-Tip.)

STEW: You didn't tell her about me.

(FITZGERALD pulls off the Q-Tip cotton. Begins to fix himself.)

FITZGERALD: I did.

STEW: Why?

FITZGERALD: Because you are, motherfucker. You're a cherry.

STEW: I told you, I'm not… not technically.

FITZGERALD: You're a cherry.

STEW: I've had sex.

FITZGERALD: Bullshit.

STEW: Not… penetration… .

FITZGERALD: Penetration is kind of an important part of the experience called sex, Stew. Get me a glass of water.

STEW: Oh, okay. Do you want ice?

FITZGERALD: No, I don't want ice. Get me a fucking glass of water so I can shoot up.

STEW: Oh. *(Exits.)*

(FITZGERALD rolls up his sleeves.)

RODNEY: What's she doing in there?

FITZGERALD: How the fuck should I know?

RODNEY: You don't think she's going through the medicine cabinet, do you?

FITZGERALD: Maybe.

RODNEY: Oh.

(STEW returns. Hands FITZGERALD the glass of water and a bottle of Red Cheek apple juice.)

STEW: I brought you some Red Cheek apple juice too since you're not gonna drink the water, right? Ha ha.

FITZGERALD: Right. *(He takes the apple juice, throws it behind the couch, and continues to fix.)*

STEW: What's she doing in there? *(Beat.)* You don't think she's going through the medicine cabinet do you?

RODNEY: She's pretty.

STEW: She is pretty.

RODNEY: She's Australian?

FITZGERALD: Their pussies're the same Down Under, Rodney.

RODNEY: I know that.

FITZGERALD: *(Pulls out a lighter, cooks his spoon.)* They don't swirl your dick around counter clockwise or nothing. *(Taps his vein.)*

RODNEY: They... they swirl your... they swirl it around?

STEW: I think so, yeah.

FITZGERALD: Shut the fuck up. You'll find out.

(Beat.)

STEW: Thanks again for the Smiths records, Mike.

FITZGERALD: Fitzgerald. I told you, call me Fitzgerald.

STEW: Sorry. Thanks again, Fitzgerald.

FITZGERALD: Forget about it.

STEW: Okay. It's just... you know, I could never find *The World Won't Listen* on vinyl. I mean a lot of the same stuff is on *Louder Than Bombs*, of course, which is kind of easy to find but *The World Won't Listen*, that's... that's a...

RODNEY: It's a good thing to have.

STEW: Totally good to have. And to play.

FITZGERALD: No... I mean, forget about it.

STEW: Oh... okay.

FITZGERALD: Shit.

(He continues preparing to shoot up. RODNEY and STEW hide their eyes. KYLIE enters. FITZGERALD shoots himself up. Lolls his head back rapidly, high as a kite.)

FITZGERALD: Shit.

RODNEY: So... how did you guys meet?

KYLIE: Oh, he phoned my agency I suppose.

RODNEY: Oh... cool.

KYLIE: Don't worry. It's all paid for.

STEW: Great.

KYLIE: We can start whenever you like.

STEW: Great.

FITZGERALD: Oh, shit.

RODNEY: Don't mind him. He's just...

KYLIE: I know what he's doing, Rodney. I'm foreign but I'm not stupid.

STEW: Oh, you're *not foreign*.

(Long beat.)

STEW: I mean, you're great. I... I think you're great.

KYLIE: Thanks, Stew. So... shall we begin?

(KYLIE removes her coat. RODNEY takes it.)

RODNEY: I'll hang this up.

(KYLIE removes her dress, stands in her bra and panties.)

RODNEY: I... I can hang that up too... if you want.

FITZGERALD: Oh, shit... Mommy?

STEW: Did Fitzgerald just say "Mommy?"

RODNEY: I think he said "Mommy."

STEW: Do you think he sees his Mom?

FITZGERALD: I don't see my fucking Mom.

STEW: You said "Mommy."

FITZGERALD: *(Gets into a reclining position on the couch.)* Would you just go feel good. Go help yourself feel good. Go be cool for fuck's sake.

KYLIE: Which one of you would like to go first?

RODNEY: First?

KYLIE: Well, you can both go at the same time if you like?

(RODNEY and STEW stare at each other.)

RODNEY and STEW: No.

FITZGERALD: Where are my cigs? *(He rises, sways, falls back.)*

RODNEY: Are you sure you're okay, Fitzgerald?

FITZGERALD: I'm fine. Go fuck.

RODNEY: Oh, okay.

KYLIE: Where's the boudoir?

STEW: Mine or his?

KYLIE: Whomever wants to start?

(STEW and RODNEY stare at each other.)

RODNEY: You start.

STEW: Are you sure? I mean you can start if you want. I can wait.

FITZGERALD: He's waited thirty years. Ha ha… *(Holds head.)* Shit.

KYLIE: Why don't we have a party. All three of us.

(KYLIE pulls STEW and RODNEY close to her body. They're sheepish but visibly excited by her warmth and strangeness.)

RODNEY: Okay. *(To STEW.)* I mean, if it's okay with you.

STEW: It's okay with you?

RODNEY: Yeah. Is it okay with you?

(Long beat.)

STEW: Yeah. I guess. *(To KYLIE.)* Is it okay with you?

KYLIE: Yes. I suggested it.

STEW: Okay.

(KYLIE removes her bra and panties. Takes their hands, leads them offstage. KYLIE kisses RODNEY deeply. RODNEY reels. They all walk offstage. Long beat. RODNEY returns.)

KYLIE: What are you doing?

RODNEY: I'm getting some CDs.

KYLIE: Great.

(RODNEY picks up some CDs.)

FITZGERALD: Mommy.

(RODNEY stares at him. Looks offstage. Exits.)

FITZGERALD: Mommy?

(Lights down.)

(Lights up. RODNEY, STEW, and KYLIE stand center stage in a bedroom, covered with rock posters and stuffed animals. A mattress on the floor.)

RODNEY: You look like Julie Christie.

KYLIE: Who?

RODNEY: Julie Christie?

KYLIE: Who's that, your ex-girlfriend?

RODNEY: Ha ha. Ha.

KYLIE: Do you want to undress?

RODNEY: Oh. Okay. *(Long beat.)* What, like in front of everyone?

STEW: He has a problem with feet.

RODNEY: I don't have a problem with feet!

KYLIE: What are you? Pigeon-toed?

RODNEY: I don't have a problem with feet.

KYLIE: It's alright. You can leave your socks on.

RODNEY: Really?

KYLIE: Whatever you want, baby. You're the boss tonight.

RODNEY: Really?

STEW: Maybe I should light a candle or something.

KYLIE: That would be lovely.

RODNEY: I'll put on some music. I brought a couple of CDs cause I didn't know how long this would take.

KYLIE: We negotiated for one hour.

RODNEY: Oh, okay. Then I guess we'll only need one... then.

(STEW removes his shirt, pants. Stands in his underwear and socks.)

KYLIE: You're leaving your socks on as well?

STEW: No. *(Removes his socks.)* I don't have a problem with feet.

RODNEY: I don't have a problem with feet!

(RODNEY plays some music.)

KYLIE: That's lovely. Who is that?

RODNEY: It's um... Nick Drake.

KYLIE: Nick Drake?

RODNEY: Nick Drake... yeah. Nick Drake.

KYLIE: Will you write that down for me?

RODNEY: What... now?

KYLIE: Before I go. I quite like this.

RODNEY: Sure. No problem. I'll even write down some other um... Nick Drake albums you might like. I can also write down...

(She moves closer to RODNEY He shrinks. She pulls down his trousers and underwear. Begins blowing him.)

RODNEY: ... the names of some of the artists he's directly influenced like The Smiths. Belle and Sebastian... of course.

KYLIE: *(Pulls back. Wipes her mouth.)* You're sweet.

RODNEY: Thanks.

KYLIE: Take the rest of your things off and lay on the bed.

(RODNEY removes his shirt and pants. Stands in his underwear and socks. Long, uncomfortable pause as he stares at his socks.)

KYLIE: Leave them on.

RODNEY: Oh. Okay.

(RODNEY reclines on the bed. STEW, who has been watching with a mixture of terror and fascination, shrugs, takes off the rest of his clothes, and joins him. KYLIE stands over them, her back to the audience.)

KYLIE: Do either of you want to eat my pussy?

(STEW and RODNEY stare at each other.)

STEW: Do you?

RODNEY: Do you? You can... if you want.

STEW: You don't mind?

RODNEY: I don't mind.

STEW: Are you sure?

RODNEY: Sure. I don't mind.

STEW: Cause if you want to… it's totally cool.

RODNEY: No, I feel the same way. It's totally cool.

KYLIE: Have you ever given head to a woman before?

RODNEY and STEW: No.

KYLIE: It's really easy. Would you like to learn?

RODNEY: Well. Um…

STEW: Maybe we should just stick to the basic stuff for now.

(KYLIE gets between them in bed.)

KYLIE: This… is… basic.

STEW: Oh.

RODNEY: Really?

KYLIE: Really. It helps put me in the mood.

STEW: Well, wouldn't the um… wouldn't the um… wouldn't the… um…

RODNEY: I'm gonna change the record. You should really hear *Pink Moon. Bryter Lyter* is like, not his best work. *Pink Moon* is… his best work. Nick Drake I mean. *(Gets up. Walks across the room. Exits.)*

KYLIE: *(To STEW.)* Wouldn't the fact that your junkie friend purchased me for an hour be enough to put me in the mood? Is that what you meant?

STEW: No.

KYLIE: Stew?

STEW: Alright… yes.

KYLIE: Look, this is your first time.

STEW: It's not my first time.

KYLIE: Don't you want it to be nice?

STEW: Yes.

KYLIE: Then put a little effort into making me happy… and I'll put a lot of effort into making you very, very happy.

STEW: Okay.

KYLIE: *(Lays back.)* Where my left and right labia meet at the top. Do you see that?

STEW: Yes. At the top.

KYLIE: Do you see the hood of skin there?

STEW: Yes.

KYLIE: Just under the hood there's a little pink bump.

(STEW moves in. Blocks audience view with his head and body.)

KYLIE: Go on lift the hood.

STEW: Okay.

KYLIE: That's my clit.

STEW: That's it?

KYLIE: That's the one. You're gonna want to concentrate on that.

STEW: I didn't know it was um…

KYLIE: On the outside?

STEW: No, I mean… I knew… um… no. I…

KYLIE: Oh, there's good stuff on the inside too. Feel free to explore, but you're going to want to stimulate my clit with your tongue. Don't forget it's there. Always go back to the clit.

STEW: How… how long does this take?

KYLIE: I usually like it done to me for about two or three hours. Then I'm ready to rock.

STEW: Really?

KYLIE: I'm kidding, Stew.

STEW: Oh.

KYLIE: You look ashen.

STEW: No. No. I'm cool.

KYLIE: You're cool?

STEW: Sure. Why wouldn't I be?

KYLIE: (*Lights a cigarette. Leans back, exhales languidly.*) Lovely. Then go to it.

(*Long beat. STEW, as hesitantly as possible, moves in for the clit.*)

KYLIE: Mmmm.

STEW: Is that… good?

KYLIE: You're doing great, baby.

STEW: Really?

KYLIE: Are you sure you've never eaten pussy before? You're a natural.

STEW: (*Laughing.*) Really?

KYLIE: Ooh. Don't tickle.

STEW: Sorry.

KYLIE: Do you like the way I taste?

STEW: Uh huh.

KYLIE: What does it remind you of?

STEW: Sake.

KYLIE: Pardon?

STEW: It tastes like sake. You know, warm, Japanese rice wine?

KYLIE: Well, that's a new one. Do you like sake?

STEW: Yes. Have you ever been to Decibel? It's a sake bar on…

KYLIE: Sustaining rhythm is an important part of this procedure, Stew.

STEW: Sorry.

(*STEW resumes head. RODNEY enters, carrying CDs.*)

RODNEY: I couldn't find *Pink Moon*, but I found *If You're Feeling Sinister*. That's Belle and Sebastian. You'll be able to trace Drake's infl… (*Notices them.*) Oh, um…

KYLIE: Come join us.

RODNEY: Okay.

(*RODNEY gets into bed. STEW pulls his head away.*)

STEW: It tastes like sake.

RODNEY: No!

STEW: I swear.

RODNEY: Really?

STEW: I swear.

RODNEY: That's so weird.

STEW: I know!

(*RODNEY tentatively moves his head in.*)

KYLIE: It doesn't bite, baby.

RODNEY: (*Sticks out his shaking tongue, comically.*) I can't.

KYLIE: Why not?

RODNEY: I just keep thinking about all the penises that have been there.

KYLIE: Well, they're not there now.

RODNEY: And the pee. I can't.

KYLIE: Well, aren't you a smooth talker. I'm nearly dry. We'd better get on with it.

(KYLIE sneers at RODNEY; grabs STEW. Kisses him, pulls him under her.)

STEW: I've got a condom.

KYLIE: I should hope so.

STEW: I'll put it on.

KYLIE: It won't do much good off.

STEW: Now? *(Rips into the condom wrapper with his teeth. Shoves it into his underpants and fiddles.)*

RODNEY: Maybe I should go.

KYLIE: No, I think you ought to watch. You clearly need a bit more help than your mate here.

STEW: Is it on?! Is it on?

KYLIE: It's on.

(She pulls him down and they begin to fuck. RODNEY stares, slackjawed. The phone rings. KYLIE begins to moan loudly. The phone keeps ringing.)

RODNEY: I'll get that. *(Finally picks it up. Answers blankly.)* Hello? Who? Oh, hi. Um… no, he's still here. Yeah. 122 Norfolk Street. Buzzer 3D. Huh? No D. Three d. Who did you say you were? Oh, okay. Okay.

STEW: Who was that?

KYLIE: Oh, nevermind. *(Pulls hair.)* Don't stop fucking me you fucking pigslut. Fuck me you dirty pig bitch.

STEW: Sorry.

KYLIE: *(Lovingly.)* That's alright, luv. *(She kisses him.)*

RODNEY: That was a friend of Fitzgerald's.

STEW: Why did you give him our address?

KYLIE: Shut up and fuck me with your dirty pig dick!

STEW: Sorry.

RODNEY: It wasn't a man. *(Long beat.)* It was a woman.

STEW: Is she coming over?

KYLIE: *(Groans.)* Alright, I've had enough of your stopping and starting. *(To RODNEY.)* You. You're on.

(She grabs RODNEY. Pulls him into her. Feels down his pants.)

KYLIE: You're already wearing one?

RODNEY: Um… yeah. I thought… um… I didn't think I'd be able to um… cause of nerves, so I put one on in the bathroom so that way I could just um… you know… into it…

KYLIE: Well are you growing into it?!

RODNEY: Not yet.

KYLIE: Why the fuck not?

RODNEY: Cause um… you're shouting at me?

(KYLIE thrusts her tongue into his ear. Grinds into him.)

RODNEY: Um… I'm growing into it… now.

STEW: I didn't cum.

(KYLIE throws RODNEY down. Mounts him.)

STEW: Aren't I supposed to cum?

KYLIE: Why don't you jerk off?

STEW: Really?

(STEW looks down. KYLIE begins to moan as RODNEY fucks her. RODNEY stares at STEW.)

RODNEY: I'm having sex.

STEW: What was her name?

(KYLIE moans loudly.)

RODNEY: Who?

STEW: The girl who called?

RODNEY: Blixa.

STEW: That's a cool name.

RODNEY: I know. *(Long beat.)* I'm having sex.

STEW: What'd she want?

RODNEY: I don't know. But she was really angry at Fitzgerald.

STEW: Really?

RODNEY: She said she needed to talk. She's coming over.

STEW: Really?

RODNEY: Yeah. *(Long beat.)* I'm having sex.

STEW: I know.

KYLIE: *(To RODNEY.)* Did you say Blixa?

RODNEY: Yeah.

STEW: That's a cool name.

KYLIE: Shit.

RODNEY: What'd I do? Am I doing it wrong?

KYLIE: That's my pimp.

STEW: Pimp?

(KYLIE pushes RODNEY off her.)

RODNEY: Was that it?

STEW: Did you cum?

RODNEY: I don't think so.

KYLIE: She's on her way here?

RODNEY: Yeah.

STEW: You're supposed to cum, right?

RODNEY: I know!

KYLIE: Shit.

STEW: What?

KYLIE: Get dressed.

STEW: It's over.

KYLIE: Now!

(KYLIE pulls the sheet over her. Lights a cigarette. Begins to pace. STEW and RODNEY stare at each other. Lights down.)

(Lights up. Bare room save a cabinet, some books, an ashtray, magazines. FITZGERALD, disheveled in a dirty suit, sits center stage with twenty glassine bags of heroin and a big pile of smack center stage. A big box of powdered Similac baby formula sits on the floor next to the drugs. FITZGERALD is inexpertly removing the heroin from the bags, filling the bags with the baby formula. Every once in a while he licks his fingers and rolls his eyes back in his head. He frequently sneezes, and takes hits from his inhaler. Rises. Reels. Lights a cigarette. The sound of a buzzer is heard. He nervously rises. Walks to answer it.)

FITZGERALD: Who's there?

VOICE: It's me.

FITZGERALD: You're early. *(Beat.)* Fuck.

VOICE: Hello? It's me!

FITZGERALD: Hang on. I'm taking a shit.

VOICE: Are you going to let me in?

FITZGERALD: Look, the whole place stinks like shit. I gotta wipe my ass.

VOICE: Fitzgerald.

FITZGERALD: Look, lemme just wipe my ass. Gimme a minute. I'll wipe my ass and light a candle or something. You're fucking early! *(Searches the room. Scurries offstage. Scurries back with a broom and a dustpan. Sweeps the heroin into the dustpan carefully. Lifts it up. Sticks his finger in. Licks it.)* Fuck.

(He looks around. Finds a cabinet, gingerly places the smack-filled dustpan in the cabinet. Shuts door. Returns to pile. Scoops up the glassine bags. Finds one particular one and places it in his pocket. Shoves the others in his coat pocket. Stares down at the white pile on the floor where the heroin was. Hesitates. Looks around. Finally kneels down, cranes his head, and licks it off the floor. Rises, reels again. Hits off his inhaler. Swallows some pills, places a record on the turntable. Lights a cigarette and returns to the buzzer.) Alright.

VOICE: Your ass is clean?

(FITZGERALD buzzes VOICE up.)

FITZGERALD: You could eat off my ass.

(BLIXA, tough in leather jacket enters, quickly.)

BLIXA: No thank you.

FITZGERALD: You know you're early.

BLIXA: I'm only ten minutes early.

FITZGERALD: I figured you'd have a hard time finding this place.

BLIXA: I've got an excellent sense of direction.

FITZGERALD: What are you? One of those aboriginals?

BLIXA: Do I look Aborigine?

FITZGERALD: You wanna beer?

BLIXA: Alright. Do you have any Foster's?

FITZGERALD: I've got Bud and Bud Lite. That's American for beer. Have a seat. I'll get you a brew. Nice and cold.

BLIXA: *(Looks around. Nowhere to sit. She finally sits on the floor.)* Nice place.

FITZGERALD: Yeah. You like it?

(FITZGERALD exits. Returns with two beers. Hands her one.)

FITZGERALD: It's a twist off.

BLIXA: *(Opens beer. Gulps it.)* American beer tastes like piss. Where's the thing we talked about? Do you have it?

FITZGERALD: You know what I always wanted to ask you people? What's up with the fucking platypuses?

BLIXA: How should I know?

FITZGERALD: They're mammals, but they lay eggs. I mean, how can they get away with that shit?

BLIXA: Where is it?

FITZGERALD: I got it. Don't worry. So how long have you been pimpin'?

BLIXA: A few months.

FITZGERALD: Wait, so you're not a pimp back home?

BLIXA: No. I work in a pub.

FITZGERALD: You're a waitress?

BLIXA: Not anymore.

FITZGERALD: Fucking incredible. So you thought you'd come to America and pimp. That's cool.

BLIXA: I couldn't get a legitimate work visa.

FITZGERALD: And this Kylie, she was down with the plan?

BLIXA: We both need the money. America is very expensive.

FITZGERALD: No shit. And this Kylie... she a waitress too?

BLIXA: She was. Now she's my bitch.

FITZGERALD: Right. And she doesn't mind all the random fucking.

BLIXA: Kylie's a smart girl... she knows herself. Very useful asset.

FITZGERALD: Sure. Sure.

BLIXA: Kylie gets blind drunk and fucks boys at random anyway. So I simply suggested we organize ourselves.

FITZGERALD: So how come she's the bitch and you're the pimp? Why not vice versa?

BLIXA: Men like Kylie better.

FITZGERALD: Why's that?

BLIXA: They tend to think I'm hard.

FITZGERALD: Aw... you're not hard. You're alright.

BLIXA: Let me ask you something...

FITZGERALD: Shoot...

BLIXA: Your two mates, are they really virgins?

FITZGERALD: Swear to fuck.

BLIXA: Amazing. Why? Fear of AIDS?

FITZGERALD: Nah. Fear of disappointing Morrisey. *(Beat.)* Say, what the fuck is Vegemite anyway?

BLIXA: It's a spread.

FITZGERALD: Cool.

BLIXA: Why is it any of your business whether or not they have sex? It's a personal issue.

FITZGERALD: How old are you?

BLIXA: I just turned thirty.

FITZGERALD: Me too. And you know what that shit's like. It's a transition. I mean, look, you packed up and moved to America to start a new life as a pimp right? That's the kind of shit you do when you're thirty. You pimp. You experiment with hard drugs. Normal shit.

BLIXA: And your mates, they're not experimental enough for you.

FITZGERALD: No. They don't experiment with dick. And it's become painful to hang out with them. Boring! They're my last two friends. I mean, you need friends, right? You, you've got your bitch. These are our friends. Who has the patience to make new ones? I'd rather keep em than be alone but they gotta loosen up.

BLIXA: Why do they have to experiment with sex and hard drugs in order to loosen up?

FITZGERALD: Cause... this is America.

BLIXA: *(Pulls a gun. Places it on the floor.)* Do you mind? It's weighing down my coat.

FITZGERALD: *(Cools significantly. Stares at it.)* No, I can hang that up for you if you want. *(Pulls out his inhaler. Takes a hit.)*

BLIXA: Are you asthmatic?

FITZGERALD: No. *(Stares at the gun again. Swallows some pills.)* You want some crackers or something?

BLIXA: That's alright. I didn't plan to stay long. I assumed I'd just get my payment and go.

FITZGERALD: Right… so I suppose you'll be wanting that… now.

BLIXA: Yes. Now would be fine.

FITZGERALD: So this chick… she's good looking, huh? *(Picks up the gun, holds it, sucks on the inhaler some more.)*

BLIXA: Careful with that. It's loaded.

(FITZGERALD puts the gun down, swallows more pills.)

BLIXA: What's that?

FITZGERALD: Vitamins.

BLIXA: Vitamins?

FITZGERALD: And minerals. Keeps you from getting cancer.

BLIXA: *(Grabs the bottle.)* Xanax. *(Long/ painful beat.)* That's a palindrome.

FITZGERALD: It's an anti-anxiety medication, alright?

BLIXA: Do I make you anxious?

FITZGERALD: Nah. I just never had a gun all up in my place before.

BLIXA: *(Takes the gun back.)* She's very attractive. Your mates won't be disappointed. Will I be disappointed?

FITZGERALD: Huh? *(Nervous.)* Nah. This is great shit. Great shit. Here. I'll prove it.

(FITZGERALD removes the single bag from his pants pocket. Opens it. Lays out a line on the floor. Pulls out a dollar bill. Hands it to BLIXA.)

FITZGERALD: Test it out, babe. On me.

BLIXA: *(Takes the dollar.)* You know when I met you at the bar, I thought you were cute.

FITZGERALD: I am cute.

BLIXA: I don't usually make these kind of arrangements. It's not really orthodox.

FITZGERALD: Yeah? You're Pimpin' for Dummies handbook frowns on it, huh? Chapter one… cash only. Chapter two, get yourself a big ass gun to enforce cash only policy. You even know how to use that thing?

BLIXA: *(Holds up the gun. Points it at FITZGERALD.)* I know how to use it.

FITZGERALD: Yeah? Cool.

BLIXA: You're very arrogant.

FITZGERALD: Thanks.

BLIXA: So are all your business transactions made with heroin?

FITZGERALD: I invested in a lot of it.

BLIXA: You don't have any cash?

FITZGERALD: I got thirty bucks… somewhere.

BLIXA: *(Takes a snort.)* It's strong.

FITZGERALD: It is.

BLIXA: It's good.

FITZGERALD: It is.

BLIXA: I'm high.

FITZGERALD: You are.

BLIXA: So where do you get it?

FITZGERALD: Oh, it's everywhere in America.

BLIXA: Wow. I'm really high.

FITZGERALD: You really are. You want another beer?

BLIXA: Sure.

FITZGERALD: You wanna mess around?

BLIXA: Maybe.

FITZGERALD: Oh yeah? Really?

(BLIXA does another line.)

FITZGERALD: I'm a little high. A little fucked up too. Maybe we could just kiss a little. That'd be good.

(BLIXA leans in and kisses him. Bites his lip.)

FITZGERALD: Ow. That's my lip, babe.

BLIXA: I know.

(They begin to make out, roll around on the floor.)

BLIXA: You have twenty bags?

FITZGERALD: Yeah. That's the deal, right?

BLIXA: You're not gonna fuck me.

FITZGERALD: Well,… I'm kinda too high. Maybe you could just gimme head.

BLIXA: No. You're not gonna fuck me.

FITZGERALD: Nah, nah. I'm all about maintaining good diplomatic relations.

BLIXA: Don't think you can burn me cause I'm foreign. I know how to use this. If I'm fucked here, I'll find you and you'll pay.

FITZGERALD: I got it. Now put away that boomerang and hunt my crock.

(He laughs nervously. She puts the gun away. They roll around again. Lights down.)

(Lights up on RODNEY and STEW's living room. FITZGERALD is comatose.)

RODNEY: You better wake him up.

(STEW leans over and shakes FITZGERALD.)

STEW: He's not responding.

RODNEY: Wake him up!

STEW: I'm trying.

KYLIE: He's overdosed.

STEW: No he hasn't.

KYLIE: Look at his skin. It's blue.

STEW: No he hasn't.

RODNEY: Wake him up!

KYLIE: You'd better get him into the shower.

RODNEY: Shouldn't we call the police?

KYLIE: You can't call the fucking police.

RODNEY: Why not?

KYLIE: Because they'll arrest you and send me back to Sydney. Do you want to be arrested?

RODNEY: No.

KYLIE: Good, cause I don't want to go back to Sydney. Run the shower. He'll be fine. We just need to shock his system.

RODNEY: Cold, right?

KYLIE: No, we're going to shock his system with lukewarm water.

RODNEY: Don't yell at me!

STEW: *(To FITZGERALD.)* Fitzgerald? Fitzgerald, if you can hear me, there's an angry pimp on her way over here so I think you better wake up.

RODNEY: Don't tell him that. He'll play dead.

KYLIE: He's going to be dead once she gets here. Blixa doesn't interrupt business unless there's something wrong, and if there's something wrong, I wouldn't want to be you, or your friend.

RODNEY: Wait, what?

STEW: Shit. Fitzgerald! Please, wake up. Please.

RODNEY: What?

STEW: Fitzgerald. Oh, shit. I don't hear him breathing.

RODNEY: She's gonna kill us?

KYLIE: Will you please just run the shower.

RODNEY: I'm locking the door.

KYLIE: It won't do any good. She'll break it down.

RODNEY: Who is this woman?

STEW: Fitzgerald, we've got trouble.

(FITZGERALD moans.)

RODNEY: Oh, thank God. *(Beat.)* Fitzgerald…

(KYLIE pushes them out of the way. Shakes FITZGERALD.)

KYLIE: Look at me…

FITZGERALD: Mom?

KYLIE: Did you burn Blixa? Answer me… did you burn Blixa.

(FITZGERALD kisses KYLIE on the lips, dreamily.)

KYLIE: She's on her way over here right now!

FITZGERALD: Aw, Mom… lemme sleep ten more minutes… willya?

(KYLIE slaps him.)

FITZGERALD: I don't wanna go to school today. I feel too good.

KYLIE: She's gonna rip your arms and legs off and kick you across the floor like a football.

FITZGERALD: That's cool.

(KYLIE slaps him.)

KYLIE: You are in danger. Great danger. If you burned her, she is going to kill you.

RODNEY: Who is this woman?

KYLIE: Do you understand the situation?

FITZGERALD: I don't know what you're talking about? Everything's fine. Everything's cool. Just relax.

RODNEY: Did you burn the pimp?

FITZGERALD: Nobody burned no one. Everything's great. Play some music, alright. Play some Stones. *Let It Bleed.* Play some be-bop.

STEW: See? Everything's fine. This is clearly some kind of misunderstanding. Everything will get straightened out.

RODNEY: Everything is not fine.

FITZGERALD: Take it easy, man… *(Rises. Looks around the room queerly…)* It's just another party. *(Vomits.)* See? Just another party.

RODNEY: I'm freaking out, Stew. I'm freaking out.

STEW: You can freak out all you want.

I'm choosing to believe that everything's fine.

(With a crash, the door is kicked open. BLIXA enters. Raises her gun and shoots FITZGERALD in the gut. He doubles over for a second.)

STEW: Or… not.

FITZGERALD: Aw, what'd you go and kick in the door for? What'd you do that for, Blixa? You didn't have to do that shit, man?

BLIXA: You fucking bitch. I told you I'd kill you if you fucked me.

FITZGERALD: Kill me? Nobody's killing nobody here.

RODNEY: Um, Fitzgerald.

FITZGERALD: Look, we can talk this out, man. Sit down. Have a smoke. We're all people here, right? Nobody's got to get damaged. Shit. This is the twenty-first century. We're enlightened and shit.

STEW: Fitzgerald. She just shot you.

FITZGERALD: No she didn't.

RODNEY: Um… yeah. She did.

KYLIE: You're bleeding. Profusely.

FITZGERALD: *(Feels his belly. Holds up his hand. Stares at the blood. Takes out his inhaler. Takes a hit.)* She shot me? *(Lights a cigarette. Sits on the couch. Smokes.)* I didn't feel a thing.

(BLIXA walks across the room. Smacks FITZGERALD in the head with the butt of the gun. He reels back. Raises himself.)

RODNEY: Jesus. Don't do that.

FITZGERALD: *(Feels his head, laughs as it bleeds.)* This is some kick ass dope.

BLIXA: Where is it?

FITZGERALD: You shot me?

BLIXA: Yes. Where's the dope?

FITZGERALD: You sure?

BLIXA: Yes.

FITZGERALD: Am I gonna die?

BLIXA: Yes.

FITZGERALD: Shit.

STEW: You're not gonna die.

BLIXA: Yes he is.

STEW: You can't just come in here and shoot our friend you know. This is America. We have rights.

(BLIXA walks over to STEW. Stares him down. He shrinks.)

BLIXA: I want my heroin and I want it now or I'm going to shoot the both of you.

STEW: Heroin?

KYLIE: What heroin?

BLIXA: *(To KYLIE.)* You shut up. Until it's proved different, you're guilty.

KYLIE: I'm not in on anything.

STEW: That's not how it works. This is America you… Australian.

(BLIXA smacks STEW. He shrinks. FITZGERALD rises.)

FITZGERALD: I didn't feel a thing. Ha ha. *(Exits.)*

RODNEY: Where's he going?

STEW: Kitchen?

BLIXA: You. What's your name?

STEW: Stewart.

BLIXA: Stewart, your friend in there? He's not your friend. He willfully put your life in danger. He promised me top grade smack and instead, he unloaded two bundles of powdered baby formula on me in exchange for my finest bitch. This is your friend. This is why I'm here… and this is why you're all gonna die unless I get my drugs. Now.

RODNEY: You'd kill four people for three hundred dollars?

BLIXA: It's the principle.

FITZGERALD: *(Reenters, drinking a beer.)* Nobody's killing nobody, here. C'mon, this is ridiculous. Let's get real here.

(BLIXA raises the gun. Fires again. Hits FITZGERALD in the chest.)

BLIXA: I'm serious.

FITZGERALD: What happened?

RODNEY: She just shot you again?

(FITZGERALD drinks the beer. They all stare in disbelief.)

FITZGERALD: What?

RODNEY: Fitzgerald?

FITZGERALD: Is it cold in here?

KYLIE: I can't believe you rented out my pussy for drugs.

BLIXA: I'm sorry. It won't happen again.

KYLIE: I'm insulted. I really am.

BLIXA: I said I was sorry, now shut the fuck up!

FITZGERALD: Is anybody else cold?

RODNEY: N… no.

STEW: Where are the neighbors? Where are the fucking neighbors? You play your Kinks records at like medium volume and they come pounding on the door… and now… nothing? Nothing!

RODNEY: This isn't happening. This is not happening. I'm not here.

STEW: Where are the neighbors?! Where is everyone?

BLIXA: Shut up.

FITZGERALD: You shot me?

BLIXA: Yes. Where are my drugs?

FITZGERALD: I'm gonna die?

BLIXA: Yes. Where are my fucking drugs?

FITZGERALD: Well… I'm not giving you no drugs now… *(Gurgles.)* You can just forget that… *(Gurgles.)* sister.

KYLIE: You're a junkie? Do you trade me for smack often?

BLIXA: This was the first time.

KYLIE: Why? Why not cash? We need cash! And you have the nerve to suggest that I was in on it? I don't do smack! Who does smack anymore? Smack is so early nineties. It's passé. What the hell are you doing getting involved in smack?

BLIXA: I was curious.

STEW: Because of Nick Cave?

(FITZGERALD rises and exits.)

RODNEY: Where's he going now?

KYLIE: Nick Cave?

STEW: Because he was a junkie? And… and… Australian?

KYLIE: No.

BLIXA: Yes.

KYLIE: Nick Cave? You did this because of Nick Cave?

BLIXA: I love Nick Cave.

KYLIE: We're in a lot of trouble. You just murdered someone.

BLIXA: I was upset!

RODNEY: Murdered? He's not dead. He's not dead.

FITZGERALD: *(Enters, wearing a long, garish, thrift store fur coat.)* Gimme a cigarette.

(BLIXA rises… hands FITZGERALD a cigarette. He lights it.)

KYLIE: Where'd you get that coat?

FITZGERALD: You like it? Nice right? *(Stares at her. Smiles. Tries to light his smoke. Takes a deep, pained breath and falls down.)*

(KYLIE crouches down. Listens to his heart. Takes the cigarette from his hand. Inhales.)

KYLIE: He's dead.

RODNEY: He's not dead.

KYLIE: He's dead.

STEW: Where are the neighbors?

BLIXA: Shit.

KYLIE: I hope you're happy.

BLIXA: Shut up.

KYLIE: We're gonna have to kill the other two now.

RODNEY: What?

BLIXA: Lock the door.

(KYLIE walks across the room toward the door. STEW follows panicked. BLIXA aims the gun.)

BLIXA: Don't fucking move.

(STEW freezes. KYLIE looks back at him.)

KYLIE: I'm sorry.

(KYLIE hands STEW the cigarette. STEW takes it.)

RODNEY: You don't smoke.

(STEW inhales. Moves over to the couch. Sits down next to BLIXA.)

RODNEY: *(Shouting.)* You don't smoke! *(Beat.)* What's happening? What's happening?

(KYLIE walks over to the couch and sits down next to him.)

BLIXA: So… how was it?

KYLIE: I've had worse.

STEW: I haven't.

KYLIE: Thanks.

STEW: Or better.

RODNEY: Can somebody please tell me what's happening? Please?

KYLIE: Where did he get that coat?

STEW: I don't know.

RODNEY: *(Moves over to the couch. Sits down.)* Please?

(KYLIE removes the coat from FITZGERALD.)

KYLIE: It's a great coat. *(She rises. Puts it on.)*

BLIXA: Alright. I've got my bearings. *(She rises.)* Let's do this and get the hell out of here.

STEW: Now? You have to do it now?

BLIXA: It's best to get it over with. I'm not a monster. I don't want to torture you.

STEW: I don't mind.

RODNEY: What's going on?

STEW: She's going to kill us.

RODNEY: No she's not. *(To BLIXA.)* You're not, are you? You're not, are you? Are you?

BLIXA: Yes. I am.

RODNEY: When?

BLIXA: Now.

RODNEY: Why?

BLIXA: You're the only witnesses.

RODNEY: You're kidding. That's… that's why? No… no… that's unacceptable. That's not… acceptable. You just killed our best friend. You owe us… not… not… we owe you… you owe us.

BLIXA: Fine… I owe you. What do you want? Another shag? Go ahead.

KYLIE: Pardon?

BLIXA: I'm sorry. I didn't mean it. I'm in shock. My nerves are shot.

RODNEY: I want more time. I wanna prepare. I wanna call my Mom. Write a will. You can't just… this is unacceptable. I'm not ready to die.

BLIXA: How much more time do you want?

RODNEY: I don't know. *(Beat.)* A lot.

KYLIE: You know it's probably not the wisest idea to be spotted running from the apartment minutes after a ruckus is heard and three dead bodies are discovered.

STEW: That is a good point. *(Long beat.)* That is a good point.

BLIXA: Well, what the fuck are we supposed to do? I'm shaking here. I'm losing it. I've never shot anyone before and now I have to do it again… twice! What the fuck do you suggest? A warm bath?

(KYLIE reaches into the pocket of FITZGERALD's coat. Holds up his smack.)

RODNEY: What's that?

KYLIE: This is heroin. It's very dangerous, and very passé, but it does fill your body with orgasmic warmth, giddy delirium, and a sense of previously unimaginable serenity. Since this is the last night of your life, would you care for some?

RODNEY: Yes.

STEW: Please.

(KYLIE kneels down and begins to prepare the drugs. Lights down.)

(Lights up. FITZGERALD is offstage. RODNEY, STEW, BLIXA, and KYLIE are high.)

RODNEY: Do you think it's disrespectful to just leave him in the tub like that?

STEW: Where are we supposed to put him? I mean… where in this apartment do you think would be more um… respectful?

RODNEY: I don't know. The bed?

STEW: The bed? You want him to get blood all over your bedding?

RODNEY: Well… does it matter… anymore?

STEW: Oh… right. Well, do you want to move him?

RODNEY: No. Fuck it.

STEW: Did you just say "Fuck it?"

RODNEY: Yeah. *(Long beat.)* Fuck it.

BLIXA: Do you two banter this way all the time?

RODNEY: I don't know... I guess so.

BLIXA: Jesus.

KYLIE: Now I know why he beat you on this shit. This is some peachy heroin.

BLIXA: You're not kidding. I can barely move.

RODNEY: Do you mind if I play some music?

BLIXA: Knock yourself out.

RODNEY: Thanks.

STEW: What are you gonna play?

RODNEY: I don't know. Remember that question like... what was it... if you were gonna die... like if a comet was gonna hit the earth in ten minutes, what would the last thing you'd um... play... be?

STEW: What?

RODNEY: This is like that question. Now.

STEW: What?!

RODNEY: Am I not making sense?

STEW: I don't know.

RODNEY: I think I'm really high.

STEW: What are you gonna play?

RODNEY: Maybe something *(Long beat.)* angry?

STEW: Angry.

RODNEY: Yeah, cause... you know... this is not a good situation, so...

STEW: Right. Like what?

RODNEY: Ministry?

STEW: Nah. Maybe something... sort of... reflective.

STEW: Reflective.

RODNEY: You know... like "what's it all about?" Leonard Cohen I was thinking.

STEW: Dylan?

RODNEY: "Knockin' on Heaven's Door." That's appropriate.

STEW: Yeah. Let's hear that.

RODNEY: *(Staggers left, toward the stereo.)* Oh.

STEW: What.

RODNEY: You know... I only have the Guns N' Roses version.

STEW: What are you doing with a Guns N' Roses album?

RODNEY: I bought it when it came out.

STEW: You did?

KYLIE: Everybody bought it when it came out.

STEW: Were Guns N' Roses really big in Australia?

KYLIE: Yes.

STEW: Well, I don't think I want Guns N' Roses' cover of "Knockin' on Heaven's Door" to be the last thing I ever hear.

RODNEY: It's not a bad cover actually... as far as Dylan covers go.

STEW: It's the last thing we'll ever hear!

RODNEY: Oh, God. We're gonna die.

STEW: We're gonna die.

RODNEY: They're gonna kill us.

BLIXA: Soon.

RODNEY: I can't believe it.

BLIXA: You've said that already.

KYLIE: About five hundred times. It's not sinking in?

RODNEY: It's not an easy thing to accept. I don't even know what stage I'm at. What are they? Anger...

STEW: Well you passed on the Ministry so I think you're beyond anger.

RODNEY: Depression.

STEW: That'd account for the Leonard Cohen.

RODNEY: What's next? Denial?

KYLIE: You're still in Denial.

RODNEY: I'm in Denial. What's next?

BLIXA: Acceptance.

STEW: No, wait... I think Denial comes before Depression.

RODNEY: What?

STEW: Denial comes before Depression. Then Acceptance. Then...

BLIXA: Death.

STEW: Right. Death.

KYLIE: I'm hungry.

RODNEY: What was I doing?

STEW: Playing music.

RODNEY: Right. God... how did Fitzgerald ever function on this stuff?

KYLIE: Would it be terribly reckless of us to order in some food?

STEW: How can you eat?

KYLIE: What? I'm not about to die.

STEW: No... I mean... I just vomited about forty times.

KYLIE: I don't know... I'm hungry.

STEW: I swear, I saw nuts and bolts I swallowed when I was six at the bottom of the bowl.

BLIXA: You swallowed nuts and bolts?

STEW: I'm oral.

KYLIE: He's oral.

BLIXA: We're not ordering food.

KYLIE: Please?

BLIXA: We've got a dead body in the bath and we're about to kill these two. You want to bring someone else into the mix?

KYLIE: Well, if he looks suspicious, we could always kill him too.

BLIXA: Are you crazy?

KYLIE: What's the difference between three bodies or four if you think about it?

BLIXA: What do you want to eat?

KYLIE: Chinese? Spicy eggplant? Hacked chicken in black bean sauce? Sizzling squid?

(STEW rises, queasy, rushes stage left. BLIXA jerks up and cocks the gun. STEW freezes.)

BLIXA: Where are you going?

STEW: I have to puke again.

BLIXA: Fine, but don't try anything stupid.

(RODNEY puts on some music. It's "To-night" from West Side Story. *They all stare at him.)*

RODNEY: Sorry... it was just a whim. *(He takes the needle off the record.)* I really don't know what to play.

KYLIE: Oh, Jesus. I'll pick something. I have good taste in music.

RODNEY: But you didn't even know who Nick Drake was.

KYLIE: Get outta my way. *(Selects a record.)* Here. This is good.

("I Eat Cannibals" by Toto Coelo plays.)

RODNEY: "I Eat Cannibals"?

KYLIE: What? It's your record.

(RODNEY walks over to the couch. Sits down next to BLIXA, defeated.)

KYLIE: Do you have any takeout menus?

RODNEY: In the kitchen. On top of the fridge.

(KYLIE exits. STEW reenters.)

STEW: Can we have some more heroin? Please?

BLIXA: You want more?

STEW: Well, it's not like I'm gonna get hooked right? Ha ha.

RODNEY: Ha. Right.

BLIXA: *(Stares at them incredulously. Laughs.)* You know... I almost don't want to kill you.

RODNEY: Really?

BLIXA: Yeah. It's almost too sad.

RODNEY: What do you mean?

BLIXA: You're both retarded.

RODNEY: No we're not.

STEW: I thought because maybe... you liked us.

BLIXA: You're okay.

RODNEY: We're not retarded. I'm not retarded.

BLIXA: You're a man child.

RODNEY: I'm not a man child.

KYLIE: *(Enters.)* Twenty minutes.

BLIXA: You already ordered?

KYLIE: Yeah. There's a phone in the kitchen.

RODNEY: There's a phone in the kitchen.

BLIXA: I've grasped the concept, thank you.

RODNEY: I'm a full-grown man, you know. I'm full grown.

BLIXA: That's apparent as well. My point is that it's a shame that I'm going to have to kill you because you very clearly haven't lived.

RODNEY: I've lived. You know it's bad enough you're going to kill me. You don't have to insult me too. I've lived. I've been to Paris.

STEW: And Prague.

RODNEY: And Prague. I've written a novel.

STEW: Unpublished.

RODNEY: Maybe somebody will find it and publish it.

STEW: Maybe.

RODNEY: Like Anne Frank.

BLIXA: Jesus. You're serious? You really believe that?

RODNEY: I don't know. Yeah.

BLIXA: You are making this very difficult.

RODNEY: What? I've lived. I'm telling you I've lived. I'm ready to die if I have to.

BLIXA: No you're not.

RODNEY: Yes I am!

STEW: *(Puts finger on nose.)* Acceptance!

KYLIE: How long ago did I say "twenty minutes"? I'm so hungry.

STEW: There's food in the refrigerator.

KYLIE: Really? What?

STEW: I can't talk about it. Just go look. Eat whatever you want.

KYLIE: Thanks.

STEW: How does she stay so thin?

BLIXA: It's her metabolism.

STEW: Hmm.

(STEW stares at RODNEY. Makes finger in mouth gag gesture. RODNEY nods.)

STEW: So, it's alright if I do a little more?

BLIXA: Help yourself.

STEW: Thanks. You know, you're not bad either.

BLIXA: Thanks.

STEW: No, really. Under different circumstances, I bet we could all hang out and have a good time.

BLIXA: I doubt it.

STEW: Well, we're sort of having a good time now… if it weren't for the murder of my best friend and the black specter of death looming over my head, I'd say this has been one of the best nights of my life.

BLIXA: Kissing my ass isn't gonna spare you, Stew.

STEW: You called me Stew.

BLIXA: Stop it. I know where this is going.

RODNEY: No. He's really guileless by nature. He's really sincere.

STEW: I am. I mean it. I'm incapable of lying.

BLIXA: Why?

STEW: Fear.

RODNEY: Fear.

STEW: But tonight… I had sex. I did hard drugs. There's music… and… and… Chinese food coming. I mean, Fitzgerald was right. It's a party. I could have been hit by a taxicab tonight on my way to the store to buy soymilk, you know?

BLIXA: How very existential.

STEW: It's true. And you know what? I've never felt less afraid and neurotic in my life than I feel right now. You're always wondering when you're gonna die, right? Well, now I know. It's a load off.

BLIXA: I think you're mad.

STEW: Maybe if you were on the other end of the gun, you'd understand, Blixa.

BLIXA: Maybe.

STEW: What were you like as a child? Tell me…

BLIXA: No.

STEW: Please.

BLIXA: No!

STEW: It's my last wish.

RODNEY: That's your last wish?

STEW: Yes.

BLIXA: You don't get a last wish.

STEW: Come on. Everyone gets a last wish. *(Does more heroin. Reels.)*

STEW: Even criminals get a last wish.

BLIXA: Your last wish is to hear about my childhood?

STEW: Yes.

(BLIXA takes the heroin away from him. Snorts some herself.)

BLIXA: Alright.

STEW: Really?

RODNEY: This isn't my last wish.

BLIXA: Alight!

RODNEY: I get a wish though, right?

BLIXA: Yes. Everyone gets a wish.

(KYLIE reenters, eating a chicken leg.)

KYLIE: Fitzgerald didn't get a wish.

BLIXA: He forfeited his last wish when he stole my drugs.

KYLIE: You know, it was my pussy he bought for free. If you think about it.

BLIXA: Don't start, Kylie.

KYLIE: No. Your whole thing is principle, but maybe there are other forces at work here. Maybe it's karmic. Maybe I was meant to give my pussy to these boys…

RODNEY: Men.

KYLIE: … as some sort of benevolent gesture. Some sort of nod to innocence. Some sort of *(Beat.)* how long has this chicken been in there?

STEW: Two days.

(KYLIE extends the chicken to STEW.)

KYLIE: Does this taste funny?

(STEW gags and runs offstage.)

BLIXA: I don't want to hear your New Age horseshit right now. I'm not in the mood.

KYLIE: You know, your lack of a spiritual side is the source of a lot of your pain, Blixa. I mean, if you were more in touch with your spirituality, maybe you wouldn't have to be a ruthless street pimp. You could be a poet, or a dancer, or a surgeon even.

BLIXA: Fuck off. Your spirituality didn't save you from being a whore.

KYLIE: Not true. My spirituality is in harmony with my vocation. I give pleasure. *(To RODNEY.)* Don't I?

RODNEY: Yes.

KYLIE: You just take… take money, take lives.

BLIXA: I said fuck off, Kylie! I'll smack you. I mean it.

KYLIE: Hard as nails. See? It's so transparent. It's because of what happened when she was a child.

STEW: *(Runs back in.)* What? What?

RODNEY: Yeah, now I wanna know too.

BLIXA: Tough.

RODNEY: No. It's my wish.

STEW: What happened?

KYLIE: She was carried off by dingoes.

(BLIXA raises the gun and points at KYLIE's head.)

BLIXA: Shut up!

KYLIE: Go on. Pull the trigger. Kill me. Your finest bitch. That's good for business.

(BLIXA shakes, begins to crack at the memory and the realization that KYLIE's right. She lowers the gun and buries her head in her hands.)

STEW: Dingoes?

KYLIE: Dingoes.

BLIXA: Dingoes.

RODNEY: How many dingoes?

BLIXA: Four.

STEW: How old were you?

BLIXA: Eighteen months.

STEW: Jesus.

RODNEY: Aren't the dingoes supposed to eat the babies?

KYLIE: Maybe they found her too sour.

STEW: This explains a lot.

BLIXA: There, you've got your wish. Now let's get this over with.

KYLIE: We can't yet.

BLIXA: Why not?

KYLIE: Food.

BLIXA: Shit.

STEW: So what did the dingoes do in lieu of… of eating you?

BLIXA: Nothing.

KYLIE: They buried her.

STEW: God. Who found you?

KYLIE: Another pack of dingoes.

STEW: No!

KYLIE: They dug her up and brought her home.

STEW: Rejected by dingoes.

KYLIE: Rejected by dingoes.

RODNEY: That's the rough.

KYLIE: It was front-page news in Sydney.

STEW: I bet.

KYLIE: Anyway, she's been extremely defensive and confrontational ever since. You should have known her in high school.

(BLIXA lets her guard down. Lets out a faint sob.)

STEW: You know… I bet we would have been friends in high school.

("Down Under" by Men at Work plays on the eighties compilation.)

RODNEY: Do you mind if I change the record?

(KYLIE grabs the gun while BLIXA isn't looking. Points it at RODNEY.)

KYLIE: You don't like Men at Work?

RODNEY: No. No. I do.

KYLIE: I'm just kidding, Rodney. Lighten up.

RODNEY: Oh.

BLIXA: Give that back.

KYLIE: Why? You don't trust me with it?

BLIXA: Kylie.

KYLIE: I wanna hold the gun.

BLIXA: Well you can't.

KYLIE: Well I am.

BLIXA: Kylie.

KYLIE: What? Maybe I'm in charge now. Huh? What do you say to that? Maybe it's a worker's revolution.

BLIXA: You're not in charge.

KYLIE: I've got the gun. Seems to me whoever's got the gun's in charge.

BLIXA: You're high.

KYLIE: So. So are you.

BLIXA: I'm going to count to three.

KYLIE: One two three. Oh, look… I've still got the gun.

RODNEY: What's happening?

(There's a buzz. KYLIE points the gun at STEW.)

KYLIE: Go get the food.

(STEW rises, gags, runs off, and hurls. KYLIE points the gun at RODNEY.)
KYLIE: Go get the food.

RODNEY: Oh, okay.

KYLIE: And leave him a big tip so he'll be happy and unsuspecting?

RODNEY: Okay.

RODNEY: *(Rises. Reaches into his pocket.)* What, like 30 percent?

KYLIE: Go!

(RODNEY moves toward the door. BLIXA lunges for the gun. KYLIE jumps back. Aims it at her.)

BLIXA: This isn't funny.

KYLIE: I think it's pretty funny.

BLIXA: Why are you doing this?

KYLIE: You sold my pussy for heroin.

BLIXA: Once! Once! I told you it was a mistake.

KYLIE: Maybe I'll sell your pussy for something insulting. How'd you like that?

BLIXA: Jesus.

(RODNEY returns with the food. KYLIE points the gun at him.)

KYLIE: Go get some dishes… and forks. I can't eat with chopsticks.

RODNEY: I could teach you. It's really easy.

KYLIE: Go.

RODNEY: Okay.

STEW: *(Returns.)* God, all you do is vomit. People pay for this stuff?

KYLIE: People kill for it. In fact, it's so precious, people will even exchange their pussies for it.

(RODNEY returns with the dishes and the food. Sets it on the coffee table.)

KYLIE: Are you hungry?

RODNEY: Yeah. It's not really what I would have ordered for my last meal but… yeah.

KYLIE: Help yourself.

RODNEY: Thanks. *(Grabs an egg roll. Bites into it.)* Wow.

STEW: What?

RODNEY: Maybe it's because it's the last thing I'll ever eat, but this is like… the best egg roll I've ever tasted.

STEW: Let me taste.

(RODNEY hands STEW the egg roll. He takes a bite.)

STEW: Wow. It is really good.

KYLIE: Hand me one.

RODNEY: Oh, well… there's only one.

KYLIE: What? I ordered three.

RODNEY: Really?

STEW: You should really check to make sure they filled your order before you let them go. That kind of thing happens all the time. You should really check to see if they charged you for three. I bet they did.

KYLIE: Shit! I really wanted an egg roll.

RODNEY: There's plenty of squid.

KYLIE: Hmm. Rodney?

RODNEY: Yeah?

KYLIE: I've got a business proposition for you.

RODNEY: Huh?

KYLIE: In exchange for the rest of your egg roll, I will give you… Blixa's pussy.

BLIXA: Not funny!

RODNEY: What's happening?

STEW: I don't know.

KYLIE: She's my finest bitch.

BLIXA: Kylie.

RODNEY: You can have the egg roll if you really want it.

(KYLIE aims the gun at his head.)

KYLIE: I'd prefer to barter for it, thank you.

RODNEY: Oh… okay. *(Beat.)* Does that mean… what… what does that mean?

KYLIE: Oh, I think you know what it means.

RODNEY: Wait… I have to… I don't have to… do I have to… ?

KYLIE: Don't you want to?

(RODNEY stares at BLIXA, who glares at KYLIE then at him.)

RODNEY: I guess.

KYLIE: You guess? This is my finest bitch!

STEW: Well, you gotta wonder… with the dingoes and all, maybe something's a little…

BLIXA: There's nothing a little…

STEW: I see what you mean about the defensive thing…

BLIXA: Why are you doing this?

KYLIE: It's the principle… *(Beat.)* plus I'm stupid high… and I'm having fun. Take your clothes off.

BLIXA: No.

KYLIE: I'll pull this trigger, Blixa. Look at me. You know I'll do it. Remember when I said four bodies is just as complicated as three when you think about it? Well… think about it.

(BLIXA begins to remove her clothes, seething.)

KYLIE: Rodney… now you.

RODNEY: Really?

KYLIE: Really.

STEW: This is the weirdest night.

RODNEY: *(Slowly begins to remove his clothes.)* Can I…

KYLIE: Yes, you can keep your socks on.

STEW: *(To BLIXA.)* He has a problem with feet.

(Lights down.)

(Lights up. RODNEY is lying on top of BLIXA, awkwardly trying to have sex.

KYLIE and STEW sit on the floor, eating Chinese food. Sunny Day Real Estate plays on the stereo.)

RODNEY: Isn't this music more appropriate?

STEW: Absolutely more appropriate.

KYLIE: Who is it again?

RODNEY: Sunny Day Real Estate.

KYLIE: I don't like it. Play something rockin'.

RODNEY: It's good. You might not get it on the first listen or two, but you should really give it a chance.

BLIXA: *(To RODNEY.)* Will you pay attention?

KYLIE: Are you starting to enjoy yourself?

BLIXA: No, but if I have to do this…

KYLIE: He has difficulty focusing…

RODNEY: I'm sorry.

KYLIE: Just try to clear your mind and be in the moment, Rodney. Don't think about anything except what you're feeling.

RODNEY: Don't think about the gun.

KYLIE: Yeah, don't think about the gun.

RODNEY: It's hard not to think about the gun.

KYLIE: Try it. Here… I'll hide it.

(KYLIE places the gun behind her. STEW eyes it. RODNEY continues to try to fuck BLIXA.)

RODNEY: Better?

BLIXA: Getting there.

RODNEY: Oh… cool.

KYLIE: Well, this is fun.

STEW: So, tell me about Australia.

KYLIE: What do you want to know?

STEW: Would I like it there?

KYLIE: Of course. It's lovely.

STEW: There are a lot of sharks right? Great white sharks.

KYLIE: I've only seen them on television, but I suppose there are some.

RODNEY: Hey, what's the difference between a kangaroo and a wallaby?

BLIXA: Jesus… Kylie, when this is over, I'm gonna… wait a minute, you're onto something there. *(Moans.)*

RODNEY: Really?

BLIXA: Don't stop. Keep doing that.

RODNEY: This?

BLIXA: Yes, goddamit!

STEW: *(To KYLIE.)* Do you watch "Neighbours"?

KYLIE: How do you know about "Neighbours"?

STEW: I've just heard about it. I've never seen it. Natalie Imbruglia used to be on it, right?

KYLIE: That's right.

STEW: And Kylie Minogue?

KYLIE: Yes.

STEW: *(Slyly reaches for the gun.)* Is Kylie a very popular first name in Australia?

KYLIE: Obviously.

STEW: Who do you think is more talented, Kylie Minogue or Danni Minogue? *(Grabs the gun. Stands up.)*

KYLIE: They're both a couple of talentless sluts if you ask me? *(She notices STEW holding the gun.)*

RODNEY: I think I'm going to cum.

BLIXA: Not yet.

KYLIE: What the fuck are you doing, Stew?

STEW: Don't move!

(BLIXA notices the new development.)

RODNEY: I can't hold it in. I'm gonna cum.

(BLIXA hurls RODNEY off her. He crashes to the floor.)

RODNEY: Shit.

BLIXA: *(To STEW.)* Now I know you don't know how to use that thing. Give me the gun.

(STEW squeezes the trigger. The bullet hits BLIXA. She stares incredulously. Tries to speak. Moves toward STEW. Falls dead.)

KYLIE: Shit. You sure proved her wrong.

STEW: Oh, my God.

(KYLIE walks over to BLIXA. Checks her pulse.)

STEW: Is she dead?

(KYLIE nods.)

STEW: Shit. Shit. I'm a murderer.

RODNEY: No you're not. It was self-defense.

STEW: It doesn't matter. I took someone's life. I'm going to go to Hell. When I die, I'm going to Hell.

RODNEY: Well, maybe we don't have to die anymore. I mean… we've got the gun now. I mean… maybe you won't go to hell… tonight.

KYLIE: Why don't you give me the gun before anybody else gets hurt.

STEW: We're not gonna die tonight.

RODNEY: Don't give her the gun.

STEW: *(Laughing.)* We're not gonna die anymore.

RODNEY: Don't give it to her.

STEW: We're not!

RODNEY: I know! I mean… things are different now.

KYLIE: Stew.

(STEW points the gun at her.)

STEW: Shut up… please.

KYLIE: Alright.

STEW: What do we do now?

KYLIE: Maybe we should put her in the tub?

STEW: Alright. Rodney. Help her put Blixa in the tub.

(RODNEY and KYLIE carry BLIXA off-stage. STEW sits down. Scratches his head with the gun. Finds the heroin. Does some more. RODNEY and KYLIE return.)

KYLIE: Don't overdo it there.

STEW: I can't stop shaking. I need to calm down. She's dead. One minute she's here, talking, having sex, threatening us, the next, she's somewhere else.

RODNEY: Where do you think she is?

(They stare at the ceiling.)

STEW: I'm high.

KYLIE: You're too high to be holding a gun. Give me the gun. I won't kill you. I promise.

STEW: You won't?

KYLIE: There's no need now. I've got just as much dirt on you as you have on me. I saw you murder someone.

RODNEY: It was self-defense.

KYLIE: You know there are ways out of this.

RODNEY: Really?

KYLIE: Give me the gun and we can figure it out, alright?

STEW: Alright.

RODNEY: No… wait. Give it to me. I'm not as high as you are.

STEW: You're not?

RODNEY: No. I mean, I'm really high, but not as high as you are.

STEW: I'm gonna give the gun to Rodney.

KYLIE: I think that's a mistake.

STEW: I'm sorry.

(STEW hands the gun to RODNEY. RODNEY trains it on KYLIE.)

RODNEY: Alright. How do we get out of this?

KYLIE: Well, the first thing we have to do is get rid of these bodies.

STEW: And then what?

KYLIE: Do the two of you have passports?

STEW: Yes.

RODNEY: Shit.

STEW: What?

RODNEY: Nothing.

STEW: What? You have a passport.

RODNEY: I do… but…

STEW: But what…

RODNEY: It's expired.

STEW: Expired? How could you let your passport expire?

RODNEY: I don't know. I mean, I wasn't planning on fleeing the country any time soon.

STEW: Well, I think we've all learned that what you're planning on doesn't really matter.

RODNEY: Well… yeah.

STEW: Didn't we learn that? Tonight?!

RODNEY: Stop yelling at me!

STEW: Why the fuck didn't you renew your fucking passport?!

RODNEY: Stew… please don't yell at me.

STEW: We could have gotten out of this… we could have gone to Australia… or…

KYLIE: Anywhere, really.

STEW: We could have gotten out of this, you stupid… stupid…

RODNEY: Don't yell. Please.

STEW: Fuck! You stupid fuck!

(RODNEY squeezes the trigger. Shoots STEW. STEW falls, hit.)

KYLIE: What the hell did you do that for?

RODNEY: What? What'd I do?

KYLIE: You just shot Stew?

RODNEY: No.

KYLIE: This is news to you? You squeezed the trigger.

RODNEY: He was yelling at me.

KYLIE: So?!

RODNEY: I wasn't... I wasn't... I didn't... know what I was doing.

KYLIE: Clearly!

RODNEY: I must have blacked out.

KYLIE: What the hell were you thinking?

RODNEY: I was thinking about my mother.

KYLIE: Pardon?

RODNEY: Yelling. The yelling. It re-minded me of... oh, God. Stew?

(RODNEY rushes to STEW's side.)

RODNEY: We were best friends. I loved him.

KYLIE: Well, I'm sorry for your loss.

RODNEY: No... I loved him...

KYLIE: You mean?

RODNEY: Yes.

KYLIE: Did he know?

RODNEY: No.

KYLIE: But you lived together.

RODNEY: Will you leave us alone for a minute? Please?

KYLIE: Where the hell am I supposed to go?

RODNEY: Bathroom.

KYLIE: There are two dead bodies in there.

RODNEY: Kitchen.

KYLIE: Fine.

(KYLIE exits. RODNEY strokes STEW's hair. Looks around. Kisses him on the mouth.)

RODNEY: Stew? I don't know where you are or if you can hear me, but... I'm sorry I shot you. It was an accident. I love you. I really really love you. Wherever you are.

(He kisses STEW.)

STEW: What are you doing?

RODNEY: (Jumps back.) You're alive?

STEW: Why were you kissing me?

RODNEY: I wasn't.

STEW: You weren't?

RODNEY: I was giving you mouth to mouth. I though you were dead. I shot you... accidentally.

STEW: I know. Why'd you do that?

RODNEY: You were yelling at me. Are you in pain?

STEW: No.

RODNEY: Cause of the heroin?

STEW: I guess. Where did you shoot me?

RODNEY: In the chest. I guess I missed a major organ.

STEW: Thanks.

(RODNEY pulls up STEW's shirt. Feels for the hole, bloodying his fingers. Holds them up. Stares at the blood.)

RODNEY: Stew?

STEW: What?

RODNEY: I do love you.

STEW: You do?

RODNEY: Yes.

STEW: Like a friend?

RODNEY: No. I think like more than a friend.

STEW: Really?

RODNEY: Yeah. Do you… do you feel the same way about me… at all?

STEW: I don't know. I'm still trying to process getting shot in the chest.

RODNEY: Okay. Well, you can figure it out… if you want. Whenever. Now that you're not dead… you can… you know, figure it out.

STEW: Okay.

RODNEY: Okay. Cool.

STEW: Why didn't you say anything?

RODNEY: I was afraid.

STEW: But you're not afraid any more?

RODNEY: No.

STEW: Rodney?

RODNEY: What?

STEW: Your eyes.

RODNEY: What about them?

STEW: There's a light behind them.

RODNEY: Really?

STEW: I can see it.

RODNEY: Really?

(STEW moves in closer. KYLIE tiptoes out of the kitchen, clutching a rolling pin. STEW and RODNEY kiss. Pull away.)

RODNEY: Did you like that?

(KYLIE smacks RODNEY on the back of the head. Knocking him out.)

STEW: What'd you do that for? We were having a moment.

KYLIE: He shot you.

STEW: He didn't mean it. He loves me.

(KYLIE kneels down. Checks RODNEY's pulse.)

KYLIE: Er… loved… a more appropriate tense.

STEW: You mean?

KYLIE: Yep. I hit him pretty hard.

STEW: He's dead?

KYLIE: I'm 90 percent sure.

STEW: So he might be alive?

KYLIE: No… he's dead.

STEW: I need another line.

KYLIE: I think I do too.

(KYLIE helps STEW up. They sit on the couch.)

KYLIE: What are you doing with a rolling pin anyway?

STEW: We make cookies. Sometimes.

(They snort.)

KYLIE: You were kissing him.

STEW: I know. He had light behind his eyes.

KYLIE: So.

STEW: It was… beautiful.

KYLIE: You have light behind your eyes.

STEW: I do?

KYLIE: Yes. I can see it quite clearly.

STEW: Really?

KYLIE: Yes.

STEW: I can't believe my best friend is dead.

KYLIE: It's for the best really.

STEW: For the best? How is it for the best?

KYLIE: His passport's expired. He'd only hold us up.

STEW: Where are we going to go?

KYLIE: Where would you like to go?

STEW: I don't know.

KYLIE: Well you figure it out. I'm going to wash up.

STEW: Will you put him in the tub… on your way? I can't look at him.

KYLIE: Alright.

STEW: Thanks.

(KYLIE drags RODNEY off.)

KYLIE: Why don't you pack up all the drugs, and whatever money you have… and some clothes.

STEW: Okay.

(STEW rises… falls back. Checks his wound. Lights a cigarette. Tries to get up again. Falls back. KYLIE enters.)

KYLIE: There's nothing wrong with his feet.

STEW: You looked at his feet?

KYLIE: I was curious.

STEW: Oh…

KYLIE: What about Moscow? You know they'd have a fuck of a time trying to extradite us. We could visit Dostoyevsky's house.

STEW: You like Dostoyevsky?

KYLIE: No. But we could visit his house.

STEW: I'm gonna die.

KYLIE: You're not gonna die. It's just a flesh wound.

STEW: I can't stand up. I feel like I'm leaving my body. I'm gonna die.

KYLIE: You're nodding. You're high.

STEW: I am?

KYLIE: Yes.

(She leans down. Kisses his cheek.)

KYLIE: You're gonna be fine. We'll stop at my place. I have a neighbor who's a pre-med student. He'll get that bullet out of you.

STEW: Won't he tell?

KYLIE: Nah. I'll fuck him.

STEW: Oh… I get it.

KYLIE: It's just you and me now, sweetheart.

STEW: You don't mind that I might be queer?

KYLIE: No. You don't mind that I sell my pussy for stuff?

STEW: No.

KYLIE: Then we've already got a better relationship than most people I know. I'm getting too old for bullshit, you know?

(She helps him up.)

STEW: Me too.

(They grab their things, stumble toward the door.)

KYLIE: Although… if you decide you're not queer and ever want to eat my pussy, that'd be nice.

STEW: Oh… okay.

KYLIE: You're a natural. An artist.

STEW: An artist.

KYLIE: Absolutely.

STEW: That's good to know. You know, Kylie…

KYLIE: What's that Stew?

STEW: I've discovered a lot about myself tonight, Kylie.

KYLIE: Self-knowledge is an important thing, Stew.

STEW: You're not kiddin'.

(They kiss. Shut out the light. Close the door. Long beat. A rustle. RODNEY enters, holding his head. Walks to the door. Turns on the light.)

RODNEY: Stew? Stew? Hello? *(Looks around. Walks over to the couch. Sits down. Rubs head again. Long beat. Smiles.)*

(Lights down.)

REALITY

Curtiss I' Cook

CURTISS I' COOK was born in Dayton, Ohio, the oldest in a family of five children. He started acting and singing while still in school. In high school, he became involved with Muse Machine, an organization that took kids from the entire county and had them perform for surrounding cities in a huge professional touring theatre in downtown Dayton. This experience helped him earn a scholarship at the Mountview Theatre School in London, where he received his BFA in acting. Today, he works as an actor, director, and playwright in New York City. His most recent play was *Greenwood*, which premiered at The Present Company Theatorium in October 2001 under the auspices of Tupu Kweli Theatre Company, which he founded and for which he serves as artistic director. As an actor, he has been seen on Broadway as John in *Miss Saigon* and as Banzai the Hyena in *The Lion King*, and on the ABC television series "The Job." He is the proud father of Curtiss Jr., Isis, and Kimani Cook.

Reality was first produced by Tupu Kweli Theatre Company on March 14, 2001, at the Grove Street Playhouse, New York City, with the following cast and credits:

Lathan Jones .... Curtiss I' Cook
Reverend Sam Sweets .... Jaymes Jorsling
Chynthia Cuffey .... Ebbe Bassey
Sabrina Harper .... Sabah El-Amin
Charles Watson .... Keith Tisdell/Michael Ealy
Thomas Wright .... Maurice Dwyer
Paulette Cuffey .... Kimberly 'Q' Purnell
Carmen Simms .... Adenrele Ojo
Bertha Jones .... Adetoro Makinde
Jimmy Cuffey .... Marcuis Harris

Directed by: Curtiss I' Cook.
Production Stage Manager: Christopher Russo
Assistant Stage Manager: Laura Canty-Samuel
Lighting Designer: Michael P. Jones
Costume Designer: Elizabeth Cline

Reality is a play inside of a play inside of the real world, i.e., the theatre space it is performed in. So the set should have a look of being very stagy, meaning that, as the play goes on, objects that at first looked real eventually come to look like set pieces or just painted-on flats. The real name of the actor playing JIMMY should be used during the play. The actor playing LATHAN should not use his real name; instead, he should use the name CURTISS (meaning that he is playing both LATHAN and CURTISS).

The use of sound is very important to me as a writer. So throughout the play, you should hear music setting moods and introducing feelings—subconsciously, as in a movie soundtrack—as well as special effect sounds for things like JIMMY walking through the fourth wall and the freeze poses. A tape or CD of these sounds is available from the author if needed.

The major thing to remember when performing *Reality* is that what the audience sees in the beginning is really just a play. It isn't until the end that we introduce them to our version of *Reality*.

I hope you enjoy.

Curtiss I' Cook

The stage is black. We hear an argument between two men.

VOICEOVER: I'm just trying to figure out what you're trying to say. All I hear is the same rhetoric you've been spewing for the past seven years, in your so-called writing!

CURTISS: Why can't you be supportive? I think there are many messages in what…

VOICEOVER: Many, many, many! What is that Curtiss… There are always many something with you. What you need to do is follow a single plot, and play it through. Leave people with many messages of one main story!

CURTISS: Forget this man. I'm an actor, not a writer.

VOICEOVER: Well act then, stop walking around here complaining about shit… focus on one thing! What you need to do is pay attention to those kids, but whatever it is, do it man and stop making excuses for things.

CURTISS: This is important to me…

VOICEOVER: Then do it! Let this be your main focus… but if you're going to do it, do it right!

CURTISS: Who's to say that I'm not doing it right?

VOICEOVER: Ok, how many plays have you written with a story line? How many plays have you written that the audiences didn't walk out thinking your ass was on drugs? How many people understand your crazy ass?

CURTISS: I've written a few plays that have touched people, and made them look at things differently.

VOICEOVER: Who are you fooling man? Because it sure ain't me!

CURTISS: What about this one?

VOICEOVER: Is it ready?

CURTISS: Yeah after a few changes and…

VOICEOVER: And and and what? Man if you don't get out of my face with that avant garde mess. Go fix your script, then come talk to me!

CURTISS: Why can't you be just a little supportive, say good job once in a while…? *(Enters the stage area.)* You fix it dammit! I quit! I don't have…

(Throws script on the floor. Realizing it does need to be altered, he picks it up and begins to write and make changes. As he does, the CAST enters the stage in a straight line; as the author makes changes, the CAST changes places until he gets it right. When this happens, the CAST leaves, and we hear the REVEREND's sermon. Lights on stage reveal a small church with nine chairs facing the audience with an aisle for the REVEREND and his podium. CURTISS continues writing, walking out into the house.)

REALITY

Set in: Dayton, Ohio.

The time: Sunday, August 9, 2000; the hottest day of that year.

The place: Inside of a very nice, small neighborhood church, roomy yet cozy, grand yet tasteful; the ideal Midwestern Sunday meeting place for the ordinary folk.

The sound of a sermon in session. As we hear the REVEREND's voice, the lights reveal the nine CAST members seated facing the audience. The REVEREND SAM SWEET is behind the podium, also facing the audience, and is finishing his speech.

REV. SWEETS: And the bible also says let he without guilt cast the first stone. But in the case of harm to your brother, let he without blinders tell the tale… meaning if you see the truth tell it!

(Sounds of "amen" from the CAST.)

REV. SWEETS: If you're exposed to the wrongs that no one else can see, make them known!

(Sounds of "amen" from the CAST.)

REV. SWEETS: But does that mean stay in your own business, Mrs. Johnson? Yes!!

(Laughter.)

REV. SWEETS: Does that mean make fun of Mrs. Johnson because the sister has a problem? No! We have to be able to help without prying, without crossing that line of nosiness and concern, without hurting our brothers and sisters because we got dirt on them that's good bathroom talk…

(Sounds of "amen" from the CAST.)

REV. SWEETS: It means being responsible for yourselves and your communities! Satan is upon us, sisters and brothers. He is here and has been here for a very long time… and he has not been more prevalent than in our own neighborhoods…

(Sounds of "amen" from the CAST.)

REV. SWEETS: …Yes! You know what I'm talking about… That feeling of not being safe walking down your own street… even for the men in our congregation… they may not want to admit it out loud in front of the sisters… but believe me it's there… Our young brothers hanging out on our corners at all times of the day and night! We need to get 'em off

that corner…! Drinking and smoking and playing loud music! We need to get 'em off that corner… Dealing and fighting and shouting obscenities to our sisters and daughters and female friends… We need to get 'em off that corner, my corner, your corner, his corner, and this corner!!

(Sounds of "amen" from the CAST.)

REV. SWEETS: …Who's going to do this? Who's going to lead the way for this righteous crusade? God is.

(Sounds of "amen" from the CAST.)

REV. SWEETS: Yes, sisters and brothers, God's hand is here to slap the stain of sin off their faces. Spare the rod and spoil the child the bible says… God's hand is heavy and His power is just. So His punishment will be harsh, final, and absolute! So *He* will lead us in getting them off our corner!!

(A roar of amens.)

REV. SWEETS: …Yes sir, thank You Lord. Thank You for Your blessings, thank You for Your gift You've given to me to lead Your sheep to Your way Lord!… Many of my brothers and sisters didn't want me here at first Lord. I heard them talking when I arrived over two years ago after our father Reverend Green passed on into Your care Lord. Some of the things they said about me Father… "What is this child doing up behind the altar?" "What can a boy his age teach me about my Lord?" And as I stand here today I give testimony to You Lord by quoting Isaiah 11:6 "…and a mere child will lead them." Once again I put all of my faith in Your divine power. When I doubted myself I went to You. When I allowed those comments to make me weak, I felt the power of Your loving spirit lifting me up. And You told me *to wait!*… To allow them to acknowledge the gift that You gave me. And I waited Lord. I waited for You to show me the right time to address this issue and You showed me through patience what *not* to do. We need to speak with our actions and not with *our* words, but *Your* words, Lord... So that's what I did, and as I look over the congregation today, over Your congregation Lord, I see individuals who wouldn't have set a foot in a house with a bible *in it* let alone the House of the Lord!

(Sounds of "amen" from the CAST.)

REV. SWEETS: Yes sir, praise Jesus! Singing and praising His name for the love He has shown and given us. Ready to rid our neighborhood of the evil in our midst!

(A woman, SABRINA, screams within the congregation. She's crying and hysterical and indicates her [unseen] baby.)

SABRINA: Please someone help me... Please someone help me... coughing... stopped!! Look, turning purple... please somebody... Please help me!!!

(The congregation jumps to its feet. Everyone runs over to SABRINA, although no one helps her. They just stand and look as she continues to scream. JIMMY CUFFEY, an African American male in his mid-thirties, pushes through the crowd and pushes SABRINA, who almost falls... Then everyone begins to scream out at the audience as if seeing something at the front of the congregation. The crowd disperses at the climax of the scene with a blackout.)

(Lights up.)

(Nine chairs have been set up over the stage inside of the church. It is eight hours later. The CAST faces the audience in their chairs. They are: REV. SWEETS, a young reverend

in his early to mid-twenties; SABRINA HARPER, the mother of the baby and in her mid-twenties; CHARLES WATSON, neighborhood businessman mid- to late twenties; JIMMY CUFFEY, a policeman; his wife, CHYNTHIA CUFFEY, late twenties/early thirties; PAULETTE CUFFEY, JIMMY's sister; BERTHA and LATHAN JONES, husband and wife, both in their mid-thirties; CARMEN SIMMS, mid-twenties; and THOMAS WRIGHT, businessman, mid- to late twenties. All characters are African American.)

(Quiet.)

REV. SWEETS: Let us pray...

SABRINA: No! I'm tired of praying, Reverend! We've been here for eight hours... Praying for guidance, asking for forgiveness, and nothing has happened. You keep telling me not to go to the police or the authorities, that God will give us the answer... Well, I've been waiting Reverend... and nothing has come! I'm being made to sit here and relive this... Do you know how hard this is ? *(Begins to cry.)* I want justice, Reverend!...

CHARLES: Sabrina, baby. Try and stay calm. It's hard I know, but it'll be a lot easier when we put Jimmy Cuffey in jail!

JIMMY: What are you talking about Chuck? Put me in jail. This is not my fault! I tried to help and I would have if...

(CHARLES and JIMMY continue to argue back and forth.)

PAULETTE: If what?... Don't try and put this on me! If you want to blame someone you should...

(PAULETTE points over to BERTHA, who begins to argue back with her.)

REV. SWEETS: Sisters and brothers, there is no need for this... The answer is coming to us. Our Lord and Savior has not forgotten us... He is waiting for the time when we are ready to receive His blessing. So I would encourage all of you to just sit in prayer and allow His words to touch us...

BERTHA: Reverend please! I'm all for the Lord coming down and helping, but we don't have time for that. First of all I have to make it known that I had nothing to do with this. I wouldn't have been here anyway if my husband didn't find the need to get all sanctified all of a sudden. But on the other hand, I know that somebody here is going to need a defense attorney. And I feel that it is my duty as a wife and mother to offer my husband's services to the highest bidder...

LATHAN: Bertha, please sit down.

BERTHA: No! I'm not sitting down! You need a case and somebody here is going to need a lawyer... the law has to be involved... waiting on some invisible answer to drop down out of the air. And you, Jimmy, a police officer too; you have to know better than this. Lathan, if you pull on me one more time I'm going to knock...

LATHAN: Bertha, honey, please you are not helping the situation... I think what is happening right now will produce its own benefits and like it or not, sweetheart, we are a part of this travesty... So please let's not make it any worse by adding our impatience to an already lengthy matter.

CHARLES: Hey, I know you. You're that guy on those commercials who's always talking about "There isn't a case that can't make money." Right?

LATHAN: Yes.

CHARLES: When did you start coming here?

CARMEN: When he found out this was my church!

LATHAN: That's...

BERTHA: What?! When he found out what?! Who are you?

CARMEN: Lathan, tell your wife who I am!

BERTHA: Do you know this woman, Lathan?

CARMEN: Yes he knows me.

LATHAN: Carmen please...

CARMEN: Don't please me...

(SABRINA screams and begins to walk over to the door.)

SABRINA: I'm going to the police!!

REV. SWEETS: *(Yelling.)* No! Sister Harper... Please give us time. We don't want worldly influences in our private dealings. I know the pain is great and it's hard for you to put your fleshly suffering to the side, but God is here! He is waiting to feel your faith, sister. He is waiting for you to accept Him with all of your heart. You do that and He will show his face on this matter.

LATHAN: Reverend, what do you expect us to do here?... We've been here for over eight hours, and I fail to see how this is benefiting anyone. I have to agree... This is a case for the authorities.

BERTHA: You're going to be a case for the authorities if you don't sit down... You shouldn't be saying nothing, other than who this Jezebel is with that tight cheap dress on.

CARMEN: Tight dress! First of all, sweetie, you don't know me well enough to be calling me out of my name! Secondly, I'm not the one you should be upset with! And as for cheap, I know you can recognize that, look at your weave!

BERTHA: What!!

THOMAS: Ladies, please!! Shut up with that Jerry Springer shit!! Excuse me, Reverend. We have a much bigger problem here! Reverend, do you still have any of those legal pads left over from the renovation meeting last month?

REV. SWEETS: I think I do. Why?

THOMAS: Because when this goes to the authorities, and it will have to, they are going to need an account of everything that happened this morning. So why don't we all take the time now and write down what we saw and experienced during the accident instead of waiting for nothing.

REV. SWEETS: We're not waiting for *nothing*, Brother Wright. We're waiting on God!

THOMAS: Yeah Reverend, but sometimes God takes a little longer than we have.

CARMEN: You know what this is: Stupid! I thought that I could help, but this is wasting my time. I'm leaving!

CHARLES: I'm with the sister with the tight cheap dress on. I tried to help too, but I think the best thing to do is turn over the man who's responsible.

JIMMY: And who would that be?

CHARLES: You! Jimmy!!

JIMMY: You are not pinning the death of that child on me! I tried to save her life!

CHARLES: Then let the courts decide

man! If you're innocent, then you'll be free.

JIMMY: I think Thomas's idea is good. Why… .

CHARLES: Thomas's idea is bullshit! And so is the Reverend's idea. You're going to jail plain and simple.

(JIMMY runs out of the church.)

CHARLES: Look, see what I mean, guilty… Waiting for God is like waiting for Godot. This is wasting time. Sabrina, come on, I'm taking you out of here and to someone who can help you. I'd advise the rest of you to do the same.

(All together.)

> BERTHA: That makes sense to me. Come on Lathan, wait until I get you home!
>
> LATHAN: I don't know if this is right, honey.
>
> SABRINA: Thank you, Charles.
>
> CARMEN: This is such a waste!
>
> THOMAS: Well I tried, Rev.
>
> REV. SWEETS: Please wait!

(JIMMY backs everyone back into the church with a gun.)

JIMMY: No! No one's leaving here until I can figure this out!

PAULETTE: James! What are you doing, are you crazy, put the gun away before you hurt someone…

CHYNTHIA: Jimmy, honey please, listen to your sister, put the gun away you're scaring me…

JIMMY: Chyn, you know I didn't do this baby! I can't let them ruin our lives like this, not now baby, not now!

CHYNTHIA: Yes, I know, but this isn't helping anyone… put the gun away. We can figure this out.

CHARLES: You had better listen to your old lady, man. What's wrong with you?… Pulling a gun out on us…

PAULETTE: Charles, just wait… let us handle this…

CHARLES: Wait my ass! Come on fellows, help me get this gun from this fool!

JIMMY: Charles, stay back man. I'm serious, I need to find out some answers… I don't want to hurt anybody so please stay back…

(The two men keep advancing. JIMMY warns again. They struggle, and two shots are fired, one hitting SABRINA in the shoulder, the other shooting CHARLES in the hand.)

PAULETTE: Oh my God!! She's dead! I know it, she's dead! Look what you've done, James, look what you've done! I told you to put the gun away, but you never want to listen to me, you never listen to me…

JIMMY: Shut up Paul!!

(The entire CAST, except JIMMY, begins to move in slow motion, reacting to the shooting.)

JIMMY: Shit, what am I going to do? What am I going to do?!

CHARLES: You're going to get your ass kicked, that's what you're going to do!!

(Slow motion stops, and everyone is moving in real time.)

CHARLES: Damn, my hand… *(He wraps his hand with his tie.)*

THOMAS: Someone please get a towel or something to stop the bleeding in her shoulder. She's going to live, but we have to get her out of here! She's losing a lot of blood. Jimmy, you're going to have to let us out and get them to the hospital!

(JIMMY doesn't answer.)

THOMAS: Jimmy, can you hear me!! We have to get Sabrina out of here.

CHARLES: You better just let my ass bleed to death, because if I get out of here I'm going to kill you!

THOMAS: Charles, hold off, we have to get her to the hospital. I'm trying to check her pulse, but I can't get it! Does anyone here know how to do that?

(CHYNTHIA walks over to SABRINA and sits her up, and begins to tend the wound as if she's done it many times before.)

CHYNTHIA: Jimmy, her pulse is low. We have to get her out of here… she's losing blood.

JIMMY: I didn't mean for this to happen!! Oh Reverend, I didn't mean for this to happen..

REV. SWEETS: I know James… I know…

JIMMY: What am I going to do…

CHARLES: Let us the hell out of here mother fucka!!

JIMMY: *(Yelling.)* Shut up! Shut up!! I have to think… I have to think!!

SABRINA: I tried to do the right thing… I started coming to church… trying to turn my life around… walk in the way of the Lord… in the way… in the way of the Lord, the way my mother did, the way my mother would have wanted me to for my child… I did it for my child… I wanted to make my life better for my child and for me… why does it seem whenever you start doing right… So much wrong is in your way… so much wrong… Who's going to care about a hooker… dead… who's going to care… Who cares?! "The serpent will get crushed by the heel of the Lord…" My baby was crushed by the heel of… Death out of life. You can't get life out of death. *(She passes out.)*

CARMEN: Is she dead?

CHYNTHIA: No, she passed out. She needs a doctor.

BERTHA: She needs a doctor and I need a drink!… This is too much drama for me…

(LATHAN grabs her.)

JIMMY: This wasn't supposed to happen… I can't get out, I'm in, and there's no one who can help me but me… Reverend, we need a prayer! We need a prayer for everyone and for me… I didn't want this to happen… Pray please, Rev.

(As the REVEREND prays, JIMMY continues to talk.)

REV. SWEETS: Please bow your heads … Lord Jesus, we come to You this evening asking that Your holy spirit touch us,

JIMMY: *(Overlapping.)* We need the words of God right about now!

REV. SWEETS: move through us with the grace of your love,

JIMMY: *(Overlapping.)* No one wants to listen to old Jimmy,

REV. SWEETS: the strength of Your all-knowing understanding and the power of Your forgiveness.

JIMMY: *(Overlapping.)* everyone thinks he done went and killed this child… They see that he's capable of doing wrong just look at what you done did now man…

(Laughs.)

REV. SWEETS: Please help this woman Lord, as she lays here in Your House.

JIMMY: *(Overlapping.)* That woman's child is dead and now she sits on the floor bleeding and you're wondering if it's right to let her get medical attention

REV. SWEETS: Do not forsake her Lord, for her journey to truth led her to You.

JIMMY: *(Overlapping, yelling.)* I didn't kill that baby!!!

REV. SWEETS: Not to be judged by men, but by the scales of glory, the scales of divinity, the scales which are held in the Lord's hands of justice.

JIMMY: *(Overlapping.)* But I am going to kill somebody in here if the answer doesn't come soon… you don't have to like me, but we are going to get some answers this day…

REV. SWEETS: And we pray for her. We also pray for Brother Cuffey and ourselves.

JIMMY: *(Overlapping.)* no more waiting… waiting… waiting!! You are not blaming me… you are not going to do that

(JIMMY fires a shot in the air. Someone in the audience reacts to the sound. JIMMY reacts as if he can see and hear the person in the audience but is not sure.)

JIMMY: Yeah!! You heard that, didn't you… all of you watching me watching me I see you… looking at me… who are you looking at me… why are you looking at me… who are you…

(The audience is gone. CHARLES begins to talk to THOMAS.)

JIMMY: Charles, you have a lot to say I see… Why don't you talk to all of us… *(Points gun at CHARLES.)*

REV. SWEETS: *(Overlapping.)* We need You Lord. We need You! Oh! God do we need You! Through Your Son's name we pray. Amen.

PAULETTE: James don't!

JIMMY: *(Pointing gun at PAULETTE.)* Or do you want to talk big sister... You always have the answers, why don't you enlighten us!

CHYNTHIA: James honey please...

JIMMY: Chyn, not now, stay with Sabrina. I know what I'm doing. I'm getting my sister to talk... right Paul?... You're going to talk to us!

PAULETTE: James, I don't know what you're talking about. What do you want me to say?

JIMMY: Anything... You and Thomas... why don't you talk about that...

PAULETTE: James, this is not the time to talk about anything other than you and this gun... you're going crazy! You need to let these people out...

BERTHA: *(Drinking from a flask.)* She sure is feisty ain't she... just answer the man's questions before we all get shot! Don't she watch primetime TV... Just answer the damn questions... shit...

(LATHAN pulls her down.)

PAULETTE: I am not going to be threatened by that gun. I know you better than this, James... You didn't mean to shoot Sabrina or Charles, and you are not going to shoot me. I'm your sister! So quit acting stupid.

(He shoots near her leg. JIMMY again becomes aware of the audience... and then he again loses this awareness.)

PAULETTE: Oh my God!

BERTHA: Oh my God!... I told you... I told you... *(She hides under a table.)*

JIMMY: Who are you?... Why are you there... who...

CHYNTHIA: Who are you talking to?...

JIMMY: *(Looks back at PAULETTE as if nothing has happened.)* I did that on purpose... Do I have to shoot you in order for you to talk?

PAULETTE: What do you want me to say?!! Thomas and I are business partners. We have been for the last year and a half. We've done a lot for this community and we plan to build a new recreation center downtown... Is that what you want to hear? I don't know why, everyone knows that! Stop this James... let us out of here!

JIMMY: Paul, don't make me have to shoot you because I will. *(Mockingly.)* This is the house of the Lord where we can lay our burdens down. I'm giving you a chance to do that, to open up, let go of all that grief you been carrying with you... *(Quick switch to evil.)* I'm going to ask you again to tell us about you and Thomas's relationship and what you do, and if you say anything else other than that I'm going to shoot you.

THOMAS: Are you all going to sit around and let him do this?! We have rights here! This is going too far!

(JIMMY shoots over in THOMAS's direction.)

JIMMY: *(Audience reaction; JIMMY stares, aware again.)* Shut up!!... Paul?

PAULETTE: *(Beginning to cry.)* I don't know how this got turned around to me...

(JIMMY waits, pointing gun.)

PAULETTE: Thomas and I... run a center for women... *(Pause.)*

JIMMY: And?...

PAULETTE: The women we help are young girls who are either in trouble with the law, have run away from home, or are poor and don't have any other recourse... We give them a place to stay and food to eat... *(Pause.)* The only thing we ask of these girls is that they work for us... that they work to help pay for their keep...

JIMMY: And what kind of work do you and Mr. Wright find for these girls to do?

THOMAS: What business is this of yours? You have nothing to do with this. We are helping this community in ways that no city official ever has... You can't stand there and judge us when you've shot two people and are holding the rest of us hostage for something none of us did.

JIMMY: Just because you and my sister give a block party every now and then or build a new community center does not give you the right to prostitute young women!!

THOMAS: Prostitution?! Who said anything about prostitution... you have no proof!! You're just some crazy ass mother fucka who goes around killing babies and holding innocent people hostage... why should any of us believe or listen to what you have to say!

PAULETTE: *(To THOMAS, indicating JIMMY.)* He's right! And you know he is... Thomas...

THOMAS: What?! Shut up Paulette... Just be quiet. I'll handle this...

PAULETTE: No. I'm tired Thomas... and people are getting hurt. If I can tell my brother the truth maybe he'll let them

out and turn himself in. So that's it James, you seem to know most of it. We sell out these girls. We make sure they are taken care of, that none of the johns they're with hurt them in any way, and we make sure they get tested regularly. Most of the money I receive is put back into the community... Like this church for instance. But normally, Mr. Wright handles the financial end of the business. We are not in the practice of hurting people...

JIMMY: Then what happened to Sabrina?...

PAULETTE: You shot her! That's what happened to Sabrina...

THOMAS: Ms. Harper didn't want to play by the rules... None of this information leaves this church, none of it...

JIMMY: Talk.

THOMAS: The girls have to go on weekly checkups, make sure the men wear condoms at all times... and take their birth control pills regularly, and they must not under any circumstances date outside of work... They cannot see *any other person* for their own recreation... Ms. Harper didn't follow any of these rules, so we had to let her go... No matter what you may think, our organization is a very well-run business. If someone doesn't want to abide by our rules, they don't have to stay. They are always free to go...

CARMEN: Wait a minute. Are you serious, this is going on right here in our town?

CHARLES: And if they got checked regularly... I'm assuming that means for disease as well as for pregnancy... How did Sabrina end up pregnant?

THOMAS: I told you Ms. Harper didn't follow any of our *rules.*

CHARLES: That's bullshit man!! Sabrina told me all about your scam and what you did to her to make sure she wouldn't steal any of your regular clients… !!

PAULETTE: What is he talking about, Thomas?

THOMAS: He's a fucking barber. He doesn't know what he's taking about.

CHARLES: But what I do know is that before you poisoned her you felt it was your right to rape her… thought you would take some of that sweet ass before it was tainted.

CHYNTHIA: Charles… Sabrina is waking up.

SABRINA: I'm cold, please somebody help me… I'm cold! Get my baby… please make sure she's all right… turn up the heat… make sure my baby is warm … I can't move… someone's holding me down please… I'm cold I'm so cold!!! Charles? Charles, are you here?… Charles?

CHARLES: Brina, I'm here…

SABRINA: Please take care of our baby; please make sure she's warm… I need your help!

CHARLES: Everything is going to be all right…

CHYNTHIA: I need some sheets or something to raise her body temperature. I've stopped the bleeding. We need to get her some more professional attention.

(CHARLES yells out of anger and frustration, and charges JIMMY. They fight; the gun flies out of JIMMY's hand. Everyone is screaming to get the gun. JIMMY is able to wrestle CHARLES into a chokehold, nearly snapping his neck. REVEREND SWEETS picks up the gun.)

JIMMY: Reverend, if you don't want me to snap his neck… You had better give me that gun.

(No response.)

JIMMY: I'm telling you right now, Rev, three seconds!

(JIMMY begins to choke CHARLES tighter, making him gag for air.)

JIMMY: Three… two…

(The REVEREND hands him the gun, and JIMMY releases CHARLES. Then he steps on his hand that's been shot. CHARLES screams.)

CHARLES: Who in the hell do you think you are?! Kill me!! I'm telling you, kill me now! Because it's over Jimmy, this shit is over, brother…

JIMMY: *(Overlapping.)* It doesn't matter who I think I am! What matters is this! *(Indicating the gun.)* Now sit over there and shut up…

CHARLES: Shut up? Man, you don't seem to get it do you?… I have a life, I have a mother, father, I have a family… up until this morning I had a newborn child… and now I'm looking at the mother of my baby die, and you want me to sit down and shut up?! I'm telling you, Jimmy… I've never been more ready to die than now… You've taken just about everything away from me that makes me who I am… My freedom, brother… You have taken my motherfuckin' freedom, and I would rather be dead than sit here for one more second…

(He charges JIMMY again. JIMMY holds him off with the gun. The strain of everything has taken him over completely.)

REV. SWEETS: Please Brother Cuffey, sit down, this is enough, sit down!

JIMMY: It's for them… Charlie, Chucky, boy… they watch and say nothing, they laugh and make comments on our lives as if they have a right to. Clean up our neighborhoods. From who? From our young brothers, that's the easy way to go. We can see what they do as they sit and watch us as if they have nothing wrong in their lives… but they do… they have many things wrong. But this gives them a chance to escape that, to get away from that bill that needs to be paid, that person who needs to be talked to… We can't get away from our problems because I'm here with this… *(Indicates the gun.)* …and we are going to talk them out, because they will help us. They will help me. I didn't kill that child! She did it! She didn't mean it… I didn't kill Sabrina. He did, with his ignorance, and he blames me for letting her die… for letting her bleed and die… Get them off that corner, whose corner, it's their corner, why should we get them off of it!! Who's inside the building that's on the corner and what are they doing? Are they helping us or themselves… they watch, I see you looking at me… Stop looking at me unless you have something to say to me… unless you want to add to what I'm saying… Stop looking at me or I'll shoot you! I'll shoot everyone! I DIDN'T KILL THAT BABY!! SHE DIDN'T MEAN TO…

(He falls to the floor and goes into a convulsion, dropping the gun. CHYNTHIA goes over and tries to help him. She can't control him. LATHAN gets up and runs out the door. REVEREND SWEETS picks up the gun and stops CHARLES and THOMAS before they can get out.)

CHARLES and THOMAS: Reverend, what are you doing? This is our chance to get out of here.

REV. SWEETS: I'm stopping you because God wants me to stop you brothers… I don't agree with Brother Cuffey's methods under normal circumstances, but this isn't normal … a lot of things are still left unresolved and they need to be. So I'm going to ask you two brothers to take your seats as Sister Cuffey tends to her husband…

(CHARLES begins to advance on the REVEREND.)

REV. SWEETS: Brother Watson, please don't make me do anything we would both regret! I'm serious about this… I need for you to take your seat.

(Seeing that the REVEREND is serious, the men find their places: CHARLES moves downstage right with SABRINA, THOMAS upstage right next to PAULETTE. REVEREND SWEETS is upstage right by the door, CHYNTHIA and JIMMY are downstage left, leaving CARMEN and BERTHA upstage splitting center. Each group sits quietly as tableau lights hit each one randomly. In the quiet, we begin to hear the sound of a clock ticking. After a period of time passes— roughly forty seconds—the REVEREND begins to sing softly an old church hymn. As he gets farther into the song, CHYNTHIA begins her monologue. While she is talking, the others, except for the REVEREND, are in the dark. CHYNTHIA is still with JIMMY; he's moving slowly, waking from his sleep.)

CHYNTHIA: We've been married for two years and I love you more than I love myself. I'm sorry, I can't give you what you want. I know you say that it doesn't matter and that in time it will take care of itself… but I look in your eyes as we make love and see how much it means to you, I see you almost wishing for it: "Maybe this will be the time…," "if I just hold her a little tighter…," "if I just love her a little more…" I see that, Jimmy, and I feel it inside of me… I want a child as much as you do… I am so afraid that you are going to leave me… I know that you don't want to, but part of me feels that if you did, you would have every right to! Don't!! Please don't, Jimmy, I love you, I don't know what I would do if you did… At work, everyone keeps asking when are we going to have children, I say we're just not ready. We just don't want children right now. But that's a lie and they know it's a lie… they laugh… they're not laughing, but I hear them laughing at us. They don't know how much you love me and I love you. They don't know how much pain we're going through. They just know their books, their TV shows that point and blame and find alternate methods… Other ways to do what's natural, what was meant to be done with the one you love the way God meant it to be done… They make me so angry!! The ones who have no right having babies three or four children, no money, three or four different men… children, dirty, crying. They shouldn't have that child, I should! I should have that baby! I want a baby, and I can't have one, but they have three or four, three or four. I have none, zero, none and it makes me angry! It makes me want to hurt them, hurt their baby!… But she had no right having a baby and I don't have one. She's a whore, she sleeps with so many men. She's sick, her baby is sick, but she has one. I have none! Now she has none because I don't want her to have one if I can't she can't if I can't… I did it for you Jimmy! So that we don't have to look at her coming here every Sunday with that child… with that sick baby that we don't have… It was wrong oh God it was

so wrong but I couldn't stop myself! I stopped it from breathing… I jumped down, covered its mouth as everybody yelled, trying not to step on it!… I just jumped down there and killed her baby, Jimmy… I did it… I killed her baby… But I meant too… I did mean it! I killed her baby…

(BERTHA goes over to comfort her as she breaks down crying. JIMMY sits up and looks at the audience. He begins to notice the people. He begins to talk as he gets up.)

JIMMY: They sit there and they judge us, how can they see me if I can't see me seeing the answers to this is in the faces of that lady looking at me… she sees… she sees but she's not really looking at me, or is she? Are you, are you looking at me too… are you staring at Jimmy and making a judgment like them two… how did you get here, why are you sitting there… in that chair staring at us as we tell of our fears. This is our life… This is no joke, but you look as if you're ready to…

PAULETTE: Someone please help my brother before he has another seizure.

(JIMMY steps through the fourth wall, disappearing to the CAST on stage. There is a hush that comes over the CAST as they look on. JIMMY, confused, examines the faces in the audience, takes a woman's program from her and begins to thumb through it. As he crosses the stage, the CAST begins to talk to each other. JIMMY looks at them from the audience's perspective.)

(All together.)

REV. SWEETS: And when there's darkness… light will come, and when there's hope… you will see my face… The Lord has spoken to us, He has given us our answer to our problems.

THOMAS: How is this an answer... a man walking through a... through a... I can't even say it.

CARMEN: A wall... he walked through the wall...

THOMAS: Yeah! A wall!

BERTHA: That's it! No more... I'm not drinking any more, when I start seeing people walk through walls and shit, that's it!!

(At that moment, JIMMY walks back onto the stage. A bright light effect. As he does, the CAST goes back to the moment right before he walked to the other side. JIMMY still holding the program, talking to himself and stunned.)

PAULETTE: Will someone please help my brother before he has another seizure? Jimmy, are you all right?

(No answer.)

PAULETTE: James?

(He just sits and begins to read the program/ bible.)

PAULETTE: Where did he get that bible from?

CHARLES: I don't know, but Sabrina and I are leaving... and once we get home, I think it's fair to tell you, I'm calling the police.

JIMMY: *(In a very calm voice.)* Charles, you're not going anywhere.

CHARLES: Come on man... I am tired of fighting with you... you're obviously not well... and your wife just confessed to killing my child... don't you think we've been through enough... Don't start this bullshit again. Now, I'm going to say this for the last damn time... I'm taking... Sabrina... before... she gets any worse!

JIMMY: No one's going to get any worse, and your baby isn't dead. *(Begins to read the program.)* Marcuis... Harris... Marcuis... Charles, they're watching us, man... They just sit and look at us as we fight, as we live right in front of them, like it's a... show.

CHYNTHIA: Jimmy, who are you talking about?

JIMMY: Them out there, Chyn. Look, can't you see them?

CHYNTHIA: No baby, that's a wall...

JIMMY: Chyn, when I walked through that wall...

CHYNTHIA: When you walked through the wall, honey?

JIMMY: I saw people watching us... I looked at them sitting in the dark holding these *(Indicates program.)* and staring... not laughing, not crying, not smiling... just watching us, watching us... watching

CHARLES: Great... well, just watch me leave...

JIMMY: You can't, the door is locked.

CHARLES: All right then, I'll just walk through the wall... Will someone please help me with Sabrina... ?

(CARMEN and THOMAS go to help.)

JIMMY: If they're watching us, and we're here... is where they are real, or is where we are real? They're watching a show like TV, like a movie like... real... what is real... is it in our minds real reality... is it... IT'S LOCKED!

(CHARLES goes over to the door; can't open it. Very angry now, trying to hold it in.)

CHARLES: Give me the key!

JIMMY: I don't have the key...

(CHARLES looks at the REVEREND.)

REV. SWEETS: I don't have the key, and I didn't lock the door.

CHARLES: Then how in the hell did it get locked!?

JIMMY: If what they see is made up, then whatever is made can be UN-made... If you believe yourself to be well, then you are... some things are changed by thought... every outward manifestation is the result of will, but this power is not always used consciously, what we consciously believe is real is...

(CHARLES goes over and takes the gun away from the REVEREND and walks up behind JIMMY.)

PAULETTE: Jimmy, look out!

CHARLES: I swear, man, you have three seconds to open that door.

(JIMMY nonchalantly turns and looks at the gun in CHARLES's hand, then turns his back on him and continues to think while CHARLES counts.)

JIMMY: That gun can't hurt me... Marcuis Harris... Michael Ealy... Ebbe Bassey... written and directed by LATHAN where is LATHAN...

(CHARLES shoots, and there's a bright light. The CAST reacts and freezes. JIMMY falls to the floor from the blast. He talks his way through.)

JIMMY: If you believe you are fine, then you are. I'm not shot; that bullet can't hurt me. I'm ok... the mind is the creator of everything, I am the controller... reality is here, this isn't real... this isn't real... there's a fine line, a line... I'm...

(As JIMMY is struggling to get up, the CAST

strikes poses, interacting with one another in reaction to JIMMY lying on the floor shot to death. Each of the three poses is struck after each of JIMMY's next three lines. CHYNTHIA cries; CHARLES just stands as PAULETTE beats him, crying; THOMAS is trying to get out of the church with CARMEN; BERTHA helps CHYNTHIA while the REVEREND tries to pull SABRINA to a safer place. JIMMY stands, crosses through the fourth wall, and looks on.)

JIMMY: I get it! Reality? A play... Then who does that make me... I'm going to see.

(Everyone on stage has stopped in a tableau of light. House lights come up about one quarter. JIMMY begins to leave the theatre as LATHAN enters through the church. He reacts to all of the frozen people. He sees JIMMY leaving and calls out to him.)

LATHAN: Jimmy... Jimmy... *(He does not cross the fourth wall at any time.)* What's going on? Where are you going?

JIMMY: I've figured it out, Lathan... "a mind can perceive that which it is told to believe." Where you are now isn't real. I'm in the real world... Right here next to this woman *(Or "man.")* wearing *(Describes what she/he has on.)* I can see so much now, I'm starting to understand so many things... I feel so free... I can't explain it... I just have to go outside man... this is too much.

LATHAN: Hold on!... What are you saying? You can't leave... you have to stay here and... Jimmy, what makes that world any more real than this one?

JIMMY: For one, someone wrote the words they *(Indicating the CAST.)* say. It only consists of three walls, and look around you, the people are frozen. Does that shit look real to you?

LATHAN: No. But hold on... We make up our minds based on what we read and hear every day. As for being frozen, I can't explain that, but what was that person doing fifteen minutes ago? *(Indicates the same audience member Jimmy referred to earlier.)* Running around this room which also only consists of three visible walls. So I'll ask my question again, what makes that world any more real than this one?

JIMMY: I don't know, but I want to live out here for a while... I'm not playing a character anymore! See this? *(Indicates the program.)* I know who I am now!

LATHAN: What, the bible? Yes, I see it... I'm glad that you feel that coming closer to God brings you closer to understanding yourself... But isn't that why we all came to church in the first place, to get a better understanding of who we are through God's eyes?

JIMMY: This is not a bible, it's a program! I don't know why you're trying to confuse me, Curtiss...

(Blackout. SABRINA changes into a clean shirt.)

JIMMY: *(Continuing his line through the blackout.)* but it's not going to work... Yeah! You didn't think I knew who you were, did you? I do, and I'm starting to know a whole lot more, and as soon as I leave this place, I know it will all make sense.

(He starts to leave. As his back is turned, LATHAN motions for the CAST to take their seats and for CHYNTHIA to begin crying over JIMMY's invisible body. Light only on CHYNTHIA; the rest of the stage is in shadow.)

LATHAN: Jimmy, what about Chynthia? You're saying this world is fake... what if this world is all you know... What if all of your dreams stem from this make-believe place... Do you care about your wife?... what happened yesterday morning... How did you know she killed that child... you and her have made a deal together, and you're just going to turn your back on that?... She thinks you're dead, Jimmy, is that fair? You have been given a gift... you say you feel free... why not share that with the person you said you'll love 'til death do you part... Why not share it with all your friends and family here... open everyone's eyes. Or are you just going to run... You can't see anything, can you!? All you see is the door, and another way to run away from your "problems"... You said you had the answer right there in your hand, man... why leave?

(JIMMY begins to leave.)

LATHAN: Marcuis!

(JIMMY stops.)

LATHAN: Let's just say I am Curtiss. I wrote this and put it all together, and you're Marcuis... I know you, man, on both sides of this line... what if I were to tell you that your life here is a hell of a lot better than the one you're trying to run to now... Your hometown of Ohio... Your mortgage on your condo is four months behind, and they're looking for you... Your children's mother...oh man! you don't want to know...

JIMMY: Do you think I'm stupid... I know your lyin'...

LATHAN: Am I?

JIMMY: I... *(Thinking.)* I can't just leave Chynthia like this... So what are you telling...

LATHAN: ...You have a responsibility to open the eyes of as many people as you can...

(The CAST assumes "Let us pray" positions.)

LATHAN: ...bring them to themselves like you are now... You'll be like a messiah and all you'll be doing is bringing them the truth...To a reality... I'll tell you what, if you can do that... touch any one of these people up here... everything that happened this morning will not have happened...

JIMMY: Let me make sure I get this... If I can make just one person understand that this is a form of entertainment, I'll go back to being Jimmy Cuffey. Instead of Marcuis Harris?

(As he talks, the CAST assumes their positions from the beginning of the play.)

LATHAN: No, you'll know everything about everything, and the choice will be yours.

JIMMY: Can I take this with me? *(Indicates the program.)*

LATHAN: Yes.

JIMMY: How much time do I have?

LATHAN: How much time do we got?!!

(JIMMY stands and thinks, while the CAST and LATHAN take their positions right after the child was killed at the start of the play. As they say their lines, everything is very robotic—i.e., everyone is taking their characterization to the extreme. When JIMMY doesn't come right in with his lines, they wait, then pick right up with their lines. Then they begin to speak faster, not waiting for him or any other cue until JIMMY stops them.)

REV. SWEETS: Let us pray...

SABRINA: *(Over the top.)* No! I'm tired of praying, Reverend! We've been here for eight hours... Praying for guidance, asking for forgiveness, and nothing has happened. You keep telling me not to go to the police or the authorities, that God will give us the answer... Well, I've been waiting Reverend... and nothing has come! I'm being made to sit here and relive this... Do you know how hard this is ? *(Begins to cry.)* I want justice, Reverend!...

CHARLES: *(Over the top.)* Sabrina, baby. Try and stay calm. It's hard I know, but it'll be a lot easier when we put Jimmy Cuffey in jail!

JIMMY: *(Looking for words.)* What are... you... talking about... Chuck? Put me in jail. This is not my fault! I tried to help and I would have if...

PAULETTE: *(Over the top.)* If what?... Don't try and put this on me! If you want to blame someone you should...

REV. SWEETS: *(Over the top.)* Sisters and brothers, there is no need for this... The answer is coming to us. Our Lord and Savior has not forgotten us... He is waiting for the time when we are ready to receive His blessing. So I would encourage all of you to just sit in prayer and allow His words to touch us...

BERTHA: *(Over the top.)* Reverend please! I'm all for the Lord coming down and helping, but we don't have time for that. First of all I have to make it known that I had nothing to do with this. I wouldn't have been here anyway if my husband didn't find the need to get all sanctified all of a sudden. But on the other hand, I know that somebody here is going to need a defense attorney. And I feel that it is my duty as a wife and mother to offer my husband's services to the highest bidder...

LATHAN: *(Over the top.)* Bertha, please

sit down. You are not helping the situation… I think what is happening right now will produce its own benefits and like it or not, sweetheart, we are a part of this travesty… So please let's not make it any worse by adding our impatience to an already lengthy matter.

CHARLES: *(Over the top.)* Hey, I know you. You're that guy on those commercials who's always talking about "There isn't a case that can't make money." Right?

LATHAN: *(Over the top.)* Yes.

CHARLES: *(Over the top.)* When did you start coming here?

CARMEN: *(Over the top.)* When he found out this was my church!

LATHAN: *(Over the top.)* That's…

BERTHA: *(Over the top.)* You shouldn't be saying nothing, other than who that Jezebel is over there with that tight cheap dress on.

CARMEN: *(Over the top.)* Tight dress! First of all, sweetie, you don't know me well enough to be calling me out of my name! Secondly, I'm not the one you should be upset with! And as for cheap, I know you can recognize that, look at your weave!

BERTHA: *(Over the top.)* What!!

THOMAS: *(Over the top.)* Ladies please!! Shut up with that Jerry Springer shit!! Excuse me, Reverend. We have a much bigger problem here! Reverend, do you still have any of those legal pads left over from the renovation meeting last month?

SABRINA: *(Over the top.)* I'm going to the police!!

REV. SWEETS: *(Over the top; yelling.)* No!

Sister Harper… Please give us time. We don't want worldly influences in our private dealings. I know the pain is great and it's hard for you to put your fleshly suffering to the side, but God is here! He is waiting to feel your faith, sister. He is waiting for you to accept Him with all of your heart.

SABRINA: *(Over the top.)* Move out of my way, Reverend!!

(By this time, the CAST is all over the place: SABRINA goes over and slaps THOMAS, who grabs her and begins to kiss her passionately; she doesn't struggle. CARMEN goes over to LATHAN; they embrace. BERTHA yells at LATHAN, who listens, then gets fed up and begins to choke her. The REVEREND talks to PAULETTE, trying to pick her up on a date, while she teases him with her body and enjoys the conversation. CHARLES looks on at THOMAS and SABRINA and begins to cry because he can't have her. All this should be done over the top as if in a dream. CHYNTHIA sits by herself holding the bloody baby and laughing.)

JIMMY: What's going on… stop it… this isn't how it was. Stop it!!

(Loud gun sound. Everyone except LATHAN and JIMMY freeze.)

LATHAN: Damn, do you know how long I've been waiting to choke her ass… You don't know what it's like having to listen to her! I'm going back over there and choke the fuck out of her, that felt good!

JIMMY: Wait a minute… this isn't what happened before.

LATHAN: Seeing through the obvious and looking at thought instead of action… not always true thought, but ideal thought. Imagination. What it would like to be. In order to move forward, we have to move past that which is a dream... and allow what we see to be our dreams and therefore become our realities...

JIMMY: What in the hell are you talking about. This ain't the damn *Matrix*...

(They both pause and look at the audience.)

LATHAN: This is what we are thinking. You can stop this by controlling your thoughts... You have to control what you see now that you can see...

(LATHAN along with the CAST reassume their beginning positions.)

JIMMY: Hold up man... You've lost me. I thought I had to convince one person of the truth. Now I'm suppose to be Keanu Reeves to your Laurence Fishburne...

LATHAN: Time is wasting.

(The CAST is still in their positions. As JIMMY begins to focus, they each begin to shift into the scene as if JIMMY is making this all happen. This time they play the scene true.)

REV. SWEETS: Let us pray...

SABRINA: No! I'm tired of praying, Reverend! We've been here for eight hours... Praying for guidance, asking for forgiveness, and nothing has happened. You keep telling me not to go to the police or the authorities, that God will give us the answer... Well, I've been waiting Reverend... and nothing has come! I'm being made to sit here and relive this... Do you know how hard this is? *(Begins to cry.)* I want justice, Reverend!...

CHARLES: Sabrina, baby. Try and stay calm. It's hard I know, but it'll be a lot easier when we put Jimmy Cuffey in jail!

JIMMY: What are you... talking about... Chuck? This... thing here is not um um... the what had happened...

(The rhythm of the scene is broken.)

PAULETTE: Little brother... you are taking too long with your lines. We can't be sitting in this church all day! Right, Thomas? We got things to do... we have ho's to sell and money to make...

THOMAS: That's right... ho's to fuck and money to make!! Making money fucking ho's... getting paid off the sweat of those shiny black asses... selling a titty for twenty... getting some booty for a Benny... letting the world know.

PAULETTE: All right Thomas! We get the picture!

REV. SWEETS: If Jesus was black, brothers and sisters, I said if Jesus was black... I bet you He would have been a Mac daddy exactly like me... Hold on... what am I saying IF He was black... I know He was black... He was poor, ain't nobody like Him, but His boys and the white women... and He wore a big ass Afro.. Now try and tell me He wasn't black...

JIMMY: Not again... how do I stop this...

CARMEN: James, you have to concentrate on what's happening... If for any reason you lose your concentration... I'm going to get Bertha over here to kick your ass... get up, Chynthia, come on over here and take care of your man... Standing around here like he doesn't know what's happening... Got the answer right there and still acting stupid...

(CHYNTHIA stands and begins to walk over to where JIMMY was lying on the floor after his convulsion. As she talks, the CAST begins to move into tableau position. Lights dim slowly.)

CHYNTHIA: Have you ever known somebody for a while, maybe a couple of years off and on… and you feel you know that person pretty well. Then you find out something about them that's very disturbing, like they've been in jail or they were raped or they enjoy bestiality. Then from that moment on, they never seem the same to you… What they say… what they do… is tainted because of the information you know, and they don't necessarily know you know it about them… Life is different when you know… and I think we all know… we just don't know that we know…

BERTHA: Close your eyes… don't look… change the reality… make them what they want to be… make them who they were …make them who we are…

(As JIMMY concentrates, the CAST gets in their position right before he walked through the wall, with the REVEREND holding the gun on CHARLES and THOMAS. LATHAN is gone. Positions are: CHARLES and SABRINA down right [SABRINA changes back into her bloody shirt, and CHARLES rewraps his gunshot hand], THOMAS and PAULETTE up left, REVEREND SWEETS at the door up right, CHYNTHIA and JIMMY down right off center, BERTHA and CARMEN down left.)

CHARLES and THOMAS: Reverend, what are you doing? This is our chance to get out of here.

REV. SWEETS: I'm stopping you because God wants me to stop you brothers… I don't agree with Brother Cuffey's methods under normal circumstances, but this isn't normal … a lot of things are still left unresolved and they need to be. So I'm going to ask you two brothers to take your seats as Sister Cuffey tends to her husband…

(CHARLES begins to advance on the REVEREND.)

REV. SWEETS: Brother Watson, please don't make me do anything we would both regret! I'm serious about this… I need for you to take your seat.

CARMEN: *(To BERTHA.)* I had this candy bar in my bag. I thought that you might like it… I'm starving… I don't know about you.

(BERTHA looks at CARMEN for a moment, then decides to take the offering.)

BERTHA: How about we split it?

CARMEN: That sounds good to me…

(They do. Then they begin to speak at the same time.)

CARMEN: Mrs. Jones?…

BERTHA: *(Simultaneously.)* Carmen?

CARMEN: Why don't you go ahead.

BERTHA: No, you… call me Bertha.

CARMEN: Ok. *(Pause.)* Bertha… I have to say, I did fall in love with your husband… But the minute I found out he was still married, I ended it… he called me, but I never called him back… I wanted to tell you, call you, and let you know, but I didn't know how… What I really want you to know is that I never intended…

BERTHA: Carmen…

(Scene shifts to PAULETTE and REVEREND SWEETS.)

PAULETTE: Reverend, I need to talk to you…

REV. SWEETS: I know… I have a very big decision to make, don't I? …

PAULETTE: Yes, you do, but I think that Thomas has been mixing with some of the other businessmen...

REV. SWEETS: Don't worry, Thomas is only the middleman. Our business is out... I can't let these people leave, knowing what we do and have it in any way tied to this church... Thomas wants to play top cat, we'll let him play top cat!

PAULETTE: So you'll take care of this.

REV. SWEETS: Don't I always... I just wished you had listened to me in the first place.

PAULETTE: Yeah, but it's too late for that now. You had better stop looking at me like that. With half of your congregation staring at us.

REV. SWEETS: Ain't nobody looking at us. Give me a kiss.

PAULETTE: No. Not here .. We have to take care of Thomas and our business...

REV. SWEETS: Leave it up to me.

(Lights down on REVEREND SWEETS and PAULETTE, and up on JIMMY and CHYNTHIA.)

JIMMY: Chynthia, I have to talk to you about something that's going to sound a little strange.

CHYNTHIA: Oh my God you scared me... You're awake... shhh, just lay still for a minute honey... don't try and move. You had another one of your seizures.

JIMMY: I know honey, but I need to ask you something very important.

CHYNTHIA: James, I know you're scared, and the right thing to do is to let these people out of here...

JIMMY: Chyn, be quiet for a minute... and listen to me... How do I do this?

CHYNTHIA: How do you do what?

JIMMY: I'm not crazy... I'm not feverish, I know what I'm about to say is going to sound very odd... but I need for you to listen and try to understand me, all right?

CHYNTHIA: All right.

JIMMY: Within everything there are many different parts... to make a sandwich, you have to have bread and something else. Right?... Right, sometimes things happen and allow you to see other parts or different parts of something that you may have never really cared about or that you didn't even know exists... Um like... a... radio... there are a lot of components that go into making a radio. What they are, how they work, we don't know unless you work on those kinds of things or you're just familiar with that stuff... but the average person doesn't know how it works or what's inside of a radio besides wires and speakers and things like that ...but...

CHYNTHIA: James, what are you talking about...

JIMMY: Hold on sweetie... I'm getting there. Now this radio falls and breaks, and you can see what's in it... it breaks open, but it still works...You can see what's in it, but you have no idea what all of it means, but you have a better understanding of how complex it is... So take this to be our life... not just yours and mine, but all of us! There's something more complex out there and you can't take it for granted. Now, if I can just make one person understand the truth, life will be wonderful for us and all this will be gone... Get It!!

CHYNTHIA: Someone broke your radio, but it still works,... Ok that's fine, I can get you another radio...

(Scene shifts back to CARMEN and BERTHA.)

BERTHA: Carmen... it's strange what you can fool yourself with... I think I knew something was going on, but I made myself believe that it wasn't there... "Oh no, not my man..." "That's for other couples. I take care of my husband... He loves me and I love him..." All the while knowing that something's not right... Why do we do that?... Why are we so afraid to look at the truth? The truth is, I'm mad as hell at you right now, but why should I be mad at you?... Maybe it's because you gave him something that I could never give him... you're totally different from me... I can't compete with that. I can't compete with something I have nothing in common with... It's like comparing apples and oranges... Don't get me wrong, I know that I shouldn't have to... But he made me have to. He made me doubt myself... Yeah, I may drink too much, but I love him, and I've done nothing wrong... He has made me go back into every conversation we've had together and try and figure out what I said to make this happen. I can't find anything... I can't find anything and I'm tired of trying to find something, but that's not going to stop me. Even after I tell him that it's over... even after I file for divorce. I'm still going to doubt me, part of *me* for this... and that's fucked up, isn't it?... We give so much power to people when we say we love them... when we spend so much time with them... So when someone abuses that power, it makes it that much harder to give it again... I am so mad at you and at me for feeling like this, Carmen... *(She*

goes for a drink, but it's empty.) Do you want to know the real fucked-up part about it... I miss him already.

(She begins to cry and CARMEN comforts her.)

BERTHA: I miss that bastard right now! I want him here with me... Oh God please... *(Still crying.)*

(Scene shift to CHARLES and SABRINA.)

CHARLES: Brina, here, I've brought you some water... Drink this. Not too fast, baby, that's it. You're going to be all right. I can feel it, we're going to be all right... I'm sorry... . I've put you through so much... I just wanted to walk away from it. I just wanted to walk and leave it up to you to handle... I know that's messed up, but I was scared, Brina, I was so scared.

SABRINA: I know...

(Scene shifts back to JIMMY and CHYNTHIA.)

JIMMY: It's not about the radio dammit... It's about life, it's about the mind...

CHYNTHIA: What about the mind...

JIMMY: The mind has depth far greater than the deepest sea, baby, with things in it that we are barely conscious of, which tell us how to act and why to act that way... Imagine that you are exposed to that... that consciousness... how much untapped power that is, to control that amount of perception... to be aware of reality...would you like that, Chyn...

(Scene shifts back to CHARLES and SABRINA.)

CHARLES: Naw, baby, you don't understand. When Cherri was killed this morning, a part of me was glad... I was thinking I didn't have any more responsibility to you or her... That's wrong, I know, but that's how I felt... I thought I was free... I didn't even think about what I had done to you or anything... If it hadn't been for Jimmy making me stay here and face you and everything, I don't know where I would be right now. But what I do know is that it wouldn't have involved you, and I would not have been complete, baby... This is going to sound like some old textbook corny shit, but Brina, I don't think I can live without you. No, I know I can't live without you, baby... I love you... all of you... and we're going to make it through this...

SABRINA: Thank you... But what about...?

CHARLES: Shhh, just let me hold you, baby... I'll take care of you...

(Scene shifts back to JIMMY and CHYNTHIA.)

CHYNTHIA: You're scaring me, I'm calling over your sister...

JIMMY: Chyn, I know that you killed that baby... I know you did it because you didn't think it was right for her to have one and you not to...

CHYNTHIA: How?... Did you see me?

JIMMY: My eyes have been opened... I've done all this for you ... Now we have a way out, baby, if you'd only listen... just like you said, "Life is different when you know... and I think we all know... we just don't know that we know."

CHYNTHIA: Paulette!?...

(PAULETTE begins to go over to CHYNTHIA and JIMMY, but THOMAS stops her.)

THOMAS: Paulette!!! Why would you tell all of our business like that? You know that you would be in as much trouble as I would... And anyway I didn't drug or hurt any of those girls... he's lying. When we decided to do this...

PAULETTE: When *you*! Decided to do this!

THOMAS: Ok. When I decided to do this and you agreed it was for the community and for these girls. You have to know that we are not part of the problem here... we are the solution... How many young women are we putting through college? How many black-owned businesses have we helped to finance? We are making a difference, Paulette. So don't let one girl and her... boyfriend ruin that!

PAULETTE: Thomas, it's going too far. And I didn't let anyone know our business, you did, by messing with the product. So if you want to blame anyone, blame your own dumb ass. I'm going to see about my brother...

THOMAS: Yeah, you do that, but I have to tell you it's... not only us, we have other investors to think about.

PAULETTE: What other investors?! This is between me and you. If you've gone out and brought other people in on this, that's you... not me... I should have known your ass was up to no good... Don't dig yourself a hole you can't get out of ... *(Heading over to CHYNTHIA.)* Yes, Chynthia.

CHYNTHIA: It's your brother... he's scaring me. Will you please try and convince him to end all of this.

PAULETTE: James, why are you doing this to your wife...

JIMMY: Paul, you love me, right?

PAULETTE: Of course, I do and so does Chynthia, but love is not the issue...

JIMMY: No! What I'm saying is... I know I've been acting strange... But you would know when I'm telling the truth, right?

PAULETTE: Like when you said you would shoot me before? Is that what you mean?

JIMMY: Yeah... No... yeah... I'm sorry about that... I wasn't in my right mind then. You know I couldn't have...

PAULETTE: And you're telling me now; you are in your right mind!?... We are still in this church, James, because of you. It's going on eleven o'clock, we still don't know who killed that child, all of my private affairs have been broadcast to everyone... we're hungry, tired, and all kinds of things and you want me to believe that NOW you're in your right mind... Ok. I believe it!... You're sane! Can we leave?

JIMMY: *(To himself.)* Make one person understand amongst a sea of people who have every reason to hate you... I can't do this... You two love me and won't believe me, how can I get these others who want me dead to understand or believe me... I can't...

That's it, Curtiss... No one believes me, I'm a madman... is that what you wanted everyone to think... even my own wife thinks I gone... And to top it all off, I can't see the people anymore. I have to stay here... I may not be able to convince anyone to believe me, but I have the real knowledge... And you can't take that from me... I've seen the reality... and this ain't it... You want to hurt me good, fine! The idea was to make just one of you see what I have seen... to know what I now know. But how can I if you know it already. Ev-

eryone here has purposely closed his or her eyes. Even the two people that love me the most won't see or I can't explain to them how to see...

(The group sighs in unison at JIMMY's rambling. He looks back at them and sees their frustration.)

JIMMY: You know what? Forget this... I'm a policeman, not a leader!. "Then everything that happened this morning would not have happened" Shit! I got better things to deal with... If you want to leave, go ahead! The door's open, Reverend.

(REVEREND checks the door, and it opens.)

JIMMY: Sabrina, do you want to be hurt?

SABRINA: No.

JIMMY: Then get up...

(She's fine.)

JIMMY: Thomas, my sister and the Reverend are using you. They're working together and plan on pinning everything on you, so I would leave the state if I were you...

REV. SWEETS: What! Paulette?

PAULETTE: I didn't tell him anything!

(THOMAS sees that JIMMY is telling the truth; he runs out.)

JIMMY: Charles, you and Sabrina can leave...

CHARLES: What about our... ?

JIMMY: Cherri is fine... although I ain't seen no baby the whole time I've been here, but trust me, she's all right... go ahead, leave, what are you waiting for...

(They do.)

JIMMY: Bertha, Lathan should be outside waiting for you... come on, everybody out, I'm tired of this... let's go... I give up. Let's end this play. I can't take this anymore...

(He pushes the rest of the CAST members out of the door... he comes back in, looks at the space realizing there's no place for him to go. He sits center as CARMEN enters.)

JIMMY: *(Sits facing the audience.)* Hello, can anybody hear me out there, I know you're there...

(CARMEN comes up behind him, trying to see who he is talking to.)

CARMEN: Jimmy, are you all right?

(JIMMY gives a startled response.)

CARMEN: I know you wanted everyone to leave... I'm just wondering if you can help me like you helped Sabrina and Charles...

JIMMY: Carmen, I'm through with helping... It's not worth it... sorry, but you had better leave.

CARMEN: Jimmy, I don't have anyone... the closest I've ever gotten to love was with a married man... don't get me wrong, I don't think I need a man to make me whole, but... *(She stops herself. Silence.)* What happened here today? One minute everything is in turmoil, then the next... I don't believe you're crazy... *(Pause.)* I do think that there is something out there and Jimmy, you may have found it...

JIMMY: Carmen, I said you had better leave...

CARMEN: Yeah, but let me just say this... By keeping us here today, you made us handle some personal demons that couldn't have happened otherwise... You

have been given a gift... *(Pause, thinking of herself.)* Don't give it away... *(Rubs stomach.)* It was given to you for a reason, you may not understand it, but we can't always understand everything...

JIMMY: *(Upset, not listening.)* I can't help you, Carmen... Please leave me alone... Leave...

CARMEN: I want you to help me, teach me what you know... so that I can tell my child when it's born, Jimmy I know you can help me... please...

JIMMY: Get out! I give up! Leave me the fuck alone!

(She begins to walk toward the door. CARMEN's voice tone changes. She is now speaking the words of LATHAN. She has no idea this is happening.)

CARMEN: You didn't even try to convince anyone... Two people... You just told two people or attempted to tell them... "I'm a policeman, not a leader" my ass, what is a policeman if not a leader. Your time is up, Jimmy, Marcuis, or whoever you want to be called...

(CARMEN stops talking; now it's LATHAN himself. CARMEN moves off, resumes the place where she was when CHARLES shot JIMMY, and freezes.)

JIMMY: You put me in a no win situation...

(CARMEN is frozen. JIMMY stares at her. LATHAN comes in the doorway.)

LATHAN: How in the hell did you know you couldn't win!... You didn't try, Marcuis. So many of us are given the answer, given the knowledge... have been shown the path... Why is it that less than half of them try and help other people...

try to make things better for everyone… it is so easy to give up! It is so damn easy to say I quit! I can't win! I got other things to deal with… It takes effort; it's a battle. People are going to think you're strange, they're going to doubt what you do, they're going to feel that they have a better way and try to bring you down… They're going to be jealous, find all of your faults and bring it out so you look bad… Sticking your head out to get patted doesn't mean it's going to get it all the time, but it will get patted a lot, if you try and try and try. Not give the fuck up!! What is that man, what is give up! Say it, and keep saying it. Believe it, live it, show… Do, man, just do and let that shit speak for itself… do something don't just give up… Yes, this is a play… it's all make believe, Marcuis, but because it's happening… now it's real… The people watching, the people performing, are real… That's the magic. Taking the known to the unknown… Pushing life, molding life, this moment right now this is Reality! What we make of it now! How we use it now is our reality. What we do with it, how we perceive it, may vary, but as long as we're doing it together…

JIMMY: You said my time was up! What now.

(Pause.)

LATHAN: You know what's now…

(LATHAN calls the CAST members back in one by one.)

LATHAN: Think… If you're not part of the solution…

(They take up their positions from when CHARLES is checking the door to see if it is locked. During this scene, JIMMY has just a slight feeling of déjà vu until the end, then it's too late.)

(CHARLES goes over to JIMMY. Very angry now, trying to hold it in.)

CHARLES: Give me the key!

JIMMY: I don't have the key…

(CHARLES looks at the REVEREND.)

REV. SWEETS: I don't have the key, and I didn't lock the door.

CHARLES: Then how in the hell did it get locked!?

JIMMY: If what they see is made up, then whatever is made can be UN-made… If you believe yourself to be well, then you are… some things are changed by thought… every outward manifestation is the result of will, but this power is not always used consciously, what we consciously believe is real is…

(CHARLES goes over and takes the gun away from the REVEREND and walks up behind JIMMY.)

PAULETTE: Jimmy, look out!

CHARLES: I swear, man, you have three seconds to open that door.

(JIMMY looks at the gun in CHARLES's hand, then realizes that this is the end. He turns back to the audience while CHARLES counts.)

JIMMY: That gun can't hurt me… Marcuis Harris… Michael Ealy… Ebbe Bassey… written and directed by Curtiss I' Cook… where is Lathan…?

(CHARLES shoots, JIMMY falls to the floor. Everyone is reacting to JIMMY lying on the floor, shot. We hear banging on the door; it's LATHAN with the police. He yells and bangs while the lights fade to black.)

LATHAN: Open the door, Jimmy… open the door. I've got the police out here, open up. Bertha, are you all right... hey somebody, open the door... open up...

(Fade out.)

(Lights continue to fade, and the CAST exits the stage getting ready for bows, but the audience still hears the knocking at the door. From behind the door, CURTISS appears, the same way we saw him at the beginning of the play. He holds his pad and pen, smiles at his work, and exits the space.)

(The end.)

THE RESURRECTIONIST

Kate Chell

KATE CHELL was born in 1976 and hails from Annapolis, Maryland. She holds BA degrees in English and drama from Ithaca College. *The Resurrectionist* was her first New York City production. She is also the author of *Wits' End* and *Breakfast with the Tiki Gods*, which was produced by Kitchen Sink Productions at the Kitchen Theatre in Ithaca, New York. Chell is a member of the Dramatists Guild of America. She currently lives and works in Brooklyn, New York.

The Resurrectionist was first produced by Yazoo City on June 11, 2001, at the Gershwin Hotel, New York City, with the following cast and credits:

Molly Lark .... Nicole Pintal
Jeffrey Rymer .... Mika David Duncan
Gabriel Shepherd .... Michael Gilpin
Erin Gallagher .... Jennifer Larkin
Thom Gilhenny .... Timothy Fannon
Connor Pond .... Jeff Coté

Directed by: David Denson
Production design: Lindsay Kaplan
Fight direction: Vinnie Penna

CHARACTERS

MOLLY LARK
ERIN GALLAGHER
DR. JEFFREY RYMER
GABRIEL SHEPHERD
DR. CONNOR POND
THOM GILHENNY

The action of the play occurs in Smithfield, London, in the year 1678.

An intermission, if desired, should follow Scene Six.

AUTHOR'S NOTES

A huge meat market has for centuries been one of the major features of Smithfield, London, but a parallel, illicit trade in flesh went on just up the street. Halfway between the Smithfield market and the whorehouses of Cock Lane was a strange triangle, the points of which were a church, a tavern, and a hospital.

The last great plague demonstrated to seventeenth century England the painful inadequacy of medical technology. The hospitals filled up with the dying and before long, the churchyards overflowed; a contemporary source writes that body parts could be seen projecting from the earth in an eerie parallel to the swellings that erupted on the body with the bubonic form of the plague. The end of the epidemic came with the fire of London in 1666. As the city rose up from its ashes, the medical community became proactive, and the study of anatomy became the vogue. The only problem was that it was illegal, and the doctors came up against no less an adversary than the church itself.

The Apostles' Creed puts it simply: "I believe in the holy Catholic church, the communion of saints, the forgiveness of sins, *the resurrection of the body*, and the life everlasting." This was a clear progression to the literal-minded world of early modern Europe, and the belief held in the seventeenth century. After all, wasn't Christ lifted, body and all, to sit at the right hand of God? The Anglican Church condemned dissection as a sure way to destroy the corresponding soul's ability to attain the everlasting.

A certain number of bodies were made available nonetheless. Since death was meted out for a wide range of misdeeds, dissection became an additional sentence for particularly serious crimes. The government mandated six bodies a year to anatomists, but with medical schools cropping up all over the city, this was not enough. The increasing demand was filled by gangs of graverobbers who became known as resurrectionists. There were numerous ways to get bodies: digging into a fresh grave and levering the body up through the broken lid of a coffin, raiding the mass graves of the poor or the charnelhouses where bodies were stored prior to burial. They were careful to leave the shrouds that wrapped the dead; clothing, unlike a dead body, was considered property and therefore stealing a shroud was technically more dangerous than absconding with a body.

In 1829 a man named William Burke was hanged in Edinburgh for a crime that is still known as "burking"—suffocation by exerting pressure on the chest and covering the mouth and nose of the victim. Burke and his partner, William Hare, perfected this method in order to procure bodies that bore no visible sign of foul play and could be sold for dissection. Not long after that, the Anatomy Act was passed in Britain, permitting medical schools to legally acquire unclaimed bodies for dissection and bringing the golden years of resurrection to a close.

SCENE ONE

A back room at the White Hart Pub in Smithfield. Three figures sit at the central table: MOLLY LARK, a woman in her mid-twenties, nursing an injured foot; GABRIEL SHEPHERD, maybe thirty-eight and huge in comparison to MOLLY's slight frame, who sits with one leg stretched out before him; and the shrouded corpse of a woman, covered over with SHEPHERD's coat. Several tankards sit on the table before them.

SHEPHERD: This ain't the way it's s'pose to go, Moll. Jesus. I mean, Jesus Christ. Bloody gaping. It's like a ravine.

MOLLY: Shut your mouth, Gabe.

SHEPHERD: Bloody gaping.

MOLLY: I said stop.

SHEPHERD: I ain't so sure about it all. I don't know. I don't. Best not to get into it. Hand her over and forget it. Or try. Have a pint, get piss-drunk, and try and forget all about it.

(Enter ERIN GALLAGHER, a barmaid of about nineteen, with a tray.)

ERIN: No more for your friend, I guess. *(She slaps the corpse on the back of its sheeted head.)* Hear that, you? You been cut off! *(She laughs in delight at her joke.)*

SHEPHERD: Goddamn it, what's the matter with you?

MOLLY: No more for either of them.

SHEPHERD: You seen the doctor?

ERIN: What's got to you, Shepherd? *(She indicates the corpse.)* Don't like me flirting with your girlfriend?

SHEPHERD: Have you seen him, for Christ's sake?

ERIN: Not yet. It's early still. Jesus. Don't take me head off, will you?

SHEPHERD: Early for a drinking man, maybe; not for him.

MOLLY: He'll come.

SHEPHERD: And if he don't? What then?

ERIN: I'll just check again for him. (*Exits.*)

SHEPHERD: Nosy bitch. Set the constabulary on us, she will.

MOLLY: She won't. Why can't you hold your peace? He'll be here. He'll take her off our hands and out of our lives, he'll pay, we'll walk out same as always, and that'll be it. Stop with your fidgeting. Drink your ale.

SHEPHERD: It don't bother you none?

MOLLY: I can be bothered for ten minutes if I'm paid for it. It's the shard in my foot bothers me more.

SHEPHERD: I just don't want to be mixed up in sommat like this. And an hour it's been, not ten minutes. Ten minutes is all right by me. An hour's too much.

MOLLY: Gabriel Shepherd, had I not the benefit of three years' acquaintance to temper my judgment, I'd swear I was looking at a frightened man.

SHEPHERD: Stop with the high talk. It don't suit.

MOLLY: You're frightened.

SHEPHERD: I dig bodies for a living, Molly; I don't guess there's nothing about one more corpse to scare me.

MOLLY: Why'd you leave the shroud on this one?

SHEPHERD: Out a' respect.

MOLLY: Respect for the body? Isn't it desecration to exhume a corpse anyway?

SHEPHERD: It's desecration enough. Anyhow, it's a lady.

MOLLY: It's a body, Gabe. You don't take the shroud because it's illegal. They send you to Newgate for it, and once you're in Newgate, like as not you'll hang. Why'd you take the shroud, Gabe?

SHEPHERD: I dunno.

MOLLY: You were afraid. The murdered sometimes walk, so I'm told; you wanted the shroud to keep her at rest. That's so, isn't it? You're scared.

SHEPHERD: Where's the goddamn doctor?

MOLLY: Where's your goddamn patience? Sit back down. Drink your pint. He's been waiting two weeks for us to bring him something.

(*Enter DR.. JEFFREY RYMER, a young doctor nearing thirty.*)

SHEPHERD: Jesus, it's about time! Where in bloody hell have you been?

RYMER: There was an emergency.

SHEPHERD: And I suppose you think I need your custom so desperately I'll stand about back here and wait on your goddamn emergencies?

MOLLY: Gabe—

RYMER: What's the matter with him?

MOLLY: Sit down. You'd better just sit.

RYMER: I thought you said to meet you out in the pub.

SHEPHERD: And where were you, I'd like to know?

RYMER: I had to call on a patient, Shepherd. It couldn't be helped. What are you lurking back here for?

MOLLY: We were afraid to leave the body out in the pub.

RYMER: Why? *(Noticing.)* It's shrouded. Isn't that—

MOLLY: That's not why. That's only part of it.

RYMER: What, then?

SHEPHERD: Bloody look at her. Go on. Have a look. Her neck—ain't much left.

(RYMER pulls back the shroud to have a look at the corpse's throat. He recoils in horror at the wide, grinning gash that ended the young woman's life.)

MOLLY: You see why we couldn't—

RYMER: Yes, yes, I see… Jesus, Molly.

SHEPHERD: You still want her?

RYMER: What?—Oh, yes, of course. Christ.

(RYMER produces a purse from his coat and hands it over. SHEPHERD takes it, counts out the coins inside, deposits some in his pocket, and tosses the rest on the table for MOLLY.)

SHEPHERD: I ain't carrying her. You do it yourself. I'm going home. Had enough for tonight.

MOLLY: Gabe, the thing's done with.

SHEPHERD: In any case, I'm done with it. I'm done. (*Grabs his coat and exits, limping exaggeratedly.*)

MOLLY: Sorry, Doctor.

RYMER: Is this how he always conducts business?

MOLLY: He'd not admit it, but he's scared. Unnerved him proper, that one did.

RYMER: Why's he limping?

MOLLY: It went badly with this one. Have you got a knife with you?

RYMER: A folder.

(He finds a folding pocketknife in his pocket and hands it to her. His attention goes back to the corpse. MOLLY goes to work removing the splinter from her foot. RYMER doesn't notice.)

RYMER: What went badly?

MOLLY: He was attacked by a hound last night taking the body away from the churchyard. I gather there was so much noise he didn't dare bring the corpse straight here, so he hid it behind a stewhouse on Cock Lane and sent me after it tonight. Said he couldn't carry it anyhow on account of his leg. Must've killed the dog.

RYMER: Here, wait, what are you doing?

MOLLY: Got a shard of something in my foot in the alley.

RYMER: Have you completely forgotten what I do when the sun's up? For God's sake, stop that. You'll mangle it. Let me see.

(MOLLY obligingly allows him to have a look at her foot.)

MOLLY: I got it already.

RYMER: I should hope so, with the digging you've done. I'll bandage it.

MOLLY: Bandage away.

(RYMER produces a handkerchief from his sleeve. There is a moment's quiet as he wraps her foot.)

MOLLY: That's the first time I've carried a body. It was horrid.

(A pause. RYMER isn't sure how to respond.)

MOLLY: So I suppose that's a first for both of us, isn't it?

(He finishes wrapping her foot.)

RYMER: Shepherd appeared hale enough.

MOLLY: He was. I don't know why he made me do it.

RYMER: You could refuse.

MOLLY: Need the money. We've been a long stretch with no business.

RYMER: Right. *(He is eyeing the corpse a bit uncertainly now.)*

MOLLY: Listen, Doctor, I don't get squeamish, really—you know that, I guess. If you need help with… her… this time, since—

RYMER: No. I suppose I'll manage. How does the dressing feel?

MOLLY: It's good. *(Pause.)* I know such things happen. It's still hard to look on.

RYMER: I think that all the time.

MOLLY: What do you imagine—

RYMER: I don't know. Somebody's hate, somebody's knife. Best not think any deeper into it. Can you go home?

MOLLY: Well, I'm not staying here.

RYMER: Have a care for yourself, Molly.

MOLLY: That's my usual practice.

(RYMER wraps the corpse in his cloak and lifts it awkwardly.)

RYMER: Until later, then.

MOLLY: Till then.

(He exits. MOLLY lifts her mug and drinks. ERIN enters.)

ERIN: Not far off, was I?

MOLLY: About what?

ERIN: Takin' me head off. Look on Gabe's face was worth a ransom. *(She begins to clear away the empty mugs.)* Bit unusual, that.

MOLLY: Say again?

ERIN: All torn up like that, and not a word about the murder.

MOLLY: These things aren't secrets. There's too many bodies for anyone to notice just one.

ERIN: You don't think we'd have heard?

MOLLY: Maybe. Did you know what went on here when you came to work?

ERIN: Everybody knows what goes on here. Bodies lined up in the windows like that all the time, people tracking grave's mud in on my clean floors, constables coming in to collect their arm-and-leg of quiet money.

MOLLY: Does it ever make you queasy?

ERIN: They're just dead things. They don't hurt no one. It took some getting used to, I guess, seeing them here and there in the tavern like it's just normal for a man to stand about naked waiting for his pint. They could leave them in those horrid sacks, at least. Ain't like a naked man's all that nice to look at before he's dead.

MOLLY: The doctors want to see what it is they're buying.

ERIN: It's all a bunch of rot, the whole business. That we get right up and walk on the Day of Judgment, rotting corpses and all? Bollocks. Let the doctors cut. Who cares. *(A look at MOLLY, who is still quiet.)* What's the matter with you, now?

MOLLY: I've never seen anything like that. Throat slit, neat as you please and deep as you can go without cutting the head right off.

ERIN: Who was she?

MOLLY: No one I knew. I don't think she was from this parish.

ERIN: Bit odd, then, being buried here. Sure someone had to have known, Molly. The pastor, certain.

MOLLY: Right, and I'll go straight up to the pastor of St. Sepulcher's Church and say to him, "Say, Pastor Grady, I sold a corpse a night or two ago was murdered, and I'd like to ask you about it, seeing it came from your churchyard." I can't do that. Ought to stop thinking about it. The thing's done. Don't much matter, I guess... (*She toys idly with RYMER's knife, forgotten on the table.*)

SCENE TWO

RYMER's basement room. He enters, carrying the corpse, still shrouded, over his shoulder, and places her on a table.

POND: *(Offstage.)* Rymer?

RYMER: Damn... who is it?

POND: Connor Pond.

(RYMER's relief is obvious. Enter POND, another doctor, just a bit older than RYMER.)

POND: I thought that was you. Working late? (*He notices the shrouded body.*) Jeffrey. You've done it, haven't you?

RYMER: I thought about what you said. It seemed to make sense.

POND: A hundred years from now these things won't even have to be secret, Jeffrey. You can be sure of that. Good God, you just went out and found one, didn't you? Bravo, Rymer!

RYMER: I don't suppose you could keep it down, could you, Connor?

POND: No need to get testy, Jeffrey. No one's about. You don't think I'd come down here yelling if there was any danger, do you?

RYMER: You'll pardon my concern. We've established that I'm going to hell; I don't want to hang, too.

POND: Once you stop jumping at shadows, that's when they get you, isn't it? When you start trusting in the safety of the night and the basement. Come along, Rymer, this is a huge leap you've taken. It's an exciting leap! Stop looking like a convict.

RYMER: All well for you to say that; I suppose when I'm a trustee I'll be a bit more carefree about things. And I have to say I'm not really sure where to begin.

POND: Did you study the book I gave you?

RYMER: Inside and out. But woodcuts are one thing. This... is entirely different.

POND: Well, let's have a look at what you've got here. Did you go to the White Hart as I suggested?

RYMER: Yes.

POND: How was the selection?

RYMER: Depends. How do you feel about damaged study material?

POND: Damaged? (*He pulls back the sheet and recoils at the sight of the gash. He turns away, his face utterly shocked.*)

RYMER: Something wrong?

POND: Good God, yes. Look at her. (*Trying to recover himself.*) What's holding the head on?

RYMER: Her last prayer, I suppose.

POND: Well, was this the only one? Did you get a discounted price?

RYMER: Christ, Connor.

POND: Well, I'm sorry. Just being practical. Sometimes there are a few to choose from.

(RYMER is staring at POND in disbelief.)

POND: She is dead, after all.

RYMER: She didn't used to be. Cover her back up.

POND: Didn't mean to be insensitive. Sorry.

RYMER: No, it's fine. Nothing really to do about it, anyhow.

POND: True. One can hardly go to the constabulary, can one?

RYMER: Hardly.

POND: I thought not. Ah, well. One dies to assist in the pursuit of life.

RYMER: Not this one.

POND: This one especially. All of them. Why not?

RYMER: Well, somehow I doubt that was the justifying thought in the head of the man who did this.

POND: We'll never know. Don't dwell on details like that.

RYMER: It's just that I thought… they'd be thieves, murderers, like the ones the barber-surgeons have. Not—nothing like a girl so young.

POND: The resurrectionists, Jeffrey, take the bodies that come easiest. Some of them arrange to dispose of the criminals. Others dig wherever there's fresh-turned earth to mark a fresh-sown body. It isn't for the anatomist to specify, really. The great Dr. Harvey dissected his own father and sister post-mortem. Think of that.

RYMER: What are you up to so late?

POND: Went out for a pint and there you were, coming back with your package. I thought I'd stop in and—

RYMER: Scare the piss out of me?

POND: Naturally. Then I thought maybe you'd like to join me for a bitter.

RYMER: It's been a long night, Connor. What with all this.

POND: Take it from a doctor, Jeffrey, who cures what ails you, that ale is what cures you.

RYMER: All I had with me I spent.

POND: They've overcharged you there at the White Hart. A girl so small shouldn't cost you more than two guineas.

RYMER: The dead don't come cheap.

POND: I'll treat.

RYMER: I can't. I do thank you for the invitation. I'm simply too strung out.

POND: Anatomist's nerves. Anatomy is a fascinating study, but it does take some time to develop the necessary… detachment? No one knows that better than I. Watch, however, that you don't push yourself too far, Jeffrey. When your nerves give you too much trouble to drink, I say you've a problem with your priorities. Very well, then. Perhaps another night. In fact, perhaps tomorrow afternoon. I have a daylight errand at the tavern that might interest you.

RYMER: All right. Tomorrow afternoon.

POND: Excellent. Enjoy your carving.

RYMER: Good night, Connor.

POND: Jeffrey.

(He exits. RYMER follows him to the door and locks it. He returns to the table, picks up the scalpel and turns it in the light for a few seconds. He considers the shrouded corpse, pulling the sheet back from her head. Finally he draws the shroud back up over her face and tosses the scalpel away. He drops into a chair, back to the form on the table, and holds his head in his hands.)

SCENE THREE

The tavern's main room, the following day. SHEPHERD sits with THOM GILHENNY, another regular, about thirty. ERIN stands behind the bar, cleaning glasses. Enter POND and RYMER.

POND: I've been wondering if it might be possible to hire this fellow as an agent for a while now.

(POND approaches the table where GILHENNY and SHEPHERD sit. SHEPHERD is balanced backward in his chair, one foot up on the table, sleeping.)

POND: You're the agent for the Company of Barbers and Surgeons, aren't you?

GILHENNY: I've been known to procure for them from time to time.

POND: Connor Pond. I'm a physician.

GILHENNY: Thom Gilhenny. And I don't care what type of medic you are.

POND: Well, no, you wouldn't, would you.

GILHENNY: I don't rise to insults, either. Say your piece and be done.

POND: May I buy you a pint first, Mr. Gilhenny? And your friend, of course.

GILHENNY: In my line the clever fellows watch their liquor. Say your piece.

POND: What kind of an agreement do you have with them?

GILHENNY: What kind are you going to offer me instead?

POND: I have a few students who could benefit from a study in anatomy. I shall need fresh specimens.

GILHENNY: And you want gallows-meat? I don't dig for my trade.

POND: I want you to act as an agent for me instead of the barbers.

GILHENNY: You couldn't pay me what their company does. I take cash to make the transaction and my commission up front. Do you carry that sort of pocket money to throw about? Enough for your several students?

POND: These men are criminals, Mr. Gilhenny. They're selling their own bodies for jail-board. How much can it possibly cost?

GILHENNY: As much as they ask. They're going to swing anyhow, and most of them'd just as soon not risk salvation without having a good many shillings to show for it, whether they can spend it first or not. And you'd have to hire me away from the surgeons. I'm on retainer, as they say in the courts.

POND: Have you ever been in a surgeon's operating theater, Gilhenny? They tie the victim—for he is a victim—they tie him down on a slab of wood, screaming, as would any sane man to see a barber with soiled overalls and filthy hands advancing on him while some assistant—probably the more capable surgeon—holds him still in his restraints. Buckets of sawdust to collect the precious blood because so much is spilled. A crowd of surgery students eyeing the fellow's torture at the hands of a stranger who wields his scalpel on the merits of the fee his father paid to secure the post.

GILHENNY: I don't do what I do for the betterment of mankind. Don't look so shocked, Doctor. I know what you lot think of us, surgeons and physicians alike. Why try to move me with horror stories? The bodies I traffic are already dead, and they don't care what catches their blood if any runs at all.

POND: The surgeons have bodies mandated by the King.

GILHENNY: Six per year, or so I understand. You've had that many off of the Scotsman there in as many weeks. I don't have the reputation I have by working for anatomists on the far side of the law, and I cost quite a lot more than a resurrectionist does. Good night, Doctor.

POND: Fetch yourself a drink, Rymer. I could use a porter, myself.

(POND sits. RYMER crosses to the bar.)

GILHENNY: You're not so conscious of the formalities when someone else invokes them, are you?

POND: We have business between us.

GILHENNY: You made a request and an offer. I said no to both, just as I'm doing now. I'm not for sale, myself, and I'm not eager to do transactions of any other kind with you, either. How long do you want to go on talking all polite this way?

POND: I suppose you didn't get your reputation by exercising a loose tongue, either?

(No reply from GILHENNY.)

POND: Then perhaps we can leave our business to lie.

GILHENNY: You do what you like. But understand: you've got no business with me.

(RYMER returns with two glasses. GILHENNY turns back to his mug as if to indicate an end to the interview. POND indicates another table and RYMER follows. They sit.)

RYMER: That didn't go so well.

POND: Disgusting, isn't it. Six bodies a year the crown mandates from the gallows to the dissection table and the bloody barbers get them all. What do they need crown bodies for when they practically manufacture corpses themselves! Why must the physicians lack what the surgeons can't make proper use of? (*He pauses for a drink.*) Incidentally, point out the fellow who sold you the girl, if he's here. Perhaps we could make use of him instead.

RYMER: One of them was the surly fellow with the surgeons' agent. The other was a girl herself.

POND: A girl? How odd. Although I know the resurrectionists sometimes send their wives to claim workhouse dead.

(RYMER glances at him, uncomprehending.)

POND: Bereaved widow, devastated mother, disbelieving sister... certainly. Works particularly well, I gather, with children, although they don't sell for much. Ninepence per foot or something like that. If you like to study that kind of thing. How did your dissection go last night?

RYMER: I'm ashamed to say I didn't even unwrap her body. I just... I just kept staring at her... throat.

POND: Well, don't let it sit too long or the rats will find it. Rats are a touch bolder than anatomists are with a body.

(RYMER looks sick. POND sips his beer.)

GILHENNY: Saw Molly come in with an odd parcel last night, Gabe.

SHEPHERD: *(Speaks without sitting up.)* What of it? Hurt my leg. Tricky carrying that with a bum leg.

(GILHENNY kicks SHEPHERD's foot off the table, bringing him crashing upright.)

SHEPHERD: Goddamn it, Thom!

GILHENNY: You're walking fine this afternoon.

SHEPHERD: Fuck off. It didn't hurt her none to do a little work for once.

GILHENNY: She does a right lot of work for you, Gabe. Most of the gangs don't have so sharp a lookout as Molly, and not many are better than she is for making sure everything's left as it was found. Don't go spoiling the good fortune you've had this time. And don't put her in harm's way.

SHEPHERD: 'Cause then you'd be out your piece of flesh, wouldn't you, Thom?

GILHENNY: Insult me all you like, but remember I'm the one knows just how lucky you've been, Gabe.

SHEPHERD: You seen her today?

GILHENNY: No.

SHEPHERD: I saw Jack Hinton down near the meat market and he said he thought he saw her coming out of the church.

GILHENNY: Lots of people come out of churches on Sunday. Do you always keep so close an eye on her whereabouts?

SHEPHERD: Don't be so bloody smart all the time, Thom.

GILHENNY: Can't help it. I was born smart. If I see her shall I tell Molly you're looking for her?

SHEPHERD: Just tell her to be here early tonight.

SCENE FOUR

The back room of the tavern. SHEPHERD is pacing angrily. MOLLY enters.

SHEPHERD: Where in bloody hell have you been?

MOLLY: Where the bloody hell was I supposed to be?

SHEPHERD: Well, pardon me if you've got better things to do, but I got to eat.

MOLLY: You're not going to starve.

SHEPHERD: Well, mayhap I won't this evening, but that don't mean I can afford not to work a night.

MOLLY: I'm here, ain't I?

SHEPHERD: I left messages for you all over the place. You're late.

MOLLY: And I'm sorry for it. Now can we get on with our lives?

SHEPHERD: What kept you, anyhow?

MOLLY: I had some business.

SHEPHERD: Jack Hinton said he saw you nosing around St. Sep's.

MOLLY: What's that to Jack Hinton or to you? Might be I wanted to sing a hymn or take communion or some such thing. St. Sepulcher's is as good a place as any for communion. What do you care?

SHEPHERD: Jack Hinton reckoned you were trying to find out about the body.

MOLLY: What body?

SHEPHERD: What body, she says. What other body is there? The tore-up one from last night.

MOLLY: And how does Hinton know about that, Gabe?

SHEPHERD: How do I know how word gets out? Could be Jack saw you come in with a shrouded corpse. Could be you been asking questions and some bloke overheard.

MOLLY: I put the thing out of my head. What's got you in such a bother?

SHEPHERD: I'm saying, maybe you got a big mouth and a loose tongue. Maybe you'll get us in trouble 'cause one body's got you green about the gills.

MOLLY: As I recall, you were the one took the shroud then ditched the damn thing, shroud and all, in the middle of an alley. You were the one who got green about the gills. Don't blame me. You likely had a pint too many and mouthed off to Jack and the rest of them yourself.

SHEPHERD: Don't start that with me, Molly Lark. All I want to say is, don't put us in danger.

MOLLY: You got nothing to worry about from me, Gabe. We've been doing this for half a year, you and I. You trust me, I trust you, nobody gets no trouble. You just keep digging, I'll keep peddling, we all get to eat and sleep decent nights. Nobody's going to put us in danger.

SHEPHERD: Have you finished?

MOLLY: Have you?

(A challenging pause.)

SHEPHERD: I got another out front. *(Drains the remains of his pint.)*

MOLLY: Already? You been busy.

SHEPHERD: Bugger off, Moll. I done my job. Do yours and keep your mouth shut. I hear any more from Hinton or the others, you'll know about it.

MOLLY: What's the matter with you, Gabe? You got ghosts following you around?

SHEPHERD: I got ghosts telling me they'll see me hung at Tyburn over this.

MOLLY: Before you start worrying over me, you make bloody damn sure you don't drop anything to your mates over your bitter this night. I hear the rumors, too, Gabriel Shepherd, and I like trouble no better than you.

SHEPHERD: Just remember that tonight, Moll. I've done.

(Exit SHEPHERD. ERIN enters as he does.)

ERIN: Hey, well done, Gabe. You got a nice one out there. I was going to tell you they fetch more with the heads attached.

(SHEPHERD only gives her an angry stare as he passes.)

ERIN: Oh, lighten up a touch, you great dizzard. Unpleasant face on that one tonight. I can't say as I envy you much, Molly. Didn't sound nice, what I heard.

MOLLY: He's drunk. No more than a mess of empty threats on a mouthful of ale. Who's in the pub tonight?

ERIN: Jack and Thom Gilhenny and the Scotsman, Braithhill. Brought another two between them. One's fresh from the gallows, the other looks to be dug. Quite a crowd of dead naked folk loitering about this tavern tonight! How these things happen in a respectable tavern is quite beyond me.

MOLLY: How tall? Short stock isn't likely to fetch much from anybody.

ERIN: The doctors like a good-sized plaything, do they? Well, I try not to look that closely, but I think not very tall, none of them. Bit sad below the waist, I thought, but I've yet to see any very impressive like that. Wonder if that affects the market value. Yours is the tallest, anyhow.

MOLLY: Much the better. Mayhap if it gets a decent price, I'll not hear any more from Shepherd. I got spotted at St. Sep's. Could be we'll have more words tonight.

ERIN: What sort of business did you have at the church in the daylight?

MOLLY: I was just curious. Nothing else.

ERIN: Did you find her name?

MOLLY: No. No way to know with most of this lot—just nameless bodies wrapped and planted quick as possible. Not much better than the trench graves they used to dig. You don't likely remember that at all. Twelve or thirteen years ago, now. So many bodies there wasn't even enough dirt to cover them.

ERIN: I remember it. I was six. Our landlord had my cat drowned to keep it from spreading the plague and we lived for two weeks on an island of boats in the Thames with others, rivermen and friends of my dad's. We'd sit, us little ones, and sing that song that goes *Ring around the roses, a pocket full of posies...* we used to sing about the contagion, you believe that? The fire was that year. I remember that best. Jacob

said once he could see the glow all the way out on Shepherd's farm.

MOLLY: We could. That might be the first time anyone's brought his name into conversation with me.

ERIN: Doesn't seem proper to. Though I've wondered how the hell either of you ever came to be bodysellers.

MOLLY: We were tenants on Shepherd's farm until a few years back when all the sheep died of the murrain. It was Jacob's idea, I think, raiding the churchyards and bringing the fresh bodies here to be sold. That's how he managed to pay our board at the farm; we'd have been turned out. It took both of them to get the bodies, but Gabe left my brother to do the selling. And then last March, Jacob—well, something went wrong, and he didn't come back one night. Shepherd thought I might earn my keep in other ways and I told him I'd pay the same way my brother did. But no one talks about Jacob. At least not to me. (*Pause.*) Erin, I have a horrid thought.

(*Enter THOM GILHENNY.*)

GILHENNY: Mistress Gallagher! They are a-callin' for a round of the house's finest, on the account of the blond gentleman there who has got not a stitch on his fine, tall body.

ERIN: Is going to pay off your account as well?

GILHENNY: That remains to be seen.

(*ERIN exits with her tray.*)

GILHENNY: (*Calls back into the pub.*) Tyler! This one's going against my merchandise, there! Take two legs this time, you bandit! (*With a laugh he allows the door to close behind him, then turns to face MOLLY.)* Molly Lark. Can't spare a smile for an old friend, can you?

MOLLY: Can't spare it, but you always take one anyhow.

GILHENNY: *(Strolls closer to where she stands.)* I'd take more than that if you'd let me. A kiss, even.

MOLLY: I know it.

GILHENNY: When's the last time you let a man kiss you, Molly?

MOLLY: You know precisely when that was.

GILHENNY: And none since?

MOLLY: Have you?

GILHENNY: Never. And I never will again, less it comes from you.

MOLLY: Your lies are almost as convincing as your kisses, Thom.

(He tries to kiss her mouth. She tilts her face out of reach.)

GILHENNY: I'm as honest a man as ever there was this side of the churchyard.

(He tries again and once more she dodges.)

GILHENNY: For Christ's sake, Molly—

(He spins her around in his grip, pulls her face to him, and kisses her. She doesn't respond.)

GILHENNY: You fight too much.

(He lets her go. Instead of moving away this time, to GILHENNY's surprise, MOLLY herself plants a kiss on him.)

MOLLY: *(Matter-of-factly.)* You wouldn't want me if I didn't.

GILHENNY: I won't lie and tell you it's not part of your charm. You drink with us, you sell with us, you swear with us, but I think you've had no real chat with a man. It'll be me when you do, Molly. And you'll forget all about kisses after that.

MOLLY: Do you believe that?

GILHENNY: I live for the day I'm allowed to prove that I'm not exaggerating my abilities.

MOLLY: I don't mean that. I mean that… I haven't.

GILHENNY: I think you haven't. But then I haven't asked, have I?

(MOLLY says nothing.)

GILHENNY: Have you, then?

MOLLY: I know what they say about me.

GILHENNY: They say it about the barmaid, too. They'd say it of anyone.

MOLLY: They believe it of me.

GILHENNY: You're not like a woman, Molly. Not like Hinton's wife or the Scotsman's mother. Of course they believe it. But I don't believe it.

MOLLY: Do you tell them I only let you kiss me? I know how they'll laugh when you come out that door. I know what they think we're doing now. They think I'm no better than the whores up the hill on Cock Lane.

GILHENNY: What do the likes of them know? Let the rest of them think what they want. We understand better, you and I.

(Pulling her into an embrace again, he puts a palm on her breast.)

GILHENNY: You're softer here.

(Now over her heart.)

GILHENNY: And here, warmer. (*He withdraws his hand.*) And I don't mind if I'm the only one who sees it.

MOLLY: I mind.

GILHENNY: Well, then, you ought to have taken up spinning. Anyhow, any fool with a pinch of sense would rather make her living with a wheel than with Gabe Shepherd.

MOLLY: What's he said to you?

GILHENNY: Nothing to me, but a blind halfwit could tell the man's had a fright. What errand took you to the church?

MOLLY: Not you, Thom. Jesus.

GILHENNY: You didn't think anyone might see?

MOLLY: Did you see *her*?

GILHENNY: Heard a lively description, I did. Is there anything really amiss with his foot?

MOLLY: Not likely. What's he care if I went to the church? I know that isn't where he found her.

GILHENNY: (*Warning.*) Molly—

MOLLY: Well?

GILHENNY: Molly, there's a church on every bloody corner. They've come up like weeds since the fire. There's no end of places to find a body if you want a body to sell.

MOLLY: Shepherd doesn't wait about for a hanged man like you do, Thom. He digs. He scavenges. And I'll tell you what you haven't heard yet; that shroud was clean.

GILHENNY: Molly, stop. Don't trust me so much. I love a good scotch whiskey too well to be trusted with the likes of that.

MOLLY: That isn't why I went, anyhow.

GILHENNY: Went over to say a prayer or so, did you, Molly? I'd believe you still say your prayers. (*Seriously.*) But I think you're best not to be seen doing it.

MOLLY: No. It's nothing to give any more thought to.

GILHENNY: Wise girl. Mind your own pints and quarts. Come and let me buy you one of each special, since my fellow's a foot taller than your sad little pesthouse corpse.

MOLLY: I'll let you buy, but with tremendous reservations. I'll certainly sell mine for twice what you manage.

GILHENNY: Molly, you're a right witch, sure as I stand here. I may even marry you.

(*They exit to the pub.*)

SCENE FIVE

The basement room. RYMER is bent over a book. The corpse is not in evidence. Noises offstage. RYMER sets aside his book.

POND: Just me, Jeffrey. (*Enters carrying a small parcel.*) For love of God, man, in this city, have you nothing better to do than hang about in the basement?

RYMER: I could ask the same of you. What's that you've got?

POND: A few cast-off instruments I came across.

RYMER: That's good of you.

POND: Anything to help the cause of knowledge. Working at last, are you?

RYMER: And not a minute too soon.

POND: A shame, isn't it; they don't last as long as they ought.

RYMER: What about you, Connor?

POND: No, no anatomy tonight. I'm on my way to a lecture. Just passing through the catacombs. (*Pause.*) I should tell you something, Jeffrey. I knew that girl. She washed linens for the hospital from time to time. I haven't quite known what to make of it. I got the impression she was a bit simple. Used to smile at all the young boys who came by in the street. Terribly trusting. She might have gone willingly with anyone. (*Pause.*) It's the constant fear of the anatomist, Jeffrey. Opening the sack to find your uncle or mother inside… I should thank God when it happened to me it was only a girl I'd seen in the hospital.

(*Noises offstage again.*)

POND: Someone there?

RYMER: Sshh.

MOLLY: Dr. Rymer?

RYMER: Molly?

MOLLY: (*Enters.*) Sorry to bother you here, Doctor—

RYMER: Why've you—here, come in…

MOLLY: I just wanted to ask you—I'm sorry; I shouldn't be here.

RYMER: No, no, it's fine. You just gave us a fright, is all.

(*He glances toward POND.*)

MOLLY: Oh—I'll come back another time.

RYMER: I think perhaps you'd best. (*Quietly*) What is it?

MOLLY: It's nothing. I just—I thought— I'll go now.

RYMER: Excuse us a moment, Connor.

(*He leads MOLLY aside.*)

RYMER: What's the matter?

MOLLY: I have to go. Really. It's nothing to do with you. Just me. Jumping at shadows, I suppose—

RYMER: It's all right, Molly; if something's wrong, you can tell me.

MOLLY: I had this awful thought—she might never have been buried.

RYMER: Who?

MOLLY: The girl—the corpse, doctor. (*Pause.*) I have to get out of here.

RYMER: You're spooking me. What could possibly have frighted you down into the basement of St. Bartholomew's Hospital of all places?

MOLLY: I can't talk about this. I have to— I wish I hadn't come. Good night.

RYMER: Molly, stop. What do you mean, she might never have been buried?

MOLLY: I only wondered if… it's really nothing to do with me now, but… I'm sick at the thought and I can't put it from my head. Her shroud is clean, Doctor. Do you understand?

RYMER: No.

MOLLY: No dirt, no mud, no *burial*, just a body and a cloth to make it look right.

RYMER: Molly, we know she was murdered already. What are you implying?

MOLLY: I don't know… but we hadn't a body for weeks! And nothing in the world could make Gabriel Shepherd steal a shroud from a churchyard when that's the only bit of the business the law takes seriously.

RYMER: Why come to tell me this?

MOLLY: It's… I thought you should know. I have to leave. This is no place for me. *(She exits, still nervous.)*

RYMER: Molly!

POND: What the hell was that all about?

RYMER: I wish to Christ I knew. Jesus, that was strange.

POND: Who was that? Pretty thing.

RYMER: A resurrectionist.

POND: I take it, the supplier of that particular specimen.

RYMER: I've never seen her in such a state.

POND: Rymer, you are pathetic to send a woman away who's come to you for counsel or comfort.

RYMER: What?

POND: That, Jeffrey, was a girl in need of male strength, and you, my dear fool, might as well have been a brick.

RYMER: Molly isn't that way. She doesn't need that from me.

POND: Well, as we are discussing a girl who happens to be a graverobber, sufficient to say you probably don't want such a thing from her, but let us observe nonetheless that some bodies still have life in them, Jeffrey. Don't become so driven an anatomist that you forget what the living are like.

RYMER: I'm sorry, Connor. If I don't get on…

POND: Oh, of course. I see. The bodies go so quickly. I'll be on my way. But—perhaps, once things… calm down… you might put me in touch with your little gravedigger.

RYMER: I assume purely for research purposes.

POND: Naturally.

SCENE SIX

The back room of the tavern. MOLLY sits at the table. ERIN GALLAGHER clears several mugs onto a tray.

ERIN: I've heard them talk about such things. Only once, though, and it was Hinton saying he didn't see how some bloke in Southwark has four bodies a week unless he hunts 'em down.

MOLLY: Who was it?

ERIN: I didn't hear. Just some bloke. Molly, Gabe Shepherd ain't that bold or that foolish. It's just the sort of story a drunk tells.

MOLLY: He was so angry, Erin. And then there was the shroud. He knows better.

ERIN: But he might have done it if he thought it would make it look like a dug body.

MOLLY: Yes.

(Enter GABRIEL SHEPHERD, furious.)

SHEPHERD: (*To ERIN*) You. Out. And keep the bloody door shut.

MOLLY: Gabe—

SHEPHERD: You heard me.

ERIN: Not on your orders, Shepherd.

MOLLY: I'll be fine.

ERIN: I got cleaning up to do.

SHEPHERD: I want that bitch out of this room, now, Molly. Tell her to leave.

ERIN: I speak the language. And, what

ought to be obvious, this ain't your house to order me out!

MOLLY: Erin, give us a minute.

(ERIN is hesitating.)

MOLLY: Go on. I'll come have a pint with you in a bit. Just... wait outside.

(ERIN nods and exits with a sharp look at SHEPHERD.)

SHEPHERD: Outside the door, I've no doubt. What's she skittish for, Molly?

MOLLY: Your tone's a bit much, Gabriel.

SHEPHERD: You waiting on that bastard doctor?

MOLLY: We got no body tonight. The doctors don't come by socially. I was talking with Erin.

SHEPHERD: You been asking about the body.

MOLLY: Which one?

SHEPHERD: You bloody well know which one I mean. The one with the flopping head, Molly.

MOLLY: I haven't, but I will now. Where'd you find her, Gabe? She didn't come from St. Sep's.

SHEPHERD: What are you asking that for?

MOLLY: I want to know if you've found a better yard. Where'd you find her? In a charnelhouse?

SHEPHERD: It ain't got nothing to do with yards or churches, Moll. You're angling straight for the gallows. You ask questions, you'll get us caught. Leave the dead to lie.

MOLLY: Fine words from a man of your trade.

SHEPHERD: I may have had a look round. It's no concern of yours where the body came from. Ain't your concern how I found it, only how much it fetched. What other questions you been asking?

MOLLY: What questions should I have done? I know my business. Come back when you're sober, Gabe, or when you got another body from wherever it is you're getting them.

SHEPHERD: Advice is it? Well I'll give you some back. Shut your goddamn mouth, Molly! Shut your goddamn mouth or someone'll do it for you!

MOLLY: I can take care of myself.

SHEPHERD: Just like your brother could, yeah?

MOLLY: I can't quite tell if that's a warning or a threat, Gabriel.

SHEPHERD: You have a care, Molly. Watch what you say.

MOLLY: I always do.

SHEPHERD: What care have you got for corpses? Half a year now we've been digging them, and I ain't never seen you like this. If I think I'm likely to wind up in Newgate because you're asking questions, I warn you, I'll find a way to shut you up. Don't doubt that.

MOLLY: Don't threaten me, Gabe. You're the one who stole the shroud. If you get caught, I'll not take the blame for it.

SHEPHERD: You'll—

(Enter GILHENNY followed by ERIN.)

GILHENNY: What's happening here?

MOLLY: Master Shepherd came with some friendly words of warning.

SHEPHERD: The shroud's gone and so's the body, Moll. Nothing left to get us in trouble but your big mouth. So keep it shut.

(Exit SHEPHERD under a glare from GILHENNY.)

GILHENNY: Molly?

MOLLY: I'm fine.

ERIN: He's different of late. Men get dangerous when they're afraid.

MOLLY: Shepherd's no danger.

GILHENNY: You said something to him?

MOLLY: Not much, but enough, I guess.

GILHENNY: Molly, I told you—

MOLLY: Did you ever know my brother when he worked with Shepherd?

(GILHENNY doesn't answer.)

MOLLY: Thom?

GILHENNY: I never met him. *(Pause.)* Did Shepherd really threaten you?

MOLLY: Just said he'd see me hung first if there was trouble. Drunk threats.

GILHENNY: Take those threats seriously, Molly. Assume he knows how to protect himself, even when he's brought the danger on himself.

MOLLY: Don't be cryptic, Thom. Just say what you have to.

GILHENNY: I sold the body, Molly.

MOLLY: What body?

GILHENNY: Jacob's. After he hung for murder and was sentenced to dissection. Sentenced for killing a girl in order to sell her. Because Shepherd made it fall on

Jacob instead of himself. He's a big, loud ox, but stupid he's not, it just serves his purposes to seem so.

(MOLLY can't speak. GILHENNY reaches for her, tries to hold her. She stands stiffly, not allowing him to comfort her.)

GILHENNY: Molly—

(She pulls gently but firmly away from him, utterly unable to respond. From the corner where she has been, forgotten, ERIN speaks.)

ERIN: It ain't possible.

GILHENNY: It is, though it surely ain't right.

ERIN: How could you not have told her?

GILHENNY: You don't understand, Erin. You think because we drink together out there, act like right mates, we don't go about scared as children that someone'll talk to the wrong doctor, to the wrong constable, to the wrong woman. You think because we seem to feel we're safe in here we don't go about fearing the gallows-hill. You think we trust each other.

ERIN: No, but I'd have thought you'd trust her.

GILHENNY: I do. I care for her. Molly, I do, but—you might be dangerous to yourself now you know. I feared you'd say things to Gabe, put his back up like you've done, get him watching you.

MOLLY: I can't believe I've never heard so much as a word—

GILHENNY: You have, only you've thought it meant other things.

MOLLY: He killed this girl, too, didn't he?

GILHENNY: He'd never tell me the truth of a thing like that.

ERIN: But he's capable.

GILHENNY: I'll only say he's done it before. Only that once that anyone knows for certain. But now you cannot—*cannot*, Molly—say to him that you know. You must stop making him wonder, because if he thinks you'll endanger him, he'll do what he thinks he has to. Just stay clear of him for a bit.

ERIN: You can stay with me if you like.

GILHENNY: You can stay with me.

(*She doesn't answer.*)

GILHENNY: But if that's not to your liking, stay with Erin.

(*A knock at the door. ERIN opens it to find RYMER standing in the doorway.*)

RYMER: Is Molly—

MOLLY: I'm here. (*To GILHENNY.*) I'll look out for myself, Thom, I always do.

GILHENNY: I know it. You're doing it right this minute, aren't you? Not tonight, then. But you know where to find my house and you know I'd look out for you if you were to knock at my door.

(*He exits followed by ERIN.*)

RYMER: What's happening, Molly?

MOLLY: We've no bodies tonight.

RYMER: I didn't come to buy and you know it. I was worried.

MOLLY: Everyone's worried on my behalf. It's making me mad. I can manage my affairs.

RYMER: Is that why you came to the hospital last night? Managing your affairs?

MOLLY: I don't know why I came to the hospital.

RYMER: Yes, you do. There's no sin in asking for help when you need it, Molly. I'm your friend.

MOLLY: You're the man who pays for dead matter. Another doctor who peddles in dead flesh.

RYMER: Don't say it that way.

MOLLY: You do. There's a strangeness in using death to learn about life, Doctor.

RYMER: You make your livelihood from it, Molly. Watch where you cast your stones. Why does this weigh on you so much?

MOLLY: Why do you think it does? I carried her body a mile at least through the witching hours and it seems to me it well-nigh broke my back and shredded my foot but the only place still hurts is my arms, do you know why? Because I had to hold her so her head wouldn't fall off! And last night I woke up thinking the blanket over my shoulders was a shroud, and if I pushed it back I'd find a grinning wound like the one killed that girl smiling up from my own throat.

RYMER: Maybe it's time for you to stop gravedigging.

MOLLY: What then? Turn whore? That's what happens to women without husbands and without livelihoods. In my worst nightmares I go from pandering for doctors who want bodies to selling off pieces of my own. They already call me that in the pub.

RYMER: Why don't you stop, then? Do something else. You could marry.

MOLLY: What kind of a man would court me? Thom plays the gallant, but I think he doesn't want a wife. And how could I marry another like me and think I'd escaped the things I've done?

RYMER: I don't mean Thom Gilhenny, I… (*Meaningfully.*) know there are other men who look at you, Molly.

MOLLY: All I know is how to dig and trade in flesh. What sort of sick parasite am I?

RYMER: You're not listening to… all right, never mind that. Molly, I don't like murder. I hate death. My entire life is built on struggling to overcome it. But you can't cling to it this way. It's what happens. The body fails.

MOLLY: And you shrug it off, don't you? It's what happens? What about the injustice? That doesn't matter to you? Doesn't matter how the life was taken, as long as you can give it back. It's just possible that even if you could staunch the freshets of blood, pour it back and seal the wound like God himself, even if all that was in your power, she might still be beyond fixing.

RYMER: Molly, just stop if it bothers you so much. It could be that simple for you. Just stop.

MOLLY: You've said that. And it's not that simple.

(*They sit silently for a moment.*)

RYMER: Do you want me to go?

MOLLY: Yes.

RYMER: I'd rather keep you company.

MOLLY: I'm not good company to keep.

RYMER: I'd rather stay.

MOLLY: No one seems to want to let me alone right now.

RYMER: Perhaps you underestimate your friends. Good night, Molly.

MOLLY: Good night, Doctor.

(*He exits. MOLLY remains, desolate. ERIN enters.*)

ERIN: Will you be coming home with me?

MOLLY: I suppose. What's wrong with me? I got to make my living.

ERIN: You could be doing worse, love.

MOLLY: I don't think so.

ERIN: (*Firmly.*) You could do worse than what you do. It ain't pretty but there's uglier faces out there in the city.

MOLLY: The only way I know is to sell.

ERIN: That gets far, far uglier than you've seen.

MOLLY: You don't know anything about us. You think it's all sitting about in a pub getting pissed while the doctors come and go and throw money?

ERIN: That ain't what I think. I think you sound a bit righteous for my taste, is all.

MOLLY: What do you mean by that?

ERIN: Just that. Folk start sounding too sorry for themselves, I start thinking about how much I love cleaning tobacco out of the mug Jack Hinton thinks is a spittoon.

MOLLY: Can you imagine carrying a woman just a touch younger than you for a mile trying to keep out of the light and hoping her head doesn't—I can't get that feeling off me! We sell flesh, for Christ's sake. Do you know what it's like to sell human flesh?

ERIN: You know goddamn well I know what that feels like.

(*A long pause.*)

ERIN: But that's neither here nor there.

Gabe's outside, Molly. I think he's waiting for you.

MOLLY: Tell him I'm staying with you.

ERIN: We're near closing. You stay back here and I'll fetch you when I'm ready to go.

MOLLY: That's fine. Thank you.

(ERIN nods and exits, closing the door behind her. MOLLY sits alone for a moment, then folds her arms on the table and lays down her head. Suddenly the door opens again. It is SHEPHERD, and he bolts the door behind him.)

MOLLY: What do you want?

SHEPHERD: What did the doctor say?

MOLLY: Nothing to do with you. He wasn't buying tonight.

SHEPHERD: What did he want, then?

MOLLY: I told you to come back when you're sober. You got nothing better to do than worry about me? Didn't Erin tell you I'm staying the night with her?

SHEPHERD: I got nothing better to do than look out for myself, and I want to have a few answers from you. Like why you been nosing around all the churches hereabouts. Like why you went to the hospital last night.

MOLLY: It's got nothing to do with you.

SHEPHERD: Then you ain't asking no more questions?

MOLLY: No.

SHEPHERD: Bloody excellent. And what about that doctor who follows you around like a puppy? What did you tell him?

MOLLY: What on earth do I have to tell anyone? What are you getting at?

SHEPHERD: You got to learn to keep your mouth shut! You got to learn this isn't a game, Molly! (Pause.) Jack says you're likely fixing to sell me off to the constabulary. That's what he makes of this business.

MOLLY: That's plain stupid.

SHEPHERD: Jack says you're probably fucking that doctor and both of you want to sell me off. Or maybe since we all know how close you and Thom Gilhenny are—

MOLLY: Are you listening to yourself? Why would I do something like that? You know I can't get a body over the churchyard wall myself. Why would I cut off my livelihood that way?

SHEPHERD: Jack and Braithhill said I was an idiot for working with a woman when everybody knows women can't be trusted. Jack says you're likely a witch. No right woman digs bodies.

MOLLY: Well, you're right. So from now on you can do it yourself. Do it yourself. This is all wrong. I've had enough.

SHEPHERD: Mayhap a witch has got better ways of getting a body to sell.

MOLLY: Like slicing her throat and hiding her body behind a stewhouse?

(A long pause.)

SHEPHERD: Why'd you say that?

(A defiant silence from MOLLY.)

SHEPHERD: I didn't hurt that girl.

MOLLY: Well, then how else did you happen across her body in a perfectly clean shroud that's never seen a grave? Why else make me carry her? Why make me carry her! Goddamn it, Gabe, why did you make me do that?

(Drawn by MOLLY's hysterical cries, ERIN tries to open the door and, finding it bolted, begins to pound on it.)

SHEPHERD: Shut up! Shut up, goddamn it!

MOLLY: Why did you make me do that?

SHEPHERD: She was already dead! Why should I let something go to waste just 'cause it was in an alley instead of the churchyard? *(To ERIN, who is pounding on the door.)* Shut up, for Christ's sake!

MOLLY: You killed her and you wanted to make sure you wouldn't get caught with the body. You made me carry it like you made my brother—

(SHEPHERD swings a punch to her mouth that sends her across the room.)

SHEPHERD: I gave you fair warning. I gave you lots of chances.

MOLLY: You gave me your murder to carry!

SHEPHERD: She was dead when I found her, do you understand? I don't know who did it, but if I have to kill you to shut you up, I will, and I'll sell you to your little doctor friend without a second thought! It ain't for you to question where I find what I sell, and if you don't like it, there ain't a bloody thing you can do about it. If you're smart you'll figure that out faster than Jacob did.

(MOLLY flies at him, clawing at his face. SHEPHERD throws her back again.)

SHEPHERD: You don't like it, do you? *(To ERIN, still pounding at the door.)* Go to hell, will you! *(To MOLLY.)* You want to stop? You want to be done with the bodies? You know how else you can earn your keep. You could have done that in the first place and saved yourself the

trouble. Now we'll talk about how things'll be from now on.

(SHEPHERD grabs MOLLY, still kicking and fighting, and drags her out a back door into the alley.)

SCENE SEVEN

The tavern, that same night. It is empty except for ERIN and GILHENNY, moving like desperate, caged animals as they try not to panic.

GILHENNY: Think.

ERIN: I am.

(Another long pause.)

ERIN: She might have gone to the church.

GILHENNY: You know I looked there.

ERIN: Thom, I don't know where she goes when she leaves here. She's alive, at least.

GILHENNY: Think of someplace! I can't just stay here and wait. Goddamn it, think!

ERIN: She'll come back here eventually.

GILHENNY: That woman is going to get herself bloody killed.

ERIN: Jesus, settle down! Shepherd's taken care of, what's there to worry about now? She'll come back.

GILHENNY: And then what?

ERIN: What the hell you mean, and then what?

GILHENNY: For a girl who's so brilliant at noticing the second a man's mug goes dry, you're awfully damn dense sometimes. Don't you ever pay attention to anything else?

ERIN: I rather thought I wasn't meant to notice anything else. Don't look at me like that. You all made sure no one talked about

Jacob, not to me or to Molly. It's your own fault she—

GILHENNY: I don't mean Jacob. I mean the dead girl.

ERIN: What, should I have told Molly? You didn't.

GILHENNY: I thought you heard.

ERIN: That sort of man doesn't worry much about being overheard by the likes of me. I heard everything.

GILHENNY: She's too goddamn fearless. I can't tell her.

ERIN: Don't tell her. Gabe's dead. Even if he said he didn't do it—

GILHENNY: Weren't you the one furious that I didn't tell her about her brother?

ERIN: What side do you want me to take? Aye, I was angry, but I saw what came of it, not you.

(GILHENNY crumples at the thought.)

ERIN: Sorry. Thom, I'm sorry; I shouldn't have—

GILHENNY: I'll figure it out when I find her. *(Exits.)*

SCENE EIGHT

RYMER's basement room. Prominent in the center of the room is the sheeted body. A covered basin stands on a table near the desk where RYMER himself sits, an unreadable expression on his face. Five knocks sound on the wooden door. RYMER starts. The knocks come again, six this time.

RYMER: Who's there?

MOLLY: Molly Lark!

RYMER: Are you alone?

MOLLY: Entirely. Let me in, Dr. Rymer, please!

(RYMER unlocks the door and opens it for her. MOLLY is bedraggled and scared, sporting bloodstains from her encounter with SHEPHERD.)

RYMER: Sweet Christ, Molly, what happened to you?

MOLLY: I threw the knife away. Into the river. Its heavy. It'll sink, I hope. Thought about burying it, but it's been rainy lately and I thought someone might find it.

RYMER: What are you talking about? Molly, sit down.

MOLLY: No. I couldn't… he was too heavy to move far. I dragged him… into an alley, but I had to leave him there. Someone'll find him—tomorrow, or the next day, but I threw the knife away so they won't find that.

RYMER: Molly—

MOLLY: If they do find it, it will be clean. No blood, no way to know whose knife it was. No one will know. Clean… even though when I threw it in it was filthy, red and filthy from blood and dirt.

(RYMER grabs her arms. She shakes him off, staring at him.)

MOLLY: I don't want anything to touch me. Ever. Not now. You know how dirty it feels when something… bleeds.

RYMER: Molly, please. Look at you—

MOLLY: I dig bodies. That's dirty. Only this—good Christ, the blood—I'm dirtier now—I feel so dirty! *(She starts to cry.)* I'm dirty!

(RYMER tries to put his arms around her.)

MOLLY: You can't touch me! *(She wrings at her bloodstained clothing.)* It might never come out. Never!

RYMER: Tell me what happened!

MOLLY: I killed him. I think… certain I did. Nobody could bleed so much and live.

RYMER: Who?

MOLLY: Who…

RYMER: Who did you… kill?

MOLLY: I didn't just kill him, Doctor. I never dug a body looks like his. It's not a body anymore. It's just—whatever's left.

RYMER: Molly, who?

MOLLY: It used to be Gabriel Shepherd, although I don't think you could tell from looking at him.

RYMER: Oh, Jesus, oh… Christ, Molly, why? Gabe? Why, Molly? You stabbed him? Tell me! What did you do?

MOLLY: Took my knife—your knife, the one you lent me, your folder with the walnut handle, Doctor—I'm so sorry I had to use your knife that way, I'm so sorry I had to throw it away.

RYMER: Never mind the knife, Molly. It's of no consequence. What matters is what happened to you tonight. Can I help?

MOLLY: Can't help Gabe anymore. Once I had him down, I couldn't stop. I just kept at him… with the knife… until I couldn't see anymore for the red. Dirty…

RYMER: Why?

MOLLY: Because it was the only way I could—because I couldn't do to him what he did to me!

RYMER: What he did—oh, God… oh, Molly, I'm so—

MOLLY: It doesn't matter.

RYMER: Never say that.

MOLLY: There won't be a child. That's something, I suppose. I wouldn't like him to be its father, and I don't think I'd like me to be its mother. I wouldn't make a good mother. You can't raise a child when you're a murderer.

RYMER: Please don't say that.

MOLLY: I murdered him. He was still on top of me, just straightening up, and I was watching the bruises come up on my arms and tasting blood on my mouth from when he bit me and salt from when I thought he might pity me if I cried, and I remembered the knife and I went after him, knocked him backwards and after I was done—and it was a while, Doctor. It was a long while, but afterwards I dragged him into an alley.

RYMER: Let me help you.

MOLLY: With what? You can help me bury the body if you want to help me.

RYMER: Why'd you come here?

MOLLY: In case someone finds the knife. It was your knife. *(Her eyes fall on the corpse.)* Might be weeks, or months. But you ought to know, just in case.

RYMER: That was good thinking.

MOLLY: If I ever unwrapped a shroud to find anything like what I left in that alley—

RYMER: Molly, are there any cuts, contusions… any wounds that might need cleaning and dressing?

MOLLY: No. I don't think so. He was really too strong to fight much. I fought, and he wasn't looking so good even before I remembered the knife, but all he had to do was hold me down.

(RYMER tries to get a look at the cuts on her face.)

RYMER: Can I look?

MOLLY: This is probably the last body I can get for you.

RYMER: Let me see your face.

MOLLY: What are you going to do?

RYMER: Just look, that's all. See if they need cleaning.

MOLLY: No. About her. *(She is fixated on the corpse.)*

RYMER: Oh. I don't know, Molly. Like you said, not much to do now.

MOLLY: You ought to go to the constabulary.

RYMER: Why?

MOLLY: Right in front of you you got a murdered body and you got a murderer. That's not reason enough?

RYMER: Molly, this does not make you a killer. It makes Shepherd a rapist that won't do it again. What... what you did, you did to save yourself.

MOLLY: But I kept doing it until I couldn't tell what was his body and what was street rubbish soaked with blood and torn-out gore! I never killed nobody! I never did, I said my prayers at night even though the only reason I ever went to the church was to break its laws! God has a place in hell for killers like me, and Shepherd'll look through the bars of his cell and leer at me because he put me there! And it's people like you that sit and watch us all run about with our knives and our ale and slaughter each other and you won't bother to do the first thing about it, not even when a murderer comes to you and tells you what she's done! Not even when you buy a body's been carved like a capon with nobody the wiser!

RYMER: You know I can't go to the constabulary.

MOLLY: You think you're protected. Special.

RYMER: Molly, I don't even know what I'm getting into yet. If I take chances, it's the end of all of this!

MOLLY: All of what? You cut up illegal corpses in a basement with stolen instruments. What is it you think you can do here?

RYMER: It's all I have! If I'm found out, I'll be arrested, excommunicated—

MOLLY: *(Yanks the sheet off of the corpse with a wild flourish.)* But you won't be dead! *(Abruptly she stops, noticing the huge wound in the stomach of the corpse.)* What is this?

RYMER: It's nothing. Dissection—it's not pretty.

MOLLY: Don't lie to me. What is this? Look at me! I've seen what doctors do. Don't lie to me. What is this mess? Jeffrey. What does this mean?

RYMER: She was pregnant.

(MOLLY slumps against the wall.)

RYMER: It's there, in the basin.

MOLLY: *(Staring at the sheeted basin.)* How old was it?

RYMER: Not sure.

MOLLY: Girl or a boy?

RYMER: It was a girl.

MOLLY: A baby. A little girl. *(Suddenly her awe wears off. She retches.)* Oh, God— tell me you can still forgive me! I'm not like him!

RYMER: You are nothing like this man, Molly. Not like anyone who could do this to a mother.

MOLLY: What?

RYMER: You're nothing like him.

MOLLY: You said he could do this to a mother.

RYMER: So I did.

MOLLY: Does that mean the bastard knew? Did he know?

(No answer from RYMER.)

MOLLY: How do you know he—

RYMER: I didn't do that. It was already there, just… hastily stitched up. After he killed her he cut into her belly.

MOLLY: Why?

RYMER: I can't answer that.

MOLLY: What if it had been me turned up dead? Dead like that? What would you have done? Something? Would you have done something?

RYMER: I'm a doctor, Molly. I can help you now, while you're alive with cuts on your face, but like this— *(He gestures at the body.)* —all I can do is mourn.

MOLLY: You're not mourning her. *(Pause)* Would you want to see him punished? The man who did it?

RYMER: Of course I would.

MOLLY: Would you try to find him?

RYMER: Molly—

MOLLY: What would you do if you knew? If you saw Gabe Shepherd walk away, fastening up his trousers, and me lying there in an alley?

RYMER: She wasn't raped, Molly. And you and I both know Gabe Shepherd didn't kill this woman.

MOLLY: If you saw him.

RYMER: I'd want to see him hang. I'd lie awake at night conjuring his ugly, suffused face. I'd make that my prayer every night.

MOLLY: Conjury and prayer, Doctor? This from a man of medicine?

RYMER: A man of medicine does not take lives. I'd want to, Molly. If I saw you— like that—I'd want him dead. I wouldn't even care how. I'd be obsessed with the many variations on that man's death.

MOLLY: But you wouldn't do it.

RYMER: Probably not. That doesn't mean I wouldn't sell my soul to have a cleaver in my hand and Gabriel Shepherd cowering at my feet and no conscience to stand between us. I'd negotiate with the devil for that.

MOLLY: That's different. Gabe's already dead.

RYMER: I want to hold you, Molly, touch your wounds and heal them, kill the pain since I can't kill him. I want to be the one that rescued you. But I can't do that, either.

MOLLY: I don't need you to heal me.

RYMER: I know you don't.

MOLLY: It's not something a doctor can heal, is it?

RYMER: That doesn't stop me wanting it.

MOLLY: I don't need a doctor.

RYMER: I don't want to be your doctor.

MOLLY: I don't need a lover, either.

RYMER: You don't need me.

MOLLY: If you love me, doctor, pretend this is me. *(Taps the sheet.)* Pretend it's me and take the outrage and find out who did this.

RYMER: What you did to Shepherd isn't enough?

MOLLY: It is enough for what he did to me, but it doesn't begin to make up for this!

RYMER: What can I do?

MOLLY: Find him! Help me find him!

RYMER: It is unjust, Molly. No human should suffer wounds like these while there is life and pain in her body.

MOLLY: It's too much, Doctor. Too much to tolerate now. He cannot be allowed to go free. Help me. You will do more good in this than you will in bandaging my face and show more love than in kissing it.

RYMER: I'm not a constable. I don't know how to do it. I wouldn't know how to begin. I'm a doctor. Please.

MOLLY: Why won't you help me?

RYMER: Why is this so important to you?

MOLLY: Are you in love with me?

RYMER: Christ! Why are you doing this?

MOLLY: I need you.

RYMER: You don't, Molly. Don't do this. You don't need me, you don't want me,

and what you do want is something I desire no part of.

MOLLY: You worry that if you start asking questions, someone will find out about the bodies? Nobody cares!

RYMER: It's not that.

MOLLY: I cannot do this without you. I need you.

RYMER: You don't, you can't even—I can't come near you, I'm afraid to touch you—

MOLLY: I cannot do this on my own! You paid for her body, her violated corpse! Doesn't that stick in your craw? Does it give you no guilt?

RYMER: Don't try to shame me! I paid, but you took the money and you no more went to the constabulary than did I!

MOLLY: I know I'm not innocent! If I were innocent I'd be clean, I'd be whole; instead I'm dirty and violated and what part of me isn't dead is dying fast— *(Pause.)* I have to go away.

RYMER: Please don't. I know... how you must be feeling...

MOLLY: You don't know nothing—

RYMER: Stay here. Not here... not... in this room—stay with me.

MOLLY: You all think you're gods.

RYMER: I know better than that. *(Pause. Withdrawing.)* You should let me take care of your wounds.

MOLLY: She trusted someone, Doctor. *(Exits.)*

SCENE NINE

The back room of the tavern, the next evening. ERIN sits at the table, head in her arms. Enter MOLLY. ERIN wakes with a start.

ERIN: Molly! Jesus, where have you been?

(No answer.)

ERIN: Molly?

MOLLY: He killed her and gutted out the baby inside her. She trusted him and in return he twisted her happiness in blood and bile. Into murder. And her baby, her little girl— If I ever see him, Erin, if I ever see the man who could do this, I might not have the strength to let him live.

(ERIN's face drops into one of utter shock. She starts to say something, cannot continue.)

MOLLY: I killed Gabe Shepherd, Erin.

(With effort ERIN shakes off the shock. Unconvincingly.)

ERIN: Well, then he won't do it again. Bastard only got what he deserved. (*Pause.*) She was pregnant? She had—

MOLLY: She had a little girl growing inside.

(ERIN cannot speak. She sits silently with her back to MOLLY, unable to answer.)

MOLLY: Did you hear the other thing?

ERIN: I saw it.

(Now MOLLY cannot answer.)

MOLLY: And you didn't—

ERIN: I couldn't get in, could I? Then I heard the other door go—I ran around, I saw—I didn't know what to do! So I ran, I slipped at the door, I wanted to find Thom, but he had gone aways up the street. I shouted, and he came back and we went back there—you were gone… and Gabe was…

MOLLY: You should have called the constabulary.

ERIN: Not for Gabe Shepherd. Not after that. I know what Gabe did to you. I understand.

MOLLY: Did they do that to you?

ERIN: That's what happens. Sometimes. Because they don't think it matters when you've let them do it before.

MOLLY: Someone will come after me.

ERIN: They won't. By tomorrow he'll be in an operating theater. Thom took him to the barbers. We sold him to them.

MOLLY: You sold him?

ERIN: They might've come for you. You said so.

MOLLY: I don't understand.

ERIN: It seemed the right thing to do. We couldn't—

MOLLY: Stop.

ERIN: (*Disbelieving.*) Are you angry?

MOLLY: What's the matter with this place?

ERIN: Are you angry with me? We did what we thought would protect you.

MOLLY: Did you at least look for me a little bit before you went racing off to the barbers?

ERIN: Didn't I ask where you've been? What's the matter with you?

MOLLY: It couldn't go to waste, could it? A perfectly good corpse. What hideous kind of world is this? Where graves spit forth their bellies for us to sell like scraps to hungry doctors? We devour our dead and sacrifice the living.

ERIN: What do you expect? Don't get righteous over Shepherd's body, Molly. He deserved what he got. And don't get righteous with me, either. (*Pause. A bit gentler.*) Smithfield's just a big market for selling dead meat. You live too long with the dead and maybe it ain't so good for you.

(*No answer from MOLLY. ERIN exits, nearly walking into GILHENNY as he comes into the room. MOLLY is facing away and doesn't see him at first. He walks up behind her, stops when her head pricks up, indicating that she has heard him.*)

GILHENNY: I wish you had come to me. I wish you had come *with* me. Are you all right?

MOLLY: I don't have anything to give you now.

GILHENNY: You mistake me.

MOLLY: I know you, with your pretty seductions and that sad tone you have now. I know what you wanted, and I don't have it to give to you anymore. (*She won't cry now, but she is shaking.*)

GILHENNY: Molly.

(*GILHENNY knows she won't ask for comforting, and puts his arms around her anyway.*)

GILHENNY: If you know me at all you know better. (*Pause.*) Where did you go?

MOLLY: I went to the doctor.

GILHENNY: Did he fix you up proper?

MOLLY: Why didn't you come and look for me?

GILHENNY: I did, Molly. I promise I did. Looked for you, shouted for you, did everything, I guess, but cross the street.

(*Enter RYMER.*)

GILHENNY: What do you want?

RYMER: (*To MOLLY.*) A few minutes with you.

MOLLY: Did you change your mind?

RYMER: Ask me anything but that.

MOLLY: There is nothing else I want to know.

RYMER: Will you excuse us, Gilhenny?

GILHENNY: Afraid not.

MOLLY: You've got nothing I want to hear, anyhow.

RYMER: Don't do this, Molly. Please. It doesn't make me your enemy that I can't be your accomplice.

MOLLY: What have you got to say to me, Doctor Rymer? Come along.

RYMER: I've been looking for you. Since last night.

MOLLY: I've not been hiding.

RYMER: Perhaps I looked in the wrong places.

MOLLY: Did you look in the churchyard? Did you look for me there? (*To GILHENNY.*) And you, where did you look? Bloody brilliant hunters you men are. Where were you looking that it took you all night not to find me?

RYMER: Is that where you've been? In the churchyard?

MOLLY: I've been in hell.

RYMER: I've been with you in spirit.

(*GILHENNY snorts derisively.*)

MOLLY: You've been in the basement at St. Bart's gutting the dead. That is where you've been, Doctor. Don't tell me about hell when the closest you've come is the morgue. *(She throws a tankard across the room.)*

RYMER: I came to make peace with her. Can you please leave us?

GILHENNY: You had your moment. Leave her alone.

RYMER: You don't have to protect her from me. She doesn't need that from you.

MOLLY: Neither of you has the right to speak for me. And neither of you has the faintest idea of what I need. Thom. Give us a minute.

(GILHENNY is angry but swallows it back. He kisses MOLLY's forehead.)

GILHENNY: You still know where to find me. There's more I want to tell you. *(Exits.)*

RYMER: You didn't ask all that of him, did you?

MOLLY: He never saw her.

RYMER: And I wish to God I hadn't, either. Ask anything else of me. Let me do anything else to give you comfort. Please.

MOLLY: I can't.

RYMER: Why not, Molly?

MOLLY: Because of what you feel for me that I can't give you back. And what I want from you that you can't give to me. Because I'll always know what matters to you in the end.

RYMER: These are opportunities, Molly. Do you see? I have a chance to do some good.

MOLLY: This isn't the way it's supposed to be! We ought to be outraged. For two deaths there ought to be punishment! And you tell me these are opportunities! You most of all should be angry. You should

want this man dead. No man should be allowed to live who calls himself a healer and commits such hideous crimes.

RYMER: Healer?

MOLLY: You know it had to be a doctor. No one else would bother to sew her back up again. You know the killer had to be one of you. *(She walks to the back of the room, leans against a section of the wall with her back to RYMER.)* Stay where you are. Just leave me for a moment.

(Enter ERIN.)

ERIN: Doctor, there's a gentleman asking for you in the pub.

RYMER: A gentleman?

ERIN: Yeah. I thought you all preferred "gentlemen" to "stuffy-lookin' Oxford gits."

(Enter POND behind her.)

POND: Jeffrey. I thought I saw you come in.

RYMER: What do you want?

(Exit ERIN, leaving the door open.)

POND: Come along, Jeffrey. Is that any way to greet a friend? I thought I might see about securing a specimen—nothing better to do with the evening. Are you alone?

(RYMER glances over at where MOLLY stands, just out of POND's view.)

RYMER: I was waiting for someone.

POND: Not your attractive little gravedigger, by any chance?

RYMER: Why?

POND: No reason. Perhaps she might allow me to view her merchandise for myself. I was thinking of procuring—

RYMER: I don't think she's likely to put in an appearance tonight.

POND: Ahh. You might find the need to turn to alternate means of acquisition, then.

RYMER: I don't believe I'll be dissecting this evening, actually.

POND: Really? Then whom are you waiting for?

RYMER: Chap I met a night or so ago. No matter.

POND: Not likely to find you easily back here, is he?

RYMER: He knows where to find me.

POND: I hope so. Otherwise you'll have to drink alone tonight. Perhaps I'll join you, unless you object.

RYMER: In that case, let us move out into the pub. This room has an unpleasant taste in the air. I dislike drinking here.

POND: Dealings in death leave their scent, do they? Taint the ale so it cannot be drunk?

RYMER: I think the corpses leave their very ghosts in this room.

POND: Oh, spare us both the morbidity. Ghosts, Jeffrey? If you go on dwelling so deeply on all your specimens you'll go mad.

RYMER: I cannot help but give it thought.

POND: Well, there's no point in harping on unpleasant realities. She's dead, and no matter who carved her up to begin with, here stand we, poised to do it again. Is that not all that matters? In the name of learning, Jeffrey.

RYMER: It's not all that matters.

POND: Don't be such a wide-eyed innocent. If death is inevitable, and incidentally, it is; I say if that is the case, then to waste the opportunity afforded us by the passing of a fellow human is a crime equal to murder itself. If we don't take that opportunity, we have only ourselves to blame for our ignorance and only our ignorance to blame for our inability to delay, even to circumvent, the inevitable. We know intelligent men ourselves who still prescribe leeches to thin the blood. Men who drone on about the humors, carry herbs to ward off foul air, still expect the king's touch to cure scrofula—men who look at the Bill of Mortality every week when it's printed and wonder why deaths stay so high. Look at the goddamn barber-surgeons, for Christ's sake! But take a man like William Harvey, an anatomist with the gall to dissect his own kin and look at what he's discovered. Blood courses through the body, it circulates; and look what he dares to study now, the very development of life in the fetus! How can we not dare that boldness, Jeffrey? *(He goes and shuts the door.)* Death can be made to serve us. It's what you did two nights ago and what you'll do every time you pay out a sum from your pocket to possess the left-behind wastes of mortality, Jeffrey. And rightly so, I say. Don't look indignant. You're an anatomist now. You'll learn to make it serve you.

(The door opens again. GILHENNY enters. His preliminary glance around the room fails to locate MOLLY.)

POND: I beg your pardon.

GILHENNY: No need.

POND: Can we help you with something?

GILHENNY: I can't imagine you've put a deposit on this room. There's no need to act as if it's yours.

(POND, with a snort, returns to the table for his beer.)

GILHENNY: *(Low, to RYMER.)* Where is she?

(RYMER nods his head in MOLLY's direction. Her look at both of them indicates confusion—she has remained out of sight and is unsure as to whether or not she ought to stay there.)

GILHENNY: Get him out of here.

RYMER: Why?

POND: Stop your whispering there, Gilhenny. We have no business, remember? Or have you reconsidered?

GILHENNY: Not here, if you please. Let's step back into the pub.

POND: No, I think I've decided not to continue any conversations with you.

RYMER: Actually, it was me he was looking for. Come along, let's find a table with service.

POND: You were meeting *him*? What for?

(GILHENNY says nothing, so RYMER supplies the [wrong] answer.)

RYMER: I'm ready for another.

POND: And he arranged it for you? No, I don't think so. He doesn't sell to our kind. *(To GILHENNY.)* What's the meaning of this meeting?

GILHENNY: Your tone is not to my liking.

POND: Your liking is none of my concern.

GILHENNY: Keep your peace, Pond.

POND: No one will leave this room until I have my answer.

GILHENNY: These are things you'd rather stayed unsaid.

RYMER: What's all this?

GILHENNY: Just another part of the anatomist's trade, right, Doctor?

RYMER: What do you mean by that?

GILHENNY: Ask your friend. Ask how he gets his specimens. He seems to think I came to tell you myself.

RYMER: What does he mean, Connor?

POND: I am not here to stand under your interrogation, Gilhenny. One homeless drab won't be missed.

(MOLLY has heard enough to understand GILHENNY's implications. She takes a step out of her hiding place.)

GILHENNY: Stop! *(To POND, who thinks this was directed at him.)* Enough's been said all round.

RYMER: *(Has forgotten MOLLY.)* Enough's been—have you all gone mad? *(To POND.)* Is this—

GILHENNY: Doctor, enough's been said.

RYMER: Don't be ridiculous, enough's been said! Connor, the man's daft, he's—

GILHENNY: We're past that, Rymer. *(To RYMER, but more for MOLLY's benefit.)* I'd rather it hadn't come out this way. I thought it might be worse if you learned on your own.

RYMER: Connor, tell me the man is lying.

POND: Enough, Jeffrey. It was an opportunity.

RYMER: What do you mean, an opportunity?

POND: For science! It was for—

GILHENNY: Your science is what others call judgment.

POND: Fine words when it's men like me put coins in your pocket!

GILHENNY: Right before they swing.

RYMER: For God's sake! How does killing a human afford you any opportunities you can't take from a corpse?

POND: The chance to observe life as it flees the body, Jeffrey! Or to understand how life comes to reside in the body to begin with. If, say, there was a fetus, one could—

(Out of POND's view, MOLLY sinks to the ground, sits on her heels with her head in her hands. GILHENNY is too disgusted to do anything but watch.)

RYMER: You couldn't! Connor—you'll... you'll hang!

POND: Have a care with your threats, Jeffrey. Since we both know where we stand. Your word against mine? Even Gilhenny has sense enough not to—

GILHENNY: Have you forgotten what you tried to hire me for? When you had the shell of a mangled little girl to be rid of? No one's untouchable.

POND: I don't recall you rising to the task, Gilhenny.

GILHENNY: I did it with Shepherd. I wouldn't bat an eye to sell you to the barbers. They'd enjoy the irony.

RYMER: How... how did you even stumble upon her? She was hardly far enough along in her pregnancy for the child even to show.

POND: She came to me, you see.

RYMER: Why?

POND: Who else would a young mother on her own come to with a child out of wedlock?

MOLLY: Stop! *(She emerges from her corner in a fury.)*

GILHENNY: Molly, stay back!

POND: What's this?

(But she is already on him, the heavy tankard in one hand, shouting furiously. POND is knocked to the floor by the force of her attack, and before GILHENNY or RYMER can react, her furious swings of the tankard have knocked him unconscious. She continues to hit him until GILHENNY, coming to his senses, hauls her off and holds her arms forcibly to her sides. She continues to shout until she starts to sob. ERIN bursts in, summoned by the noise and, seeing POND's motionless body, shuts the door immediately behind her.)

RYMER: Christ. Christ Almighty.

GILHENNY: Molly. Quiet now. Shh. Settle down, it's over.

ERIN: Is he dead?

RYMER: Is he—

MOLLY: Dead! Is he dead, have I—

(She chokes and can't finish. Shaking off the shock, RYMER kneels to check.)

RYMER: He's unconscious. He'll wake.

ERIN: Won't wake as pretty as he was before.

(RYMER stares at her in disbelief.)

ERIN: *(Irritably.)* What?

MOLLY: He deserves to die.

GILHENNY: Yes, he does.

RYMER: What are you going to do?

GILHENNY: What do you care? *(RYMER says nothing.)* Whatever she decides.

MOLLY: Doctor? Will you leave us, please?

RYMER: Molly—

MOLLY: Don't try saving me now. Please. You know you don't want to be in this room.

RYMER: I'm not leaving.

MOLLY: Get out! There's no place for you here, there's nothing you can do. And that's what you wanted. Get out.

RYMER: Can I—

MOLLY: You can't. Not tonight or ever. I know what mattered to you.

(RYMER exits. ERIN remains by the door. MOLLY and GILHENNY stand side by side looking at POND.)

MOLLY: You didn't tell me because you thought I'd kill him?

GILHENNY: The more fool me, I didn't tell you because I thought you'd get yourself killed.

ERIN: Could you really sell *him* to the barbers?

GILHENNY: Aye. But he'd have to be dead first.

(MOLLY is silent.)

ERIN: Well, you can't just leave him here. *(To MOLLY.)* You said it yourself, if you ever—

GILHENNY: Blood isn't bleach. Every one of us knows that.

ERIN: What, then? Just go on and pretend it's all done with, just because it's over?

GILHENNY: Yes. Because it's over.

MOLLY: I want to drag him still breathing to the churchyard and bury him alive. *(A pause. To GILHENNY.)* Would you try and stop me?

GILHENNY: No, I wouldn't. But you couldn't order me away as easily as that doctor, either.

MOLLY: I don't know where I can go. But I want to go home.

GILHENNY: All right. *(He indicates the door.)* I'll wait.

(GILHENNY exits, followed by ERIN. MOLLY stays, staring at the body.)

MOLLY: This ain't the way it was s'posed to go.

(She exits, leaving POND alone, unconscious in the dark.)

(End of play.)

BUNNY'S LAST NIGHT IN LIMBO

Peter S. Petralia

PETER SALVATORE PETRALIA was born in Melbourne, Florida, on January 22, 1974. He attended Warren Wilson College in Asheville, North Carolina, for two years; and then he matriculated in the Experimental Theatre Wing of NYU's Tisch School of the Arts for one year before running off to join the circus in San Francisco. While in San Francisco, Petralia experienced and explored a variety of new theatrical techniques, after which he returned to New York City to focus on developing new work. He acts as co-artistic director of proto-type in New York, which he co-founded in 1996. In 1999 he directed his play *Poor Angels* at the tenth annual American Living Room Festival at HERE Arts Center. He recently directed *The Twilight Series* at HERE and was a guest artist at Warren Wilson College in North Carolina in the fall of 2001 where he directed his newest play, *Cheap Thrills*. He is the Development Director at HERE Arts Center. He lives in Brooklyn, New York, with Aaron and his kitty.

Bunny's Last Night in Limbo was first produced by proto-type on March 16, 2001, at HERE, New York City, with the following cast and credits:

Bunny .... Tom Pilutik
Sister .... Stephanie Sanditz
Mother .... Lu Chekowsky
Father .... Dan Sherman
Boy .... David Sochet

Director: Peter S. Petralia
Assistant Director: Laura Klein
Music: Max Giteck Duykers
Costumes: Michelle Shaffer
Lights: Rebecca M. K. Makus
Sets: Betsy Ayer
Makeup: Claudia Pedala
Stage Manager: Ariana Valera
PA/Photographer/Choreographer: Jung E. Chu
Artistic Consultant: Tamar Kagan
Artistic Consultant: Karen Sackman

Special thanks to the following: E. Davis, Ricky's NYC (www.rickys-nyc.com), *Time Out New York*, S. Petralia, G. Astles, L. Rawlings, D. Erickson, N. Kontos, G. and A. Paul, O. Anders, V. Truesdale, L. Klein, J. Eun Chu, M. Duykers, J. Duykers, M. Weaver, S. Shaw, Glen Orenstein Graphics, C. Manson and Big Art Group, S. Kashar, S. Dali, K. Kimbrough, and the staff at HERE.

Music for *Bunny's Last Night in Limbo* is available by contacting proto-type, 136 McKibbin Street, #5, Brooklyn, NY 11206, 212-252-5526, or info@proto-type-home.com. Please indicate the format in which you would like the music (CD, tape, score) when making requests.

Dedicated to O. Anders and the Petralia sisters.

CHARACTERS

BUNNY: A young boy, scrawny, awkward, and confused. He is going through a journey—an awakening to not only his own sexuality but also the disturbed nature of his family. This is Bunny's story.

SISTER: Bunny's sister. She is slightly older than Bunny—hungry for attention, confused, and obsessed with beauty products. She is in the midst of discovering her sexual power (especially the pleasures of masturbation) amidst the awkwardness of being pre- or barely pubescent. She spells words as she speaks.

MOTHER: Bunny's mother. Mid-40s—wears several huge wigs. She is a faded beauty queen who has lived in a small town forever, always taking care of Father. She is a heavy drinker. She loves dressing up, and, throughout the piece, her crazy ensembles begin to deteriorate. She looks a bit like Divine but without the huge forehead. She loves Bunny the way an owner loves a dog, and she is bitter toward him and Sister for ruining her beauty. She does not face up to anything—she is a bit of an actress.

FATHER: Bunny's father. Mid-40s—toupee. Obsessed with television and the media. He is a heavy drinker who sits watching TV most of the time. Although he seems angry and often unloving, it comes from a place of frustration with his inability to have a "normal" family life.

BOY: Three/four years older than Bunny. He is a mysterious and fickle boy. He awakens Bunny to his sexuality. He is sexy and playful.

A NOTE ON THE ACTING STYLE

This text is meant to be deeply felt but not overly acted. It requires a sensitivity to having fun with the material without pushing it into stereotype or melodrama. As much as possible, the actors should not use gestures that are normal to them in their own life—instead they should create a physical life for the characters that supports the story and text. The text should not be treated as precious, but instead should provide a ground for a physical and spatially oriented performance. Above all, the story must live in the bodies of those who embody these characters. In addition, a full soundtrack of music should be used throughout to further develop the psychology and emotion of the piece.

SPACE

There are three main playing areas: the house, the woods, and the theatre. The house should be made up of the fractured remains of suburbia. There should be no attempt to be realistic, only suggestive of domesticity. The more psychological the playing space can be the better. The house should have a distinct area for the kitchen and a space for BUNNY's room and SISTER's room. Along the downstage edge of the stage is a somewhat transparent curtain that blocks the house from view. It should be made of some sort of shimmery material, and it can be opened and closed by the actors. When this curtain is closed, the area downstage of the curtain can be used for scenes in the theatre. There should be a microphone on a stand in this area for the actors to speak into as indicated. The woods should likewise be suggestive only but must have two ropes or rope swings and fake grass. Lighting and music should support and develop the emotional and psychological aspects of the play. Scenery can be suggestive with a focus on the lights setting the picture.

When the audience enters the space, the curtain is closed on the stage.

PROLOGUE: "BUNNY'S DREAM"

Location—theatre. After a brief moment of silence and darkness, BUNNY enters the stage awkwardly through the curtain, unfolds a piece of paper, and reads. During this speech, BUNNY is holding a light that illuminates his face and the curtain behind him—like a nightlight. The lights should not fully reveal him.

BUNNY: "Dreams." My dreams used to scare me so much when I was a child that I couldn't sleep alone in my room. I would get up just after everybody was asleep and drag my pillow and a blanket into the doorway of my sister's room. I'd sleep like that—half in the hallway and half in her room until the morning hoping that if something terrible happened in my dream and I never woke up I would at least be discovered quickly. I always woke up. Most of the time just before anyone else so I could sneak back into my room, but sometimes I overslept and got caught. Eventually my parents made me stop.

Sleeping alone in my room, I rarely slept through the night. Until something happened.

Now I spend all day waiting to fall asleep so I can dream. Well, anyway, that's what this is all about. This is my recurring dream of being little—a spell, I suppose—what happened when I closed my eyes and never woke up.

My name is Bunny and this is my dream. It's called: Bunny's Last Night in Limbo.

(Playful music begins. It is a jalopy of sounds lumbering along.)

SCENE: "MUD PIES"

Location—house. SISTER emerges, hiding something behind her back. She pushes BUNNY down to a sitting position on the floor stage right. SISTER goes to the edge of the stage where she finds a bucket, a pie tin, and a can of whipped cream. She is very intent on what she is doing, and she occasionally giggles. BUNNY seems excited. She's putting the mud from the bucket into the pie pan. SISTER makes a mud pie as she speaks.

SISTER: No peeking! Chocolate! Y-u-m! This is for being so good, Bunny. This is for your birthday. This is for y-o-u... little Bunny birthday boy. (*Sings.*) Happy Bunny day to you, happy birthday to Bunny, Happy birthday Bunny boy, Happy Bunny boy birthday. Okay. You can l-o-o-k now.

BUNNY: A pie!

SISTER: You better e-a-t up, Bunny boy.

BUNNY: I'm gonna use my hands.

(BUNNY puts his hand into the pie, and then he lowers his head to it and shoves a huge handful into his mouth. It takes him only a short moment to realize it is mud. SISTER laughs.)

BUNNY: Ugh. Pthuh. Kuh. It's mud. Jerk!

(BUNNY throws the mud on SISTER. They have a mud flinging fight.)

SISTER: Uhhh. You little j-e-r-k!

BUNNY: I hate you!

SISTER: I hate y-o-u!

(They can say what they want here... groan, whatever. The flinging becomes very physical. SISTER gets BUNNY down to the floor and gets on top of him. The mud flinging has turned into a wrestling match... she is choking him. He spits mud in her face and then flips her over his head... she rolls into a summersault. BUNNY gets up and jumps on her. SISTER screams.)

BUNNY: Why are you so mean?

SISTER: I'm not mean. You're just a w-i-m-p. You gotta learn to take it like a man, Bunny.

BUNNY: I'm a wimp? You look pretty wimpy from where I'm sitting. You're jealous. That's what I think.

SISTER: I am not jealous. You just g-e-t everything.

BUNNY: Yeah, right. I get everything. You're dumb.

(BUNNY tickles SISTER.)

SISTER: Oh my god! Stop it.

(SISTER laughs. She begins to tickle BUNNY back. They end up tickling each other... until they are eventually both sitting facing each other... laughing.)

SISTER: I'm sorry.

BUNNY: I know.

SISTER: Pattycake?

BUNNY: Okay.

BUNNY and SISTER: (*Play pattycake.*)
    Pattycake
    Pattycake
    Baker's man
    Bake me a cake as fast as you can
    If you don't
    What'll I do?
    I'll punch you in the face
    till you're black and blue
    Pattycake
    Pattycake...

(MOTHER appears upstage. She stands looking at SISTER and BUNNY.)

MOTHER: Bunny! Bunny!

BUNNY: What?

MOTHER: (*As if calling from a distance.*) Bunny, come over here. Momma's got a surprise for you!

BUNNY: A surprise? This is my lucky day.

SISTER: You're spoiled.

BUNNY: You're mean. Bye. *(Sticks his tongue out at SISTER.)*

SISTER: Bye, Bunny.

BUNNY: You're a mess.

MOTHER: *(To SISTER.)* It better be clean in here before dinner.

(SISTER shoots BUNNY a bird. BUNNY leaves. SISTER immediately becomes bored. She sticks her middle finger in the mud bucket from earlier. She pulls her finger out and licks it. She makes a nasty face and freaks out for a few seconds. Then she picks up the bucket and wipes up some of the mud with a rag.)

SISTER: Um. Cleaning could be fun.

SCENE: "LIPSTICK"

Location—house. SISTER is cleaning up, grudgingly, singing.

SISTER: Down down baby
    Down by the roller coaster
    Sweet sweet baby
    Sweet sweet don't let me go
    Chimmi chimmi coco puff
    Chimmi chimmi ra-ah
    Chimmi chimmi coco puff
    Chimmi chimmi ra-ah

(She is finished cleaning and has begun playing with poses and dance routines. She begins to sing into the microphone, getting taken over by the fun of her song. She camps it up big time. During this she starts drawing on her lips with lipstick.)

SISTER: I met a boyfriend, a biscuit
    He so sweet, a biscuit
    Like my cherry pop, a biscuit
    Ooo Sabrina
    Walk-in down the street
    Ten times a week

    I said, I meant it, I gave your momma credit

(She stops, laughing at the song. The following is spoken into the microphone.)

SISTER: I love l-i-p-s-t-i-c-k. All kinds. I've got ten shades of red and five browns. "I have a color to match my every mood." I got that from a Revlon commercial. Do you know the one I mean? It's with Lynda Carter. You know, Wonder Woman? She's in the swimming pool? Never mind. I can't imagine the world without lipstick… it'd be pretty boring. I'd lose my favorite snack treat. *(She puts lipstick on and then bites a chunk of it. Then she puts it in her pocket as she chews the bite she took.)* L-i-p-s-t-i-c-k is the world's most overlooked source for nutrition. It's packed full of healthy stuff like vitamins and oils. It goes on smooth and digests right away. Mmmmm. Mary Margaret says l-i-p-s-t-i-c-k is made out of bat poop, but I don't believe her. She doesn't know anything about beauty anyway. Her mom won't even let her wear l-i-p-s-t-i-c-k. My mother thinks beauty is important. That's why she is so pretty. She lets me wear makeup because she wants me to be pretty too. I'm glad 'cause being pretty is fun… and important. I'm good at it, aren't I? I get all the boys to look at me. "My lipstick makes me look… kissable." That's Maybelline. The boys in Mrs. Harper's class can't stop staring when I come in. I don't blame them. The other day on the playground I kissed a boy. He wasn't that good at it. I had to hold him down. He was chicken. He said he never kissed a girl before so I asked if he had ever kissed a boy and then he bit my lip. I got really mad so I told everyone that he liked boys. He's dumb anyway. Everyone made fun of him. He's a fag, I'm sure. *(She takes out the lipstick again to take another bite. But it's empty—no more lipstick in the tube. She sticks her tongue into the tube, trying to lick out every last bit.)* Hmmpf. I'm gonna have to get some more. I think I want "Tragic Diva" this time, from Urban Decay. It tastes better than Maybelline. I think it's because it costs more. They put special things in it that make it good… and it stays on longer. I hope it's not bat poop. That Mary Margaret is crazy. They wouldn't put bat poop in there.

(She tosses the lipstick down as MOTHER, BUNNY, and FATHER turn around.)

MOTHER: DINNER!

SCENE: "SWANSON'S"

Location—house. The members of the family all stand facing each other in a circle at the center of the space. BUNNY and SISTER stand across from each other, FATHER and MOTHER stand across from each other as well. A subtle light fills this "table" area with cool light. They are passing TV dinners around rapidly. They don't start passing until FATHER finishes his first line.

FATHER: Now I say my grace I eat to bless this house and fill this seat with health and heart and money.

MOTHER: Amen.

FATHER: Amen.

SISTER: My f-o-o-d is c-o-l-d.

BUNNY: Mine too.

SISTER: No it's not. I got first prize in jump rope. Mary Margaret lost big time.

MOTHER: Daddy, are you tired?

SISTER: I kept going for t-e-n minutes. That's longer than you can any day, Bunny.

MOTHER: Stop spelling. *(To FATHER.)* You had a long day. You look tired. I did Alice's hair today.

FATHER: Alice?

(A distinct lighting change occurs. MOTHER, SISTER, and FATHER stare at BUNNY briefly as he begins speaking the following lines into the microphone. They immediately begin talking amongst themselves again, ignoring him; their speech is improvised and indiscernible to the audience.)

BUNNY: I hear them. They are definitely talking. I wonder what the weather is like in China. They have silk shoes and panties. Those must feel good. I don't like meatloaf. Mother loves it. Meatloaf. Loaf. Gross word. Loaf. Loaf. Loaf. Loaf. Sounds like shoes. In China there are a lot of people and they all have black hair. Really black. I saw a picture with a tree that had pink flowers and a man standing under it wearing a red coat. His hair was so black. Black and shiny. I stared at his hair and deeply hidden in it I saw the faint outline of a bunny. Funny. Bunnies are pretty funny, you know. I don't know any Chinese people. I don't even know how far away it is. It's not close.

(Everyone pauses for a second, looks at each other, and begins talking again.)

MOTHER: Bunny. Eat your dinner.

FATHER: Did you watch the news today? It was on again.

SISTER: I learned a new song today.

FATHER: I had short hair. Did you see, Mother? On TV. Did you see?

MOTHER: I'll cut your hair. I will.

FATHER: How's Alice? I'm not tired.

SISTER: Hey. Hello? I learned a new s-o-n-g today.

MOTHER: A song? That's lovely. Did you hear that Bunny? A song. Bunny knows a song, too. Don't you Bunny?

BUNNY: I know a song.

SISTER: It rhymes, but I can't remember the tune.

BUNNY: Is it far to China?

FATHER: Did Alice say hello to me?

SISTER: I think it was high. Yeah. There were a lot of high, high n-o-t-e-s.

MOTHER: Let's see, you do need a haircut. It's a bit shaggy. Shaggy dog.

FATHER: Not shaggy.

SISTER: Oh. I remember.

(SISTER suddenly breaks out in song into the microphone. The family stops for a second and stares at her as they did earlier to BUNNY. They then immediately begin talking in low voices again. BUNNY stares at his SISTER.)

SISTER: "Cabin in the Woods," by Me.
    I saw a little cabin in the woods,
    a cabin, a cabin, a little cabin in the
        woods.
    I walked up to a cabin in the woods,
    and guess just what I saw.
    I saw a w-o-l-f, a big bad w-o-l-f, with
        one big furry nose.
    He huffed and puffed and snorted at me
    but he could not catch me at all.
    So I ran, I ran, I ran down the path
    to a little cottage gate.
    And I knocked and knocked and I
        knocked real hard
    on the little cottage door.
    With a clank and bang and a jug jug jug
    the door it opened wide.
    There inside oh there inside oh
    was a little funny man.
    And he took me in and he shut the door

so the w-o-l-f could not get in.
And that's why they say oh that's why
    they say
don't go to the cabin in the woods.

(Everyone pauses for a second before resuming his or her conversation.)

FATHER: Let's watch TV.

MOTHER: TV! That's a great idea.

BUNNY: No.

MOTHER: Yes, hon. *(Clicks the remote control in the general direction of a TV, and the programming switches to some random soap opera.)*

SISTER: I'm not hungry. Can I leave the table?

MOTHER: Let's see. What's today?

BUNNY: Tuesday.

MOTHER: Is today Wednesday?

FATHER: It's Tuesday.

SISTER: Can I leave the table?

MOTHER: Oh. Tuesday.

(SISTER gets up without being excused.)

BUNNY: May I be excused?

MOTHER: Oh. Bunny. Are you all finished?

BUNNY: Yes.

FATHER: What is this shit on TV?

MOTHER: Bunny-wunny. You are so…

BUNNY: Thank you.

(BUNNY gets up and walks over to where SISTER stands. They close the curtain. The lights on the table area fade down to a low level as MOTHER and FATHER continue talking in muffled tones. Meanwhile

BUNNY and SISTER say the following lines to each other into the single microphone.)

SISTER: They really like TV.

BUNNY: They're weird.

SISTER: You're weird.

BUNNY: I know.

SISTER: Did you have a good day today?

BUNNY: No.

SISTER: Me neither. I hate Mary Margaret.

BUNNY: I hate this place.

SISTER: Me too.

BUNNY: We have to stick together.

SISTER: I know.

BUNNY: I'm going to go for a walk.

SISTER: Have fun.

(The lights fade on BUNNY and SISTER. MOTHER and FATHER move offstage as BUNNY begins to walk around the stage.)

SCENE: "JUNGLE FEVER"

Location—woods. A light reveals BOY standing on a step stool, stage left next to a long rope, which hangs from the ceiling. BUNNY's walk turns into a run. He begins running in a circle stage left. BUNNY cannot see BOY. Another long rope is hanging straight down in the center of BUNNY's circle. BUNNY is out of breath. He sees the rope and stops, having arrived. BOY watches BUNNY. BUNNY stands next to the rope. SISTER, MOTHER, and FATHER are on stage in the house.

BUNNY jumps onto the rope. He climbs about halfway up the rope and stops. He wraps the rope around him into a cradle so he can sit in the rope while holding it closed. He looks out at the world. There is a light on BOY as he watches intently.

BUNNY: "A Confession for the Trees." Hello? Hello? Is it lonely being a tree? Do you get in trouble? Oh boy. Um. Last week something happened. We were stealing underwear. I wasn't, really. Not underwear. They were. I don't even know them. I mean, not really. My bags were full of expensive things that I can't have. I had a stolen Buddha made out of plastic. Buddha was all red and cute. Do you believe in Buddha? I am considering it. We were done except for Missy's underwear. She was getting one last pair. Pink, I think, with lace. Probably sexy.

(BUNNY begins to unravel the cradle of rope so he can swing around on it. He is holding onto it with his hands and his feet, but his torso is free from the rope. He begins to swing himself and the rope around in a twirling manner. He starts spinning faster and faster until the spinning gets so fast that he stops spinning it and coasts along until the rope slows and he slides down the rope landing on the floor, bottom first. BUNNY sits on the floor and looks straight up, then he gets up and back on the rope as he continues.)

BUNNY: Um. We were taken to the employee area of the store. It was claustrophobic back there. I had to keep breathing. The handcuffs hurt. The police took us to their shiny cars and we were separated. When we got to the police station the light was almost gone. My legs were cold. That ink stays on your fingers. The flash makes you blink. My eyes were red and my nose was running but they couldn't find Mother. It was almost Halloween. That's my favorite. No sign of Mother in her short skirt. I'm in trouble.

I don't know where she is. Mother? I don't know where she is. Mother? Officer. I don't know where she is. I really didn't. She was in a red Camero and she smelled of smoke, and sex, and something like medicine. She seemed so lucky with her torn tights and smeared lipstick. I wanted to take some lipstick, but I didn't.

She took me. Home.

The worst part was—no Halloween party.

(BUNNY slowly slides down the rope until he lands on the ground again.)

BUNNY: Are you listening to me? Do you have a good time out here? Things are so easy for you. I guess that's okay, though.

Well. See you later.

(BUNNY walks stage right and returns to his bed. BOY'S light is still on. He is smiling. BOY disappears. Lights fade to black.)

SCENE: "HOT TRAFFIC"

Location—bedroom and kitchen. It is night. FATHER is restless. He is walking from room to room checking on the sleeping family. BUNNY sleeps near SISTER. MOTHER sleeps alone.

FATHER: Bunny? Are you sleeping?

BUNNY: What?

FATHER: You're awake.

BUNNY: No, I'm sleeping. What's wrong?

FATHER: Feeling strange. Do you ever feel strange, son?

BUNNY: Yeah. I feel strange now.

FATHER: Did I tell you about the television?

BUNNY: I don't remember.

FATHER: I had a yellow Jaguar when you were born. Your mother and I bought it used from some pathetic people.

BUNNY: I'm tired.

FATHER: That car was beautiful. I drove it across the state once looking for a bed for you. I found the right one. It's a good bed.

BUNNY: Is that why you feel strange?

FATHER: No. Where is your sister?

BUNNY: She's sleeping. Are you okay?

FATHER: No, I'm not.

BUNNY: What's wrong?

FATHER: *(To SISTER.)* There you are. Are you dreaming, little girl? I dream about TV. I was on TV.

BUNNY: I'm tired, Daddy. Can I just go back to sleep?

FATHER: Don't you ever want to listen?

SISTER: Bunny? Daddy? What's happening?

BUNNY: *(To FATHER.)* I'm just sleepy, that's all.

FATHER: Don't talk to me like that you little turd.

SISTER: Leave him alone.

BUNNY: I'm tired and you are being weird. I don't like when you're like this.

FATHER: You both better listen up. Two little turds. Fuck.

BUNNY: It's late.

SISTER: Bunny, let's get out of here.

FATHER: Don't you even try it.

SISTER: Just leave us alone.

FATHER: I'm going to tell you.

SISTER: Stop it!

BUNNY: I'm going back to sleep.

FATHER: She used to be sweet to me. Now she's a fucking zombie. You two turds. I could have been famous. Did you know that?

SISTER: Why don't you just go throw up and pass out already?

(FATHER hits SISTER.)

FATHER: It was an accident. I was stuck in traffic for a long time—there was a car wreck or something. It was hot and the air didn't work so I got out of the car and sat on the hood smoking a cigar.

BUNNY: I'm scared.

SISTER: Me too.

FATHER: I'm just smoking my cigar when I hear a commotion going on behind me. I turn around to see what it is. It's a camera crew, about six people with cameras and mics and lights. I didn't want to get involved so, I just turned back around and ignored them.

BUNNY: You don't make any sense.

FATHER: Then all of a sudden the cameras are right up on me. They wanted to talk to me. I didn't really want to be bothered with them. I mean, I was aggravated about being stuck—the last thing I wanted was to deal with a camera… so I just told them I wasn't interested in being interviewed and I got up to go sit in my car.

BUNNY: Can you please go to sleep, Daddy? It's okay. Just go to sleep. Please.

FATHER: Am I boring you?

SISTER: Yes. I'm going to sing a song.

FATHER: I don't know what's wrong with everyone. No one listens. Those TV people—they kept filming me anyway. I told them to leave me alone again, but they still didn't get it.

(The following lines are spoken simultaneously.)

BUNNY: I wish I lived in China.

SISTER: *(Simultaneously, sings softly.)*
    When you're walking down the street
    And your pants begin to leak
    Diarrhea, drip, drip, diarrhea
    Some people think its funny
    But it's really green and runny
    Diarrhea, drip, drip, diarrhea
    When you're sliding into first
    And your pants being to burst
    Diarrhea, drip, drip, diarrhea
    When you're in the bathroom stall
    And there's no toilet paper on the wall
    Diarrhea, drip, drip, diarrhea
    So you take it like a man
    And you wipe it with your hand
    Diarrhea, drip, drip, diarrhea

FATHER: *(Simultaneously.)* I finally got out of the car and punched the reporter right in the jaw. That ended that. Everyone just stood around looking stupid after that. They left me alone… and I sat to wait the traffic jam out. I waited for another hour before the traffic started moving again. That was a beautiful car. About a month later I get a call from Channel Six News saying they want to use a clip of me from that day on their new traffic update trailer. They wanted me to sign a contract with them, but then they gave me a big check. I was on News Six for the next year and a half. I was a celebrity. *(FATHER is dazed.)*

BUNNY: I'm going for a walk.

SISTER: Be careful. It's late for a walk by yourself.

BUNNY: Bye.

(BUNNY begins walking away. SISTER goes to sleep. FATHER is in a stupor.)

FATHER: Do you hear me. I was a celebrity. I even got an agent. She used to love me. I'm not a stupid person. I'm not.

(Lights fade to black.)

SCENE: "JUNGLE FEVER P2"

Location—woods. A light reveals BOY standing on a step stool, stage left next to a long rope, which hangs from the ceiling. BUNNY's walk turns into a run. He begins running in a circle stage left. BUNNY cannot see BOY. Another long rope is hanging straight down in the center of BUNNY's circle. BUNNY is out of breath. He sees the rope and stops, having arrived. BOY watches BUNNY. BUNNY stands next to the rope. SISTER, MOTHER, and FATHER are in the house. BUNNY jumps onto the rope. He climbs about halfway up the rope and stops. He wraps the rope around him into a cradle so he can sit in the rope while holding it closed. He looks out at the world. BOY is watching intently.

BUNNY: Hello trees. Hello? Hmmm. It's cold up here. It feels like it's gonna rain. I should've stayed home.

BOY: *(Whistles.)* Psst.

(BUNNY turns around quickly, looking for where the sound came from. He doesn't see BOY.)

BUNNY: Who's there?

BOY: Somebody.

(BUNNY looks around again. He still doesn't see BOY.)

BUNNY: I see you. What do you want? I don't have anything.

(BOY stands on his step stool and jumps onto his own rope as he says his next line.)

BOY: You don't see me.

BUNNY: *(Sees him.)* Oh. Hello.

BOY: Hello.

(BOY is swinging next to BUNNY. He is a little higher than BUNNY.)

BOY: Did you get in trouble?

BUNNY: For what?

BOY: For the underwear.

BUNNY: No. Yes. Not really.

BOY: What kind?

BUNNY: I didn't take underwear.

BOY: Oh, yeah. Buddha.

BUNNY: Yeah. How'd you find out?

BOY: Here. *(Reaches out and tugs on BUNNY's rope.)* Grab my hand.

BUNNY: Why?

BOY: Just do it. It'll be fun.

(BUNNY does. BOY holds onto BUNNY's hand tight.)

BOY: Hold on. *(BOY starts the ropes swinging.)*

BUNNY: Okay…

(They swing in a slow arc at first. Then they get faster. They are still holding hands. They start laughing as the swinging gets wilder. When they are really swinging fast and wide, BOY lets go of BUNNY's hand and they both slide down the ropes to the ground.)

BOY: I beat you.

BUNNY: Did you? Who are you?

BOY: Who are you?

BUNNY: My name is Bunny.

BOY: Did you ever kiss a boy?

BUNNY: No. Not really.

BOY: I have.

(BOY leans over and kisses BUNNY briefly. They laugh.)

BUNNY: Oh boy.

(BUNNY suddenly leans over and kisses BOY, knocking him over until BUNNY has pinned BOY to the ground. They wrestle and kiss. The sound of rain is heard. SISTER enters the scene and she shines a flashlight on them. BOY stops suddenly.)

SISTER: Bunny?

BUNNY: Sis?

SISTER: Are you alright? What are you doing?

BUNNY: Um.

BOY: I have to go. *(Stands and collects himself. He begins to leave.)*

SISTER: Who is that?

BUNNY: Go? Oh. Yes.

SISTER: Bunny!

BOY: I'll see you later.

BUNNY: Bye.

SISTER: You better come with me.

(BUNNY jumps up awkwardly; suddenly able to take in the fact that he just kissed a boy willingly—and even eagerly—as he and SISTER exit.)

BOY: Bye. *(Disappears.)*

BUNNY: Bye. *(Smiles, confused.)*

SCENE: "CLEANING HOUSE"

Location—house. This scene follows quickly after the previous one. SISTER and BUNNY move into the house space and they sit stage right. MOTHER and FATHER are sitting upstage center. The following lines are spoken simultaneously. BOY is in the woods.

SISTER: Who was that?

FATHER: *(Simultaneously.)* What time is it?

BUNNY: I don't know.

MOTHER: *(Simultaneously.)* It's late. What does it matter?

SISTER: You kissed him.

FATHER: *(Simultaneously.)* I feel sick.

BUNNY: I know

MOTHER: *(Simultaneously.)* Let me get you something.

SISTER: Was it nice?

FATHER: *(Simultaneously.)* Get me a drink.

BUNNY: Yes.

MOTHER: *(Simultaneously.)* Yes.

(MOTHER moves to the edge of the stage; she sees BUNNY and SISTER.)

MOTHER: What are you two doing awake?

SISTER: Talking.

MOTHER: Oh.

BUNNY: Are you okay?

MOTHER: Fine. I'm fine. I'm so happy. I dyed Betty's hair for the first time, today. It looked so good. She'll be back, for sure.

SISTER: Is Daddy okay?

MOTHER: (*Looking for beer bottle.*) Where is that bottle?

BUNNY: He came and talked to us the other night.

MOTHER: (*Finds beer bottle.*) Oh, here it is.

SISTER: Are you listening?

MOTHER: Go to bed, will you?

SISTER: Yeah.

(*MOTHER moves back to FATHER, gives him his drink, and sits down with him again. The following lines are spoken simultaneously.*)

BUNNY: Do you think they love each other.

MOTHER: (*Simultaneously.*) Here's something for my little pumpkin.

SISTER: I don't know.

FATHER: (*Simultaneously.*) It's too warm.

BUNNY: Have you ever kissed anyone?

MOTHER: (*Simultaneously.*) Just drink up, sugar.

SISTER: Uh-huh.

FATHER: (*Simultaneously.*) I talked to Alice today.

BUNNY: It's nice.

MOTHER: (*Simultaneously.*) How did her hair look?

SISTER: Yeah. Are you a fag?

FATHER: (*Simultaneously.*) She talked to me too.

BUNNY: I don't know.

MOTHER: (*Simultaneously.*) Was her hair nice?

SISTER: Well, you kissed a boy. I think that makes you a fag.

FATHER: (*Simultaneously.*) Never mind.

BUNNY: Don't tell them.

SISTER: I won't.

BUNNY: I need to sleep now.

SISTER: Pleasant dreams.

(*SISTER goes to sleep and BUNNY returns to the woods. MOTHER and FATHER go to sleep. The lights fade to black.*)

SCENE: "SEDUCTION"

Location—woods. MOTHER, FATHER, and SISTER are in the house. BOY is in the woods. BUNNY walks into the woods eating candy as he whispers something to BOY. They use the rope swings as they play and laugh.

BOY: Who told you that?

BUNNY: No one told me. I read it. In a book. Not a magazine.

BOY: Not a magazine? What is that supposed to mean?

BUNNY: It means it wasn't a magazine.

BOY: Oh. Bunny? How many more do you have?

BUNNY: Five more.

BOY: I have something for you.

BUNNY: What?

BOY: It's up here.

BUNNY: Up there? What is it? (*Stands up and tries to see what BOY has.*) What? Do you have something?

BOY: I do. Sit on my lap.

BUNNY: Oh.

(BUNNY gets on BOY'S lap. They are face to face.)

BUNNY: I feel it. What now?

BOY: I have an idea.

(BOY puts BUNNY's hand on BOY's crotch. BUNNY and BOY kiss and go down to the ground. The lights fade down on BUNNY and BOY quickly.)

SCENE: "COCKTAIL/TANGO"

Location—house. SISTER remains asleep. Tango music starts. MOTHER and FA- THER dance and fight. As they move around the space dancing/fighting, the ten- sion builds. The following lines are said with their slow, deep tango.

MOTHER: I can't breathe.

FATHER: I love the smell of your hair.

MOTHER: You're holding me so tight.

FATHER: You're so tense. WHY DON'T YOU LOOSEN UP, HUH?

MOTHER: Don't tell me to loosen!

FATHER: I'm gonna squeeze the spit right out of you.

MOTHER: Let me go.

FATHER: Pour me another. Bitch.

MOTHER: Pour me another.

(FATHER throws the contents of his glass on her face.)

MOTHER: Fuck face.

FATHER: You can't take your liquor.

MOTHER: I can't breathe.

FATHER: That little squint in your face is so sexy. *(Licks the spot on MOTHER's face.)*

MOTHER: Umm. Feels so good.

FATHER: You like that? Bitch.

(FATHER throws MOTHER to the ground and then jumps onto her. He picks her up by the arms and looks her in the face. The scene has become more violent.)

MOTHER: I can't breathe.

FATHER: I love the smell of your hair.

MOTHER: You're holding me so tight.

FATHER: You're so tense. WHY DON'T YOU LOOSEN UP, HUH?

MOTHER: Don't tell me to loosen!

FATHER: I'm gonna squeeze the spit right out of you.

MOTHER: Let me go.

FATHER: Pour me another. Bitch.

MOTHER: Pour me another.

(FATHER throws the contents of his glass on her face.)

MOTHER: Fuck face.

FATHER: You can't take your liquor.

MOTHER: I can't breathe.

FATHER: That little squint in your face is so sexy. *(Licks the spot on MOTHER's face.)*

MOTHER: Umm. Feels so good.

FATHER: You like that? Bitch.

(BUNNY enters their scene and sees FA- THER on top of MOTHER. MOTHER and FATHER see BUNNY and are still. No one says anything. MOTHER begins

throwing up blood in a bucket. FATHER takes his belt off. He is mumbling incoherently… and crying. BUNNY slowly walks past his father, not saying anything, and grabs a cup of water. Then he goes to his sleeping area, drinks his water, and returns to sleep. MOTHER and FATHER are now on opposite sides of the stage. MOTHER has stopped throwing up. She takes up her glass and continues drinking. FATHER is drinking out of his glass as well.)

MOTHER: I'm tired.

FATHER: Yeah. It's bedtime.

(They walk to one another. MOTHER slaps FATHER hard on the face. FATHER walks upstage. MOTHER is breaking down. She walks to the microphone and speaks. There is an echo and reverb effect on her voice that gets progressively worse until near the end of the speech when it tapers out to a very clean, un-effected sound.)

MOTHER: Fucking bedtime. Fucking bed. That little fucker hurt me when he came out. My skin was like a spongy Jell-O stretched full of water. I could feel it. I was filled up with waves of water, pounding outward. It came on suddenly. I had to breathe to keep the water down. It reached up inside me and came out of my mouth in a scream. Fuck! Lights and cars and the hospital. I was laid out, strapped down. Swollen. Too many eyes seeing me there like a giant walrus. They all groped me with their cold fucking hands. Ufh. My head was so dizzy from the pounding in my gut and in my cunt that I thought the water rolling inside me would rush up and drown me. I lay spinning, sweating. My eyes were stinging from the sweat. I wanted someone to wipe my forehead but I couldn't get the words out of my mouth. I wanted someone to knock me out.

There were too many eyes. I couldn't count. And the rubber hands pulling inside me… shit… that little fucker didn't want out. I felt like I was shitting all over. Then a rip. My whole bottom half fell out. Then a knocking sound and a beep. I woke up covered in blood.

(MOTHER is suddenly still.)

MOTHER: I did not celebrate. I wasn't included in the party—my job was done. Everyone smiled. No one saw me, though. I was not offered a cigar. I just rubbed my loose Jell-O stomach, touched the pink lines. Felt the pounding ache. My body was soaked.

I am not one of the boys.

(MOTHER goes to sleep, and the lights dim to black.)

SCENE: "A VISITOR"

Location—house. The family sleeps. BOY walks slyly into the house, looking for BUNNY. MOTHER wakes when he speaks.

BOY: Hello? Bunny?

(BOY approaches where BUNNY sleeps and is about to wake him with a kiss when MOTHER approaches BOY and taps him on the shoulder, scaring him. He jumps and almost makes a noise, but MOTHER blocks his mouth with her hand.)

MOTHER: Excuse me. Who are you?

BOY: Um. A friend. Of Bunny's—just thought I'd pay a late night visit.

MOTHER: You almost woke him. He needs his sleep, you know.

BOY: Oh. I know. Sorry.

MOTHER: He needs his sleep.

BOY: Yeah. I heard that.

MOTHER: Don't you have a home?

BOY: Of course, I…

MOTHER: Like a drink, then?

BOY: A drink?

MOTHER: Come here, you.

(MOTHER moves to the other side of the stage, leading BOY. She pours a drink of a dark liquid for herself and for BOY.)

MOTHER: It is chilly out. This will warm you up.

(MOTHER holds out the drink, but BOY does not take it.)

BOY: I should go. *(Starts to leave.)*

MOTHER: So soon? We have hardly gotten to know one another.

BOY: Oh. Um. Right. Well, my name is…

(MOTHER gets very close to BOY, pressing herself near to him.)

MOTHER: Please… don't be so formal, call me…

(BOY breaks away to take the drink from MOTHER's hand.)

BOY: I think I will have that drink.

MOTHER: Tasty isn't it…

BOY: Yeah, it is.

MOTHER: Another?

(MOTHER gets very close to BOY again. He does not resist as much this time.)

BOY: Perhaps.

MOTHER: I think you could be a good friend to my son.

BOY: Um. Yes.

MOTHER: *(Holds out another drink.)* Want this?

BOY: Yes.

MOTHER: How about a little kiss then?

BOY: That might be interesting.

(They kiss. BOY steps back and looks at MOTHER.)

MOTHER: Nice. Very tender.

BOY: I liked that, I think.

MOTHER: Of course you did.

BUNNY: *(Wakes up.)* Hello?

BOY: Um. Bunny. Hi.

BUNNY: Oh. Hi.

MOTHER: Who's this, Bunny?

BUNNY: A friend.

BOY: Just wanted to say hi.

BUNNY: Hi.

MOTHER: Hi.

BOY: I better go.

BUNNY: Goodnight.

(BOY leaves.)

MOTHER: Seems like a nice boy.

BUNNY: He does.

MOTHER: Go to bed.

BUNNY: Nite.

(BUNNY goes to sleep. MOTHER paces for a second and then makes a loud screaming sound.)

MOTHER: WAKE UP. IT'S TOO DAMN QUIET IN HERE.

(Everyone wakes and goes back to sleep.)

SCENE: "WE WANT YOUR BRAIN"

Location—house. BUNNY and SISTER are in the house. BOY is in the woods. FATHER starts pacing as MOTHER tries to get him to tango.

MOTHER: It's another day. Isn't it dear?

FATHER: I have been trying to tell you.

MOTHER: Are you feeling sick, sugar bear?

FATHER: Yes. I am feeling sick. I am feeling sick of this place.

MOTHER: Why don't we watch TV.

FATHER: I fucked Alice again today.

MOTHER: Oh.

FATHER: It wasn't as good as it was yesterday.

MOTHER: Should we watch the news again?

FATHER: Are you listening to me?

MOTHER: Yes. I am.

FATHER: I'm sorry. I can't do this.

MOTHER: You can't?

FATHER: I'm going to leave now.

MOTHER: Okay.

FATHER: You are pathetic.

MOTHER: Okay.

(FATHER leaves. There is the sound of a slamming door. Everyone turns from where they are to look at MOTHER, who is standing, watching a TV.)

SCENE: "TALK TALK"

Location—house. FATHER is gone. The scene is as before, except that the actors who play BUNNY and SISTER come downstage to speak the following lines into the microphone, calmly, but with a sadness to their voices which is genuine.

BUNNY: Well. What do you think about that?

SISTER: I'm not surprised. That's about it.

BUNNY: Yeah. It's a bit of a relief, actually.

SISTER: You don't feel sad?

BUNNY: I guess I should. But no, not really—he scared me.

SISTER: So, what now?

BUNNY: Well. I kind of have to pee.

SISTER: I see. Do you sit when you pee? Or do you always stand?

BUNNY: It depends. If I am at home I sit, elsewhere I stand.

SISTER: Oh. I always sit.

BUNNY: That's nice.

SISTER: Yeah. Something strange happened to me.

BUNNY: Oh. Did you meet a boy too?

SISTER: No. It was better than that.

BUNNY: Oh. What happened?

SISTER: Nothing.

BUNNY: Nothing?

SISTER: Let's just say I discovered an interesting way to entertain myself.

BUNNY: Oh. Well. I'm going to bed again.

SISTER: Nite.

(The lights dim as the family goes to sleep.)

SCENE: "ANOTHER VISIT"

Location—house. The family sleeps. BOY walks slyly into the house, looking for BUNNY.

BOY: Bunny?

BUNNY: Hello?

BOY: Shh.

BUNNY: What are you doing here?

BOY: Just came to give you a little something.

BUNNY: Is it what I think it is?

(BOY gives BUNNY a stuffed bunny.)

BOY: I thought you might like this.

BUNNY: It's very… pink. And sweet.

BOY: Go to sleep. I'll rub your head until you dream of sweet nothings.

BUNNY: Okay.

(BUNNY lays down and BOY strokes his hair. MOTHER watches while BOY sings the following and watches.)

BOY: Sleep, sleep, it's time for dreaming.
  I know a magic spell.
  It's for dreaming, for dreaming.
  Sleep, sleep, time is slipping.
  I cast a spell.
  It's for dreaming, for dreaming.
  Sleep, sleep…

(BUNNY has fallen asleep. BOY kisses his forehead and stands up. He walks backwards a few feet and bumps into MOTHER. She turns him around, and they face each other.)

MOTHER: I knew you'd be back for more of me.

BOY: Yeah. I knew I would be back too.

MOTHER: A kiss?

BOY: How about something more interesting.

(The lights fade as BOY goes down to his knees and puts his face into MOTHER's crotch. She moans as he eats her out. At her climax, SISTER wakes and begins the next scene.)

SCENE: "TWISTER SISTER"

Location—house. MOTHER and BOY are still in the house in their sexual situation. SISTER is onstage pacing. As she paces, she pulls the hair out of a Barbie doll's head. The lights are dim, and she is wearing a nightgown. She stops every now and then before she continues her pacing. She does this for about ten seconds. She stops pacing, goes to a microphone, and speaks. The microphone sound should have lots of delay so that her voice seems to echo after her—making everything she says happen twice. During SISTER's speech, BOY sneaks over to BUNNY, who is sleeping. When he gets there, he crawls under the covers and starts being sexual with BUNNY.

SISTER: Who is it? Hello. Hello. Miss Susie? *(She paces some more. Then…)* Mother?

MOTHER: *(Responds from upstage.)* Yes?

SISTER: What is happening to us?

MOTHER: It's hard to say, dear.

SISTER: Um. Okay.

MOTHER: Go to sleep.

SISTER: Um. Okay. *(Begins pacing again. She stops every now and then before she continues her pacing. She does this for about five seconds. She stops pacing, goes to a microphone, and speaks.)* Bunny?

BUNNY: *(Responds from his place on the floor with BOY.)* Hello?

SISTER: Bunny, are you scared? Do you want to sleep on my floor tonight?

BUNNY: No. I'm dreaming of the woods tonight.

SISTER: Um. The woods?

BUNNY: Yeah.

SISTER: Okay.

BUNNY: Go to sleep.

SISTER: Okay. *(Begins pacing again. She stops every now and then, and then she continues again. She does this for about five seconds. She stops pacing, goes to a microphone, and speaks.)* Bunny?

BUNNY: *(Responds from the floor.)* Yeah?

SISTER: I love you?

BUNNY: Yes. I love you too.

(SISTER goes to sleep as the lights fade to black.)

SCENE: "CIGARETTES AND SUGAR CUBES"

Location—house. MOTHER and SISTER are in the house. BOY and BUNNY are under the covers together, naked.

BOY: You sure you've never done that before?

BUNNY: I'm sure. My head feels like it's gonna pop open.

BOY: I'm tired.

BUNNY: That was rough. It's kind of like using Scott Tissue instead of Charmin.

Charmin is softer and thicker but it doesn't last as long and the little cotton fibers get stuck on your bottom. Scott is cheaper. Cheaper, but rougher. Maybe rougher is better. *(Opens his eyes and takes a drag on the cigarette.)* These are a little rougher. But it's worth it. When I feel tied up inside— these unleash something. They don't really unleash it. They relieve it. Each time I puff it out I fill up with relief. Puff. Relieve. Puff. Relieve. Puff. Relieve. Puff. Relieve. Puff. Relieve. *(Starts to hyperventilate, but stops before it gets too out of control.)*

BOY: Bunny? Calm down.

BUNNY: I can't sleep.

BOY: Then write me love letters until you pass out.

BUNNY: No. I can't while you are here. I only do it when I am alone.

BOY: Do you want a sugar cube?

BUNNY: Of course I do.

BOY: What will you do for it?

BUNNY: Just give it to me and I'll be able to sleep.

BOY: Beg.

BUNNY: Beg?

BOY: Beg.

BUNNY: Come on. Please, please. Please, please, please, please.

BOY: Okay. Here.

(BOY puts a sugar cube on the tip of BUNNY's tongue.)

BUNNY: Be right back. *(Exits the stage.)*

BOY: Poor kid. Slipping away with sugar cubes. I bet he's keeping them tucked under his pillow or in a box somewhere.

Saving them to build a sugarhouse. What a funny house it'll be. Bunny inside, sleeping on a pillow of sweet dreams. I imagine Bunny's little house of sugar standing still in front of me and my, cock out, and suddenly yellow, warm—melting the sugar crystals down… to juice. Silly Bunny left dreaming in a puddle of sweet piss. Just like where he came from. Then my arms, bigger than sugar, would wrap poor wet Bunny, in my folds. That's love. Love coming to the rescue.

(BOY eats a sugar cube. BUNNY enters again.)

BUNNY: Did you miss me?

BOY: Bunny? Are you in love with me?

BUNNY: I don't know.

BOY: You don't know?

BUNNY: Can we do it some more?

BOY: Of course.

(Lights fade to black.)

SCENE: "HUNGRY MAN"

Location—house.

MOTHER: DINNER!

(The members of the family gather. BUNNY and BOY scramble to get dressed. BOY tries to sneak out of the house without being seen, giving BUNNY a kiss, but SISTER sees him. The others all stand facing each other in a circle at the center of the space. BUNNY and SISTER stand across from each other, MOTHER in the same spot as before. A subtle light fills this "table" area with a cold light. They are passing TV dinners around rapidly. They don't start passing until MOTHER finishes her first line. The dialogue is said awkwardly.)

MOTHER: Amen.

SISTER: This is weird.

BUNNY: Yeah.

MOTHER: Daddy? Oh.

SISTER: He's not here.

MOTHER: I know. I know.

BUNNY: Sorry my new friend woke you up.

SISTER: "Friend"?

BUNNY: Shut up.

MOTHER: I did Betty's hair again today. She needed a haircut.

BUNNY: That's great.

MOTHER: I did Betty's hair again today. She needed a haircut.

SISTER: We heard you. Maybe I should sing a song for you. Like old times.

MOTHER: I'm too tired for a song.

BUNNY: A song? Sing it.

(SISTER suddenly breaks out in song into the microphone. The family stops for a second and stares at her. MOTHER begins mumbling to herself pretty much right away. BUNNY stares at SISTER in amazement.)

SISTER: "The Pussy Song," by Me.
    In the morning when I wake
    I stretch my stringy arms
    and I look around the room
    for my little pussycat
    pussycat
    pussycat
    where are you
    pussycat?
    When pussy hears my call
    she jumps up on my bed
    and she cuddles me
    and she snuggles me

she licks me up and down
licks me
licks me
pussy licks me
up and down
Then I take pussy in my arms
I squeeze her really tight
and I shake her silly body
like a pussy piggy bank
piggy bank
piggy bank
I shake pussy like a
piggy bank
Pussy meows and howls
she claws me with her nails
and she seems to be unhappy
but I squeeze her anyway
Squeeze her
Squeeze her
I scare my pussy when I
squeeze her
She tries to get away
I finally set her free
then I watch her run
and I laugh at all my fun
I laugh
I laugh
My pussy makes me
Laugh

(Everyone pauses for a second before resuming their conversation.)

BUNNY: Wow.

SISTER: It's the most fantastic song ever.

MOTHER: TV! That's a great idea.

SISTER: What?

BUNNY: No.

MOTHER: Yes, hon. *(Clicks the remote control in the general direction of the TV.)*

MOTHER: Let's see. What's today?

BUNNY: Tuesday.

MOTHER: Is today Wednesday?

SISTER: It's Tuesday. Can I leave the table?

MOTHER: Oh. Tuesday.

(SISTER gets up without being excused.)

BUNNY: May I be excused?

MOTHER: Oh. Tuesday.

BUNNY: Yes.

MOTHER: Oh. It's Tuesday.

(BUNNY gets up and walks over to stage right. The lights on the table area fade down to a low level as MOTHER talks to herself and to the empty space where FATHER used to sit. Meanwhile, BUNNY and SISTER say the following lines to each other into the microphone.)

SISTER: She's lost it.

BUNNY: Uh-huh.

SISTER: Oh well.

BUNNY: I guess.

SISTER: You guess what?

BUNNY: I guess, "Oh well." I can't take much more of this.

SISTER: Oh. Well. Good luck doing anything about it.

BUNNY: Thanks.

(BUNNY and SISTER close the curtain.)

SISTER: No problem.

BUNNY: I think I understand what happened to you now.

SISTER: Really?

BUNNY: Yeah. Something like that happened to me too. With that boy.

SISTER: You mean you did it.

BUNNY: Uh-huh.

SISTER: Wow. I think I need to have some private time to think about that.

BUNNY: It was fun.

(The lights fade out on BUNNY and SISTER. MOTHER is still holding her dinner plate.)

SCENE: "ANOTHER VISIT"

Location—house. The family sleeps. MOTHER is awake but in a daze—she is mumbling to herself. BOY walks slyly into the house, looking for BUNNY.

BOY: Bunny?

SISTER: *(Wakes up.)* Hey.

BOY: Oh. Hi.

SISTER: Are you coming to see Bunny?

BOY: Yeah. Is he sleeping?

SISTER: Out like a light. Maybe you should let him sleep.

BOY: Oh. Okay. Yeah. Well, I'll see ya later.

SISTER: He really likes you.

BOY: That's sweet.

SISTER: Yeah. How come you never come over during the day?

BOY: Oh. I just don't, I guess.

SISTER: Oh. Anyway, be nice to my brother, okay?

BOY: Of course.

SISTER: Okay.

BOY: Nite.

SISTER: Nite.

(SISTER goes back to sleep. BOY starts to leave as MOTHER's mumbling becomes words. He hides as MOTHER starts talking—unsure where she is, what's going on at all.)

MOTHER: Did something happen? When I was little the world was a different place. The cellar was scary and dark. I had to take the garbage down. I hid some kittens down there once and got in trouble. In the back of the cellar were some stairs and they led up to the yard. We were not allowed in the yard unless to retrieve something blown off the line or some such reason. Other kids were allowed in their yards, but Mrs. Murray wouldn't allow us. I shared the back bedroom with Daisy and it was usually a mess because she was a slob. When I got old enough to care I did the cleaning in that room and all the others. I had my first sexual experience in that back bedroom. Sixteen with the man I would eventually marry. It was a big mess in there. Directly below us lived Mrs. Bateman and her husband Davis. I never called her anything but Mrs. Bateman but I think her name was Debra. They were older than my parents. More like grandparents. Mrs. Bateman taught me how to crochet, how to make tea with evaporated milk, how to wash stockings in cold water and store them in the ice cube tray in the freezer—in her "ice box." Whenever I was sick, which was a lot, she took care of me. We did puzzles, read, played cards. I was anxious for my mother to come home from the factory for lunch. We would sit and sing "Calling Mrs. Weaver" over and over until she got there.

(BOY approaches MOTHER and puts his hand on her shoulder. She does not move. As he talks to her in the following dialogue, she becomes more and more distant and disturbed. Her story slowly becomes violent and highly hallucinatory as she goes on. BOY becomes more and more sexual with her as she speaks.)

BOY: Shh… Um.

MOTHER: Mrs. Bateman taught me how to bake cakes and to make Jell-O.

BOY: I dreamt about you last night.

MOTHER: We used to let it sit a while and then beat in some evaporated milk and it made it come out pink and foamy but solid.

BOY: I fell out of bed twice.

MOTHER: Foamy but solid.

BOY: How about a little something. Been thinking about me?

MOTHER: I think I had a lot of warm good stuff there. There was no fighting down there.

BOY: Do you hear me sweet lips?

MOTHER: Mrs. Bateman is the reason I went to the Ulmstead Vocational High School for hairdressing.

BOY: Listen.

(BOY and MOTHER roll around on the ground together. He sings as he makes out with her, and she continues in her rambling violence—their lines overlap.)

MOTHER: She taught me to respect the way we can make ourselves look. Our power is in our powder puff. Bunny? Bunny? Where are you? It was just for fun. Bunny? My cottontail is hopping down. Do you want a carrot? What's a bunny to do, Bunny? You were named after his father. It was Bunny, it was, Bunny, it was Bunny…

BOY: *(Overlapping.)* I've got the whole world in my hands, I've got the whole world in my pants, I've got the whole world in some ants, I've got the whole world in a chance. I've got the whole world in my hands, I've got the whole world, I've got the whole world in your pants, I've got the whole world. I've got the whole world.

(MOTHER lets out a loud squeal as she lifts her skirt over her head repeating "It was Bunny." SISTER wakes up.)

SISTER: HEY!

(This wakes BUNNY up.)

BUNNY: What? What's happening?

(BOY stands quickly. MOTHER just remains where she is on the floor in a mess.)

BOY: Hi Bunny. I was just coming over to…

BUNNY: Were you… ?

MOTHER: Oh. Bunny.

SISTER: Bunny he was…

BOY: Bunny. Let's go to the woods.

BUNNY: I think I'm going to throw up.

BOY: Um. Shit.

SISTER: You should leave.

MOTHER: How about it? Bunny? Bunny? How does that sound?

BUNNY: No. It sounds miserable. You make me sick. Oh my god.

BOY: Bunny.

BUNNY: You make me sick. Leave.

SISTER: Um…

BOY: I'm sorry. Bye. *(Leaves.)*

SISTER: Oh my god.

MOTHER: Something about Bunny. Yes.

BUNNY: Jesus.

(BUNNY goes to his bed. SISTER looks at MOTHER.)

MOTHER: It was all Bunny. Bun. Bun. Bunny.

SISTER: What is wrong with you?

MOTHER: Bunny.

(MOTHER stops moving, exhausted from her outlay of emotion. SISTER stands still.)

SCENE: "MOTION SICKNESS"

Location—house. The scene remains as before, MOTHER is still on the ground. SISTER speaks into the microphone.

SISTER: So Bunny, what do you think of all this?

(BUNNY walks over to the microphone and speaks.)

BUNNY: Oh. You know. I'm kind of pissed actually.

SISTER: I see. What do you think of my dress?

BUNNY: It's nice. I suppose.

SISTER: So. What about that cute boy?

BUNNY: Fucker.

SISTER: Yeah.

BUNNY: Her too. But she was crazy.

SISTER: Yeah. She was crazy.

BUNNY: I suppose.

SISTER: She was definitely crazy.

BUNNY: He broke my heart.

SISTER: I'm sorry.

BUNNY: Yeah. I guess we are on our own now.

SISTER: Yeah. I guess so. How does that make you feel?

BUNNY: Hungry. Do you want to go get a bite to eat?

SISTER: Yeah. And a beer.

BUNNY: Great.

(SISTER leaves the stage, closing the curtain on her way. All music stops.)

EPILOGUE: "BUNNY'S DREAM"

Location—theatre. After a brief moment of silence and darkness, BUNNY speaks the following lines. BUNNY unfolds a piece of paper and reads into a microphone.

BUNNY: "Bunny's Last Night in Limbo." I call it Bunny's Last Night in Limbo because it's the last dream of my childhood. That's all there is. Dreams. I had a different dream last night. In it I was flying like a superhero. I had a blue cape and purple tights. I looked pretty silly, but I felt good—with the wind blowing through my hair (which was ridiculously long in my dream). I felt sexy. Like Fabio. I was flying over a strange landscape of candy-coated buildings and there were all these tiny people moving around below. It looked like a bizarre map of the world drawn in black magic markers. The people below were building something. Something out of yellow sugar cubes. I just kept flying and flying but I had no idea where

I was going. I wanted to stop and check out all the cubes of sweetness, but I just kept flying. I don't know why. All I know is when I woke up I felt safe, alone, and a little bit wet. Well, that's all I wanted to say. Thank you for staying awake. Have a good night.

(End.)

SUMMERLAND

Brian Thorstenson

Born in Oregon, BRIAN THORSTENSON is a playwright, poet, and actor who lives in San Francisco. His first play, *Heading South*, was produced at the Studio at Theatre Rhinoceros, The 450 Geary Studio Theater (Bay Area Critics Circle Nomination), and was part of the 1996 Berkeley Art Center's performance series. His plays *The Trick* and *Cul-de-Sac* received staged readings as part of the GreenHouse Series and the One Act Fringe Festival at San Francisco State University. *Summerland* received the 2000 Highsmith Playwriting Award, was one of six plays selected for the 2000 Bay Area Playwrights Festival, and was produced as part of the 2000 Z Festival of New Performance in Santa Cruz, California. Thorstenson's poetry has been published in *Transfer* and *Six Thousand Five Hundred*. As an actor, he has worked at the Magic Theatre, The Eureka Theatre, Intersection for the Arts, and Theatre Rhinoceros. He was a founding member of the Z Collective, a San Francisco-based theatre company known for its site-specific productions. He recently completed work on his first feature film, *Haiku Tunnel*, written and directed by Josh and Jacob Kornbluth. Thorstenson has received writing residencies from the Djerassi Resident Arts Program and Blue Mountain Center. He has a BA in theater from Willamette University in Salem, Oregon, and an MFA in creative writing from San Francisco State University.

The New York City premiere of *Summerland* was produced by Wings Theatre Company (Jeffery Corrick, Artistic Director; Robert Mooney, Managing Director) on January 4, 2001, at the Wings Theatre, with the following cast and credits:

Aura .... Dolores Kenan
Bud .... Ivan Quintanilla
Doreen .... Barbara Ayres Bruno
Tom .... John Coleman
Skye .... Eric Conley
Sam .... Mitch Poulos

Director: Sam Sommer
Lighting Design: David Castaneda
Costume Design: Tom Claypool
Scenic Design: Sam Sommer
Fight Choreography: John Coleman
Stage Manager: Parys Le Bron

Summerland was developed at the Bay Area Playwrights Festival 23, Jayne Wenger, Artistic Director; and at the Z Space Studio, San Francisco.

Acknowledgments: Claire Chafee, Roy Conboy, David Dower, Brighde Mullins, Daniele Nathanson and Camille Roy for their acute dramaturgical advice. I am deeply indebted to a group of talented actors whose work informed the writing of *Summerland* over the course of several readings and workshops: Frances Lee McCain, Kenny Neal Shults, Nicola Harwood, J.M. Beck, Matthew Chavez, Robert Parsons, David Cramer, John Ficarra, John Cowen, and David Perry. Tracy Ward first staged the play with an eye on the horizon line and an ear attuned to the wind of the plains. I owe much to Sam Sommer who picked *Summerland* "out of the pile" and shepherded it through the New York production with such grace and ease. Sam and the entire cast welcomed me into the process with a warmth and consideration that was disarming. Thank you. Barb Fraser, a native of South Dakota, let me borrow her grandmother's name, Aura. Kathleen Norris's book *Dakota: A Spiritual Geography* was a continuing source of inspiration. To Dave Gleba for much-needed business advice and financial support, Harriet Barlow and the staff of the Blue Mountain Center where the first draft of *Summerland* was completed, and Tom Caldarola for 11 years of support, goading, and potent conversations. Thanks to Martin Denton for including the play in this anthology and his enthusiastic support. To Nicola Harwood, whose voice echoed in my head while I was writing Doreen, for her triple duty as divine actress, inspired dramaturge, and staunch friend, I owe my deepest gratitude. Thank you girlfriend.

Summerland is for my great-grandmother Maude Amelia Moore Orr, 1882–1978.

CHARACTERS

BUD: 18 years old.
DOREEN: 45. A waitress and diner owner. Bud's mom.
TOM: Mid- to late 20s. A rancher.
SKYE: Late 20s. A wanderer.
SAM: Mid- to late 40s. A trucker.
AURA SIGURDSON: Doreen's grandmother. An apparition.

SETTING

Various locations in western South Dakota.

TIME

The last two weeks of August.

NOTES ON THE SETTING

The various locations should be suggested by simple set pieces, e.g., a bench for the rest area, a counter for the diner. The rest of the locations can be defined by lights and the actors' visual imaginations. Most of the outdoor scenes should be staged on an empty stage. One scene should move seamlessly into the next. No blackouts!

NOTES ON THE TEXT

A line usually follows the one immediately before it, but when one character starts speaking before the other has finished, the point of interruption is marked with an asterisk.

ACT I
SCENE 1

Summer night. Late. BUD sitting on a rest area bench, waiting. DOREEN at the diner counter, waiting. Wind. Dust blowing. DOREEN and BUD look up. AURA appears. She is very real, but something about her clothes, her presence, tells you that she is from a different time period. That she has just been blown in by the wind. She looks at DOREEN, then at BUD, then listens to the wind.

AURA: The wind. Times it howls so loud have to shout to be heard. Workin out-doors all day it made ya dizzy, ya went to bed with a ringin in your ears. Leaches all the moisture outta the land. Outta your skin. Summerwind—nice enough for the current it makes, for the movement in the heat—could turn a field to dust in no time. Blow away anything you planted. Dim the sun.

Winter time a Chinook wind'll melt the snow away in a day.

Days and days a wind. Drives some folks crazy. Drives em away. I saw that happen. Days and weeks of it. And us always waitin for rain. Always.

Couldn't have been more shocked when I first came to Dakota. Nothin but sky, endless endless sky and empty land. Couldn't see past that for a long time. The desolation. I was afraid to go too far from our claim. Afraid, with no landmarks, I'd never find my way back. People said "It's just three miles from the buffalo waller. Just remember that, you'll be fine." But if I wandered too far I couldn't even find that waller. Thought we'd prove up our claim and move on.

Then I started noticin how bright the moon and stars were. How the air sat on my lips like ripe fruit. How that desolation became this quiet, a quiet that worked its way into my bones. Became a craving. Became a balm. You hesitate before you give that up.

Over time I started "seein," started recognizin things—other shacks on the horizon line, tufts a prairie grass—greasy grass is what the Indians call it—the break on the west forty, herd a antelope racin away.

One time a group of women rode in eighteen miles just to say hello. Saw them comin an hour ahead of their arrival.

Distance-vision.

Comes with time out here.

(AURA looks at DOREEN and BUD again and then exits. Lights shift.)

SCENE 2

DOREEN still at the diner counter. BUD still sitting on the rest area bench, a rest area on a deserted stretch of South Dakota Highway. BUD is facing the parking lot. The headlights of a truck swing onto stage, lighting up his face. Country and western music from the truck radio. The radio goes off. Sound of truck door opening and closing. Truck lights still on BUD's face. TOM enters.

BUD: Hi.

TOM: Hey. *(Pulls out a revolver from his pants, swings around and shoots out one of his truck's headlights, then the other.)*

BUD: Jesus.

TOM: Better?

BUD: What?

TOM: That's better.

BUD: You don't have any lights now.

TOM: Still got my fogs.

BUD: Jesus.

TOM: Whatcha doin?

BUD: Just, you know… sittin.

DOREEN: Sittin.

TOM: I've been drivin. Good night for drivin.

BUD: Yeah?

TOM: Wanna go for a drive?

BUD: You don't have any headlights.

TOM: Take your car.

BUD: I hitched here.

TOM: Damn. *(Pause.)* Just sittin on a summer night. That ain't good.

BUD: Depends.

TOM: Depends?

BUD: I've been waitin.

TOM: Well that's different ain't it. That's a reason to be sittin. *(Takes out his gun and tries to blow out one of the rest area lights.)*

BUD: Cut it out.

TOM: *(Tries again. He misses again.)* Dammit.

BUD: Cmon, cut it out.

TOM: Shut up. It's my gun.

BUD and DOREEN: Stupid.

(DOREEN exits.)

TOM: Wanna drink?

BUD: Um…

TOM: Cmon, have one. Might as well if you're waitin. *(Goes and sits by BUD on the bench.)* Here. Go on.

(BUD takes a drink.)

TOM: Good shit huh.

BUD: Yeah.

TOM: This here's premium shit. Don't get shit like this all the time. Not this premium. If you're gonna drink why drink crap. Right?

BUD: Yeah, guess so.

TOM: Have some more.

BUD: Nah, I'm fine.

TOM: Pisses me off. Waitin. Waitin for anything. Waitin for people, waitin in line, waitin for summer. All of it. Pisses me off.

BUD: Tom.

TOM: How'd you know my name?

BUD: We've been here before. Together.

TOM: *(Holding the gun to BUD's head.)* Stupid fuck. How'd you know my name? Huh? Huh? How'd you know?

BUD: Put the gun down.

TOM: Tell me you little fuck. Tell me how you know my name.

BUD: You told me.

TOM: Shut up. *(TOM still has the gun to BUD's head.)* Now tell me how you know my name.

BUD: I told you, we*

(TOM sits down. He puts the gun down on the bench between him and BUD.)

TOM: *(Overlapping.)* Fuckin lucky guess. That's what I think. Tom. Any stupid fuck could come up with that. That what it was? Fuckin guess? That it?

BUD: You told me your name was Tom. We went for a drive in your truck. You said we should meet here. Next week. Same time. You know who I am. Don't you.

TOM: *(Gets up from the bench.)* You think someone's gonna show up here. Rest stop. Middle of the night.

BUD: Yeah.

TOM: Who? Who's gonna show up here, in the fuckin middle of the night?

BUD: You did.

TOM: Yeah. So?

BUD: You said you'd come back.

TOM: And you've been waitin since then?

BUD: Every Friday and Saturday night.

TOM: You're crazy. You know that? Fuckin loopy. Waitin. For a goddamn month. That's nuts. *(Starts to leave.)*

BUD: Where are you goin?

TOM: I'm gettin the fuck away from you.

BUD: Say my name.

TOM: No.

BUD: Say it. *(Picks up the gun.)*

TOM: Shoot me.

BUD: Say my name.

TOM: *(Turns around.)* Pull the trigger.

BUD: Say it.

TOM: Cmon. Shoot me. Cmon. Shoot me. That what you want? Huh? Huh?

(BUD lowers the gun and sets it down on the bench.)

TOM: I seen you.

BUD: What?

TOM: Seen you sittin here. Middle of the night. Waitin.

BUD: Why didn't you stop?

TOM: You fuckin creep me out man. Hate that. Hate that more than waitin. I'm outta here kid. *(Exits.)*

BUD: Wait. Wait.

(TOM doesn't turn around. Truck starting. Radio. Fog lights on BUD's face. Sound of the truck driving away fast.)

BUD: Stupid.

(BUD takes the gun and points it toward a rest area light. Pulls the trigger. It's out of bullets. He puts the gun down and starts to leave. He stops, turns around, and looks at the gun. He goes back to the bench, picks up the gun and pockets it, then exits. Lights shift.)

SCENE 3

Morning. Two-lane highway. BUD on the side of the road trying to hitch a ride home. No cars or trucks in sight, no sound, just the morning heating up a day that will top 100

degrees. You can already smell the heat coming off the blacktop. The sound of a car approaching. The car goes by, a radio blasting.

BUD: Fuck. Tourists! Don't forget to stop at Wall Drug. Get your free ice water, get your five cent coffee, get your stuffed jackalopes. Fuck you.

(The sound of another car approaching. BUD resumes his hitchhiking pose.)

BUD: Cmon, cmon, cmon. Stop this time. Stop.

(The sound of the car stopping and someone getting out. SKYE enters, a look of deep concentration on his face.)

BUD: Hey. Hey. Dammit. Hey.

SKYE: Shh. *(SKYE sits cross legged, takes a pair of dice out of a pouch. He takes a deep breath and exhales on a vocalized "Ahh.")* Ahhhhhh. Seven.

BUD: Which way you headed?

SKYE: *(Not looking at BUD.)* Shh. *(He throws the dice.)* Seven-out. *(He gets the seven.)* Alright. Eight.

BUD: Looks like you're headed east.

SKYE: Shhh. Eight. *(He throws the dice. He doesn't make the eight.)* Damn. Eight, eight, we're running late. *(He throws the dice. He doesn't get the eight.)* Man oh man oh man oh man.

BUD: Can you give me a ride? I can't stand here watchin you do… whatever… if you're not gonna give me a lift. I gotta pay attention.

SKYE: Concentrate. Eight. *(He throws, he misses again.)* Irritating. Really irritating. *(He looks up at BUD.)* Hey bud.

BUD: What?

SKYE: Hey.

BUD: No. My name.

SKYE: What about it?

BUD: How did you know my name?

SKYE: I don't.

BUD: You just said it.

SKYE: Are you high or something?

BUD: Bud. That's my name.

SKYE: For real?

BUD: How'd you know my name?

SKYE: Bud's like an all purpose word. Your name really Bud?

BUD: Yeah.

SKYE: Like flower bud?

BUD: No, just Bud Bud.

SKYE: Huh. Never met a Bud before. My name's Skye.

BUD: Sky? Like…

SKYE: Like *(Points up.)* with an e trailing along at the end.

BUD: What kinda name is that?

SKYE: Hippie parents.

BUD: Oh. I need to get home. It's not that far.

SKYE: Wanna play? Perfect spot to roll the bones. Flick a the wrist, elbow shake. Simple as can be. I'm stuck at eight. Eight's my dilemma.

BUD: Jesus.

SKYE: Take a twirl Bud.

BUD: *(Starts to leave.)* I've had enough kooks for one day.

SKYE: Sit and play the cubes man. Help me get past the weight of eight.

BUD: Will you give me a ride then?

SKYE: Eight Bud. I gotta get to ten.

BUD: *(Sits.)* You're throwin em all wrong.

SKYE: Show me.

BUD: Like this. *(Throws the dice. He gets eight.)*

SKYE: Yes! Eighter from Decatur.

BUD: Let's get out of here.

SKYE: Man, you've got the hands Bud.

BUD: Do nine and ten then let's go.

SKYE: Let me see em.

BUD: Do the nine and ten.

SKYE: Your hands man. Gimme your hands.

(Takes BUD's hands and studies them, turning them over. He traces the lines of BUD's palm with his finger.)

SKYE: Life line. Love line. Nice hands Bud.

(Finds a piece of gravel in BUD's hand.)

SKYE: Gravel.

BUD: Where?

SKYE: Gotta a little piece … stuck … there. Gone.

(BUD takes his hands away from SKYE. SKYE smiles.)

BUD: Do the nine and ten.

SKYE: Nine. *(Throws the dice.)* Carolina Nine. Yes!

BUD: Ten.

SKYE: *(Takes a deep breath, exhales, and does the ten in focused silence.)* Double fin. Yes yes yes. *(Collects the dice and puts them back in his pouch. He looks at Bud as if seeing him for the first time.)*

(Silence.)

BUD: What? You got the ten so let's go.

SKYE: *(Looks out into the distance.)* God. Watched a rainstorm come in yesterday. Miles aways, truckin across the plains. Whoosh, it was on top of me. Bang. I'm drenched. Ten minutes and it's flying further east and I'm baking in the sun again. You've got some hands Bud. Can I trust them?

BUD: Yeah, sure. Why not?

SKYE: Why not, huh, why not.

(SKYE reaches out and places his hand gently on BUD's face, palm open, then draws his fingers together as he draws his hand away from BUD.)

SKYE: Which way?

BUD: Why'd you do that?

SKYE: I'm hitting the blacktop.

BUD: Why'd you do that.

SKYE: You got the eight Bud.

BUD: Yeah.

SKYE: I got the ten but you got the eight.

BUD: So.

SKYE: Come on then.

(BUD doesn't move.)

SKYE: Or stay. *(Starts to leave.)*

BUD: Wait.

SKYE: You trippin again?

BUD: Tell me why you did that?

SKYE: Come with me and find out.

(BUD doesn't move. SKYE starts to leave again.)

BUD: Wait. Wait.

SKYE: Yeah?

BUD: Ok.

SKYE: Point the way dude.

(Lights shift.)

SCENE 4

Morning. A diner. Music from a jukebox. DOREEN is behind the counter reading the newspaper. A TRUCKER is sitting alone drinking a cup of coffee.

DOREEN: Warm up?

TRUCKER: What?

DOREEN: Can I warm up your coffee? You ok?

TRUCKER: Hot one, huh?

DOREEN: 105. Second week, every day over a hundred. Must all be crazy to live here.

TRUCKER: Yeah. Sure. You finished with the funnies?

DOREEN: Yeah.

(She takes him the funnies, bringing a coffee pot with her.)

DOREEN: Never did think they were very funny. Make no sense to me. Always some damn monster in a closet or somethin jumpin out and scarin the bejeezus out of some kid with funny hair. Seem like a waste of time to me but you're welcome to em.

TRUCKER: Need a chuckle every now and then. *(Picks up his coffee cup to take a drink, but his hands are shaking and he spills most of it.)* Dammit!

DOREEN: It's what rags are for.

TRUCKER: Hands don't seem to wanna behave today.

DOREEN: *(Wipes up the coffee.)* You on a run?

TRUCKER: Just finished one. Headed home. East river. Up near Aberdeen.

DOREEN: Got cousins in Barnard. You know the Tjenstrom's?

TRUCKER: Heard the name. Heard they're good folks.

DOREEN: That they are. There. You sure you're ok?

TRUCKER: The funnies'll help.

DOREEN: Could use a laugh myself today. *(Takes a postcard out of her apron pocket.)* See this? Postcard from my ex-husband. Came this morning. Like I need to be reminded of him. You know what I mean? First time I hear from the son of a bitch in eight years and it's a goddamn postcard. Isn't much, picture of a Travelodge in Billings. You know, the kind they leave in your motel room. Couldn't even take the time to write a proper letter. Signed M, for Marvin, on the back and three words: "I - was - here." Postmarked "Moose Jaw, Saskatchewan." This card, it traveled from Montana to Canada till the words faded, changed from I am to I was.

You married?

TRUCKER: Divorced.

DOREEN: You an asshole to your ex?

TRUCKER: Like to think I'm not.

DOREEN: Odds aren't on your side. Thought I saw Marvin once, at the Harley rally in Sturgis. Watched this man gettin off his bike, adjustin his Levi's, pullin up the back with a quick hitch, just like Marvin always did. Couldn't stop starin. This guy noticed, cocked his head to one side like he was tryin to figure out who I was, then straightened it like the answer came to him. I started across that street, didn't know what I might say or do. Just goin. This guy sees me comin, jumps on his Harley and takes off. Mighta been him. Or it mighta been some other asshole runnin from a woman.

TRUCKER: Well at least he wrote somethin.

DOREEN: Whoop-de-do. We'll give him an "A" for effort.

(DOREEN goes back behind the counter. TRUCKER reads the comics. BUD enters.)

DOREEN: You want somethin?

BUD: Coffee.

DOREEN: I could fix you some eggs.

BUD: Just the coffee.

DOREEN: When was the last time you ate?

BUD: Leave it.

DOREEN: You look like you been up all night.

BUD: Suppose I do.

(TRUCKER chuckles at the comics.)

BUD: What's his problem?

DOREEN: Thinks the funnies are actually funny.

BUD: Trucker?

DOREEN: Been here since I opened. You need to eat somethin.

BUD: Got any of those cinnamon rolls?

DOREEN: Some real food.

BUD: Just a cinnamon roll.

(DOREEN plates a cinnamon roll.)

BUD: You alright?

DOREEN: No use complainin.

BUD: Even if stuff bugs ya?

DOREEN: Doesn't get you anywhere.

(BUD pulls the gun out of his pants and sets it on the counter.)

DOREEN: What're ya doin with that?

BUD: Got it from a guy.

DOREEN: What guy?

BUD: Just this guy.

DOREEN: You buy it from him?

BUD: No. He sorta left it with me.

DOREEN: What d'ya think you're gonna do with a gun?

BUD: Thought it might come in handy.

DOREEN: For what? Put it away. Don't look good.

BUD: People seen guns before.

DOREEN: Crazy idea. Stupid, if you ask me, carryin a gun around.

BUD: Wasn't plannin on havin one, this guy just sorta… forgot it.

DOREEN: Well that don't make any sense, somebody just forgettin a gun.

BUD: Yeah, well…Guess he's just a forgetful person.

DOREEN: Are you in some sort of trouble?

BUD: No.

DOREEN: Well, with that gun and all.

BUD: I told you some guy left it with me.

DOREEN: Looks like trouble.

BUD: I'm not in any trouble.

DOREEN: Hope he doesn't come lookin for it.

BUD: He won't.

DOREEN: Finish your cinnamon roll.

BUD: Don't want any more.

DOREEN: And put that gun away.

BUD: I don't see what the big deal…

TRUCKER: I was in Butte yesterday morning. Traveled I-90 through Bozeman, Livingston, Billings. Swung down into Wyoming right around dusk. Stopped in Spotted Horse for a Snickers bar and a fill up. Bout 15 miles south of there I see a truck pulled up on the side of the road, no flashers goin off, just kinda pulled off at a kittywampus kinda angle. I pull up behind him and head up the road to see if everything's ok. Get to the driver's side of the truck and yell up. No answer. Try again. No answer again. So I climb up and open the cab door. This guy's sittin with his back against the passenger side door, feet on the seat, knees up to his chin, hands in his lap. Whole cab smells like Jack Daniels. "You need some help?" I ask him. "Don't come in here" he says in this shakey voice. "I won't, just wanted to make sure there wasn't somethin I could do, someone I could call, you know. "Back off" he says. Then he lifts his hands and points a gun right at my head. "Back off, step down and shut that door." "Now I ain't tryin to be troublesome, just wanted to see if I could give you a lift or anything." "You deaf? Back off." Then he thrusts the gun forward and shoots right past the left side a my head. Wasn't gonna count on his aim bein off a second time so I step down, got back on the road. Kinda shakey for awhile but I started feelin better by the time I was headin outta the Black Hills so I flip on my CB to get some company. The wires are buzzin. It's all anyone can talk about. Seems that some other trucker stopped same as me. Only this time the guy with the gun was dead. Shot himself. After he shot the lady that was travelin with him. At least that's how it looked. I drove till I saw your place, pulled in and waited till you opened.

(BUD puts the gun back in his pocket and starts to leave.)

TRUCKER: Leave the gun.

BUD: Mister it isn't any of your…

TRUCKER: Leave it.

BUD: You coulda just made that up.

DOREEN: Bud!

BUD: Well he could have.

TRUCKER: Doesn't matter.

BUD: Go back to your funnies. *(Starts to go.)*

TRUCKER: You know how to use that thing?

(BUD doesn't answer.)

TRUCKER: That gun, it'll always tie you to somethin or someone. Waitin for somethin or someone. Waitin for somethin to happen.

BUD: How'd you know about that?

DOREEN: About what?

BUD: Nothin.

TRUCKER: *(Gets up and starts toward BUD.)* Give it to me.

(BUD doesn't move.)

TRUCKER: Now.

(BUD takes the gun out, walks past TRUCKER, and sets it on the counter, then starts toward the door.)

DOREEN: Where're you goin?

BUD: Home. I'm goin home. Happy?

DOREEN: Get some sleep. Ok?

(BUD exits. TRUCKER opens the gun and check for bullets.)

DOREEN: What'd you mean about waitin?

TRUCKER: We're all waitin for somethin aren't we? I should get back on the road.

DOREEN: You ok to drive?

TRUCKER: Yeah. Fine. Thanks. *(Starts to take his wallet out to pay.)*

DOREEN: On me today.

TRUCKER: I'll be sure to stop by again.

DOREEN: Yeah, do that.

TRUCKER: *(Gestures toward the road.)* Yeah. Guess I should…

DOREEN: Ok then.

(Pause.)

TRUCKER: Good pie. You got good pie here. I'll be back.

DOREEN: Make one special for you next time. Thanks, uh…?

TRUCKER: Samuel. Sam.

DOREEN: Doreen.

SAM: Doreen. *(Pointing to the gun.)* I can get rid a that for you.

DOREEN: I'll take care of it. Thanks Sam.

SAM: See ya in the funny papers. *(Exits.)*

(Lights shift.)

SCENE 5

Evening. Rest area, same as Scene 2. BUD sitting counting the cars that have come and gone.

BUD: Fifteen.

(SKYE appears behind Bud.)

SKYE: Bud.

BUD: *(Turning around and seeing it is SKYE.)* Oh. Didn't get very far. Havin trouble with that eight again?

SKYE: My rollers keep sending me up one side of the highway and back down the other. Like I'm stuck in some sorta traveling black hole, some sorta mobius strip of a trip.

BUD: Maybe you should throw the dice away and go in one direction for a while. Decide for yourself.

SKYE: This place has got some kind of hoodoo, put some sorta trance on my travels.

BUD: If I was you I'd get the hell out of here.

SKYE: I'm thinking I need to stay around here for awhile.

BUD: Why would you want to do that?

SKYE: Why don't you show me around. Gimme a night on the town Bud. I'm a wandering tourist and you know the territory.

BUD: There's not a town worth spittin at around here. Hardly any people and the ones that there are aren't particularly interesting.

SKYE: Gotta be someplace you like. It's better than sitting and doing nothing.

BUD: Better than travellin in circles you mean. I'm fine right here.

SKYE: What are you waiting for?

(BUD doesn't answer.)

SKYE: One day I said, Skye, it's time to move, time to get out, see what's happening past the outlines of your bedroom window. Cause there's something going on out there, there's a pulse in the air. Nobody here can tell you about it cause they don't know. They aren't feeling it. They sat down, decided not to get up again. Or they're waiting, for some person, some god, some sorta omen to point the way. This nagging ache, this ache inside wasn't going to go away sitting at my window watching the clouds collect. So I left. Hit the blacktop. Skiing the white line.

BUD: Did you find it?

(Pause.)

(Lights shift.)

SCENE 6

Split scene: DOREEN and AURA at the diner; BUD and SKYE in the Badlands. Night. AURA at a diner table doing a crossword puzzle. DOREEN enters.

AURA: What's a six letter word for "exit undetected"?

DOREEN: *(Starts to exit.)* You're not gonna be here when I come back.

(AURA smiles and goes back to her puzzle. Lights up on BUD and SKYE in the Badlands.)

BUD: Full moon. Clear night. Best time to be out here.

SKYE: Eerie Bud. Really eerie.

BUD: Mako sica.

SKYE: What?

BUD: Mako sica. It's the Indian name for this place. Land Bad. Badlands. All chiseled and chipped. Corroded. Like fractured cathedral spires stuck on burial mounds.

DOREEN: *(Enters with a bottle of Jack Daniels.)* What are you doin here?

AURA: Crossword puzzle.

(DOREEN sits down and pours herself a glass of Jack Daniels.)

AURA: You gonna share some of that.

DOREEN: Bottle's right there.

(AURA pours herself a drink.)

SKYE: Man, look at those colors, jumping from one spire to the next. Connecting lines. Like it used to be one piece. Solid.

BUD: Dinosaur time it was.

SKYE: Purple, grey, cobalt. Man oh man oh man.

BUD: It's different during the day. Cream, tan, and deep deep rose.

SKYE: Not a tree anywhere. Like some weird ancient skyline. Desolate and deserted.

BUD: And lonely. Really lonely.

DOREEN: He's left. He's not comin back.

AURA: You don't know that.

DOREEN: Don't know where he is, who he's with, only that he's not sleepin at home, sleepin in his bed. I saved three months a tips to buy that bed and it doesn't look like it's been touched in a week.

AURA: He'll get hungry. Come home for dinner at least.

DOREEN: Not tonight. Not tonight. Gotta keep up. You gotta keep up. You gotta story for me? Huh? You got somethin to get me through the night. Make one up for me. Better than a book. So what's the story, huh? All about this woman who puts two plates on the table. Two napkins. Two forks. Two... what? What else?

(AURA doesn't answer.)

DOREEN: Well just two of everything you need for dinner. Then she waits. Dinner's ready. And she waits. Then she makes a deal with herself—if he isn't back in half an hour she'll eat alone. Half an hour comes and goes, her sittin at the table with two plates, two forks, two of everything you need for dinner. The macaroni and cheese gets cold, sticks to the edges of the pot, skins over. Dark. Hard. She thinks about callin around to find him. But who? Doesn't know anyone who he might be with, who might know.

BUD: I met this guy...

DOREEN: She thinks about burnin the rest of his dinner,

BUD: Guy named Tom.

DOREEN: throwin the plates against the wall,

BUD: Thought he was… you know… a friend.

DOREEN: turnin on the water in the sink,

BUD: Anyway,

DOREEN: lettin it run over onto the floor. Flood the whole damn place.

AURA: Went to Rapid. Saw a movie. Couldn't get a ride back. Probably sittin at Denny's, drinkin coffee. Talkin to the waitress.

DOREEN: That the story?

AURA: Could be. Why not?

BUD: Met him hitchin a ride back from Rapid City. Came out here in his pickup. Like tonight but no moon. Pitch black, and this storm comes in from the west. Lightning… thunder, lightning, thunder, lightning thunder. It would be totally dark, then flash—four, five, six fingers of lightning. White. Purple. Blue. Like a flash photo. Those three spires just sittin there posin for us, just for the two of us. The storm swept right over the top of us. Then pitch dark. Just sittin in his pickup.

SKYE: I feel like I'm floating.

(DOREEN pours another drink.)

AURA: You're just like Vic. That man liked his Jack Daniels.

SKYE: I could just take off. Fly right through those creases and crevices.

AURA: There was this one time, what was it?

SKYE: Glide over the canyons.

AURA: Musta been '34? '35? Depression days.

SKYE: Be like flying through hell. Only

safe cause I wouldn't touch down.

AURA: Vic says to me, "Aura, they're launchin a big balloon up into space, from some place near Rapid, some sorta scientific thing, sendin men up into the stratosphere, whatever that is, and we're gonna go watch." I thought Vic was a little… you know… thought it was some crazy story, somethin he probably heard from Elmo or Hugo. But those years any distraction was a good one, even a trip to nowhere and back.

'34. I was pregnant with your mom.

Vic wasn't makin anything up though. Drove the Ford right through this pasture to the rim of a cliff overlookin this bowl in the land. Us and hundreds a other folks who had the same idea.

DOREEN: Crazy idea if you ask me. Stupid.

AURA: You should a seen it. It was a sight. Hundreds of people scurryin around, adjusting ropes, working the generator, laying out this big circle of white canvas— looked like a giant griddlecake. And in the middle of it all was this huge shiny white balloon. Musta been over 300 feet high. Whole thing lit up by dozens a floodlights so bright you could actually read a newspaper. Air was so still that balloon hardly had a ripple in it, just hovered there, strainin against the ropes.

I don't know… it was somethin… somethin about seein all those people workin together, workin together to get a silly balloon up into the air that was… well… made some sorta sense. Like things'd work out. You know?

DOREEN: It's past four. Highway patrols gonna call any minute. He's dead. On the side of the road somewhere.

(AURA looks at DOREEN.)

DOREEN: Ok. Not dead. He's not dead. Just hurt. Yeah. Hurt.

AURA: Phone's not ringin though is it? Hasn't rung all night. Gotta keep up. Gotta change the story.

BUD: Gravel… that gravel. That piece you picked out. Last night I was runnin to get to the rest area, runnin on the side of the highway. I tripped, skidded through the gravel, stopped two inches from the blacktop. Spent the night pickin bits of gravel out of my hands, tryin to stay awake. Every time I heard a truck door slam, or a radio, or saw someone's headlights cuttin through the dark I knew it'd be Tom. Knew last night he'd show up.

SKYE: Did he?

BUD: He tells me he doesn't know who I am. Like he's never seen me before, like we never went for a drive, never came out here, never…

AURA: Stayed up all night, Vic and me, sittin on the hood of the Ford, watchin that balloon, readin, talkin every now and then. Around five, whole bowl started gettin busy: Jeeps leavin, crew gettin ready, men runnin to grab the ropes. Then everyone got real still, like they all just been touched in a game a freeze tag. A minute or two of nothing… then "Cast off" echoes up the bowl, the men start droppin their ropes and that balloon… well… it just, real slow and quiet started risin up into the air. All this shimmerin white in the blue dawn. I put one hand on my belly, closed my eyes and made a wish. One wish. Simple really. One wish on that balloon risin up into the air. Then, whoosh, the balloon cleared the rim of the bowl and took off east, risin up and up into the air, risin up into

territory no one had ever been before.

DOREEN: I gotta extra room I don't want. Find a sledge hammer, knock the walls down, make it disappear like it never existed at all. Burn his clothes, melt the extra silverware, throw his bike off a butte. When there is only one of everything. Then I'll be able to sleep. But only when there's one. *(Exits.)*

(SKYE turns toward BUD and reaches out to touch his face again. BUD draws away.)

BUD: Why do you keep doin that?

SKYE: Wipe it away. Get rid of it. Clean.

BUD: That won't do anything. Won't help. Stupid.

SKYE: Most people don't like carrying that kind of stuff around.

BUD: You don't know anything about me.

SKYE: Tell me.

BUD: No.

SKYE: Well, how I am supposed to know…

BUD: Just don't do that again.

SKYE: Come on. Tell me.

BUD: I don't want you takin things away from me.

(Lights shift.)

SCENE 7

Morning. Diner. AURA is at a table doing a crossword. DOREEN enters. She is very hung over.

AURA: Sit down. Have some coffee. You could do with some coffee.

(DOREEN starts to go for the bottle of Jack Daniels.)

AURA: You're a difficult one aren't you. Used to make your mother nuts. She had to put you on a leash when she took you out cause you was always runnin off somewhere.

DOREEN: How long you plannin on bein around?

AURA: Course that's from you grandfathers side. Flighty bunch. Specially the women. Always moanin about it bein too cold, or too hot, or too windy. Didn't like the dust, didn't like the sky.

DOREEN: How long?

AURA: Can you imagine that? Someone livin out here and not likin the sky. Never made any sense to me. Now your grandfather,

DOREEN: Just tell me.

AURA: solid as the Black Hills he was.

DOREEN: How long?

AURA: Drink your coffee.

DOREEN: Grandma…

AURA: Doreen! How many time have I told you not to call me Grandma. Oh. Hate that word. Makes me feel old. Don't like feelin old.

DOREEN: Don't see how it matters now.

AURA: What's a three letter word for "This is your life."

DOREEN: Go. Just go. Just get outta here.

(BUD enters.)

DOREEN: Where the hell have you been?

AURA: That mouth of yours Doreen.

DOREEN: Shut up.

BUD: I didn't say anything.

DOREEN: I wasn't talkin to you. Grandma you stay* out of this.

BUD: *(Overlapping, simultaneously with AURA.)* Grandma?

AURA: *(Simultaneously with BUD.)* Honestly. I'm gonna have to gag you.*He can't see me.

DOREEN: Where have you been? What?

BUD: Finish the whole bottle yourself?

DOREEN: Don't you start…

BUD: Looks like it.

AURA: He can't see me.

DOREEN: So you're just hauntin me.

AURA: *(Simultaneously with BUD.)* I'm not hauntin anyone.

BUD: *(Simultaneously with AURA.)* I'm not hauntin anyone.

AURA: Christ on a cracker.

DOREEN: Make him see you.

AURA: Can't do that.

DOREEN: Make him hear you.

AURA: I can't do that either.

DOREEN: Great. Just great. *(Sits down. To BUD.)* Where have you been? You look like hell.

AURA: How would you know?

DOREEN: Get out here! Just get out of here.

(AURA exits. BUD starts to leave.)

DOREEN: *(To BUD.)* Where do you think you're goin?

BUD: Gettin away from your crazies. Seen enough of em before.

DOREEN: Sit down. Tell me where you've been.

BUD: Don't start.

DOREEN: You tell me right now.

BUD: Out.

DOREEN: That's no answer

BUD: Only one you're gonna get.

DOREEN: Well aren't we the man.

BUD: Didn't say that.

DOREEN: What's got into you lately? Stayin out all night, I don't know how many times…

BUD: Ten…

DOREEN: Draggin yourself home* lookin like some sorta apparition.

BUD: In the past month.

DOREEN: Like you're workin on some sorta badge.

BUD: Why not.

DOREEN: Who is she?

BUD: What?

DOREEN: I can hear you sneakin out. Sneakin out goin to meet some girl. Who is she?

BUD: No one you know.

DOREEN: She from around here?

BUD: No.

DOREEN: Then where?

BUD: Around.

DOREEN: What's her name?

BUD: Not sayin.

DOREEN: Tell me her name.

BUD: I'm not sayin.

DOREEN: Where'd you meet her?

BUD: Around.

DOREEN: Well is she nice? Is she pretty?

BUD: I don't want to talk about it.

DOREEN: Jesus. No more stayin out all…

BUD: I'll do whatever I want.

DOREEN: You will not.

BUD: I'm eighteen. I know what…

DOREEN: You don't know anything.

BUD: More than you think.

DOREEN: You knock her up?

BUD: What's with this motherly concern shit?

DOREEN: I'm not spendin another night* sittin up for you.

BUD: You're always on about how much money you don't have or lookin for the bottle you just bought.

DOREEN: I'll do what I want in my own house. Don't need some kid…

BUD: I'm not some kid. I'm your kid.

DOREEN: You tell me where you were* last night.

BUD: I told you. Out.

DOREEN: Afraid your drunken ol mom will embarrass you?

BUD: Don't let anyone tell you you ain't good at somethin. That's why dad left.

DOREEN: Your father was nothin* but a…

BUD: Isn't? Couldn't stand bein around you* anymore.

DOREEN: Your father's* got nothin to do with this.

BUD: I'll go live with him.

DOREEN: You don't even know where* he is.

BUD: I'll find him.

DOREEN: He don't want to be found.* Not by me.

BUD: We'll find each other.

DOREEN: And not by you.

BUD: I should know. I should. But you never want to talk about him. Never what to tell me shit about him. Every time I ask all you have to say is nothin to tell. Nothin to tell.* Nothin to tell.

DOREEN: I don't know! I don't know what happened! He just left. Didn't say a damn thing. He just left.

BUD: That's not* good…

DOREEN: Enough.

BUD: Enough? Nothin about this place is enough. Nothin. *(Exits.)*

(Lights shift.)

SCENE 8

Night. The floor of the Stratosphere Bowl outside Rapid City. BUD and SKYE come running in.

BUD: Ha! Beat you.

SKYE: No way.

BUD: Got here first.

SKYE: One second man. One second.

BUD: I'm the winner. *(Sing-song.)* Doo doo doo doo doo. I'm the winner. Wanna go again? Huh.

SKYE: You couldn't handle it.

BUD: Oh yeah?

SKYE: Yeah.

BUD: You're on.

(They stand side by side, ready to race.)

SKYE: Go.

(BUD starts to go. SKYE stands still.)

SKYE: Psych.

BUD: You're gettin it.

(BUD goes after SKYE, grabs him, pulls him to the ground, and starts to tickle him.)

SKYE: Get off. Get off. Oh. Oh. Stop it. Stop it. All right.

(SKYE gets the upper hand, flips BUD over and pins him.)

SKYE: Now who's the winner.

BUD: I am.

SKYE: Who?

BUD: Ugh! I am. I'm the winner.

SKYE: Then get up.

BUD: I'm the winner.

SKYE: Come on Bud. Get up.

BUD: Urgh.

SKYE: Uh-huh. Who's the winner?

BUD: Ok. Ok. You are.

SKYE: Who?

BUD: You are. Skye's the winner.

SKYE: That's right.

(SKYE still on top of BUD. A moment that could be a kiss but isn't. SKYE rolls off. Pause.)

SKYE: What is this place?

BUD: The Stratobowl. Used to send men up into the stratosphere from here. This national geographic scientific thing.

SKYE: In rockets?

BUD: No. These big helium balloons.

SKYE: Trippy. You ever see one?

BUD: Before I was born.

(Pause.)

SKYE: Man look at all those stars.

(SKYE gets up and starts to spin around face to the sky. BUD joins him till they both fall down laughing and out of breath.)

BUD: Wow.

SKYE: Yeah.

(Silence. They stare at the stars.)

SKYE: See that? That's the Northern Crown.

BUD: Where?

SKYE: See that one radically bright star?

BUD: Yeah.

SKYE: The mother jewel. Middle of the crown. Four arcing up from it and three arcing down. See?

BUD: Yeah.

SKYE: The Shawnees said it was a circle of star maidens dancing in the sky. But the circle's not complete cause one of the maidens fell in love with a mortal dude so she danced down to earth to live with him.

BUD: How'd you know that?

SKYE: Gabriel. He told me.

BUD: He's your friend?

SKYE: More than that. You know.

BUD: No. Not really. Well sorta.

SKYE: We started this road trip, me and him. Aretha on the tape deck, pack a Marlboros on the dash, 24 ounce Slurpees from 7-11. Whizzing down the blacktop, windows down, singing along with Aretha. "What you want, baby I got it. What you need, baby I want it."

BUD: Where is he?

SKYE: Gabe knows how to do it man. He knows the road. You know what I mean? First time I felt the heft of a tunnel, tasted kisses like red dirt and peaches, went subterranean in tandem.

BUD: Where is he?

SKYE: He'd get these twinkle eyes, little creases around the corners, lids quivering, sparks shooting out. Always knew we were headed into adventure when he got those eyes. They'd articulate the horizon, point me across state lines, then bring it down to the blacktop. Look, he'd say, check out the dotted whites. Watch em curve over the ground. Which side? Which side you wanna go down? Today. Just for today. Just lay it down for today. We'll decide again tomorrow.

BUD: Where is he?

SKYE: We followed the whites together for awhile. Then last week we were throwing the cubes. Got to ten. He said left. I said right.

BUD: You miss him?

SKYE: Sometimes.

(Pause.)

BUD: Look. Shooting star.

SKYE: Where?

BUD: There. See it?… And another.

SKYE: …And another.

BUD: Three at once. See em?

SKYE: We've dialed into the meteor shower channel Bud.

(They watch the meteors.)

SKYE: What's the big one Bud?

BUD: Big what?

SKYE: You know. The big one. The big daydream. The movie on repeat in your head. The one that keeps you from checking out.

BUD: Oh. Not sure I, um …

SKYE: Tell me. I wanna know.

BUD: When I was ten my dad took us to Chicago. It was right before he left. Or disappeared. Or whatever he did. We went everywhere. The zoo, the aquarium, museum of natural history. But I liked the tall buildings the best. Whooshin up in an elevator to the very top. One of em had this open air skywalk a thousand feet above the street. We were there just as the sun was going down and all the city lights were turnin on. Whole grid of the city comin to life. All the intersections made sense, you know. I could have stayed lookin at that all night.

SKYE: I wanna see the ocean. In California. Just once, that's all. You ever seen the ocean?

BUD: Nope.

(Silence.)

BUD: Wow. Look at all of em.

SKYE: Yeah. Make a wish.

BUD: What?

SKYE: On one of the shooters. Make a wish.

(BUD watches for a shooting star, then closes his eyes and makes a wish.)

BUD: Your turn.

(SKYE does the same thing.)

BUD: What was it?

(SKYE puts his finger to BUD's mouth.)

SKYE: Shh. Won't come true then.

(SKYE traces the outline of BUD's lips. BUD takes SKYE's finger into his mouth. SKYE moves in to kiss BUD. BUD pulls away.)

BUD: Did you hear somethin?

SKYE: No. There's no one here.

BUD: Got a feelin.

SKYE: No one's here. Come here. Look at the stars.

(They watch the stars, then BUD moves toward SKYE and kisses him. They pull apart and the… Lights fade.)

ACT II
SCENE 1

Diner. DOREEN at work. TOM sitting alone drinking a cup of coffee.

TOM: Hey. *(Pause.)* Hey!

DOREEN: Yeah?

TOM: Coffee? Got an empty cup here.

DOREEN: *(Puts the pot on the counter.)* Help yourself.

TOM: Ain't it your job, to bring it over?

DOREEN: Depends.

TOM: Depends?

DOREEN: On my mood.

TOM: And?

DOREEN: You want some or what? No? *(Starts to put the pot away.)* Gotta keep it warm.

TOM: Dammit. *(Gets up and pours himself some coffee.)* Forget about a tip.

DOREEN: Damn. And me plannin my Hawaiian vacation with that money.

TOM: You got a mouth on ya, don't ya.

DOREEN: Finish your coffee. Can't have people hangin around all day. Doesn't look good.

(TOM goes back to his seat. SAM enters.)

SAM: *(Clearing his throat.)* Hello... Doreen.

DOREEN: Sam. Hi. How ya been?

SAM: No use complainin right?

DOREEN: Guess not. Guess not.

(Small pause.)

SAM: I was in the area.

DOREEN: Which way you headed?

SAM: Not on a job.

DOREEN: Oh.

SAM: I was wonderin... if that... the pie... that pie offer. The one you made last week. Wonderin if... if I could take you up on that.

DOREEN: Long way to come for a slice a pie.

SAM: It's good pie.

DOREEN: Thanks.

SAM: Got no place to be for a couple of days.

DOREEN: You stayin in the area?

SAM: Depends. I guess.

DOREEN: Oh.

SAM: Thought you might like some company.

(Small pause.)

DOREEN: Have some coffee.

SAM: Need to park my rig first.

DOREEN: Ok.

(SAM exits.)

TOM: Hey, you know a kid named Bud?

DOREEN: Who wants to know?

TOM: This kid. He's what...? Seventeen, maybe. Eighteen.

DOREEN: Uh-huh.

TOM: Seems like you know a lot of the folks around here.

DOREEN: Never seen you before.

TOM: I'm lookin for him. This kid Bud.

DOREEN: Wadda ya want with him?

TOM: He's got somethin of mine I wanna get back.

DOREEN: And what would that be?

TOM: You know where he is?

DOREEN: No.

TOM: Like to believe you.

DOREEN: Don't care if you do or don't.

TOM: Well if you see him…

DOREEN: Doubtful.

(He downs his coffee, throws a dollar on the table, and starts to leave.)

TOM: Had better coffee. That's for sure.

DOREEN: This what you're lookin for?

(DOREEN has taken the gun out and placed it on the counter. Her hand rests lightly on the gun.)

TOM: *(Turning around.)* Might be.

DOREEN: Well is it or isn't?

TOM: Looks kinda familiar.

DOREEN: Who are you?

TOM: Let me look at it.

DOREEN: Stay right there. What's your name? Answer me.

TOM: Tom.

DOREEN: Where you from?

TOM: Around.

DOREEN: This Bud kid, how do you know him?

TOM: Just give me…

DOREEN: Tell me.

TOM: Look I don't want to…

DOREEN: Tell me.

TOM: Picked him up, hitchhikin.

DOREEN: And?

TOM: Gave him a ride.

(SAM enters.)

SAM: Got some trouble?

DOREEN: It's nothin. Sit down. Help yourself to some coffee.

TOM: Waitress who don't wait on people.

DOREEN: Shut up.

SAM: Doreen I can, maybe…

DOREEN: This is the guy Bud got the gun from. Isn't it?

SAM: What's he want?

DOREEN: Isn't it Tom.

TOM: Maybe.

DOREEN: Maybe? That ain't an answer.

TOM: Yeah. Yeah it's my gun.

DOREEN: How'd he get your gun?

TOM: I sorta left it with him.

DOREEN: Uh-huh. People don't sorta leave guns with other folks.

TOM: Sorta forgot it.

DOREEN: Well, that's a stupid thing to do.

TOM: Look lady…

DOREEN: Shut up. What'd you two do?

TOM: Didn't do anything.

DOREEN: Tell me.

TOM: Went for a drive.

DOREEN: Where.

TOM: Around.

DOREEN: What else?

TOM: Talked. Just give me…

DOREEN: Better not be anything else you want to tell me.

TOM: Nothin else.

DOREEN: *(Gesturing toward the gun.)* So you want this back? That right Tom?

TOM: Yeah.

DOREEN: Or maybe you want to see Bud again.

TOM: Just wanted to get my gun back.

(DOREEN picks up the gun and aims it at TOM.)

SAM: Doreen…

DOREEN: I got this Sam.

Now you listen to me. You turn around and walk out that door and don't you ever come back here again. And if you ever see Bud, anywhere, you turn your ass around and go the other way. And you go fast. Understand?

TOM: Yeah.

DOREEN: So do it. Now.

TOM: Not without my gun.

SAM: Doreen…

DOREEN: I know what I'm doin Sam.

SAM: Nothin but trouble.

DOREEN: And givin it to him'll make it go away?

SAM: Brought him here in the first place.

TOM: He's right.

SAM: Get rid of the gun and him. He won't be back. Will you Tom?

TOM: No sir.

SAM: You'll do what she says. Won't ya?

TOM: Sure.

SAM: And if you don't, I'll…

TOM: I got it!

(SAM moves to DOREEN and extends his hand, asking for the gun.)

DOREEN: I'm not givin him this gun.

SAM: Stupid havin a gun. You said it yourself Doreen.

(SAM puts his hand on the gun while DOREEN is still holding it.)

SAM: I'm goin to take this. He won't be back.

(SAM removes the gun from DOREEN's hand. He checks for bullets.)

SAM: *(To TOM.)* Head towards the door. Facin me.

(TOM backs to the door.)

SAM: If I ever see your face again…

TOM: You won't.

(SAM gives TOM the gun.)

SAM: Now, get out of here.

TOM: You're crazy lady. You know that. Fuckin loopy.

DOREEN: Get out of here!

(TOM exits. Pause.)

SAM: You ok?

DOREEN: That was none of your business Sam.

SAM: Best thing though.

DOREEN: Is it? Is it?

SAM: Wasn't your gun Doreen.

DOREEN: And Bud's not your kid. *(Pause.)* I got work to do. *(Exits.)*

(Lights shift.)

SCENE 2

Night. Late. Rest area. Trucklights swing onto the stage. Sound of country and western music, lights go off, then a truck door opening and shutting. TOM appears on stage. He walks around the rest area bench. Sits down, take a flask out and takes a swig. Puts the flask away and takes out his gun. He aims it at one of the rest area lights and shoots. He misses.

TOM: Dammit. Godfuckingdammit. *(Takes another swig from his flask, returns it to his pocket, picks up his gun, and tries to shoot out the light again. He hits it this time.)* That's better. Ain't it better? Yeah it's better. Thought you'd like that better. Have a drink? Hate doin it by myself. Fuckin hate that. Waitin and drinkin alone. Waitin. on a summer night. Fuckin hate it. You know? Got my lights fixed. Wanna go for a ride? Good night for a truck ride. Yeah. Night ride. Joyride. Good night for that. Don't you think?

Yeah. Good night for that.

A good night.

(Lights shift.)

SCENE 3

Evening. Diner. DOREEN cleaning up. SAM enters. DOREEN's back is to the door and she doesn't see who it is.

DOREEN: We're closed. *(Turns around and sees SAM.)* Oh.

SAM: I'll come back then.

DOREEN: Come in if you're here.

SAM: *(He reveals a bouquet of flowers.)* Here.

DOREEN: Oh. Let me get somethin to… you know… a thing… you know… for you know… *(Exits.)*

SAM: *(To DOREEN offstage.)* You keep this place real nice.

DOREEN: Thanks.

SAM: A lot of these places I eat at on the road, well they could use some fixin up. There's one up in Rock Springs looks like it'd fall over if you laughed too loud.

DOREEN: Rock Springs?

SAM: Montana. North a Miles City on 312. You ever been up there?

DOREEN: *(Returning with flowers.)* Montana?

SAM: Yeah.

DOREEN: No. Been into Wyoming. That's all. Casper, Douglas. That area.

SAM: Rock Springs's right in the foothill of the Rockies. Great drivin country, watchin the mountains steppin down and givin into the plains. Like you've been up in the sky and you're pullin parts of it down with you. Pullin it down and spreadin it out. Never get tired of that country.

DOREEN: Don't think I'd like to be hemmed in by mountains.

SAM: Doesn't feel that way. None of the towns are up high—too much snow—so it's like the mountains are always to one side.

DOREEN: Yeah, well.

(Pause.)

SAM: Listen about today… um… I'm sorry if I you know… If I was outta line.

DOREEN: You were.

SAM: I was just you know… worried that…

DOREEN: Don't need a fairybook hero Sam.

SAM: Yeah. Well?

DOREEN: You hungry? I could make some supper.

SAM: That'd be nice.

DOREEN: Fine.

SAM: I'll go wash up.

(AURA appears as SAM exits.)

AURA: Who's the man?

DOREEN: Sam.

AURA: Sam. Kinda ordinary name isn't it?

DOREEN: It's a fine name.

AURA: You know what you're doin?

DOREEN: Haven't got the vaguest idea.

(Some music starts playing. SAM has put a slow song on the jukebox.)

AURA: Ohh. He's a romantic.

DOREEN: Go.

AURA: Awful pushy Doreen. Gets you into…

DOREEN: Grandma.

AURA: All right. Don't need to stay here and be insulted. You seen my puzzle book?

DOREEN: Behind the counter.

(AURA gathers her book. Sam reenters.)

SAM: Hope you don't mind I…

DOREEN: I like that song.

SAM: Would you like to dance?

DOREEN: Dance?

SAM: Yeah, you know…

DOREEN: I know what it is Sam.

SAM: Well?

DOREEN: What are you doin here Sam?

SAM: You asked me to supper.

DOREEN: No. I mean…

(Pause.)

SAM: This was a dumb idea. I should go.

DOREEN: Suit yourself.

SAM: Be easier wouldn't.

DOREEN: Marvin always complained about everything. House was a mess, where was his denim shirt, didn't want meatloaf for supper. All the time downin another six pack. I called my mother a coupla times, asked her what I should do. She says "You stay with your husband Doreen. That's what you do." Damn stupid thing to say.

(AURA disappears.)

DOREEN: See his eyes, they changed. Got this look a distance in em. Like that stretch of two lane between here and Mud Butte.

SAM: That's lonely country.

DOREEN: That distance kept growin and growin, takin up more space. When he left my mother told me to wait for him. "If you're worth it, he'll be back." Ha! Worth it. Finally told my mother to go to hell, packed up Bud and me, and moved here. Opened this place up.

SAM: And since then?

(DOREEN doesn't answer.)

SAM: My wife… my ex-wife, she loved my hands, said they looked like they knew things, hands with their own particular wisdom. She'd trace and retrace the lines like she was planning a trip. Told me those lines looked like the Missouri. Wide. Deep. Bein fed by all its tributaries as it rolled towards the Mississippi. Told me they were the first thing about me she was taken with, that she was attracted to. That's what she said. Later.

Sometimes I lose em. I look down and think—whose hands are these? They just stop belongin to me. Sometimes lasts all day, sometimes just a minute or two. Never told her that though. Never told her that the day we got married, wasn't my hand she was slippin the wedding ring onto. That my hands weren't mine that day. All day. Might be why it didn't last. Or something else. Never know.

You're really pretty Doreen. Noticed it the first day I stopped in here.

DOREEN: You always lie like that?

SAM: No. I did.

DOREEN: Well, I wouldn't kick you outta bed for eatin crackers.

SAM: Ha! It's an awful nice song.

(SAM reaches out his hand to DOREEN. A gesture to dance.)

DOREEN: And your hands? Today?

SAM: All mine.

DOREEN: Haven't done this in a very long time.

(DOREEN gives SAM her hand.)

SAM: I'll have to make sure I stop by more often then.

(SAM twirls DOREEN in a very slow circle and they dance. Lights shift.)

SCENE 4

Night. The Badlands.

SKYE: Darker than last time.

BUD: Yeah. See how the spires have changed, different deeper shades of blue.

SKYE: Mako sica. *(SKYE starts humming "All I Want" by Joni Mitchell. His humming moves to soft singing, to himself.)*

BUD: What's that?

SKYE: Joni.

BUD: Who?

SKYE: Joni Mitchell.

BUD: Never heard a her.

SKYE: Really?

BUD: Sing some more.

(SKYE sings some more, teasing and seducing BUD. BUD responds to SKYE's singing until the two move together and kiss. They start to make out more heavily, shirts and pants starting to be unbuttoned. Headlights from a truck light them up. Sound of a truck door opening and closing.)

BUD: Shit.

TOM: *(Enters, drunk.)* Hey. Wanna lift?

BUD: No.

SKYE: We're fine.

TOM: Uh-huh. Good night for a drive.

BUD: Don't want one. *(To SKYE.)* Come on, let's go.

TOM: That's what I've been doin. Drivin. Drivin around. Drivin and watchin. Wanna drink?

BUD: No. Thanks.

TOM: Good night for a drink.

SKYE: Really, we're cool. Thanks.

TOM: I like givin people rides.

BUD: Just get in your truck and get outta here.

TOM: What's the matter? Don't like trucks? I'd a thought you wouldn't like to walk. Wouldn't want to get all sweaty and hot.

BUD: Just don't want to get in your truck. Tom.

SKYE: Tom?

BUD: Come on.

(TOM pull out his gun and shoots it into the air. BUD and SKYE stop.)

TOM: That's better. Turn around. I'm being real polite here offerin you a ride and all, offerin you a drink, goin outta my way to help. People that aren't appreciative? Folks that aren't polite? You know? That don't got any manners? Now that pisses me off. Really pisses me off. For example, Bud, you ain't introduced me to your friend here. That's just bad manners ain't it. Your mom wouldn't be happy about that. Not that she's got any manners herself.

BUD: You don't know anything about my mom.

TOM: Got my gun back didn't I.

BUD: What'd you say to her?

TOM: Nothin. Nothin to say. Just got my gun back. So who's your friend?

BUD: None of your business.

SKYE: Skye.

TOM: You shut up. See? What was I just sayin, what was I just talkin about. Manners. Bud and I were havin a nice conversation and you just butt right in. See that pisses me off. It really does. Just pissed me off Sky. What kinda stupid name is that. Sky. Shit.

SKYE: Let's go Bud.

BUD: What'd you tell her?

TOM: Ain't ya gonna listen to your girlfriend. Huh?

SKYE: We're not looking for any trouble.

BUD: Tell me.

TOM: Fuckin fags.

BUD: What?

TOM: You heard me.

SKYE: Bud, come on.

BUD: Wait. What did you say?

TOM: You heard me. Fuckin fags.

BUD: Fuckin fags? That what you were thinkin when we were sittin in your pickup. When we were sittin in your pickup and the windows were gettin fogged up from both of us breathin so hard* and

TOM: You don't know what I think.

BUD: you're askin me to trace that scar on your arm and then you're tracin it with me* and

TOM: Makin up shit stupid stories again.

BUD: then you reach over and grab my hand and before you know it you got your mouth on *my mouth

TOM: Shut up!

BUD: Your mouth on my mouth and you're undoing my pants and then you got your mouth on my

TOM: *(Overlapping.)* I said Shut up!

BUD: Cocksucker!

(TOM backsides BUD with his hand. BUD falls to the ground.)

TOM: You fuckin freak.

(TOM raises his gun and aims it at BUD.)

BUD: Shoot me. Come on. It's what you came for, isn't it Tom. Isn't it? Huh?

I didn't think so.

TOM: SHUT UP. Just fuckin SHUT UP. *(Moves toward BUD.)* That's where you belong you fuckin freak. In the dirt. Under my boot. Ground to a pulp.

(TOM raises his gun toward BUD. SKYE goes up behind TOM and grabs him before he can shoot. TOM and SKYE struggle. The gun goes off. SKYE gets shot in the arm and falls.)

BUD: Skye!

TOM: Tell your boyfriend to get up.

BUD: Get out of here.

TOM: What's wrong? He get hurt?

BUD: I said get out of here.

TOM: Fuckin freaks, the both of ya.

(BUD lunges toward TOM and lands a punch on TOM. TOM falls. The gun falls. BUD grabs the gun and starts kicking TOM.)

BUD: Leave me alone. Just leave me alone. Leave me the fuck alone. *(Cocks the gun and aims it at TOM's head. Pause. He uncocks the gun and backs up to SKYE.)* Get in your truck and get out of here.

TOM: *(Gets up.)* Freaks.

(TOM exits. Headlights leave the stage. The sound of a truck leaving. Lights shift.)

SCENE 5

The diner. DOREEN, SAM, BUD, and SKYE.

DOREEN: Who is he?

SAM: Doreen get me a rag.

BUD: Why'd you give him that gun?

DOREEN: What?

BUD: You gave him back that gun didn't you.

SAM: Doreen, now.

(DOREEN goes to get a rag.)

SAM: Where's the nearest hospital?

BUD: *(To SAM.)* Can't you do anything?

DOREEN: *(Returns with a rag.)* Rapid. Here.

SAM: I'm gettin my truck.

DOREEN: Take my car.

BUD: Don't let him die. Please. Don't let him die.

DOREEN: It's right in front.

BUD: Please. Don't let him die.

SAM: He's not gonna die. Just needs some stitchin up.

(SAM starts to pick SKYE up.)

BUD: Skye.

SKYE: Yeah Bud.

BUD: I'm right here. I'm not goin anywhere.

SKYE: It's cool Bud, really.

SAM: Get out of my way.

BUD: I'm comin with you.

(AURA appears.)

DOREEN: Let him go Bud.

SAM: I'm sorry.

DOREEN: Go. Go.

(SAM and SKYE leave.)

BUD: This is all your fault.

DOREEN: I told him to stay away from you. I told him to…

BUD: When are you gonna quit messin up my life.

DOREEN: Who is that?

SAM: *(From offstage.)* Cmon, Bud.

BUD: I'm comin.

DOREEN: Is that where you've been. Is it?

(BUD doesn't answer.)

DOREEN: Is it?

BUD: I'm goin. *(Leaves.)*

DOREEN: I told that guy to stay away from Bud. I told him to…

AURA: Oh stop it Doreen.

DOREEN: Don't you get on me.

AURA: Somebody's got to.

DOREEN: Who was that?

AURA: Stop it. Right now. Just stop it. I didn't leave St. Louis to settle here and have a buncha stupid family. You gotta start listenin to people. Start noticin what's around you.

DOREEN: Don't you start tellin me what to do. Everytime I listen to someone, somethin goes wrong. And the last time I listened to family I got stuck with a stupid drunk of a husband.

AURA: This is different.

DOREEN: How? Still family tellin me what to do. My own mother

AURA: *(Overlapping.)* It wasn't her fault.

DOREEN: Yes it was.

AURA: I told her the same thing.

DOREEN: What?

AURA: About her and your dad.

DOREEN: Why?

AURA: I know. Stupid now. But you, you gotta…

DOREEN: This can't be, this just can't be, any of it.

AURA: Shut up. "This can't be. This just can't be." That's what I said. When I moved here. Didn't stop me though. Didn't stop me from makin gravy outta grease when we ran outta bacon, pullin up dried prairie grass when we ran out of coal, buryin water to keep it cool durin hot spells. Didn't stop me from provin up that land. There was no time to be homesick and no time for self pity. That's the deal you make with this land. With this land and with each other.

DOREEN: What have I got to do with that?

AURA: You been waitin ever since you got here. Waitin since Marvin left. And now look…

DOREEN: That man…

AURA: Was a sorry son of a bitch. I know that. Told you that when you married him. Be glad he ain't around anymore.

DOREEN: What do I have to do?

AURA: Pay attention Doreen. That's all you gotta do. Pay attention.

DOREEN: Whata you think I've been doin.

AURA: You gotta try harder Doreen. You gotta "see." Watch the thunderheads roll through on a summer's afternoon. Look out for blizzards. Listen to the dust blowin. Get some dirt on your hands.

DOREEN: And then?

AURA: Up to you ain't it. Then it's up to you.

(Pause.)

DOREEN: That boy with Bud? He's…?

AURA: What?

DOREEN: They're not just friends. Are they?

AURA: What do you think?

DOREEN: I… I don't…

AURA: You wanna know?

DOREEN: I don't know.

AURA: It's all there. All there in Bud's face. You just gotta look. You just gotta pay attention. *(Small pause.)* Love's gotta be proved up too.

(Lights shift.)

SCENE 6

Diner. Sound of summer heat. DOREEN working. She stops for a moment and looks up, moves as if to the front door and looks out at the sky. She's trying but it's not easy.

DOREEN: Sky. Summer sky. Stretched out. *(A moment of exasperation.)* Sky. It's just sky, just sky like… like… like the day I moved here. Huh.

Didn't have any notion where I was headed. Knew I had to get somewhere, somewhere else, somewhere that wasn't that little town full of nothin. Nothin but waitin. Ended up here and… well… guess I just wanted to sit for awhile. Sit and watch. Is that such a bad thing? Watch the weather go by, watch myself gettin older, watch the truckers come, and go. Funny now, bein here, in a smaller place than I started. Always expected it to be a bigger one. How'd this happen? Guess you never know till… guess you never know…

Haven't seen a sky like this for a while. Not for a long while.

(AURA enters doing a crossword puzzle. DOREEN doesn't turn around.)

AURA: It precedes "Blastoff!"

DOREEN: *(As much to herself and the sky as to AURA.)* One.

AURA: O. N. E. Perfect.

(BUD and SKYE enter.)

DOREEN: How's the arm today?

SKYE: Getting there. *(Moves his arm up and down as far as he is able.)*

DOREEN: It's somethin.

BUD: How ya doin?

DOREEN: I'm fine.

BUD: Good. So you're ok?

DOREEN: I'm fine Bud. Just fine.

(Pause.)

BUD: Mom. I'm… I'm…

DOREEN: You want something to eat?

BUD: Mom, listen…

DOREEN: Got some of those cinammon rolls.

BUD: Mom I'm…

DOREEN: Or some eggs. That's simple.

BUD: Mom. Look at me.

(Pause.)

AURA: Doreen.

(DOREEN turns and looks at BUD.)

BUD: Mom, I'm leavin.

SKYE: You are?

BUD: We're leavin. Together. *(To SKYE.)* That ok? *(To DOREEN.)* I'm leavin.

(Pause.)

DOREEN: When are you goin?

BUD: I was thinkin about today.

DOREEN: Never get anywhere if you think about it.

BUD: Today. We're leavin today.

DOREEN: Which way are you headed?

BUD: Not sure. West maybe.

DOREEN: Well is it west?

BUD: Probably.

DOREEN: Well decide. At least decide what direction.

BUD: Ok, Ok.

SKYE: West. We're goin west.

DOREEN: Here. Tips from this morning. All I got on me right now. *(Takes some money out of her pocket.)*

BUD: No, you need that.

DOREEN: Just take it.

BUD: Ok. Thanks.

DOREEN: If you wait till I close I got some more back at the house.

BUD: Think we'll be leavin before then.

DOREEN: Well, that's something.

BUD: Well… guess I should. *(Starts to leave.)*

DOREEN: Bud.

BUD: Yeah?

DOREEN: *(Finds the postcard from Marvin and gives it to BUD.)* Here. Take this. Postcard from your Dad. I burned all his stuff when he left. Take it. Or throw it away. I don't care. Only thing I have might help you find him.

BUD: You really don't know where he is do you.

DOREEN: No Bud. I don't.

BUD: Or why he left.

DOREEN: Don't know that either. Really never knew. *(Beat. DOREEN takes a good hard look at BUD.)* Always thought when I looked at you it was your dad's eyes I was seein. But today… well… I was wrong. Weren't his eyes I was seein. Wasn't his look of distance. It was my grandmother's. Aura.

AURA: One wish. Simple really.

DOREEN: A wish on a balloon.

AURA: Balloon takin men where they'd never been before.

DOREEN: A wish that her folks'd be pioneers. Like her. I think she hoped it'd be my mom. Or me. But we spent most of our time… well it just wasn't us. It's you Bud. You're her wish. You've got Aura's distance vision Bud. Don't forget that. Ok?

BUD: Ok. When we get someplace I'll… I'll let you know.

(BUD and SKYE start to leave.)

DOREEN: Skye?

SKYE: Doreen.

DOREEN: You take care of him.

SKYE: Bud, he's got it all together.

DOREEN: Still…You two. You both take care.

SKYE: We will.

(SKYE gives his bag of dice to DOREEN.)

SKYE: Here.

DOREEN: What…?

SKYE: Just get to ten.

(BUD and SKYE leave.)

AURA: He's a strange one that Skye.

DOREEN: Suppose he is.

AURA: Wonder where they'll end up.

DOREEN: Does it matter?

AURA: And this trucker. Think he'll be back?

DOREEN: Don't know.

AURA: Could do worse.

DOREEN: Already have.

(Lights shift.)

SCENE 7

Daytime. BUD, SKYE, and AURA at the geographical center of the United States.

BUD: This is it?

SKYE: What's the sign say?

BUD: *(Reading.)* The geographical center of the United States.

AURA: *(Opens her palm and a handful of dirt falls out.)* Dirt. Dust. Mud.

SKYE: Yeah. This is it.

AURA: The Gumbo.

SKYE: Too much. It's too much.

AURA: Dry it's creased liked the wrinkled face of an old man, ripplin out across the plains. Wind kicks it up, rest on your hands, on your face. A second skin.

BUD: Thought it would be somethin different, somethin more, more than just a little sign on the side of the road.

SKYE: Doesn't matter. Stretch it out Bud. Out the end of your fingertips. Coast to coast, Canada to Mexico. Man. Trippy. *(Slowly spins around in a circle with his arms outstretched.)*

AURA: Rain comes the soil "rolls," an inland ocean of mud. Sticks to you, like clay, balls up on your shoes, works its way into your clothes, under your nails, into your bones.

(SKYE stops spinning.)

SKYE: Wow. Cmere.

AURA: *(To BUD.)* Dry or wet you can't get rid of it.

BUD: Why?

AURA: *(To BUD.)* Ya always carry part of it with you.

SKYE: Just cmere. Stand here.

(BUD and SKYE stand side by side.)

SKYE: Look. Bullseye in the center Bud. Whole country radiating out from this single point.

(SKYE puts his arms around BUD. They draw in close and kiss.)

AURA: Don't really know what to make of that. Seem content though. Seem, seemly. *(A sigh.)* Makes me feel old.

SKYE: I was doing it all wrong, thinking in lines and right angles, hard edges. Circles. Circles this time. Moving out from this starting spot.

(Beat.)

BUD: Summer's ending.

SKYE: Yeah. Fall.

BUD: Yeah. I'm scared.

SKYE: Yeah. Nothing wrong with that.

AURA: Nothing wrong with that.

(Silence. BUD and SKYE standing a moment before they start their journey. AURA looking on. Wind. BUD and SKYE start walking, walking in concentric circles out from the geographic center. BUD and SKYE pass AURA, and she disappears. BUD and SKYE walking as the lights fade.)

(End of play.)

PLAYS AND PLAYWRIGHTS
for the
NEW MILLENNIUM

Edited by Martin Denton

A collection of eight exciting new plays which electrified audiences in New York City throughout 1998 and 1999. These gifted and talented young playwrights are boldly pushing contemporary theatre into the 21st century, helping to shape and define the themes and structures of the next wave of American drama.

Midnight Brainwash Revival by **Kirk Wood Bromley** — a revel for the new millennium.

Horse Country by **C.J. Hopkins** — a dizzying joyride through the American landscape.

When Words Fail... by **David Dannenfelser** — a tender comedy of the human spirit.

Making Peter Pope by **Edmund De Santis** — an epic comedy of a young gay man.

Crunching Numbers by **Lynn Marie Macy** — three linked one-acts about turning thirty.

Café Society by **Robert Simonson** — a cockeyed satire of contemporary urban America.

"So I Killed a Few People..." by **Gary Ruderman & David Summers** — a serial killer's chilling monologue.

Are We There Yet? by **Garth Wingfield** — a comic drama of renewal and rebirth.

Retail: $14.00

Additional information can be found on the web at http://www.nytheatre.com/nytheatre/books.htm

Available in bookstores and on line or order directly from the publisher

Send a check or money for $14 (plus $3.50 for priority mail) to:

The New York Theatre Experience, Inc.
P.O. Box 744, Bowling Green Station
New York, NY 10274-0744

PLAYS AND PLAYWRIGHTS 2001

Edited by Martin Denton

Nine outstanding new plays from off- and off-off-Broadway's 1999–2000 season.

Washington Square Dreams by **Gorilla Repertory Theatre** — eight ten-minute plays set during an outdoor performance of *A Midsummer Night's Dream*.

Fate by **Elizabeth Horsburgh** — romantic flights of fancy in a compact comedy about a pair of passionate strangers.

Velvet Ropes by **Joshua Scher** — two innocents trapped in an art museum contemplate the nature of humor, performance, and art.

The Language of Kisses by **Edmund De Santis** — an estranged mother and daughter come to terms with the past and themselves in this moving drama by the author of *Making Peter Pope*.

Word to Your Mama by **Julia Lee Barclay** — channel surfing through a turn of the millennium mind.

Cuban Operator Please... by **Adrian Rodriguez** — short play about the effects of exile and death on the relationship between a father and son.

The Elephant Man—The Musical by **Jeff Hylton & Tim Werenko** — John Merrick gets to sing and dance on Broadway.

House of Trash by **Trav S.D.** — a raucous populist musical farce about a garbageman moonlighting as a Baptist preacher.

Straight-Jacket by **Richard Day** — brilliantly funny and incisive satire of Hollywood and hypocrisy.

Retail: $15.00

Additional information can be found on the web at http://www.nytheatre.com/nytheatre/books.htm

Available in bookstores and on line or order directly from the publisher

Send a check or money for $15 (plus $3.50 for priority mail) to:

The New York Theatre Experience, Inc.
P.O. Box 744, Bowling Green Station
New York, NY 10274-0744

ABOUT THE AUTHOR

MARTIN DENTON is executive director of The New York Theatre Experience, Inc. He is the founder, reviewer, and editor of nytheatre.com, one of the premier sources for theatre reviews and information on the Internet since 1996. Denton is a member of the American Theatre Critics Association and The Drama Desk. He is the author of *The New York Theatre Experience Book of the Year 1998* and the editor of *Plays and Playwrights for the New Millennium* and *Plays and Playwrights 2001*. He is passionately committed to discovering and fostering interesting new American drama wherever it can be found. He lives in New York City with his two Siamese cats, Logan and Briscoe.

THE NEW YORK THEATRE EXPERIENCE

The New York Theatre Experience, Inc., is a nonprofit New York State corporation. Its mission is to promote and increase awareness of and interest in theatre and the performing arts locally, nationally, and globally in order to inspire more people to attend and support live performance theatre. The principal activity of The New York Theatre Experience is the operation of a free website (http://www.nytheatre.com) that comprehensively covers the New York theatre scene—on, off, and off off Broadway. The New York Theatre Experience also publishes books of theatre reviews and features as well as newly written and produced plays.

If you would like to contact Martin Denton or would like to know more about the current and future plans of The New York Theatre Experience, Inc., please send an e-mail to mddenton@botz.com.